TRANSLATING BLACKNESS

TRANSLATING BLACKNESS

Latinx Colonialities in Global Perspective

LORGIA GARCÍA PEÑA

Duke University Press *Durham and London* 2022

Printed in the United States of America on acid-free paper ∞
Typeset in Warnock Pro by Westchester Publishing Services

Library of Congress Cataloging-in-Publication Data
Names: García Peña, Lorgia, [date] author.
Title: Translating Blackness : Latinx colonialities in global perspective / Lorgia García Peña.
Description: Durham : Duke University Press, 2022. | Includes bibliographical references and index.
Identifiers: LCCN 2021055647 (print) |
LCCN 2021055648 (ebook)
ISBN 9781478016038 (hardcover)
ISBN 9781478018667 (paperback)
ISBN 9781478023289 (ebook)
Subjects: LCSH: Black people—Migrations. | Latin Americans—Migrations. | Black people—Latin America—History. | African diaspora. | Decolonization—Latin America. | Latin America—Emigration and immigration. | BISAC: SOCIAL SCIENCE / Black Studies (Global) | SOCIAL SCIENCE / Ethnic Studies / American / Hispanic American Studies
Classification: LCC F1419.B55 G37 2022 (print) | LCC F1419.B55 (ebook) | DDC 980/.00496—dc23/eng/20220214
LC record available at https://lccn.loc.gov/2021055647
LC ebook record available at https://lccn.loc.gov/2021055648

For Black Women
Black Migrants
Black Queers
Black Colonized
Black Minoritized
Black Otherized
here, there, and in vaivén

CONTENTS

Note on Terminology · ix
Acknowledgments · xi

INTRODUCTION: Race, Colonialism, and Migration in the Global Latinx Diaspora · 1

PART I. **ON BEING BLACK AND CITIZEN: LATINX COLONIAL VAIVENES**

1 A FULL STATURE OF HUMANITY
Latinx Difference, Colonial Musings, and Black Belonging during Reconstruction · 29

2 ARTHUR SCHOMBURG'S HAITI
Diaspora Archives and the Epistemology of Black Latinidad · 79

PART II. **BLACK FEMINIST CONTRA*DICTIONS* IN LATINX DIASPORAS**

3 AGAINST DEATH
Black Latina Rebellion in Diasporic Community · 113

4 THE AFTERLIFE OF COLONIAL GENDER VIOLENCE
Black Immigrant Women's Life and Death in Postcolonial Italy · 153

5 SECOND GENERATION INTERRUPTIONS
Archives of Black Belonging in Postcolonial Diaspora · 193

CONCLUSION: Confronting Global
Anti-immigrant Antiblackness · 233

Notes · 241 Bibliography · 279 Index · 303

NOTE ON TERMINOLOGY

One of the impulses that led me to write this book is precisely the imperfections of translating racial meaning and racial politics across languages, cultures, and geographies. The terms I use throughout the book are insufficient for describing the ethnic, cultural, and racial experiences of people across geographies and times. The following list highlights some of the most common identity terms used throughout the book, with a brief explanation of how I use them.

AMERICAN: The term *American* refers to the entire hemisphere and its people (North America, Central America, the Caribbean, and South America). I otherwise use specific terms like *US Americans, US Black,* or *Latin American* to refer to specific areas or national groups.

BLACK: A global category for naming peoples and cultures of African ancestry, recognizing that different nations and cultural groups use a diversity of terms to name race.

BROWN: Mixed-race blackness and mulataje, used particularly when engaging with nineteenth-century Caribbean people.

HABESHA: People from regions in Ethiopia and Eritrea. In the diaspora, it became a term of inclusion and intra-ethnic solidarity for some people. Over the past thirty years, it has become a politicized ethnic term to destabilize the national bordering project that has separated people from the East African region. I use it following the activists and artists I interviewed who define themselves as Habesha.

LATINX: A gender-inclusive/neutral term that names people who identify a link to Latinidad either through Latin American ancestry or to cultural belonging to communities in the diaspora.

MULATO/A: A category of privilege within the racial hierarchies of the nineteenth-century Hispanic Caribbean. The term refers to a mixed-race Afro-descendant person of light, medium, or dark-brown skin. I use this term only when speaking about nineteenth-century subjects who self-identified as such. Otherwise I use Brown. I use the gender binary *(mulato, mulata)* given this is not a contemporary term and the people I engage in the book identified themselves in binary language.

QUEER: A term used to encompass a diversity of people who do not identify with the heteronormative hegemony, who identify as LGBTQI, or who do not conform to the gender binary.

SECOND GENERATIONS: A politicized yet contested term, used in Italy to name children of immigrants born in the diaspora and those who migrate at an early age. The term highlights the political dimension of citizenship exclusion experienced by people who are cultural citizens of the nation but not always recognized—legally and otherwise—by the state.

WOMEN: People who identify as such regardless of how the state or institutions defined their biological sex at birth.

WOMEN OF COLOR: I use this term here in two ways: first, to highlight the contributions of late twentieth-century Black, Brown, Indigenous, mixed-race, and Asian feminists in the United States who articulated a project of transnational solidarity with the oppressed and colonized across the globe; and second, to take seriously the ways in which minoritized nonwhite women living in the Global North name themselves and build solidarity across ethnic and racial groups.

ACKNOWLEDGMENTS

It takes a village to write a book. My village is multilingual, transnational, and multigenerational. It is inhabited by ancestors, warrior women, scholars, family, and friends. I will not be able to name each member of my village, though you know who you are; and you know my heart. Thank you to each of you for being on my corner and helping me, in your own distinctive way, to complete this book.

I want to say gracias to the Black Latinx migrants who have been sharing their stories with me for more than a decade. It was those stories, shared informally in various languages and moments over many years, that led me to think about Black Latinidad in vaivén and beyond. The epistemological journey to Italian blackness was wonderful and challenging. I am grateful for the generosity, kindness, kinship, and love I received from Anacaona Mujeres Dominicanas en Italia, especially Marlene de la Cruz, Milagros Guzmán, Thiara Garden, Melania Cruz, and Fredamily Santana Guzmán, who shared their wisdom and opened their home to me and my son for seven summers, every year. Gracias also to the Dominican Consulate in Milan for connecting me with multiple Latinx immigrant organizations and for sharing its archives of stories and documents. Grazie especially to Medhin Paolos, who opened my eyes to the incredibly rich Habesha archive that lives in the geography of Porta Venezia and who introduced me to the amazing activists who founded Rete G2 in Rome. Your generosity and wisdom, Medhin, made my research in Italy possible and introduced me to important ways of theorizing and thinking about nonhegemonic blackness.

My gratitude goes also to the activists who shared stories, resources, and testimonies with me over the years, especially Mercedes Frías and Tess

Asplund, whose badassness continues to inspire a generation. Grazie mille to Claudia Fezzardi and Veronica Saba, who guided me the first two summers in Italy, serving as diligent research associates and connectors to a world I was only beginning to discover. I will be forever grateful to the people at Rainbow Café in Porta Venezia for graciously allowing me to spend countless hours in "my office," reserving that corner end table with reliable Wi-Fi and the coldest AC, summer after summer, and for supplying me with the right amount of café and spritz needed to survive the long hours of work.

The work of Italian studies scholars and artists who made inquiries into Black italianità, Italian colonialism, race, and immigration made my writing this book possible. I want to especially acknowledge Gaia Giuliani, Mauro Valeri, Alessandro Triulzi, Jacqueline Andall, Wendy Pojmann, Derek Duncan, Cristina Lombardi Diop, Caterina Romeo, and Graziella Parati. Thank you also to Igiaba Scego, Camilla Hawthorne, and Alessandra di Maio for the dialogues and for producing inspiring work that revolutionized how we think about italianità.

The central axis of this book is Black Latinidad as it manifests through geographies and historical periods. As I conceived my argument and obsessed over historical figures like Arturo Schomburg and Gregorio Luperón, I was fortunate to have Black Latinx studies interlocutors like Miriam Jiménez Román (who hated what she called the "entrepreneurship" of Schomburg and pushed me on every single argument) and Juan Flores (who was delighted to hear me think out loud about Luperón and Douglass). I am sad they are not here in the flesh to see this project completed, but I do hope this book honors their legacy. Thank you also to Silvio Torres-Saillant for the productive conversations on Dominican blackness and to Bernardo Vega for his feedback on nineteenth-century US-Caribbean relations. The field of Black Latinx studies is a promise that comes true in the (forthcoming) work of young scholars and graduate students. I am excited to see in the next years books by Rebeca Hey Colón, Paul Joseph López Oro, SA Smythe, Regina Mills, René Cordero, Omaris Zamora, and Genesis Lara, among many others, who engage blackness and Latinidad across geographies and through multiple methodologies. As I complete this book, I am also excited to join the ranks of Yomaira Figureoa and Tiffany Florvil, whose work rethinks hegemonic conceptions of blackness, and diasporic imaginaries.

George Lipsitz and Yolanda Martínez-San Miguel are the most generous readers a scholar can ever hope to encounter. They came out to Cambridge for a book workshop in spring 2019 and over the years continued to read multiple versions of the manuscript, providing incisive and valuable insights along the way. Thank you, George and Yolanda, for your rigor and generosity. April Mayes, Christina Davidson, and Raj Chetty read chapter 1 and provided feedback that was critical as I theorized Black Latinidad through the stories and words of Gregoria Fraser Goins. My conversations with Margarita Cordero, Yolanda Garden, Tirso Medrano, and Fafa Taveras helped me understand Black Dominicanas' role in the 1965 revolution and beyond. Laura Briggs and Durba Mitra were incredibly generous readers; their feedback helped me think deeper about the ways in which gender violence, migration, and blackness intersect. Feedback from Arlene Dávila, Paula Moya, Michaeline Crichlow, Tommy DeFrantz, Josie Saldaña, Nicole Guidotti Hernández, and Frances Negrón-Muntaner at various stages of the writing process challenged me in the best possible ways. Several chapter workshops and presentations in the Departments of African American Studies at Princeton; Social Cultural Analysis at New York University; Latino Studies at Northwestern; Black Studies at the University of California, Santa Barbara; Race, Colonialism, and Diaspora at Tufts; and African and African American Studies at Duke yielded valuable feedback and incredibly productive conversations with colleagues and students. The Ford Foundation awarded me a postdoctoral fellowship in 2015 that allowed me the time to conduct archival research and oral interviews in Italy. In 2018 the Massachusetts Institute of Technology awarded me the MLK fellowship, which gave me the time to write, and which provided me with a treasured intellectual community; thank you to Joaquin Terrones and the Program in Women and Gender Studies at MIT for this opportunity. The Weatherhead Center for International Studies and the Dean's Competitive Fellowship at Harvard provided financial support for travel to different archives in Europe, the Caribbean, Washington, DC, and New York City.

I finished writing this book amid a pandemic while archives shut down and libraries went remote. At times, checking citations and accessing documents seemed an impossibility. The staff at the Dominican Studies Institute, especially Sarah Aponte, Jhensen Ortiz, and Anthony Stevens, were always incredibly generous as were the staff at the Dominican National Archive, particularly Aquiles Castro; I want to thank also the Moorland-Spingarn Research Center (MSRC) at Howard University, the Schomburg Center for Research in Black Culture at the New York Public Library, and the Special Collections Research Center at Syracuse University for facilitating my research over this past decade. I am grateful also to colleagues who shared books and scanned documents and manuscripts I could no longer access due to pandemic restrictions and closures, particularly April Mayes, Christina Davidson, Alex Gil, Nelson Santana, Ginetta Candelario, Quisqueya Lora,

Pablo Mella, Aquiles Castro, and Elizabeth Manley. Writing can be a very isolating process; I am grateful for the writing companionship of Raj Chetty and Genevieve Clutario and for the generous invitation to be part of the Writing Collective de las Nenas organized by Yolanda Martínez-San Miguel at the University of Miami.

Norman Storer, Catie Peters, Alondra Ponce, and Arisleyda Dilone provided valuable research support as I tracked down documents and images in archives across continents and sites over the years. Massiel Torres Ulloa transcribed several interviews and Megan Bayles went above and beyond copyediting duties to provide the right doses of "what is this?" and "clarify that," which ultimately made the book more accessible to readers. My gratitude goes also to the Duke University Press anonymous reviewers for their thoughtful and incisive comments, to Sandra Korn for her diligence in the manuscript preparation process, to Courtney Berger for believing in this project from its conception, and to Alex Guerrero for taking the essence of the book and turning it into a stunning cover image.

The completion of this book came during a particularly challenging time in my life as I struggled to survive the institutional violence that led to my being denied tenure at Harvard, during a pandemic and amid a global climate of antiblackness, xenophobia, and anti-immigrant violence in our nation and the world. It would have been too easy to give up writing this book, and I would have, had it not been for the encouragement, kindness, love, and support of so many people in my life: my parents, Maritza Peña and Julio García, who have written the manual on unconditional love; my son, Sebastián, who, at his young age, has the most ethical sense of justice I have ever seen in a human being; my brother, Albin, whose quiet but constant presence has always made me feel safe in this world; my incredible tribe of *guerreras* and accomplices, Chandra Mohanty, Angela Y. Davis, Keish Kim, Josefina Báez, P. Gabrielle Foreman, and Catherina González Seligman, who always had my back. Thank you to my wonderful students who made a home for me beyond institutions and whose tireless support inspires me every day. Gracias also to my dearest friends Eric Gómez, Lauren Kaminsky, Irene Mata, Sharina Maillo-Pozo, Pam Voekel, Adnaloy Espinosa, Afia Ofori Mensa, Mé Lo, Claudio Mir, Nuna Marcano, and Kirsten Weld, who fed me, nurtured me, went on masked socially distanced walks with me, and made me laugh out loud with silly memes and Zoom happy hours as I edited notes and complained about absolutely everything. Above all, thank you to my ancestors on whose backbridges I still walk in radical hope toward a future free from white supremacy, racial capitalism, and colonial violence. *Grazie mille de todo corazón.*

INTRODUCTION

Race, Colonialism, and Migration in the Global Latinx Diaspora

My name is Jovanna. I was born in Milan. I speak only Italian and a few words in bad Spanish. I went to school here. . . . Yes, I am Black; yes, I am Latina, but those are races, not countries. Everyone deserves a country. . . . I know a piece of paper will not guarantee my happiness. But people in Italy need to recognize and be aware that my lack of this "piece of paper" limits even the most mundane of activities. That it erases me from this country in which I was born. —JOVANNA RODRÍGUEZ, 23, ethnic Peruvian, born in Italy, from a speech delivered in Milan in 2015

My name is María. This is my country—the only one I have ever known. Here I learned to walk, to talk, and to write my name, María. My parents came here to give me a better life. I have broken no laws. Yet I am treated worse than an animal, like a goat, like a cow brought up to exist without identity. I have no papers. Yet here I am, belonging to no other nation than this one. Why do they do this to us? My only crime is that I was born to poor Black immigrants who followed the route to work and survival. —MARÍA PIERRE, 19, ethnic Haitian, born in the Dominican Republic, from a speech at a rally in Santo Domingo in 2013

My name is Elizabeth. I am undocumented. I was brought to this country when I was five years old. . . . My parents made a choice to move here in an effort to provide a better life for their children. . . . I was enrolled in American elementary school. I take all AP classes. I play violin for the youth symphony. I get good test scores, and I participate in my community. Yet my opportunities get slimmer and slimmer due to recent legislation. . . . This reminds me of Jim Crow, when customers were turned away with cash in hand . . . all because they were a different race. . . . How could someone who doesn't know me judge and reject me? . . . I broke no laws. I am not a criminal. Please don't let them treat me this way. —ELIZABETH GARIBAY, 19, ethnic Mexican, born in Mexico, from a speech delivered in Atlanta in 2011

This book is born from my own experience as a Black Latina immigrant scholar living in constant *vaivén* (coming and going) between belonging and unbelonging. It emerges out of the necessity for what philosopher Jonathan Lear calls radical hope: the commitment to dream of the possibility that "from this disaster, something good will emerge. . . . The hope is held in the face of the recognition that, given the abyss, one cannot really know what survival means."[1] In the face of oppression and obliteration, hope and action for another way of being—for a future free from colonial exploitation—is indeed a radical act of possibility. In that sense, this book is a radical act of hope that contra*dicts* impossibility and interrupts the colonial structures that have led us to live "in the wake" of slavery that erases the possibility of Black humanity in the streets and the archives.[2]

Translating Blackness proposes Black Latinidad as an epistemology—a way of understanding and producing knowledge from the site of unbelonging in what Christina Sharpe calls the "unfinished project of emancipation."[3] "Unfinished" implies an opening: that which is not finished is still in the making. Black Latinidad is thus not an embodied identity or a social construct but a point of entry and a set of methods that move us beyond homogeneous concepts of racial and citizenship exclusion. My analysis of Black Latinidad denaturalizes the nation as a site of belonging and invites us instead to learn from a productive detour away from and in contra*diction* to the colonial order that sustains national notions of citizenship and belonging. While these are lessons that can be deduced by reading archives in contra*diction*, against dominant versions of history and accepted hegemonic "truths," this book asks new critical questions to theorize blackness in translation. To think through Black Latinidad—to see the world through the epistemological contributions of Black Latinx humanity—is a project of Black possibility, Black living, and Black being.

Three testimonies open this book, delineating the geographies, axes, and *vaivenes* that structure my conceptualization of Black Latinidad as a site for critical engagement and a political articulation of the intersections of race, colonialism, and immigration in the twenty-first century. The three places embodied by each of these minoritized undocumented women—the United

States, Hispaniola, and Italy—fatefully and symbolically map my conceptual understanding and genealogical framework of Black Latinidad in constant vaivén as it intersects immigration with national belonging and unbelonging. More importantly, these testimonies exemplify the continuum of colonialism and the ruptures of colonial oppression as they appear and reappear in newer sites of racialization and unbelonging for Latinx migrants, such as Italy.

My previous book, *The Borders of Dominicanidad: Race, Nation, and Archives of Contradiction*, closed with the words of Elizabeth Garibay and María Pierre. I open this book with their voices—adding Jovanna Rodríguez's to the chorus—as a reminder of how struggle and oppression operate on a continuum. The similarities among these three experiences of unbelonging are undeniable: Garibay, who was born in Mexico and brought to the United States as a child, was excluded from civic life due to her undocumented status. Pierre, in the Dominican Republic, and Rodríguez, in Italy, were both disavowed from the countries in which they were born due to their parents' immigration status. All three women experience both racial and juridical exclusion—colonial consequences of racial oppression. They speak back to the nation in the language of racial justice *and* immigrant rights.

In the field of Latinx studies in the United States, Latinidad has been imagined as a concept that engages the experiences, histories, and cultural productions of US Latinx people. The geographical and historical borders of Latina/o/x studies have meant that most of our intellectual corpus is centered on the post–civil rights movement era and dominated by conversations about immigration and experiences of the US-Mexico border. In my previous work, I proposed a disruption of the hegemonic conceptualization of Latinidad by centering Hispaniola's encounter with the US empire in the nineteeth and twentieth centuries as another possible site of analysis.[4] My disruption in no way proposes a merging of Latinoamericanism with Latinx studies; these are two distinct concepts and fields. Rather, I suggest an engagement with the former via the Hispanic Caribbean and Haiti as a point of encounter and a reexamination of the geographical boundaries of Latinx to include new diasporas and the experiences of what Jorge Duany calls the culture of vaivén through which diasporic subjects travel back and forth between home and diaspora, participating in the life, culture, and politics of the nation they associate with their ethnic identity as well as the one in which they reside.[5] If Latinidad as an ideology first emerged in contradistinction with the US empire as a site of transnational contestation, as I argue in chapter 1, then that history is very much a part of what we understand to be Latinidad today. The vaivenes of the term are also crucial to understanding its genealogy. Further, the detours of Latinidad through Latin Americanness via the Caribbean are key to recovering and recentering Latinx blackness.

Translating Blackness intervenes in Latinx studies by geographically and conceptually expanding Latinidad to include the study of Latinx peoples, cultural products, and political processes in diaspora beyond the United States. In *The Borders of Dominicanidad,* I proposed decentering the US-Mexico border as the focal point of US Latinidad, instead thinking conceptually and geographically through US imperialism as constituent of the racial and ethnic production of Latinx as a category beyond the United States. In this book, I further expand Latinidad by examining its multiple vaivenes through blackness as a global racialized category. In so doing, *Translating Blackness* traces how theories and bodies intersect in various geographical and colonial/colonized spaces—Latin America, the United States, and Europe—to map a new cartography for understanding the convergences of colonialism, immigration, and blackness that shape Black Latinx lives in diaspora. The transnational and transatlantic triangulation of Black Latinidad this book proposes explains the implications of blackness as what Frantz Fanon called a "lived experience" while tracing how the construction of racial difference and blackness are the projects of nations as well as of the communities that define, translate, and remake the meanings and entanglements of blackness.[6] People confronting racism ultimately find ways of belonging, engaging terms and ideologies in their particular realities in ways that contra*dict* the persistent violence of colonialism that perpetuates xenophobia and antiblackness across the globe.

Setting off from Frederick Douglass's interpellation of Black Latinidad as *different from* (read: inferior, less civilized) US blackness in chapter 1, *Translating Blackness* historicizes multiple vaivenes, (mis)translations, and detours of Latinx colonialities through what I call hegemonic blackness—blackness defined through US culture, politics, histories, and the Anglophone experience (which sometimes includes the Anglophone Caribbean and South Africa via iconic representations of popular and political figures such as Bob Marley and Nelson Mandela). Attending to the various ways US blackness has itself migrated through imperial impositions, cultural expansion, academic discourse, and political diction, I argue that from the middle of the nineteenth century to the present, hegemonic blackness has shaped how global Black experiences, particularly those of Global South migrants and their descendants, are understood, analyzed, engaged, and translated around the world. This book thus historicizes Black Latinidad in the context of global blackness and in relation to hegemonic blackness. Thinking about the Caribbean, Édouard Glissant proposed the idea of "relationality" to help us consider the ways people—particularly Afro-diasporic people—are connected through their shared experiences, through what Glissant calls "shared knowledge."[7] Following Glissant, *Translating Blackness* brings attention to how Black Latinxs living in the Global North access the knowledge they share with other Black subjects in ways that indict their common colonial experiences of violence and exclusion and summon the historical legacy of resistance from which Black people across the globe have demanded inclusion and belonging throughout modern history. In so doing, I propose Black Latinidad as a category from which we can better understand the vaivenes of colonialism and migration that shape Black experiences in diaspora.

This book expands the geographies of Latinidad, and more specifically of Black Latinx colonialities, through my engagement across geographies: the Dominican Republic, the United States, and Italy. In turning to Italy, I analyze a region that does not immediately come to mind as critical to the geography of Black Latinidad. Yet the case study of Italy speaks to the global dimensions of blackness across overlapping histories of colonialism and racism. While the United States is the largest and most significant location of Latinidad outside of Latin America, Latinx migration has, since the mid-twentieth century, increasingly diversified because of the labor demands of global capital, shaping not only the experiences of migrants and their national cultures but also how people who identify as Latino/a/x imagine themselves in an ever-diversifying diaspora. What I find most interesting about these new Latinx migrations across the United States and Europe is how Second Generations (children who migrate at an early age and those born abroad to immigrant parents) living all over the world create new transnational imaginaries through claims to a global blackness that defies national borders. I analyze how these global Black diasporas, from the Dominican Republic to Italy, look to the cultural and political production of established Black diasporic enclaves in the United States to shape their political and cultural language vis-à-vis the dominant hegemonic and often white supremacist cultures of their new nations: that is, how and why a Second Generation woman of Peruvian descent from Italy like Jovanna Rodríguez, whose words open this book, looks to New Jersey rather than Lima to find a political language with which to talk back to Italy, translating Latinidad through US experiences and political frameworks of blackness.

Translating, Mistranslating, Untranslating Blackness

In his 1923 essay "The Task of the Translator," Walter Benjamin asserts that translation participates in the "afterlife" (Überleben) of the foreign text, enacting an interpretation informed by history.[8] This interpretation does more than transmit messages; it re-creates the significance of the multiplicity of experiences amassed by the word/text over time that attempts to "make visible" the meanings that have been invisibilized by hegemonic language. For Lawrence Venuti, translation is never perfect, but it is always an antihegemonic project of bringing forth that which is not at the center.[9] I argue, following Benjamin's and Venuti's interventions, that to translate thus presents us with the possibility of *seeing* the Other. This act of seeing is also an act of recognition that can contra*dict* hegemonic knowledge. Interpolating these understandings of textual translation with the political interjections of people and institutions speaking to the nation and beyond, I argue that translating coloniality into hegemonic blackness can be a strategy for making visible the experiences of Global South Black people by asserting their belonging in a global network of anti-colonial contestation. But counterhegemonic translation is never a gentle process of historical summoning. Rather, as Gloria Anzaldúa asserts, it is always a violent process of erasure—an act of terrorism because foreign words cannot encompass the specificity of the experience being translated.[10] Brent Edwards taught us that the process of translation for Afro diasporic people is always messy, sometimes even a failure in which not even the very basic "grammar of blackness" can be translated.[11] Translations are thus always lacking, always amiss. For Black Latinx immigrants living in the Global North, translated half truths often separate them from Black nationals, further marking their unbelonging to the nation. The impossibility of full recognition leaves them, as in the case of Black Latinxs in the United States, outside of even minoritarian discourses of contestation (Latinidad and hegemonic blackness), their blackness called into question because of their linguistic and cultural differences.

Blackness is a local and global construction that, though historically and geographically specific, develops as a process of vaivén across geographies, histories, markets, and polities through formal and informal channels. The construction of blackness is always situational. However, hegemonic globalized versions of ethno-racial concepts dominate popular perceptions, intellectual discourse, social and popular media, and, at times, even legislation, shaping people's actions and encounters with race and coloniality. Confronting these hegemonic racial meanings thus also requires an intentional translation that engenders a larger network of recognition and inclusion. For undocumented Latinxs in Georgia like Elizabeth Garibay and Black Latinx Europeans like Jovanna Rodríguez, the language of Black resistance—often framed through US hegemonic discourse—provides a platform from which to speak back to the nation while garnering a larger network of transnational political solidarity.

Translating Blackness proposes translation as a metaphor for understanding how dominant ethno-racial labels are used by multiple communities to make visible the historical processes that (re)produce their minoritized subjectivity: colonialism, global capitalism, and migration. At times, as in the case of Black Latinxs in the United States, the translation of blackness has been part of national projects of self-definition vis-à-vis colonial impositions by the United States and Europe. At other times, as in the case of migrants and new Black diasporic sociopolitical movements in Europe and Latin America, translations of blackness summon common historical experiences to garner inclusion and political representation. In both cases, the translation goes beyond a literal understanding of the ethno-racial hegemonic label "Black" to the circulation of knowledge about the historical processes informing the lives of human beings living the social costs of racism and exploitation that result from the colonial regimes that engender blackness as exclusion.

In *Translation and Subjectivity*, Naoki Sakai exposes the challenge of translating belonging because the subject in translation, as Sakai explains, is in tension, struggling with the ownership of words and meaning.

> The translator must be responsible for her translation, for every word of it, but she cannot be held responsible for what is pledged in what she says. For she is not allowed to say what she means in what she says in translation—she is supposed to say what she says without meaning. At the same time that the translator must be absolutely responsible for what she says, her task begins with her pledge to say what the original addresser means to say. *Her responsibility consists in her commitment to withdraw her wish to express herself* from what she says even though she has to seek and interpret what the addresser means in the first place. Therefore, the translator is also the interpreter.[12]

Bearing in mind the "task of the translator"—their responsibility as an interpreter of lived experiences—*Translating Blackness* proposes translation as an expression of belonging that seeks to conjure unbelonging: to make visible the colonial/colonizing process that engenders human exclusion. It challenges the monolithic representations of Black people and Black histories that dominate hegemonic narratives, archives, and the public sphere through an engagement with the internal and transnational colonial regimes that operate within and across states, communities, and institutions that force people to "withdraw their wish to express" their sense of belonging. Yomaira Figueroa-Vásquez argues that to label people as Black without nuance is an act of violence; it is to "reduce the complexity of Black life."[13] Simply naming all Black experiences through hegemonic blackness can lead to a "withdrawal of the self"—to the erasure, mistranslation, and silencing of the specific experiences of nonhegemonic Black people. *Translating Blackness* moves away from the simplistic grouping of Black experiences to complexify the narrating, sharing, and historicizing of the multiplicity of global and relational Black experiences. At times, as we will see throughout the book, translating blackness leads to transnational, intra-ethnic political solidarity; at others, it erases nonhegemonic Black experiences. For Black Latinxs in the Global North, particularly in the United States, translating blackness can simultaneously confront the internal borders that produce them as foreign (and therefore Other within the nation) and the pervasive dominance of Hispanicity and *mestizaje* that erases them from the dominant understanding of Latinidad and Latinx diasporas. Translating blackness is thus always in tension with hegemony, exposing the experiences of nonhegemonic Black subjects living between belonging and unbelonging.

Black *en inglés*: The Latinx Colonial Difference

The significance of US Black politics and the legacy of US Black struggles for freedom have undoubtedly made visible a multiplicity of colonial exclusions and discriminatory regimes as well as the resistance to these forms of exclusion that US Black people have exercised for centuries. Angela Davis writes, "Black struggles in the United States serve as an emblem of the struggle for freedom"; she goes on to note that the Black radical tradition is relevant not only to Black people in the United States but also to "all people who are struggling for freedom," including Latinxs, LGBTQI people, immigrants, Palestinians, Indigenous, and incarcerated people.[14] Engaging US blackness as Davis describes is an example of "translating blackness": embodying, engaging with, interpolating, and dialoguing with hegemonic Black struggles for equality and freedom. By translating their experiences through hegemonic blackness, historical actors, organizations, and communities across the globe make their experiences of unbelonging visible to a larger, more powerful constituency, gaining solidarity in their assertions of belonging and their strug-

FIGURE I.1 Swedish activist Tess Asplund interrupts a neo-Nazi march in Borlänge, Sweden, May 1, 2016. AP images.

gles for freedom. I argue that translating blackness makes coloniality visible, transforming the epistemological, historical, and cultural experiences of a small collective into a recognizable global marker to gain access and mobility and produce social change. Translating blackness conjures the universal violence against Black bodies and calls upon the poetics of blackness as a series of cultural and linguistic codes that go beyond the particular experience of exclusion from the nation-state. Translating blackness contra*dicts* and transcends the nation, claiming Black humanity as a global category of belonging.

On May 1, 2016, Tess Asplund, an Afro-Latina Swedish activist, translated her blackness to the world when she stepped out in defiance of white supremacy, her clenched fist raised in front of three hundred marching neo-Nazis from the Nordic Resistance Movement in Borlänge, Sweden (see figure I.1).[15] Asplund was born in Cali, Colombia, in 1972 and adopted by a Swedish family at seven months old.[16] While Sweden prides itself on progressive ideals of inclusivity and social justice, race and multiethnicity are not part of that inclusive agenda. In fact, like most of Europe, Sweden imagines itself as nonracial and insists on assimilation to Swedish values and identities as the only road to national inclusion.[17] Thus, Asplund grew up Swedish, distanced from Colombian linguistic and cultural heritage, while simultaneously suffering racism and exclusion due to her racial and ethnic identity as a Black

Colombian. Legal adoption and Swedish citizenship did not exempt Asplund from anti-immigrant racist violence. Asplund identifies as Black, Latina, immigrant, and ethnic Colombian.[18] As she explained to me, her Black Latina identity comes not only from her ethnic background but from the experiences of unbelonging that shaped and gave meaning to her everyday life in Sweden—from being singled out at school to being asked for a passport on a train to being at the receiving end of racial slurs and anti-immigrant violence.

The photo of this petite Black woman standing in defiance of white supremacy resonated with Black activists around the world. Asplund's heroic actions earned her the respect and admiration of many, including recognition by the BBC as one of the most influential women of 2016.[19] Reflecting on her actions and on the overwhelming global reception of the photograph, Asplund stated that her bravery was fueled by the urgency of this moment in which "racism has become normalized."[20] It was thus her hope that people would think about her action as a symbol of what one person can do if they get out of their comfort zone and fight for what is right. "I have been fighting against these people for twenty-seven years," she said. "If you stay at home, they have won."[21]

In their article "From Afro-Sweden with Defiance: The Clenched Fist as Coalitional Gesture?," Nana Osei-Kofi, Adela Licona, and Karma Chávez analyze the symbolic significance of Asplund's performance of anti-racist defiance, referring to her clenched fist as a "coalitional gesture" that defies global racism: "In the case of Asplund, we contend that the image of her clenched fist acquires its power by doing *historical, political, and relational memory* work as it gets linked to earlier anti-racist struggles, while at the same time making visible a *contextually specific* expression of the movement against racism in Sweden."[22] Asplund's clenched fist—her Black Latina body's interruption of state-sanctioned white supremacist violence—summons the memory of twentieth-century Black resistance we associate with the US Black Power movement that, as Davis argues, shapes how we understand anti-colonial resistance and freedom struggles across the globe.[23] Asplund herself says she was inspired by Malcolm X, Nelson Mandela, and Angela Davis—further evidence of her translation of blackness through the global narrative of anti-racist, anti-colonial struggles for freedom and justice.[24] As Osei-Kofi, Licona, and Chávez argue, Asplund's raised fist sparked "relational memory work," allowing a transnational audience to engage with Asplund through their own affective, political, historical, and cultural understandings of her raised fist.[25] Visual artists from all over the world interpreted Asplund's gesture (see figure I.2), while memes and videos inundated social media. Political actions by women of color of multiple ethnicities and identifications

FIGURE I.2 Luiso García, *Viva la gente de color*, 2016.

that mimicked Asplund's protest spread across Europe and Latin America in defiance of the growth of the extreme Right that seems to be spreading like a virus across the globe.[26] In the process, these interpretations consecrated Asplund as a global icon of anti-racist resistance.

Asplund's embodiment of Black political performance against white supremacy points to two significant processes that are foundational to my theorization of translating blackness: the cultural translation of specific local contexts to the world through the interpolation of recognizable symbols and/or the language of hegemonic blackness, and the contextually specific engagement of racialized immigrants' experiences through the language of Black liberation and resistance. Asplund's blackness is translated to a global audience through a recognizable symbol of Black Power: the fist. In turn, this translation establishes her belonging and solidarity beyond the nation. Her identity as a Black Latina Swede, however, shifts and refocuses her historical interpellation of the fist, summoning a specific colonial-diasporic experience—the confrontation with white supremacy in Sweden's anti-immigration climate following the 2015 "refugee crisis." Black Latinidad contra*dict*s her oppression and reminds us of the parallels and intersections between race and migration in the present day.

Translating blackness can be an effective political strategy for shattering the hegemony of white supremacy and nation-states through cultural, political, and social media translations historically grounded in racial struggles for liberation and citizenship, as seen in Asplund's case. But it can also reproduce other forms of erasure and unbelonging for Black communities across the globe: the image of Asplund does not immediately summon a confrontation with xenophobia and anti-immigrant violence as she intended. It produces Asplund as a Black woman protesting white supremacy rather than a Black Latina facing antiblackness due to the rise in anti-immigration, anti-refugee sentiment in contemporary Europe. That is, Asplund engages hegemonic blackness via an emblem of the Black radical tradition to be visible in the world. Hegemonic blackness, in turn, gains her access to a discourse of political dissidence, historical belonging, and global recognition. Her translation allows the world to *see* her and, in this seeing, formulate questions that may inform a dialogue about nonhegemonic blackness (e.g., What is happening in Sweden? What are the experiences of Black Swedes?). Or, as Asplund explained to me, "People saw this little Black woman and recognized what I did as something we must do. We have done. But the picture allowed me to connect with Colombia. To find my family, to talk about the way this [white supremacist violence] is affecting all of us [nonwhite people,] you know, like Muslims, and Asians, and Latinos."[27] Translating blackness is only the first step; to be seen as a Global South person in the world requires the audience to reach beyond the universalizing hegemonic symbol and ask questions about specifics. To translate blackness can lead to contest exclusion and demand Black belonging, protection, and rights within the nation.

Historical representations of US slavery and emancipation, Jim Crow, the Harlem Renaissance, and the global significance of the US civil rights, Black Power, and most recently Black Lives Matter movements, in addition to the cultural representations of US Black global icons of success, have made US blackness appear to be the *only* way to be Black *and* a citizen. Put another way, to have access to political power, historical presence, and representation as a Black human, one must necessarily engage blackness as it is understood, produced, and mediated through US discourse. The translation of multiple forms of oppression, colonialism, and exploitation to US blackness can successfully speak to a global public—even when one's nation is not listening. Asplund's raised fist gestures toward a global understanding of Black Power grounded on the historical experiences of US Blacks. It also inserts her—and by extension, her local struggle—into globalized conversations about Black belonging and antiblackness. As such, her story and her struggle, symbolically encapsulated in the image of her raised fist, are situated within a historical continuum. Translating blackness requires the simultaneous reminder of difference and the demand for inclusion by virtue of the shared experience of colonial oppression and contestation.

Terry Cochran argues that translation is intrinsically linked to national bordering.[28] The need to translate presumes the existence of a hegemonic language—and in the case of Black Latinxs in the diaspora, of a normative way of being Black. In the early twentieth century, Black Puerto Rican bibliophile Arthur Schomburg and Nuyorican poet Piri Thomas struggled to find belonging within the Black literary and intellectual circles of New York. Their ethnic, linguistic, and cultural identities as Puerto Ricans marked them as different from US Blacks, making their integration into US Black political and cultural movements arduous, to say the least. A century later, Black Latinxs still must explain their *other* blackness to a larger US constituency. In February 2018, during an interview with Black American actress Zendaya, popular hip-hop icon Cardi B responded to an inquiry about her racial identification by saying, "I don't got to tell you I'm Black. We came over here the same f*cking way."[29] Since her rise to fame in 2017, the Caribbean American singer has been questioned about her blackness and light-skin privilege by an audience unaccustomed to heterogenous, multiethnic blackness. Antonio López argues that the social difference that blackness makes in the United States is central to Black Latinidad: "how an Anglo white supremacy determines the life chance of Afro-Latinos hailed as Black and how a Latino white supremacy reproduces the colonial and postcolonial Latin America privileging of *blanco* over *negro* and *mulato* [mixed-race] identities, now on behalf of white Latinas/os who may themselves face Anglo forms of racializing discrimination."[30] This logic of hemispheric white supremacy also determines whether one is "white enough or the right kind of white or less black or the right kind of black to receive or be denied rights and advantages based on how one speaks (or doesn't) in English, Spanish, or both."[31] The linguistic experience of diasporic Black Latinxs, Yolanda Martínez-San Miguel argues, is also intrinsic to what she calls the "coloniality of the diaspora" that divides Black people between national subjects (e.g., US Blacks) and minoritized citizens from post/neocolonial spaces (e.g., Black Puerto Ricans living in the United States).[32]

Following Martínez-San Miguel, I argue that the experiences of Black Latinxs also differ from those of other racialized nonwhite national subjects because for them the nation-state is both a colonial power and a bordering agent producing the legal structures of citizenship and belonging. Marked as foreign due to their legal status and/or cultural or linguistic difference, Black

Latinx diasporic subjects struggle to find a political and cultural place within the nations in which they reside as immigrants (or as descendants of immigrants) while simultaneously facing similar forms of racism and exclusion to those confronted by US Blacks: they can be shot by the police *and* arrested by the immigration authorities. For Black Latinxs, translating their racialized immigrant Latinx exclusion by aligning with US Black historical experiences can help them become legible to the nation, access resources, and build antiracist and anti-colonial solidarity.

The contradictions and (mis)translations of Black Latinidad through US coloniality in these examples produce Black Latinxs as both Black and other-than-Black: simultaneously foreign to the nation and constituents of it. This tension is intrinsically linked to the relationship between race and immigration shaping our current global economy—a relationship that stems from the same colonial legacy that produced Black people as inferior, superfluous, and expendable. At the same time, these translations of blackness engage historical legacies of slavery and migration and point to the processes that have consistently shaped Black diasporic solidarity and cultural, political, and social movements across the globe for nearly two centuries.

Colonial Migrations of Black Latinidad

Central to *Translating Blackness* are the colonial structures that link anti-immigrant racism and antiblackness in the twenty-first century, producing globalized categories of human beings "susceptible" to exclusion, in David Hernández's terminology: ethnic minorities, immigrants, and racialized nonwhite subjects.[33] Contra*dicting* the practices that often separate the work of racial justice from that of immigrant rights, this book also grapples with the multiple ways people who are deemed to "unbelong" create collective possibilities of being and belonging through cultural and political acts of alliance building that translate historical experiences of colonial exclusion (such as slavery and segregation) into present-day political contestations of immigrant/minoritized human belonging (such as #BlacksLivesMatter and #NoHumanBeingIsIllegal).

In 2011, after the University of Georgia banned undocumented students from accessing its public universities because they were thought to be "taking seats away from citizens," I joined a group of activists, including students, professors, and community members, to create an alternative school for undocumented students.[34] We called it Freedom University Georgia, following in the footsteps of the Black Freedom Schools that decades before sustained liberationist education models in the US South. It opened its doors to thirty-two undocumented students in October 2011. Freedom University was a direct response to a racist policy that sought to exclude undocumented students from accessing higher education. It also became a national model for resistance when anti-immigrant sentiment was on the rise, evidenced by the passage of the historic Arizona SB 1070 in 2010, popularly known as the "Show Me Your Papers" law, which required police officers to inquire about people's immigration statuses; the US government's Secure Communities program, which targets Mexican and Latinx immigrants for deportation; and a national financial crisis that led, as they historically have, to a rise in deportation and widespread mistrust of immigrants, particularly those of Latinx descent.[35]

I learned many lessons as a Freedom University teacher, organizer, and co-creator. I learned to be an effective, engaged scholar. I learned to teach in ways that are transformative, create community, and promote social justice. I also learned the very tangible, intrinsic, and often subtle ways anti-immigrant racism is entangled with antiblackness—how, as Garibay explained in her interpellation of Jim Crow that opens this book, anti-immigrant racism emerges out of the same colonial capitalist structures that engendered slavery and continue to sustain the existence of Black and Brown immigrant subjects in the afterlife of slavery, suspended in unbelonging to the nation and the world.

I came to clearly understand twenty-first-century anti-immigrant violence as an iteration of colonialism one afternoon in September 2011 in Pinewoods, a trailer park in Athens, Georgia, where most of the residents are undocumented immigrants. A dozen of us were sitting outside the trailer of Athens's immigrant advocate Beto Cacao, organizing to support undocumented students when Linda Lloyd, a US Black woman from Georgia, walked up. She walked around Cacao's yard, nodding to each of us before standing in the very center of our improvised circle to address the group. "I have been here before," she said by way of introduction, "and we cannot, we will not let it happen again." Lloyd came of age in post–Jim Crow Georgia and, like many young activists of her generation, worked to end segregation and integrate a deeply fragmented community. Since the 1980s, she has fought for equality in Georgia. She eventually became the director of the Economic Justice Coalition, a grassroots organization that seeks to end economic inequality and disparity in Athens.[36]

For Lloyd, the passage of the ban against undocumented students was clearly another iteration of what many Black people from Georgia experienced under Jim Crow: a painful border that divided humans into two categories, belonging and unbelonging. Like Lloyd, US Black leaders John Lewis and Angela Davis showed their support for undocumented Georgia students in the wake of the ban by publicly linking their exclusion to the history of racial segregation. As Davis put it, "The discourse of 'immigrants' draws from and feeds on the racisms of the past, the racisms that have affected people of African descent, of Native American people. So, it seems to me that the struggle for immigrant rights is the key struggle of our times. And it is a struggle for civil rights. It is a struggle for human rights."[37] Their recognition of the historical intersections of immigrant and Black struggles for freedom provided undocumented students in Georgia with a larger, stronger, and more historically grounded political sustenance from which to speak back to the state and the nation.

As a scholar of US Black Latinidad, I was very familiar with the history of Jim Crow and the social movements that ended segregation in the United States. But having grown up in the Northeast, I had never been immersed in a community that lived "in the wake" of Jim Crow until I moved to Georgia.[38] Lloyd and other locals brought their acute awareness of that recent past to the immigrant struggle, shaping the nature of our organizing, teaching, and solidarity. It also profoundly redefined how I, as a Black Latina Dominicana and a scholar of Black Latinidad in the United States, conceptualize, define, understand, and experience the relationship between blackness, immigration, and Latinidad as a continuation of colonialism—as entangled experiences of past and present colonial oppression. Sharpe argues that the project of emancipation is incomplete, and therefore Black people live in what Saidiya Hartman calls "the aftermath of slavery."[39] But slavery was a product of colonial capitalism. We must thus recognize, as did Lloyd, that the same colonial logic that convinced the world that it was acceptable to profit from capturing and enslaving Africans and Indigenous people continues to sustain "immigrant" as a racialized subhuman category of unbelonging, and racialized immigrant subjects as disposable, consumable bodies without history, aliens to the nation-state at the service of the global capitalist machinery. Following this logic, I argue that racialized nonwhite Latinx immigrants like the women whose testimonies open this book are also living in "the aftermath" of colonialism: their everyday lives are shaped by the continual intersections of antiblackness and anti-immigrant sentiment that produce new categories of "undesirables," to borrow Hernández's term, in the nation. The exclusionary category "immigrant" is an iteration of the global colonial capitalist regime of human exploitation.

Sylvia Wynter argues that our present struggles "with respect to race, class, gender, sexual orientation, ethnicity, struggles over the environment, global warming, severe climate change, the sharply unequal distribution of the earth resources" are a result of colonial structures that define people as human or less than human through colonial categories of citizenship based on race, ethnicity, bodily ability, or what I call belonging and unbelonging.[40] For Lisa Lowe, one significant effect of these colonial categories of humanity is the emergence and dominance of an archive that defines humanity through proximity to European values, cultures, and whiteness.[41] In the United States, these categories of belonging and unbelonging determine who goes to prison; who gets pulled over by the police; who must show identification in public spaces; who is left out of institutions, archives, and other sites; and who can run, nap, read, or watch birds in peace.[42] If humans (those who belong) are defined by their proximity to Europe, as both Wynter and Lowe have argued, then lesser human, racialized nonwhite, minoritized, and immigrant subjects (who unbelong) are presumed to be expendable, durable, and uncivil—now, as in the fifteenth and sixteenth centuries.

In many Global North colonial powers such as the United States, these dynamics of belonging and unbelonging manifest through a discursive and economic replacement of the slave with the immigrant of color. As Hernández argues, race and noncitizenship work together as "intertwined vulnerabilities that make whole communities susceptible and at times defenseless against constitutional status."[43] Immigrants now do the labor that enslaved Black and Indigenous peoples and Asian indentured servants were once forced to do all over the Americas. They also occupy the place of liminal humanity that sustains the nation. The oppression of Black people and immigrants must therefore be confronted together.

Nicholas de Genova argues that the category "immigrant" is a modern fabrication that hinges on our collective belief in the nation-state as a "quasi-natural space" rather than the exclusionary regime of the practice of bordering.[44] That is, "immigrant" and "citizen" are "bordered identities" defined through statutory, often arbitrary regimes of human belonging that hinge on notions of presumed legality and illegality.[45] That certain immigrants are presumed to be "illegal" also shapes how citizens who share the ethnic or cultural identity of a racialized immigrant group, such as Latinxs in the United States, experience everyday racism and civic exclusion. For many immigrants of color in the United States—particularly those of Latinx descent—noncitizen discrimination (the presumption of illegality) and racism intersect, shaping their access to civic mobility, from driving to higher education. The intersections of race and immigration shape their unbelonging to state institutions and the nation.

Since the conception of the United States as a nation, citizenship has been equated with whiteness. The Naturalization Act of 1790, in which citizenship was restricted to "any alien, being a free white person" who had resided in the United States for two years, relied on a racial hierarchy rooted in white supremacy and measures of difference, including gender, sexuality, class, bodily ability, religion, and political ideology.[46] Immigrant belonging continues to depend on assimilation to acceptable versions of whiteness that shift over time. As European migration to the United States decreased in the second half of the twentieth century, "immigrant" came to signify a racialized nonwhite category of exclusion—a locus of political and legal negotiation of the nation-state and its narrowing racial and ethnic borders. While European immigrants from the early nineteenth to the mid-twentieth centuries experienced hardships upon their arrival in the United States, they were eventually able to assimilate (albeit not equally, as we know from the experiences of Irish Americans and Italian Americans) into the white American "melting pot," becoming unhyphenated citizens. By contrast, Black, Asian, Native, and Brown immigrants who arrived in the United States throughout the nineteenth and twentieth centuries never became "just American." Rather, their insertion into the nation has always been and continues to be conditional to what Gustavo Pérez Firmat has called the "hyphen" (an ethnic and racial qualifier to national identity required only of minoritized citizens) and dependent upon successful performances of white American civility.[47] This hyphenated state of deferred and conditional belonging is due in part to the fact that these immigrants were and are colonial subjects of the expanding US empire (most notably in the cases of Puerto Ricans, Cubans, Dominicans, and Filipinos who migrated throughout the twentieth century), and in part because the United States has not yet resolved the internal borders that exclude Afro-descendants, Indigenous people, and Mexicans—who were never immigrants—from full citizenship. The exclusion of Black, Brown, Native, and Asian peoples from American citizenship at the conception of the nation-state continues to shape present-day ethnic identifications that border notions of national belonging for many of us (presumed illegal) immigrants. The racialized production of "immigrant" sustains the ethno-racial borders of the US nation by excluding racialized nonwhite immigrants and their Second Generation descendants from becoming full citizens by withholding their belonging to the nation through "hyphenated" identities and exclusion based on race. In the current political climate, "immigrant" is thus a category of political and legal restrictions, human negation, and border making, particularly in Global North immigrant-receiving postcolonial nations like the United States. The legal status and social condition we typically associate with "immigrant" in fact signify, as de Genova argues, a "heterogenous spectrum of legal distinctions and social inequalities" that shapes people's identities and relationships to different forms of belonging.[48] If the law as de Genova argues is the device that produces the universality of "citizen" (belonging to the nation), then "immigrant" functions as its opposite (unbelonging). Immigrant belonging is thus an impossibility.

On Possibility: Black Latinx Belonging

But resistance has always come from impossibility. Haven't all social, political, economic, and cultural counterhegemonic movements been grounded on experiences of unbelonging and the radical hope for belonging?

Black Latinxs living in the Global North—particularly in the United States and Europe—carry slavery and immigration with them as colonial experiences of unbelonging, often while navigating other forms of internal and transnational colonialities. Their subjecthood and bodies are bordered through palimpsestic colonialisms. Their experiences and histories, I argue in this book, can help us make sense of how "Black" and "immigrant" intersect in the twenty-first century, producing other forms of colonized oppression. More importantly, Black Latinidad can help us see possibilities for transnational anti-colonial and anti-racist forms of contestation that go beyond the nation and challenge hegemonic notions of racial and ethnic identification.

My conceptualization of Black Latinidad is guided by the intersections of colonialism, diaspora, migration, and blackness that shape the historical processes and experiences of diasporic Black people who are linked—by birth, language, culture, or ancestry—to Latin America and who are immigrants (whether by their own or their parents' displacement) in the Global North. Black Latinidad differs from Afro-Latin Americanness in the experience of migration. This plurality of diasporas means that Black Latinx people confront and navigate multiple contradictory regimes of coloniality and racial hierarchies: those produced through the colonization of Latin America by the Spanish, French, British, and Portuguese, which shaped their ethno-racial identities and experiences at "home," as well as those imposed by the internal bordering of racialized citizen/immigrant subjects "abroad." The dialectic between here and there, and the symbolic and historical vaivén between sites of belonging and unbelonging, is constitutive of Black Latinidad. Duany has used the notion of vaivén—coming and going—to highlight the transnational experience of Puerto Rican people in the United States as subjects and nations on the move.[49] In the Dominican Republic, "vaivén" signifies ambivalence and uprootedness. My use of the term departs from Duany's framework and Dominican popular ideology to insist on its dynamic possibilities: to be coming and going to and from the nation and hegemonic notions of belonging is to challenge the social order, the structures of the market, and the ideologies of national identifications.

Translating Blackness engages Black Latinidad as a theoretical category through which to understand the historical intersections of race, ethnicity, migration, and citizenship that have led to the present-day production of minoritized citizens of color. The vaivén of blackness through Latinidad and the multiple colonial entanglements that shape the conceptualization of a global Black Latinx collective exemplify how race and citizenship travel across national paradigms through the movement of bodies, words, and objects. In turn, their vaivenes shed light on colonialism and coloniality in the contemporary globalized nation-state. Translating blackness makes these colonial entanglements visible. Visibility, in turn, places local anti-colonial struggles within a recognizable global historical continuum.

Italy as a Site of Vaivén

People are often puzzled to find out I engage Italy in my research about Black Latinidad. But understanding Italy as a site of postcolonial encounters, as a gateway to the European Union, and as a nation that imagines itself as "clean" from the history of colonization and slavery—and therefore free from the afterlife of slavery—leads us to look at the Black experience beyond the hegemonic narratives and common locations we have come to anticipate as associated with blackness. As SA Smythe argues, "A postcolonial understanding of Black life in Italy creates a spatial transnational continuity with other European countries which also have colonial histories, reinforcing the idea of diasporic communities that share a colonial legacy."[50] Studied in tandem with other sites and historical processes, as it is in this book, Italy can be incredibly productive as a site for understanding contemporary experiences of blackness. In this way, it contributes to the goal of building a more robust articulation of global blackness as we strive to end antiblackness, white supremacy, and violence against immigrants of color.

I began to think about this project in 1998, when I was nineteen years old, a recent college graduate working as a journalist for a nongovernmental organization in Latin America. I was tasked with reporting on the conditions on the ground in the aftermath of natural and human disasters. In the fall of that year, Hurricane George hit the Caribbean, taking a toll on the southwestern border region of the Dominican Republic, and I was sent to write stories about how people were coping after the storm. In late September, I arrived in the village of Postrer Río, a community of about seven thousand people located in Independencia Province in the southwestern Dominican borderlands. Postrer Río had suffered greatly due to the hurricane. As I talked to people, I noticed that there seemed to be no women in town. Or rather, there were grandmothers and little girls, but all the working-age women were gone. I began to ask around about the women, and one man told me, "They have all gone to Italy." As I later confirmed, Postrer Río, as with the rest of the Neyba Valley and Jimaní Basin area, had experienced a gigantic increase in migration to Europe—mostly of women—since the early 1980s.[51] In the eighties, most migrants went to Spain, but by the late nineties they began increasingly to migrate to Italy.

I was aware of Dominicanas' migration to Spain. In fact, I had two cousins working as nannies for wealthy Spanish families in Madrid. But I can say with certainty that at the turn of the twenty-first century, there was no public or scholarly conversation about Italy as a migration destination for Dominicanas. Rather, most of the attention about Dominican migration centered around the United States, Puerto Rico, and, to a lesser extent, Spain. I became obsessed with the subject and set out to research it. I gathered the little information that was accessible at the time: a few articles by sociologist Luis Guarnizo, some short pieces on the crowning of Denny Méndez as Miss Italia in 1996, and several social science articles on migration to Spain that included statistics or brief mentions of other sites of Latin American migration to Europe, including Italy.[52] I also began to read more generally about Italy as a migrant destination for Global South women.[53] Notably, throughout my two decades of work in and about Italy, I gathered anecdotes and stories, asking friends and family members in the Dominican Republic if they knew of a Dominicana who had moved to Italy. Sure enough, many people had heard of or knew someone who had moved to Italy, and slowly I began to build a network of amazing informants who shared their experiences and connected me with friends and family in Italy willing to share their stories.

By the time I began to travel regularly to Italy to conduct research for this book in 2013, it had become the "door" to Europe for asylum seekers from Syria, Eritrea, and Somalia as well as a contested location for citizenship rights for descendants of immigrants. My interest in Dominicanas' migration to Italy transformed into a project about the ways Black migrants—particularly those who also identify as Latinxs—experience belonging and unbelonging as they navigate overlapping colonial histories and their place as immigrants in the Global North. The Dominican experience that led me to these questions continued to inform my analysis and bridge my research as I found myself in a long detour through the vaivenes of Black Latinidad in the twenty-first century. Moreover, the Dominicanas who first pointed me toward Italy also led me to the questions that inform this book: How do colonial histories shape the way Black Latinx migrants and their descendants understand and translate race and national identity in the diaspora? How is blackness named, translated, politicized, and historicized in postcolonial nations that did not participate in the colonization of the Americas and the slave trade? And how do these translations of blackness intersect with the experiences of immigration, colonialism, diaspora, and ethnicity in the context of globalized antiblackness?

Over seven years of qualitative research in Italy, I learned about the experiences of people who are Black, migrants, and postcolonial subjects. In turn, my understanding of blackness, Black history, and Black futurity also expanded in ways that at times took me by surprise and at others confirmed what foundational Black Latinx scholars like Gregorio Luperón and Arthur Schomburg seemed to have been suggesting since the late nineteenth century: that "Black" transcends nations, and as such, nations are not sufficient frameworks with which to explain or contain Black belonging. Black Latinidad, in particular, emerges through the Italian experience as a valuable human and epistemological category for understanding the world today: how global antiblackness operates in this historical moment and, more importantly, the possibilities for detours, change, and hope.

Still, Italy is but one of the examples I present in this book. My hope is that my engagement with it opens the possibility for more transnational, global conversations about the intersections of blackness, colonialism, migration, and belonging in immigrant-receiving sites beyond the predominantly studied locations of Latinidad (the United States, Latin America, and Spain). Further, my analysis of Italy insists on the expansiveness of Black Latinidad not only as a category of identification but also as a method of inquiry and an epistemology. Read in dialogue with the Caribbean and the United States as sites of Black Latinidad, Italy offers an immense opportunity to expand the fields of Black and Latinx studies as well as our methods of inquiry through the analysis of overlapping histories of colonialism in present-day manifestations. So while this is not a book specifically about Italy, I ask you, the reader, to accompany me through my own critical vaivén through Italy, linking US abolitionist Frederick Douglass to Black Italian beauty queen Denny Méndez to Black Latinx scholar Arthur Schomburg to the lives of Black migrants in contemporary Italy.

Black Citizen / Latinx Difference

The first section of this book, "On Being Black and Citizen: Latinx Colonial Vaivenes," interrogates the relationships between citizenship, blackness, and colonialism in the United States from Reconstruction to the civil rights era. Centering Hispaniola's relationship to the US empire as critical to the articulation of Black Latinidad, this section traces the genealogy of Black Latinx intellectual and political discourse and its vaivenes and detours through US Black political thought, highlighting the importance of Black diasporas outside of Africa and Africanist discourse. While acknowledging the violent legacy of slavery and colonialism, my analysis pushes against the dominance of Afropessimism as the lens through which to understand the lived experiences of Black people, insisting instead on the ways Black people within and beyond the United States have constructed being and belonging in contra-*diction* to slavery and colonialism.

Chapter 1, "A Full Stature of Humanity: Latinx Difference, Colonial Musings, and Black Belonging during Reconstruction," poses a conversation between nineteenth-century Black intellectuals and freedom fighters Gregorio Luperón and Frederick Douglass, exploring the significance of the two men in the production of Black Latinidad as a category of belonging in the face of US colonial expansion during Reconstruction. This conversation is framed by the vaivenes of Black Latina musician and writer Gregoria Fraser Goins. The lives of the two men intersect in Fraser Goins's own through a series of familial and political ties that emerge as a result of Douglass's trip to the Dominican Republic in 1871 as part of the Commission of Inquiry to annex the country to the United States. Through Fraser Goins, we witness the tangible effects of the relationship between the two nations on her sense of belonging and her identity as a Black/Brown Latina.

Chapter 2, "Arthur Schomburg's Haiti: Diaspora Archives and the Epistemology of Black Latinidad," analyzes how diaspora, migration, and citizenship are constitutive of early articulations of Black Latinx thought. Through a close reading of Black Puerto Rican scholar Arthur Schomburg's writing, archival ethos, and lived experiences, this chapter illustrates the emergence of Black Latinx intellectual discourse, epistemology, and thought in dialogue with the notion of diaspora. Schomburg's sophisticated intellectual project is grounded on the intersections and vaivenes of colonialism, migration, diaspora, and blackness that shape Latinx struggles for citizenship and belonging in the United States and beyond. Like other Black Latinxs for generations to come, Schomburg struggled to belong within US blackness due to his Puerto Rican cultural and linguistic identity. Yet he did not fully belong in Puerto Rico either, in part due to his migratory experiences and in part due to his awareness of the pitfalls of the Latin American independence projects he once supported. These projects were grounded on myths of racial inclusivity and mestizaje that ultimately erased Black people, Black histories, and Black knowledge from the nation. Translating the multiplicity of his own post/colonial vaivenes through blackness and Latinidad, Schomburg dedicated his life to a "Negro nation without a nation."[54] This "Negro nation," as Schomburg imagined it, was a global collective united by common histories, the acceptance of linguistic, cultural, and ethnic diversity, and, most of all, a desire for equality and historical transcendence.

The book's second section, "Black Feminist Contra*dictions* in Latinx Diasporas," foregrounds gender and sexuality as essential to theorizing Black Latinidad in the diaspora. Centering the lives, work, experiences, and articulations of belonging of Black women living in the afterlife of colonialism and slavery in the diaspora, this section historicizes the colonial violence that has produced Black women as objects for consumption, the systemic state-sponsored violence that leads to Black women's deaths, and the effects of antiblackness and colonialism that prompt Global South Black women to migrate north. In analytical vaivén between colonialism and migration, this section also shows how Black migrant women and their children contra*dict* colonial and state violence through private and public acts of re-membering that interrupt the colonial archive and its afterlife. This section is also in transatlantic geographic vaivén, following the physical, historical, and symbolic movement of Black Latinas through the United States, the Caribbean, Europe, and Africa.

Chapter 3, "Against Death: Black Latina Rebellion in Diasporic Community," examines the civic, social, and physical deaths of Black women in the Dominican Republic as an effect of the alliance between US colonialism and the Dominican state. Through analyses of photographs, interviews, pamphlets, oral histories, and literary texts produced by Black Dominicanas living in the United States, the Hispanic Caribbean, and Italy, the chapter traces the significance of radical Black Latina feminist activism in shaping transnational dialogues around antiblackness and immigrant rights. The chapter engages original testimonies from women who fought in the Dominican Civil War of 1965 and were forced to migrate as a result of their radical political views. Unlike previous work on the women of the 1965 war that focuses on middle- and upper-class Dominicanas, this chapter investigates the lives of working-class Black guerrilleras in the aftermath of the war, following them through their migrations and vaivenes in diaspora. The chapter maps radical Black Dominicanas' migration and historicizes the Caribbean Latina political legacy of Black contestation that emerged in Italy in the 1980s and 1990s within socialist and feminist migrant women organizations.

Chapter 4, "The Afterlife of Colonial Gender Violence: Black Immigrant Women's Life and Death in Postcolonial Italy," investigates what happens to Black Latina women in Italy in the twenty-first century as the country shifts from being an immigrant-sending nation to an immigration hub. The chapter sets off from an analysis of the posthumous representations of Carolina Payano, a twenty-one-year-old Black Caribbean immigrant murdered in Milan in 2012, in dialogue with colonial photographs, documents, and depictions of Eritrean women during the Italian colonization of Eritrea (1888–1945). It traces the entanglement of multiple colonial regimes in the production of Black women as exoticized, disposable objects of consumption. The media portrayal of Payano exoticized her blackness and the "backwardness" of her embodied Caribbean "essence" even after death, adding to the sensationalism of the tragedy while at the same time erasing the structural violence, colonial legacies, and persistent anti-immigrant legislation that produced the precarious conditions that led to Payano's death. The chapter engages these narratives in the larger context of Italian sex tourism in the Caribbean, paying close attention to how Black immigrant women organize and resist oppressive regimes through acts of solidarity and transnational networks of information and political involvement.

Chapter 5, "Second Generation Interruptions: Archives of Black Belonging in Postcolonial Diaspora," focuses on the cultural, political, and social interventions by Black Second Generation activists in contemporary Italy. Through a comparative analysis of a novel, a film, public speeches, and songs, the chapter proposes Black Latinidad as a framework for understanding the multiple ways Black Second Generation subjects translate hegemonic terms (e.g., Black, Afro, immigrant) to build transnational networks of inclusion that help them challenge the colonial legacies sustaining racism in their nations. The chapter shows how colonial histories shape the lives of Black immigrants and new citizens in postcolonial diasporic communities as they negotiate multiple conceptualizations of race while asserting national belonging. I theorize what I call "archival interruptions" as the method by which Second Generations build alliances with other marginalized communities and contra*dict* the colonial and white supremacist logic of the nation-state. Using art and social media, they translate their local struggles into a global language of resistance grounded in Black freedom. In so doing, they can attract a larger constituency, and at times produce effective local, national, and transnational changes.

Read together, the two sections of this book produce a more complete narrative of Black Latinidad that insists not only on its intellectual history—produced by elite men of letters—but more importantly on the epistemological contributions of people often omitted from or silenced in historical archives. This book, then, reads Black Latinx archives and stories as constitutive of global blackness. *Translating Blackness* is about violence and rebellion, migrations, vaivenes, and returns. It is about belonging and unbelonging. And most of all, it is about Black knowledge and radical existence across place and time against colonial violence and antiblackness.

PART I. ON BEING BLACK AND CITIZEN

Latinx Colonial Vaivenes

1 A FULL STATURE OF HUMANITY

Latinx Difference, Colonial Musings, and Black Belonging during Reconstruction

In 1901 Gregoria Fraser entered Syracuse University, her mother's alma mater, to study art and music.[1] She was a talented young woman who had grown up surrounded by culture and unique experiences; she had lived and studied in Europe and Latin America and was fluent in English, Spanish, French, and Danish. Her mother, Sarah Loguen Fraser, was one of the first Black women to practice medicine in the United States, and her father, Charles Fraser, was an accomplished pharmacist and businessman. Gregoria had grown up in economic comfort, surrounded by a transnational community of Black intellectuals, artists, and political figures that included US abolitionist Frederick Douglass and her namesake, Gregorio Luperón, the Dominican general who led the war against Spain (1863–65) that delivered the country's independence. Both men were her godfathers.[2]

Sarah Loguen Fraser was the daughter of Reverend Jermain Wesley Loguen, an abolitionist and bishop in the African Methodist Episcopal (AME) church who had escaped bondage at the age of twenty-one and who, along with his wife, Caroline Storum, ran a major depot on the Underground Railroad in Syracuse (see figure 1.1).[3] Sarah Loguen came of age surrounded by

FIGURE 1.1 Dr. Sarah Loguen, photographer unknown, ca. 1875. Syracuse University Portrait Collection.

intense political work for Black liberation and gained practical medical experience as she helped care for injured people escaping enslavement. When she graduated from Syracuse University in 1876, she became one of the first Black woman physicians in the United States; she practiced medicine until the end of her life. Frederick Douglass, a mutual friend, introduced her to Dr. Charles Fraser, a wealthy pharmacist and plantation owner of Caribbean Afro-Danish descent who lived in Puerto Plata, Dominican Republic, whom she married in 1882.[4] Shortly thereafter, Loguen moved to Puerto Plata and became the first woman to practice medicine in the Dominican Republic. Gregoria, the Frasers' only child, was born in 1884. When Gregoria was ten years old, her father died after suffering a devastating stroke. Newly widowed, Sarah Loguen Fraser returned with her daughter to the United States to live near her family. They moved in with her sister, Amelia, and her husband, Lewis Douglass (Frederick Douglass's son), in 1895.[5]

Unfortunately for Gregoria Fraser, the students and faculty at Syracuse University did not see her fascinating family history, her worldly experiences, or her refinement. All they saw was "a Negro, a Black woman"—a fact that shaped her experience as a student.[6] Her classmates whispered racial slurs as she walked around the Fine Arts building. Professors dismissed her, believing, as one teacher remarked to her, that Fraser "should realize that dishwashing and scrubbing floors would unfit [your] hands for piano work."[7] But Fraser had never scrubbed floors or washed dishes. In fact, as she responded to her professor, her class privilege meant that "back in Puerto Plata, Dominican Republic, where I am from, we had servants to do this kind of work."[8] But Fraser's upper-class status did not exempt her from racism at Syracuse as it had done in the Dominican Republic—a majority Black and Brown nation where upward mobility, respectability, politics, and prestige were mediated primarily by class and economic status rather than exclusively by color.[9] Despite her class status, the professor did not *see* Fraser; all he saw was a Black woman destined for hard labor.

Only Joseph Carl Seiter, a dean and professor of piano, was kind to Fraser during those difficult years at Syracuse. She recalled him remarking "on cold and snowy days, loud enough for others to hear: 'I know you wish you were home in Santo Domingo' so students could hear him. . . . He knew how stupid white *North Americans* were about the American colored. . . . It did no good."[10] After months of racial aggression—from classmates yelling "coon" at her in the hallways, to professors refusing to let her perform in class—Fraser suffered a nervous breakdown in February 1903 and left the university. Her mother returned to her alma mater to collect her daughter and bring her back to Puerto Plata, where she nursed her back to wellness. In the fall of 1903, after months of care and sunlight at home, Fraser returned to Syracuse to complete her studies.[11]

While neither Gregoria Fraser nor her mother ever lived on the island again, returning only for visits, their sense of belonging to Puerto Plata followed them through a multiplicity of vaivenes and returns until the ends of their respective lives. They retained their home in Puerto Plata, sending money and construction materials for decades to keep it in good condition. They maintained relationships with Dominican friends through letter writing and occasional visits in other cities such as New York and Paris. Upon Dr. Loguen's death in April 1933, the city of Puerto Plata honored her with nine days of mourning that culminated in a magnificent funeral mass attended by almost the entire city.[12] The two women remained connected to the island of Fraser's birth and the adoptive home that afforded Dr. Loguen more than a decade of career satisfaction and the joy of living "her full stature" as a human being.[13]

As an Afro-Latina Dominican woman scholar working and living in the United States, I cannot help but feel a peculiar sense of intimacy with the lives of these two amazing women who in some ways mirror my own vaivenes between belonging and unbelonging despite the difference in our class statuses and the historical processes that separate our migrations. Their vaivenes through different conceptualizations of blackness, their encounters with freedom and belonging, and their experiences of overlapping diasporas are at the core of what I hope to describe and analyze in this book. As I read—full of gratitude—through the letters, manuscripts, and other documents that Gregoria Fraser collected to memorialize her mother's life, I felt closer to her. I understood her pain, hope, and nostalgia in my own skin. I, too, left the Dominican Republic around puberty, just old enough to remember but too young to articulate the pain and desolation migration causes. How hard it must have been for her to trade sandals for boots, to walk in snow and ice, to experience her unbelonging in skin that dried and grew brittle in the cold weather she was so unaccustomed to, and with the coldness of her classmates' harsh racist remarks. As I read through "Miss Doc," Fraser's unpublished biography of her mother, I wondered what she must have thought and felt as she walked through those hallways at Syracuse University—as people stared at her and wished her ill. Did she close her eyes and imagine the green-blue sea of Puerto Plata? Did she feel displaced and foreign? Did she find refuge in the US Black community? Did her Latinidad distance her from US blackness? How did her Latinidad shape her sense of belonging and unbelonging in the United States in the early decades of the twentieth century? How did she translate her (Latinx) blackness?

In 1939, more than three decades after leaving Syracuse, Fraser reflected on similar questions in a letter written aboard a boat taking her home to the Dominican Republic.

> I am sure you did not realize that I had come to *crossroads* in my life and that after much meditation and prayer I finally made the break, and here I am on the Atlantic homeward bound. . . . You see, Sally, *I am brown* and all the other passengers are white Americans. . . . *Tomorrow I will be on native soil and being brown will not matter.* As you know, it

> has been thirty-six years since I have been in these waters and having lived in the United States the life of repression and suppression that is exacted of one born and brought up in Southern Republic, I have grown so clothed with layer upon layer of apparent indifference and callousness that I am wondering if I will ever feel *like a real human being again*, or go on forever being an animated automaton? Yes, I made the island trip but with a bad taste in my mouth.[14]

Gregoria Fraser's musings beautifully encapsulate her lifetime of detours and vaivenes through blackness and Latinidad. Identifying as "brown"—which a contemporary reading understands as a way to name Latinx blackness and Hispanic Caribbean *mulataje* (mixed-race blackness)—rather than Negro, Fraser distances herself from "North Americanness" and from the "repression and suppression" of a US racial system that did not allow her to live "like a real human being."[15] Her origins and upbringing in the Caribbean, and her multicultural and multilingual identities, produced her unbelonging in the United States in spite of her upper-class status, US citizenship, and community of powerful US Black scholars, businesspeople, and artists. Living through the vaivenes of a double diaspora—Black and Latinx—at the turn of the twentieth century in the United States was an unbearable task for anyone. As we will see in chapter 2, Black Caribbean immigrants often opted to identify as Negro in order to find belonging within the binary US racial system.[16] For Fraser, however, being *just* US American was not an option. She did not want to erase her Dominican origins. Her connection to the island of her birth and her Caribbean roots were central to her identity as a Black woman. Moreover, her sense of citizenship, belonging, and worth was intrinsically tied to her belief that elsewhere, race functioned differently, and there were other ways to be and belong as a Black woman in the world.

Fraser's optimism about the possibilities of belonging in the Dominican Republic was not only the result of her personal journey as the daughter of an upper-class Black family in Puerto Plata. It was also influenced by the well-established reasoning of US Black intellectuals and thinkers of the late nineteenth century who, in the face of the denial of Black lives in the postbellum United States, looked to the Caribbean—particularly Haiti and the Dominican Republic—as a potential location for Black citizenship, Black futures, and Black belonging. Fraser's birth and her contra*dictions* and vaivenes resulted from the idea that Black North American migration to the Caribbean was the answer to US racial problems. Gregoria's mother migrated to Puerto Plata in the 1880s, as did many other educated US Black people, in search of a better future, and to grow professionally as a doctor.[17] For Gregoria, however, her birth in the Dominican Republic and migration to the United States meant she was an immigrant—a citizen of what I have elsewhere called El Nié, that liminal location between here and there that is home to those of us who live in vaivén in physical and symbolic bordered sites.[18] Fraser's early life was lived between two worlds that, less than a decade after the betrayal of radical reconstruction, were worlds in the making.[19]

By the time she attended Syracuse University in 1901, however, those worlds had been made—sadly, differently from how many Black thinkers and liberators had dreamed of during Reconstruction. Jim Crow was in full effect and the Ku Klux Klan had gained strength across the US South. Meanwhile, the end of the Spanish-American War in 1898 solidified the Caribbean as a site for US colonial expansion. Fraser's life, as well as her ethnic and racial identities, had been defined by hope—by a moment that had, in the two short decades from her birth to young adulthood, dissipated. Still, the moment that engendered her existence—the radical hope that shaped her mother's migration to Puerto Plata—is key to understanding Black belonging and Black citizenship as integral to the anti-colonial thought that produced what we have come to understand as Black Latinidad: the epistemology; lived experiences; and historical, cultural, and political productions of people who are Black, of Latin American ancestry, and diasporic or immigrant subjects living in the Global North.

To understand Fraser's vaivenes and contradictions, this chapter turns to the thoughts and lived experiences of her two godfathers, Frederick Douglass and Gregorio Luperón, focusing on the relationship between Fraser's two *patrias*, the Dominican Republic and the United States, between 1867 and 1880, as both countries were recovering from civil wars. This chapter uses the words, actions, and impacts of Douglass and Luperón to analyze the relationship between the project of US imperial expansion over the Caribbean and the project of US Black citizenship during the two decades that followed the US Civil War. I argue that this relationship is central to Black Latinidad. In the postbellum era, US Americans began to translate Latinidad—and, by extension, Latin blackness—as inherently different from Anglo-Americanness (white and Black). Through the language of civilization versus barbarism, republicanism, and Manifest Destiny, Latin American republican projects were imagined by US Americans as less developed, inferior, and in need of North American guidance. Grappling with the contradictions of simultaneously living in a republic and an empire, elite US Black subjects like Douglass felt at times that supporting imperial expansion projects was both their new duty as citizens of the United States and an opportunity to expand democracy, freedom, dignity, and civility for people of color across the hemisphere. In this framework, annexing the Dominican Republic was an opportunity to create a larger form of Black solidarity and ensure the expansion of the Anglo-American civilizing project. I argue that it is precisely during Reconstruction and US expansion, as US Black subjects grappled with the contradictions of citizenship and empire, that we find the roots of a hegemonic narrative of blackness—shaped by the US empire—that continues to dominate transnational conversations, political processes, and intellectual and cultural discourses across the globe. That is, the impetus for Douglass's decision to support the annexation to bring civilization and citizenship to the "southern Latin republics" and the narrative of the "Black man's burden" that shaped colonization projects throughout the end of the nineteenth century are intertextual to the hegemonic discourse through which we define and translate Black lives, Black histories, Black knowledge, and Black political movements today.[20]

It is precisely this misunderstanding that separated Gregoria Fraser's two *padrinos* in the nineteenth century, keeping them from seeing their shared political investment in Black citizenship. It is my intention in this chapter to historicize, in part, the roots of the "mistranslations" that continue to separate US Black and Black Latinx struggles. The wedge that kept Douglass and Luperón from seeing their struggles as one, as this chapter will show, was very much driven by nationalism and a perception of the nation as the central site of struggle for racial justice. While we have made progress in the creation of transnational interventions, we still have a long road ahead when it comes to acknowledging the multiple and overlapping ways racism and colonialism affect people's understandings of themselves and others. Black is a global category of oppression, but it is also a site of contestation; to translate blackness can be a contra*diction* of the colonial order that negates Black lives.

The first of the American colonies to become independent, the United States maintained the colonial order and its economic system of oppression through the continued enslavement of Black people for nearly a century. Unlike Haiti, Cuba, and the Dominican Republic, the US independence project did not consider Black lives or the possibility of Black citizenship. After the US Civil War, however, the question of how to reconcile the categories of "Black" and "citizen" continued to haunt the nation and the lives of Black people. One of the solutions to the "question of blackness" that dominated US politics during Reconstruction was the possibility of annexing Black nations in the Caribbean to ship freed Black people to, to get them off the mainland. From 1867 until the middle of the 1870s, Congress debated annexing the Dominican Republic. In 1871 US president Ulysses S. Grant appointed Frederick Douglass, an abolitionist and rising political figure, to the Commission of Inquiry for the annexation of Santo Domingo to the United States of America. With this appointment, Douglass was cast in a new light: he was concerned not only with domestic reforms but also with the expansion of the US empire abroad. In one of the earliest documented cases of political tokenism, the appointment of a Black man to the annexation commission was meant to assuage internal opposition to the colonial project. Douglass was charged with convincing the American public that annexing the Dominican Republic would be a good deed. To justify his involvement, Douglass cited US "civility" and Dominican "barbarism": the very language of colonial dominance that was used to enslave Black people for nearly three centuries.[21]

That Douglass became an arm of the US empire in 1871 seems like a contradiction to the Black abolitionist's previous anti-colonial struggles. In fact, later in life, he took an active role in defending Cuba from impending US colonization. Douglass, like many late nineteenth-century republicans in the Americas (including José Martí, Juan Pablo Duarte, and Ramón Emeterio Betances), believed in the nation as a universal institution of citizenship and inclusion. He believed inserting people in the fabric of nation—even if that meant through colonialism—would allow them to finally access equality and citizenship. For Dominicans, who had endured two other annexation attempts and increasing pressure from the United States and Spain to abandon their national project, however, Douglass's invitation to civilization and citizenship seemed suspicious, at the least. But the fact that he was Black also confused Dominicans. Addressing that confusion, mulato general and intellectual Gregorio Luperón warned Dominicans not to be misled by "the yankees" and to remember that despite being Americans, despite color, they were "Anglo-American," and "we" (Dominicans) are "Latin Americans."[22]

Frank Guridy, Millery Polyné, Antonio López, April Mayes, and Nancy Mirabal have studied the significance of Black Panamericanism in the late nineteenth- and early twentieth-century Caribbean as key to the conceptualizations of diaspora, Black internationalism, and Latinidad. Building on their important research, my investigation into Black Latinidad as a concept and theory begins with US Black liberation. I argue that it is during Reconstruction—a period of mass US expansion over the Americas—that the notion of a "Latin difference" is articulated and expanded to include US blackness as different from other forms of blackness. As US Blacks were invited into the nation through the passage of the Fourteenth Amendment, they were also invited into US imperialism. The contradictions of being citizens of a nation and an empire shaped the relationship of US blackness to the world, and in particular to Latin American republics. These contradictions also shaped how Black Latin Americans imagined themselves in relation to and against Anglo-Americans. This "Latin difference," which Luperón articulates in 1871, is foundational to the production of Black Latinidad in the United States as an ethno-racial category that is different from and oppositional to US blackness.

One of the ways this dynamic plays out in the contemporary diaspora is through the conflicting and competing relationship between Black Latinx and US Black people in the urban United States that at times, as Mark Sawyer argued, hinders coalition building in the fight against white supremacy.[23] Allow me to share an example. On June 2, 2020, during the massive protests in response to the police murder of George Floyd, looters destroyed a number of small immigrant-owned businesses in the Bronx and Manhattan. Video that night captures a group of mostly Black Dominican men chasing a group of presumably US Black looters from their neighborhood. The footage, which received hundreds of thousands of views on Instagram and Twitter, underscored racial tensions between US Black residents and Dominican residents in this part of Manhattan. The following night, a group of protesters—most of them Dominican—marched on Dyckman Street in New York to demonstrate against the looting. The video, and the anti-looting protests that followed, made #Dominicans a popular anti-Black hashtag on social media. Memes declaring that Dominicans "don't know they are Black" flooded Twitter, while more serious calls were made to "cancel Dominicans" and call out Latinx antiblackness. Similar scenes played out across the United States in the wake of the Black Lives Matter protests in the summer of 2020, leading to confrontations between Latinxs and US Black subjects and exposing Latinx antiblackness. Non-Latinx critics on social and mainstream media expressed surprise that there could be antiblackness within the Latinx community, demonstrating a lack of understanding of both Latinidad and white supremacy. The anti-looting protests on Dyckman Street were grounded on a generalized misunderstanding of the fact that blackness is a global category of oppression. That the media identifies Dominicans as "ousting Black people" mistranslates their blackness, erasing the fact that the "ousters," in addition to being Dominican, are also Black.

During Reconstruction, US Black intellectuals, religious leaders, and political figures began to imagine themselves as part of the US empire.[24] Their role within the imperial project, as articulated by Henry Blanton Parks at the end of the century, was to "bring civilization to the colored races"—to advance the project of Black citizenship through imperial expansion and a language and logic of dominance and superiority.[25] As intellectuals in Hispaniola grappled with the threat of US imperial expansion, they began to conceptualize themselves as different from both Black and white North Americans, articulating said difference as an anti-colonial political project. For Luperón and his contemporaries, the "Latin difference" became a unifying rubric against US colonialism: "no hay asimilación posible, en nada podrán entenderse, mucho menos al avenirse; la guerra sin cuartel será el idioma mas inteligible por la heterogeneidad de las razas" (there is no possible assimilation, they [Latinos and Anglos] will not be able to understand each other, much less in the advent of an unwarranted war; there will be the utmost unintelligible language due to the heterogeneity of the races).[26] While "Latin America" eventually came to be identified as both a region and an idea that encompasses all of Central and South America and the Caribbean, the intellectual, political, and military struggles that engendered Latinidad as an ethno-racial, cultural, geographic, and political concept emerged as a political and intellectual project in Hispaniola during the intense period of expansionism that followed the end of the US Civil War (1865–98). In Hispaniola, the idea of Latinidad was intrinsically shaped by a preoccupation with multiracial citizenship ("heterogeneidad de las razas") in the face of US imperial expansion, in contra*diction* to the violence of slavery and the ever-present specter of European coloniality embodied in white criollos and caudillos. Over time, as April Mayes describes, Latinidad came to signify a predominantly mestizo and Hispanic ethno-racial concept that allowed Dominicans to exist in racial ambivalence—neither Black nor white. In its conception, though, the conceptualization of Latinidad advanced by Luperón was grounded on an understanding of multiracial citizenship that included—and at times centered—blackness.[27] The fact that Haiti was the model, as well as the site, for the articulation of the Americas' anti-imperial solidarity further solidified Black freedom and multiracial citizenship as central to Latinidad.

National projects in Haiti, the Dominican Republic, Cuba, and Puerto Rico all attempted to produce racially inclusive citizenship that guaranteed national belonging to all people. As imagined by Luperón in 1865, citizenship was grounded on emancipation and liberation, and thus necessarily included Black people in the national citizenry. In expanding freedom throughout the Caribbean (via the Caribbean Confederation) and the rest of Latin America (through the concept of Latinidad), Luperón imagined liberty as a contra*diction* to "la esclavitud con todo su despotismo" (slavery in all its despotism).[28] Imperialism and colonial expansion threatened the project of a "raza unida," forged through sovereignty and emancipation.[29] For Cuban José Martí, decades later, Latinidad offered the possibility of substituting nation for race to guarantee that all people, regardless of the color of their skin, became one under the principles of justice, freedom, and patria.[30] With the benefit of hindsight, we know these projects of racially inclusive citizenship failed.

Douglass and Luperón were both very beloved Black people who fought for Black freedom and racially inclusive citizenship in the nations they helped build. And yet they found themselves in opposing positions in 1870 when the United States attempted to annex the Dominican Republic. Douglass believed the Dominican Republic "could not survive on its own" and needed the United States to become a bastion of republicanism and civility where people of all races could thrive.[31] He envisioned a Dominican state as part of the North American republic and a potential refuge for US Blacks seeking freedom and fortune during Reconstruction. To Luperón, who had gone to war to guarantee citizenship and freedom for all Dominicans, regardless of color, Douglass was a traitor to the race, a "yanki" seeking only greed and expansion.[32] Though they did not see eye to eye, both men imagined worlds in which blackness was not a deterrent to growth. In many ways, their hopes and contradictions intersected in their goddaughter's life. Gregoria Fraser's vaivenes through Dominican and US blackness—her two padrinos' political and symbolic projects—at different times merged and were in conflict within her as she attempted to make sense of the intersections of race, migration, and colonialism that shaped her being and belonging as a Black Latina. I read her vaivenes as constitutive and representative of the Black Latinx experience in the diaspora. My purpose here is to consider Black belonging through the lens of Latinidad, and to examine the vaivenes and detours of blackness and Latinidad away and through each other. To do that, this chapter attempts to bring Douglass and Luperón into conversation, to ask them to sit together and *see* their goddaughter and, in her, their contributions and contra*dictions*. In so doing, I hope to remind us that Latinidad was grounded, imagined, and founded through blackness—specifically, the possibility of anti-colonial freedom and Black citizenship in Hispaniola, in contradistinction to US hegemony and expansionism. This chapter thus theorizes Latinidad as a site of anti-colonial, racially inclusive citizenship that begins with the possibility of Black belonging.

Black Citizenship and US Imperial Scheming

After the Civil War (1861–65), the United States had to grapple with the meaning of Black citizenship and belonging in the wake of emancipation. Reconstruction (1865–77) brought a short yet forceful wave of hope for Black belonging as US Blacks attempted to redress the inequalities of slavery and its political, social, and economic legacy. During this period of transformation, the Thirteenth, Fourteenth, and Fifteenth Amendments altered established notions of US citizenship, abolishing slavery, granting Black citizenship, and allowing Black men to vote. Parallel to Reconstruction was a renewed energy for the project of territorial and economic expansion that had begun with the Monroe Doctrine (1823) and was paused during the tumultuous years leading up to the Civil War.[33] As historian Eric Love argues, expansionism "survived the Civil War and at the same time was transformed by it."[34] Indeed, race—and in particular concerns regarding Black citizenship—shaped the United States' imperialist project throughout the second half of the nineteenth century.[35]

In this climate of expansion, the Dominican Republic represented a strategic military location for securing the US borders from the threat of European economic and political dominance.[36] As President Grant would later state, "A glance at a map will show that England has now a cordon of islands extending from southern Florida to the east of the island of Cuba. . . . In case of war between England and the United States, New York and New Orleans would be much severed, as would be New York and Calais, France."[37] England, Spain, and France still held several colonial possessions in the Caribbean. For Grant and his supporters, owning Hispaniola would therefore mean carrying out the Manifest Destiny and protecting the Americas against European colonial expansion. The Dominican Republic was seen as the gateway to that project, with the idea that reluctant Haiti would later be coerced, followed by the entire Gulf of Mexico and Panama's Darién province.

In the contradictory environment of Black citizenship and US imperial expansion, US Black emigration to the Caribbean was revisited as a solution to the "free Black problem," as intrinsic to the mission of post-Emancipation US colonialism, but also, as Nicholas Guyatt argues, "for abolitionists who recognized the radical potential of creating 150,000 new American citizens in the Caribbean, annexation became (in the words of one proponent) 'the key to Southern reconstruction.'"[38] The proposal of Black emigration as a solution to the "racial problem" was not new. Rather, as Love notes, it dated back to the foundation of the US nation. In "Notes on Virginia" (1781), Love writes, Thomas Jefferson argued that Black emigration "would not only rid the United States of the barbarism of slavery"; it would save the country from the "catastrophe" of miscegenation.[39] In the early nineteenth century, the American Colonization Society took the idea further, organizing a mass emigration of Black Americans to Africa and the Caribbean. While thousands moved to Liberia, Haiti, and the Dominican Republic's Bay of Samaná, the colonization project was widely opposed by US Blacks, who believed they had the right to US citizenship and freedom within the continental borders of the nation they had helped build, rather than on foreign soil.[40]

US Black emigration reemerged in postbellum political rhetoric as both sides of the political spectrum struggled with the idea of Black citizenship and belonging. For abolitionists like Douglass, the annexation of a Black and Brown republic seemed like an opportunity to extend American republicanism while also providing Black people in the US South a way out of poverty and disenfranchisement. He wrote, "All signs indicate that the continent, the whole continent and nothing less than the continent is ultimately to belong to us. . . . Mexico, Central and South America and all the isles of the Caribbean Sea must eventually yield to our irresistible power of expansion."[41] Advocates of Black emigration began to look to the Caribbean—specifically the Dominican Republic—as a potential site for US Black citizenship. The island's strategic location and natural resources as well as years of imagining the Dominican side of Hispaniola as a racial paradise—a perfect mix of white, Black, and Brown people, in contradistinction with "Black Haiti"—made the country attractive to investors, politicians, and Black freedom advocates alike. Annexing the eastern portion of the island of Hispaniola and encouraging US Black emigration became an alternative plan to combat the continued disenfranchisement, destruction, and unbelonging of Black people on the mainland.

For Grant, who spearheaded the efforts to annex the Dominican Republic from 1869 to 1872, US Black emigration opened the possibility of reconciliation in a deeply fragmented United States, something he made clear in his 1869 memorandum "Reasons Why Santo Domingo Should Be Annexed to the United States."

> Caste has no foothold in San Domingo. It is capable of supporting the entire colored population of the United States, should it choose to emigrate. The present difficulty in bringing all parts of the United States to a happy unity and love of country grows out of the prejudice to color. The prejudice is a senseless one, but it exists. The colored man cannot be spared until his place is supplied, but with a refuge like San Domingo his worth here would soon be discovered, and he would soon receive such recognition as to induce him to stay: or if Providence designed that the two races should not live together, he would find a home in the Antilles. . . . San Domingo is weak and must go somewhere for protection. Is the United States willing that she should go elsewhere than to herself? Such a confession would be to abandon our oft-repeated "Monroe doctrine."[42]

Two contradictory racial visions shaped Grant's impetus for annexation: Black belonging through racial reconciliation and Black unbelonging through racial exclusion. The latter contains the implicit desire to secure a white continental republic and a Black overseas state ("or if Providence designed that the two races should not live together, he would find a home in the Antilles") to assuage white fear of Black citizenship. Yielding to white fragility and supremacy while recognizing the unfairness of the situation, Grant looked to the Dominican Republic as a solution to the predicament in which he found himself as a newly elected president whose triumph was the first to be secured through an alliance between Black voters and white allies.[43] He owed his office, in great part, to Black voters, yet his integrationist campaign had very much hurt his popularity among rich and powerful southerners. Grant envisioned that the annexation of Santo Domingo would allow him to have his cake and eat it, too: to support Black citizenship and assuage white fear of US Black belonging.[44]

Grant lamented the failure of the annexation project years later in an interview with the *Chicago Tribune*: "We should have made St. Domingo a new Texas or a New California. If St. Domingo had come we should have had Hayti. A power like ours makes us masters of the Gulf of Mexico."[45] That the Santo Domingo debate coincided with the passage of the Fifteenth Amendment, which in 1870 gave Black men the right to vote, and the Ku Klux Klan Act, which gave the president the power to declare martial law and impose punishment to terrorist organizations, added to the urgency of solving the problem of securing Black citizenship in the wake of emancipation. For Grant, the Dominican Republic was a possible solution. He believed it to be, after all, a place where "caste has no foothold"—a racial paradise that would enable Black citizenship and teach southern whites a lesson. As one Black Uncle Sam cartoon illustrates (figure 1.2), expansion to Hispaniola signified not only an economic transaction but also a potential transformation of US citizenship beyond the borders of the continental United States.

The slippage between Black belonging and unbelonging in Grant's annexation defense has been the subject of multiple studies about racial politics during Reconstruction.[46] For some scholars, Grant was a racist who wanted to deport all Black citizens to the Caribbean; for others, he was an idealist who imagined extending US citizenship to Black and Brown people in the Caribbean to ameliorate the violence and exclusion still faced by Black people in the US South. While both views raise valid points, I argue that Grant's position on annexation and Black citizenship were guided by the contradictory desire for expansion and freedom that shaped all political and economic projects during

FIGURE 1.2 "The Last Real Estate Transaction." *Frank Leslie's Illustrated Newspaper* 30, no. 757 (April 2, 1870): 48.

Reconstruction. Grant's 1869 memo and his *Chicago Tribune* interview a decade later point to three axioms guiding his annexation proposal: (1) the Dominican Republic represented an important economic and political asset for the US empire; (2) racism and prejudice made Black citizenship in the United States an impossibility; and (3) Black people, in both the United States and the Caribbean, were sources of labor: cogs in capitalist machinery securing the prosperity of white-dominated enterprises. The annexation of the Dominican Republic was therefore imagined as an economic solution to the "Black problem" in a capitalist regime accustomed to functioning through free Black labor.

Meanwhile, in the Dominican Republic, where independence from Spain was gained twice by a majority Black- and Brown-led army, the dominance of caudillos and the colonial desire of the white elite after the Restoration War (1861–65) continued to threaten sovereignty and limit progress for the majority of Black and Brown Dominicans.[47] The white and light-skinned Brown and Black elite, led by four-term dictator Buenaventura Báez, welcomed annexation as a solution to the economic and political crisis that had followed the war and a potential answer to the regime's inability to unite the fragmented nation.[48] At the same time, Black and Brown leaders such as Gregorio Luperón saw annexation as a threat to freedom, autonomy, and the project of color-blind citizenship that Juan Pablo Duarte and others had envisioned in 1844.[49] By the time Báez assumed his fourth term as president in 1868, the country was struggling with insurmountable debt, a decreasing population, and increasing internal conflicts. With growing discontent among the population and the increasing power of the disjointed leadership of local caudillos, Báez sought US annexation. Grant welcomed Báez's invitation to annex the country in exchange for clearing their debt and granting all Dominicans US citizenship.[50] After a series of secret meetings and conversations between the Báez administration and US annexation proponents, US representative Council General Raymond Perry and Dominican representative Manuel María Gautier signed an annexation treaty drafted by US Secretary of State Hamilton Fish that included annexation and the purchase of the Bay of Samaná for US$2 million on November 29, 1869.[51]

Over the next few months, Grant dedicated his time to convincing the Senate to ratify an irregular and secretive diplomatic process between the United States and the Dominican Republic because for Grant, the means justified the end. Given that the annexation document assured "the Dominican state is following the wishes of its people," Grant saw the annexation as a gift the United States could not refuse and a manifestation of the United States' "destiny" to own the island and, by extension, the entire Caribbean.[52] Let us remember that in 1870, as the annexation debate was taking place, Hispaniola was the only island in the Caribbean not occupied by a European colonial power. It was thus the only island that could be possessed without risking war with Europe. But contrary to Báez's assurances that the people of Santo Domingo had "willingly and willfully" offered up their country for annexation, there was persistent armed and political resistance on the island and among the Dominican exile population across the Caribbean. Luperón, who was living in exile on the island of St. Thomas, led the resistance. From St. Thomas, he orchestrated various military attacks against Báez with support from members of the Partido Azul (Blue Party), including Generals José María Cabral and Antonio Pimentel, as well as allies across the Caribbean—in particular, Haitian president

Jean-Nicolas Nissage Saget.[53] Allies saw in the project of Dominican independence another symbol of Black liberation.[54] This transnational Caribbean network of freedom fighters, along with local armed resistance, sustained La guerra de los seis años (1868–74), as the conflict came to be known.

The armed struggles were a response to the newest threat to republicanism in the Americas: US expansionism in the region. In a letter to US Senator Charles Sumner in January 1870, Luperón wrote:

> Proscrito del suelo que me vio nacer y que contribuí a liberar del dominio español durante la gran lucha de los años 63, 64 y 65, véame [contrariado] al contemplar, sumido en una dolorosa impotencia. . . . Tras el infame que . . . a la patria el vil tirano que después de haberse adueñado de sus destinos se ha propuesto oprimirla y deshonrarla, ese mismo hombre que era ayer necesario instrumento de la política europea, reanudó el hilo de sus traiciones . . . ofreciéndola a América del Norte.[55]

> [Outlawed from the ground that witnessed my birth and which I helped to liberate from Spanish domination in the great battle during '63, '64 and '65, you find me now [upset] in contemplation, sunk in painful impotence. . . . After the infamous deed that . . . the vile tyrant has done to my homeland after taking possession of her, he has resolved to oppress and dishonor her, this very man that yesterday was the tool of European politics has gathered the thread of his betrayals . . . offering it to North America.]

Comparing the United States' annexation to Spanish colonialism ("gathering the thread of his betrayals"), Luperón notes the inconsistencies of the Monroe Doctrine that in effect usurped rather than protected the sovereignty of the young republic. Contra*dicting* Báez and Grant, Luperón insists that annexation was the will of one powerful man ("a vile tyrant"), who had taken over the country by force, against the will of the people, to dishonor it. His letter calls attention to the fraudulent assurances made by Báez that the country had "voted almost unanimously in support of annexation," while simultaneously holding the US government complicit in the violation and betrayal of Dominican freedom. He adds:

> Los más ilustrados como los más dignos representantes de la nacionalidad dominicana, no quieren que la anexión de esta débil república a la poderosa Unión sea consumada por las vías que han adoptado los poderes de ambos países ni por ninguna otra vía que no entrañe la verdadera expresión de la voluntad popular. Dicha mayoría protesta con

armas en mano por hace mas de dos años. . . . Tres grandes buques de la marina de Guerra Norte Americanas imponen sobre todo el litoral de nuestra patria la voluntad del traidor y comprimen con su presencia la decisión de los pueblos. . . . Hacen mas eficaz esa presión los dineros que Báez ha recibido de EU.[56]

[The most enlightened and worthy representatives of Dominican nationality do not want the annexation of this weak republic to the powerful Union to take effect in the way that the powers of both countries have decided it or by any other way that does not involve the true expression of the popular will. Said majority has been protesting with weapons in hand for more than two years. . . . Three large North American Navy ships occupying the entire coastline of our country impose the will of the traitor and with their presence suppress the decision of the people. . . . The money that Báez has received from the US makes this pressure more effective.]

Luperón's written and military protests eventually gained enough media traction that Grant decided to take anti-annexation leaders seriously. Grant responded by offering Luperón a bribe: $500,000 and the title of governor of Santo Domingo if he agreed to support the annexation project. Luperón responded to Grant with these words:

No se borra una nación por pequeña que sea, como una huella estampada sobre arena. . . . La repetida doctrina de Monroe tiene sus vicios y sus delirios, nosotros creemos *que la América debe pertenecer a sí misma,* y alejada de toda influencia europea, vivir como el mundo Viejo, de su vino propio, local e independiente; pero no pensamos que la América deba ser yankee. De un hecho al otro hay una gran distancia que no se puede salvar. . . . La respuesta que dio Washington a los ingleses cuando éstos le pedían un puerto en el litoral norte, para el establecimiento de una escala: "Cada pulgada de territorio americano cuesta al pueblo una gota de sangre." La República Dominicana es un pedazo de tierra bien pequeño, que ha abortado grandes calamidades para las naciones que han pretendido usurparlo.[57]

[No matter how small a nation may be, it cannot be simply erased like a footprint in sand. . . . This redundant Monroe Doctrine is vile and delirious. We believe that *America must belong to itself* and be free from all European influence, to live like the Old World, on its own, locally and independently; but we do not think that America needs to be yankee. There is a great distance from one thing to the other. . . . The answer Washington gave to the British when they asked for a port to establish a layover was: "Every inch of American territory costs our people a drop of blood." The Dominican Republic is a very small piece of land, but one that has provoked great calamities to those nations that have attempted to take us over.]

Luperón, and by extension his Caribbean network of anti-colonial resistance, articulated a political language of anti-annexationism to combat Grant's plans and Báez's colonial musings.[58] Insisting on Dominicans' republican enterprise as part of a broader struggle for independence and freedom in the Americas, Luperón challenged the US empire. He highlighted the hypocrisy of the Monroe Doctrine while asserting Dominicans' right to independence precisely as part of the very republican tradition the United States was so proudly defending. While Grant and the US annexationists largely dismissed Luperón and the other anti-annexation leaders as "criminals," "pirates," and "bandits," it was the concerted efforts of anti-annexationists—from military actions to media campaigns to letter writing—that led to the divided 5–2 vote by the Senate Foreign Relations Committee in March 1870 that forever ended the annexation project.

As a result of Dominican opposition led by Luperón, Cabral, Tomás Bobadilla, and others, the US Senate, as well as US public opinion regarding the racial impact and impetus of the annexation project, began to be divided. For some, the fact that the Dominican Republic was a nation of Black and Brown people was positive: the emigration of US Black people would be a logical outcome, while the annexed state would provide a good example of racial democracy in the region for places like Cuba, which still maintained a slave economy. For others, however, the idea of intervening in a free "colored republic" during Reconstruction sent the wrong message to US Black people and to the free world. One of the concerns often articulated was precisely that the Dominican Republic shared the island with Haiti, a symbol of Black liberation throughout the world. Gerald Horne historicizes this debate, focusing on how senators who sat on opposing sides of the issue deployed Haiti as a justification both for and against annexation.[59] Senator Fernando Wood of New York, for example, thought the annexation project was "designed to overawe Haiti and protect American interests," which was why "the United States had dispatched three ships of war of our small Navy to "Samaná Bay."[60] Senator Carl Schurz also argued that the annexation would be a threat to Haitian sovereignty; he asked, "Is there a man on the floor of the Senate who thinks that when we have the one half of that island we shall stop before we have the other?"[61] Predicting the trajectory of US colonialism in the Caribbean that would manifest between 1898 and 1916, with the possession of Cuba and Puerto Rico and interventions in the Dominican Republic and Haiti, Senators Wood and Schurz warned about the perils of imposing US will in the Caribbean and taking away Haiti's powerful and symbolic liberty just as the United States was struggling to enact Black citizenship and Black freedom.

For more than half a century, Haiti had been an important symbol of Black liberation and freedom all over the Americas, particularly in the United States. But it was precisely because of Haiti, Samuel Howe argued, that the United States felt destined to acquire Santo Domingo, despite the opposition of "foreign powers which disfavor the growth of our political influence in the West Indian islands."[62] It was the duty of the United States, according to Howe and others, not only to defend the Americas from potential European expansion in the Caribbean, as stated in the Monroe Doctrine, but also to protect the Dominican Republic—and its white and light-skinned Brown (mulato) citizens—from the threat of Haitian invasion and the potential results: the extermination of white people and the blackening of the island. In the eyes of Howe and others, the fact that Luperón was Black and half Haitian, and that he launched his military campaign with explicit Haitian military support, made him, as Howe declared, an enemy of the Dominican nation.[63]

In previous works, I have argued that the United States played a significant role in establishing the racial borders of the island of Hispaniola by producing the Dominican Republic as an "other-than-Black," mixed-race, almost-white nation, in contradistinction with Haiti, which was understood as blacker and therefore more savage than the Dominican Republic.[64] In this view, Haiti was unsalvageable and thus not a prime site for colonization, while the Dominican Republic's light-skinned Brown population and ("inferior") Latin whiteness offered a presumed malleability that could lead to civilization. Or, as Howe put it: "The Dominican Republic is worth more to us than even Cuba would be" since "it has no slaves. More than half of its population is of the white race (in the Southern sense of the word), they are democratic in their disposition and have a spirit of progress."[65] The rhetoric of Dominican mestizaje and Latin or "southern" whiteness in Howe's letters and speeches actually entered into use as early as 1845 (one year after Dominican independence from Haiti), when a US commission assessed the country's ability to self-govern.[66] This narrative was solidified throughout the nineteenth and early twentieth centuries in the rhetoric of US imperial expansion (1869–1872) and, later, in the actions of US colonial occupation (1916–24).[67] But Haiti was not only a concern because of its presumed racial inferiority. Postemancipation, following the ratification of the Fourteenth and Fifteenth Amendments, the idea of taking the liberty of the first Black nation against its will would surely have been met with heavier criticism from liberals, abolitionists, and the growing Black voter population than would the idea of taking its eastern neighbor, which already had a murky history of sovereignty and colonial desire in addition to a presumed identity as a "Latin" or "southern" white and light-skinned Brown nation. Dominican mulataje and proximity to whiteness was imagined as a favorable potential allegiance with American whiteness and white interests. In his defense of annexation, for example, Senator Howe wrote that "Dominican people are of a high type of physical organization, and may be properly classed in the white race."[68] While the plan, as both Guyatt and Horne have argued, was to take Haiti too, the first step in the process was to seize the more sympathetic, weaker, "whiter" neighbor.[69]

In the tension between US colonial expansion and Caribbean anti-colonial resistance, Latinidad and, more specifically, a "Latin difference" came to be articulated and deployed as decisive and intrinsic to the republican understanding of the relationship between race and citizenship by both anti-annexationists and annexationists on the island and the mainland. While the terms *Latinx*, *Latino*, and *Latin* were not yet commonly used—though some variations of *Latino* began to surface as early as the 1850s—the use of *raza*, *Hispanoamérica*, *southern races*, and *Latinoamericano* can be read as nineteenth-century corollaries. Mayes argues that Latinidad emerged as a unifying principle of raza for Latin American nations but that it was viewed as an inferior category in the United States.[70] US Americans came to imagine Latinidad as, at best, a mark of underdevelopment or, at worst, a sign of potential barbarism. The US colonial gaze viewed "Latin people" as inherently weaker and unfit for self-governance due to, as Douglass put it, "a deficiency inherent to the Latin American races" and the legacy of Spanish, Portuguese, and French colonialism.[71]

Frederick Douglass: Black Citizenship, Empire, and the Emergence of Hegemonic Blackness

Despite the failed annexation vote in Congress, Grant pushed on, getting the Senate Foreign Relations Committee to agree to the creation of the Commission of Inquiry to travel to the Dominican Republic to assess the state of the country and the will of the people regarding the project of annexation.

Perhaps it was in reaction to the debate over annexation that President Grant appointed Frederick Douglass, a strong admirer of Haitian freedom, to the Commission of Inquiry in 1871. Douglass was one of Grant's most important supporters. The Republican Party had buttressed the ratification of voting rights for US Black men, and thus US Blacks, particularly in the South, had supported Grant's presidential candidacy en masse in 1868. Douglass, who had become an important political voice in the struggle for Black citizenship, saw in Grant an ally to Black political enfranchisement and to the project of Reconstruction. During the annexation debate, Douglass stood by Grant, costing him his friendship with longtime ally and fellow abolitionist Senator Charles Sumner and inviting the criticism of radical Pan-African thinkers of his generation.[72]

Along with politicians Benjamin Wade, Samuel G. Howe, and Andrew White, journalist Henry Blackwell, and a team of botanists and businessmen, Douglass sailed to the Dominican Republic on January 18, 1871, once again lending his unwavering support to the Republican Party. During his eight-week stay on the island, Douglass met with leaders of the Báez administration, gave speeches, and interviewed US Black émigrés who resided in the country, particularly in the Bay of Samaná, to assess the state of the nation and the willingness of the people to annex the country.[73] The commission's report was favorable to annexation. Douglass and the journalists who accompanied the commission were convinced annexation would be mutually beneficial—an assertion that shaped Blackwell's extensive media campaign in the months to come. Blackwell believed there was no discrimination in the Dominican Republic, and that this racial harmony would be contagious. He wrote, "We forgot all about color, and ceased to notice the accident of complexion." This experience led Blackwell and others to believe that "the key to Southern reconstruction is the annexation of Santo Domingo."[74]

From 1869 to 1872, and especially during the months following his return from Santo Domingo in March 1871, Douglass gave a series of speeches (see figure 1.3), wrote opinion pieces, and otherwise publicly and privately advocated for the annexation of the Dominican Republic—a surprising turn, given that he had maintained such a strong anti-colonial position before and during the US Civil War. But Reconstruction, the triumph of the Republican Party, and the overall sense of hope and optimism for the promise of Black citizenship produced a sense of national belonging among many US Blacks who, like Douglass, began to see the possibility of an integrated national future in which Black people could finally live full and successful lives.

FIGURE 1.3 James Earl Taylor, drawing of Frederick Douglass giving a speech in the Bay of Samaná, Dominican Republic, 1871. *Frank Leslie's Illustrated Newspaper* 31, no. 806 (March 11, 1871): 437. Courtesy of the Image of the Black in Western Art Project and Photo Archive, W. E. B. Du Bois Research Institute, Harvard University.

Because of Douglass's active support in favor of the annexation, the 1871 National Black Convention, the African Methodist Episcopal Church, and many journalists and Black elite entrepreneurs also endorsed it. In his autobiography, *The Life and Times of Frederick Douglass*, he wrote,

> My selection to visit Santo Domingo with the commission sent thither, was another point indicating the difference between the old time and the new. It placed me on the deck of an American man-of-war, manned by one hundred marines and five hundred men-of-wars-men, under the national flag, which I could now call mine, in common with other American citizens, and gave me a place not in the fore-castle, among the hands, nor in the caboose with the cooks, but in the captain's saloon and in the society of gentlemen, scientists, and statesmen.[75]

His appointment to the commission solidified for Douglass the possibility of belonging, for him and possibly for all new Black citizens. Through the language of expansion and domination symbolized in the diction "man-of-war,"

Douglass affirmed his place as a supporter of US expansion—a colonial project that was integral to US patriotism and the notion of citizenship belonging.

Amid this climate of patriotic optimism, Douglass saw annexation in a new light: as a possibility for bringing unity to the races and glory to the United States. He wrote, "I was for limiting our dominion to the smallest possible margin, but since liberty and equality have become the law of our land, I am for extending our dominion whenever and wherever such extension can peaceably and honorably, and with the approval and desire of all the parties concerned, be accomplished."[76] In his 1871 defense of the Dominican annexation, recovered by historian April Mayes, Douglass further insists that his change of heart is beneficial to US Americans and Dominicans alike.

> Were I a citizen of Santo Domingo I would hold up both hands from the rising till going down of the sun if need be, in favor of the annexation of that country to the United States, for I see no better way to improve the fortunes and promote the highest interests of that country. In coming into the American union, in renouncing separate nationality, Santo Domingo takes no step backward. *She simply swaps impotence and decay, for activity and growth.* She parts with danger for safety, isolation and weakness for union and strength.[77]

Recording the results of the interviews he conducted in the April 1871 report submitted by the commission, Douglass concluded that the "Latin" influence over Santo Domingo had led to the failure of the republic and annexing the country to the United States was the only solution to the calamities and "backwardness" to which the country was victim. He argued that people overwhelmingly favored annexation because they were "tired of war and they think that under the Government of the United States they will have peace and prosperity."[78] Douglass, and by extension the commission, relied on interviews and testimony as well as the results of the 1870 plebiscite that, according to Báez, demonstrated that nearly 100 percent of Dominicans favored annexation. However, as Diómedes Núñez Polanco argues, the extreme repression of the Báez regime would not have allowed for a different result: "[El plebiscito] Estuvo lleno de irregularidades. No solo porque había siete buques de guerra estadoaunidenses en las costas dominicanas, sino además, por los mecanismos de repression internos . . ." (It [the vote] was full of irregularities. Not only because it took place while seven war ships surrounded Dominican coasts, but also because of the repression mechanisms used internally . . .).[79] The fact that an insurrection was taking place, to which Douglass and the rest of the commission were witness, did not seem to alter

Douglass's belief that the Dominican Republic was united in its desire for annexation. Dismissing the Luperón-led anti-annexation protests as a revolt by Haiti-supported "criminals and pirates," Douglass sided with Báez's Hispanophile criollo annexation project, actively participating in suppressing the Black- and Brown-led anti-colonial resistance.[80]

Douglass's support for annexation was sustained by a belief that the United States was superior to Latin America. Yet, as Millery Polyné and others have argued, he also believed that he truly was serving the interest of his race by expanding American citizenship to other "colored people." Douglass considered Dominicans to be among the "Negroes who made up the 1,470,000 in the Spanish colonies."[81] As Polyné argues, "Thus his support of US foreign policy initiatives, was influenced by several factors in which race played an integral role: the protection and advancement of US African American rights in the United States; the security of sovereign governments to rule without unsolicited US intervention; and the modernization of nations that had been devastated by racial slavery and European colonialism."[82] Douglass thought the Dominican Republic and the United States could together create colorblind citizenship that would strengthen the civilization and advancement of Black people across the hemisphere. He wrote, "The true cure for the spirit of caste, in our country and Santo Domingo, has been found in the Fifteenth Amendment of the Constitution of the United States, the one that guarantees color blind citizenship."[83]

The Dominican Republic's reputation in the United States as a multiracial society was, for Douglass as for white pro-annexationists, an advantage to the project of Reconstruction. Like Grant, Douglass saw in the Dominican Republic the possibility of a site where Black citizenship could be realized without the interference of racial prejudice—a thought that persisted even when annexation failed. The United States, being the "superior" and more equipped of the two nations, could provide the republican backbone, while the Dominican Republic, as a place that "knows no caste," could provide the fertile ground for the experiment of color-blind US citizenship. Years later, as Douglass retracted the idea that US colonialism could equal freedom for Black people in the southern republics, he continued to look to the Dominican Republic as a refuge, encouraging others—including his son Charles, as well as Gregoria Fraser's mother, Sarah Loguen Fraser—to move to the Dominican Republic to find the possibility of full humanity that the United States denied.[84] By the middle of 1872, Grant was in the midst of a reelection campaign and once again recruited Douglass to support him. Douglass accepted, leaving behind any involvement in Hispaniola politics for two decades. In July 1889,

Douglass was once again called upon to serve American interests on the island when President Benjamin Harrison appointed him minister to the Republic of Haiti and counsel to the Dominican Republic. This time around, Douglass refused to serve US interests in pressuring the Haitian state to accept the acquisition of Môle Saint-Nicolas, a fact that cost him his post and led to a media campaign aimed at discrediting him.[85]

Throughout his political life, Douglass struggled with his position regarding US expansion and colonialism. This ideological vaivén, I argue, is critical for understanding the contradictions of Black citizenship and belonging in the United States and its present-day iterations. Douglass's assessment of Latinx people and Latin American government reflects an ideology that perdures and shapes today's engagement with US Latinxs and Mexican migrants, as well as the United States' present-day relationship with Haiti and other parts of the Caribbean and Central America. While ideas of racial equality and color-blind citizenship were central to Douglass's desire for the annexation of Santo Domingo, he cast "Latin" people as inferior, impotent, and unfit for self-government, and therefore in need of US guidance. Echoing the diction of the scientific racism he had been so openly against, Douglass argued that Latinidad was inherently different from North Americanness because of its roots in the Southern Hemisphere.[86] The argument around the separation of races due to "natural" factors, including weather and disposition, dominated the political sphere in the middle of the nineteenth century. During the annexation debate, both anti- and pro-annexationists argued that the United States was an "Anglo-Saxon Republic" and therefore had the "natural" preponderance to dominate other races. Even Senator Sumner, who opposed the annexation, used scientific racism to argue that "the African belongs to the equatorial belt and he should enjoy it undisturbed."[87]

Although Douglass fought the ideas of scientific racism, as they had been used to justify slavery and the subjugation of Black people in the United States, when it came to "Latin" people, he asserted their "inferiority" and "weakness" were reasons that "Latin" people were unfit for self-governance. Latinos, Douglass argued, exhibited a "low state of civilization," which was due in part to the "demoralizing influence of long continued Spanish tyranny, and perhaps a *deficiency inherent to the Latin races*."[88] It was this "inherent deficiency" that caused the "many drawbacks to the full comprehension of the principles of republicanism. In most of the South American republics we notice the same condition. The party beaten in an election takes up arms, and in the end it is brute force that decides the contest."[89] The rhetoric of civilization versus barbarism was central to the republican enterprises of the mid-nineteenth-century Americas. Argentine writer and politician Domingo Faustino Sarmiento, for example, wrote extensively about the perils of barbarism as embodied in the Native peoples of the Americas, and of the need to civilize them through Eurocentric ideas of education and civility. During his term as president of Argentina, these ideas shaped the internal borders of the nation, leading to the mass dispossession of Black and Indigenous Argentines. In the Dominican Republic, César Nicolás Penson, Manuel de Jesús Galván, and Félix María del Monte employed these same narratives during the second half of the nineteenth century, leading to the erasure of African cultures and heritage from the narrative of dominicanidad and its displacement onto neighboring Haiti. Ultimately, this displacement led to the construction of the internal borders in Hispaniola that have produced Dominicans and Haitians as racial antagonists, and the former as less Black than the latter.[90]

The concern with progress and civilization in the young nineteenth-century American republics was rooted in a colonial desire to assimilate to Europe. American republics from the United States to the Southern Cone built governments, educational curricula, and civic institutions modeled after France, England, and Rome, which were viewed as the pillars of civilization. Yet the centrality of Europe in American republicanism and civility necessarily meant the erasure of Black, Brown, and Native epistemes and the negation of Black, Brown, and Native people as citizens and producers of their own histories. Articulating Black belonging within this colonizing order left Black thinkers in support of US expansion with two options: engage the rhetoric of civilization versus barbarism to justify the possibility of color-blind citizenship through inclusion, or risk complete exclusion. Ironically, in order to promote the possibility of a trans-American color-blind citizenship, Douglass had to argue against Latino civility, presenting them as "brutes" and untamed people in need of US guidance.

Douglass's position on the question of US expansion and Black citizenship thus demonstrates the challenges of being Black and a citizen in the United States. The process of becoming a Black citizen during Reconstruction demanded that Black people be citizens first and Black second, while simultaneously being excluded from full national belonging precisely because of their race. The contradictions of color-blind citizenship demonstrated that civilization via expansion meant erasure rather than inclusion and progress for all human beings. The postbellum era inspired nationalism among some US Black people who, for the first time, believed in the possibility of citizenship and belonging in the United States. But US nationalism also meant a commitment to supporting the imperial project. How, then, to reconcile race and nation when Global North nations depend on racial subjugation, racial hierarchies, and racial exclusion to maintain their power? How can a Black citizen of a Global North empire be loyal to their race and nation when one's nation oppresses one's race both at home and abroad?

Writing about the role of US Black citizens in the project of US imperialism at the end of the nineteenth century, Michele Mitchell argues that imperial expansion gave US Black citizens an opportunity to contrast the feminization of Black masculinity with a rhetoric of virility and manhood: "Significantly, the majority of extant Afro-American commentary on race and empire was produced by ambitious men within the aspiring and elite classes." These men, Mitchell argues, were most likely to view imperialism as an opportunity to improve their status and "fortify black manhood." Even aspiring and elite men who were initially hostile to the idea of expansion bought into the trope of manhood constructed around the possibility of upward class mobility imagined through territorial expansion.[91] Participating in the imperial project was thus not only a duty for the new US Black citizen; it also, as Lauren Hammond argues, opened the possibility of expanding the number of Black voters, thereby strengthening Black political power in the union.[92]

Scholars generally historicize the solidification of the US empire in 1898 as a direct result of the Spanish-American War. Such peculiar ideological periodization has meant ignoring the significance of Reconstruction and the project of Black citizenship in shaping American expansion. That the attempt to annex the Dominican Republic did not result in colonial possession of the island, as it did for Puerto Rico thirty years later, does not erase the fact that in 1868 the United States invaded the Dominican Republic as part of its imperial expansion plan. It also does not change the fact that this early colonial ploy shaped the logic of expansion that would later lead to colonial possessions in the Caribbean and the Pacific. Thinking through the 1867–72 annexation attempt and Douglass's contradictions can help us better understand how the US imperial project that was solidified in 1898 came to be imagined, articulated, and defined through and against Black citizenship.

Douglass's philosophy is grounded on the impossibility of the coexistence of US superiority and Black freedom. In her essential study of Douglass, Juliet Hooker argues that he envisioned a "composite nationality" anchored in the idea of a universal human right to migration and the Americas' political legacy as a multiracial space: "Reading Douglass as a democratic theorist thus reveals how his arguments about US and Latin American racial politics intersect to formulate a black fugitive democratic ethos."[93] Through a hemispheric reading of Douglass alongside Argentine Domingo Faustino Sarmiento and Mexican José de Vasconcelos, two Latin American thinkers who engaged notions of citizenship and race in their conception of the nation, Hooker presents Douglass as a figure who bridges the history of racial political thought in the Americas and a "radical democratic thinker" whose ideas shaped democratic theory.[94] The thread that unites Douglass's apparent political contradiction is, according to Hooker, "his commitment to multiracial democracy."[95] The abyss between what Hooker calls Douglass's "black fugitive democratic ethos"—his simultaneous support of a composite nationality and immigration—and his colonial interest in Latin America is exemplary of the contradictions of being Black and US American that continue to separate US Black struggles for democracy and freedom from other transnational anti-colonial struggles. The creative and destructive tension between US superiority and Black freedom marks the urgent need to translate blackness as a way of contra*dicting* state-colonial hegemony that shapes belonging and unbelonging.

Before Reconstruction, the place of Black people within larger hemispheric and global anti-colonial struggles for democracy was clear: the United States and Europe were the definitive enemies of Black freedom; internal colonial borders were illuminated through the institution of slavery, which in turn defined the external colonial projects of bordering and expansionism. Prior to Reconstruction, Douglass opposed American expansionism. He was untrusting of the nation-state as an institution of freedom, an idea he articulated in his best-known speech, "What to the Slave Is the Fourth of July?," delivered on July 5, 1852, in Rochester, New York: "Would you have me argue that man is entitled to liberty? That he is the rightful owner of his own body? You have already declared it. . . . The feeling of the nation must be quickened; the conscience of the nation must be roused; the propriety of the nation must be startled; the hypocrisy of the nation must be exposed; and its crimes against God and Man must be proclaimed and denounced."[96] But the idea of national belonging summoned him—and all US Black men—to partake in the promise of citizenship and participate in the project of the US empire, as the US nation and the US empire were and always have been entangled. In accepting US belonging, Douglass was thus also complicit in the expansionism that would strip the freedom and citizenship that Black and Brown people in Latin America had earned against another colonial power.

I have struggled for years to make sense of this contradiction in Douglass's life and political work. On the one hand, as Hooker articulates, Douglass's work, as well as his relationships to Haiti, Cuba, and other parts of the Americas, reveals a critical awareness of the significance of Black liberation and the possibility of hemispheric blackness through shared principles of republicanism and civility. On the other hand, his political role in US imperialism during Reconstruction, and his prejudice against Latinos as an "inferior race," shaped not only his actions during that period but also the legacy of US Black exceptionalism that continues to shape the conversation around race and belonging for Black Latinxs throughout the hemisphere and, as Brent Edwards argues in his engagement of early twentieth-century black internationalism, "In effect, transnational black solidarity is traded in for a certain kind of national currency, an anti-racism in one country."[97] Consciously or not, Douglass heralded US Black leadership and dominance over hemispheric blackness. If white Americans like Grant and others believed themselves to be "protecting" Black and Brown "southern republics" from European colonialism through absorption and expansion, US Black subjects like Douglass believed they could teach Latinos how to be citizens of color—Black, civil, and free. The structures laid out during Reconstruction, in part through Douglass's prominent role in the production of Black and Brown Latinidad for a US audience, also shaped Black Latinxs' understanding of themselves as different from US Blacks. As Luperón put it in his 1871 letter to José Gabriel García, the annexationists and Dominican "traitors" supporting the annexation were protecting the colonizing interests of the United States.[98]

Nationalism is a European construct. In the Americas, nationalist projects were built on the backs of enslaved people and mirrored the exclusion of colonial projects. But as Cornel West reminds us, the problem of nationalism for "Black folk—who are victimized mainly by Europeans tied to vicious notions and practices of white supremacy—using a European ideology to counter" is that it limits the possibility of unity; it obscures how "morally tainted it [nationalism] is in terms of not allowing our internationalism and universalism to become more pronounced."[99] In many ways, Douglass's endorsement of expansion was also a search for belonging—for a place where he could finally realize his "full stature as a man." Throughout the twentieth century, Black intellectuals pushed against expansionism and colonialism as a path to Black belonging, instead articulating Pan-Africanism and diaspora as the only true "home" for Black people. Still, the contradictions that shaped Douglass's vaivenes in 1871 were very much part of Black and Brown peoples' struggle to be recognized as capable of self-government and deserving of the protections and responsibilities of citizenship. In many ways, we are still in the midst of this struggle: we push the nation to fulfill its promise of citizenship for all people, and at the same time we see that promise leads to the exclusion, incarceration, and disenfranchisement of colonized others.

In the second half of the nineteenth century, Black and Brown men like Douglass could not yet see that the promise of citizenship would be broken—that Black belonging would not be possible in the United States. Or perhaps Douglass did see it clearly and hoped for a trans-American allegiance that would change the color composition of citizenship and tip the balance.

However Douglass envisioned the future, his actions and words in the annexation debate were impactful on the island as well as the mainland. The speeches he gave in Black churches across the United States, for example, had a lasting impact on how church leaders, such as AME missionary secretary Henry Blanton Parks, viewed the role of Black people in the US imperial project, moving them to concretely articulate colonization projects between 1888 and 1910 that positioned US Black citizens as carriers of imperial will across the globe.[100] While Douglass was not a proponent of mass emigration, his view of US Black men as superior men of color began a long and lasting tradition of US Black imperialism, from the AME missions and African emigration projects of the late nineteenth century to the twentieth- and twenty-first-century intellectual, political, and cultural projects that cast Black Latinxs as "negrophobic" or less capable of understanding and producing Black political and cultural thought.[101] US imperialism has contributed to the continued erasure of Black Latinidad from the sociopolitical history of blackness in the Americas through the very rhetoric of US exceptionalism that shaped Douglass's political engagement with Latin America. This narrative continues to inform transnational dialogues about race and citizenship between Latinx and Black people in the United States today. Understanding this legacy—in all its complexity and contradictions—is important for understanding the historical nexus that produced hemispheric blackness and transnational Black solidarity among Latin and North Americans for more than a century.

A New Raza: Luperón's Anti-colonial Struggles for Freedom

In 1875 Charles Douglass, Frederick Douglass's son, expressed a contra*diction* of US media's assessment of Gregorio Luperón and other Dominican rebels—as an "outlaw" leading "an uneducated mass" to its ruin."[102] He wrote:

> A few such men as Luperón down South would relieve the Government of the United States of much of its anxiety concerning the Negroes' protection, and would bring about a more fraternal feeling between the races. He would be a Toussaint to them there and would command respect from all parties for his manhood, courage, and undoubted

> honesty and patriotism. At the time the annexation question was before the United States Senate, Luperón was represented by the press of this country as a cut-throat and barbarian of the worse kind. He is just the opposite of this. A kind, courteous and benevolent disposition is what all who have the honor of his acquaintance accord him. He has been received into the highest courts of Europe with the greatest considerations of respect; and if his own countrymen would listen to his advice, they would soon become happy and prosperous people.[103]

In this, Charles Douglass provided a glimpse of the advent of the project of transnational Black solidarity that, as Frank Guridy has shown, shaped the relationship between US and Caribbean Blacks at the turn of the twentieth century.[104] Charles Douglass had accompanied his father on the Dominican Republic expedition in 1871. Four years later, Grant appointed him as consul to Puerto Plata, where he served until the death of his wife in 1879 forced him to return to the United States. The time that Charles Douglass spent in Puerto Plata coincided with Luperón's return to his native city and the end of Báez's dictatorship, along with his ploys to sell the Dominican Republic to the highest bidder. Following the triumph of the anti-annexation revolution he had led, Luperón directed his political and intellectual energies, along with Puerto Rican thinkers Ramón Emeterio Betances and Eugenio María de Hostos, into organizing the fight against Spanish colonialism in Puerto Rico and Cuba and the threat of US imperial expansion throughout the Americas. Luperón traveled all over the Caribbean, Latin America, and Europe, meeting with Latinx exiles and expatriates to spread his ideas about a united Latin America. It was during those years that Luperón and Betances founded La Sociedad Latinoamericana in Paris; it was the first documented diasporic Latinx organization in Europe. La Sociedad's goal was to "share the common experiences and cultures of Latin Americans and to promote unity among Latin American emigrants, students, and expats residing in the Old World."[105]

While lesser known than Puerto Rican Ramón Emeterio Betances and Cuban José Martí, Gregorio Luperón (1839–97; figure 1.4) was one of the earliest Caribbean proponents of what came to be known as the Confederación Antillana: a project that sought the political unification of Cuba, Puerto Rico, and the Dominican Republic against US imperialism and Spanish colonization under the ideals of freedom, justice, and racial equality.[106] Yolanda Martínez-San Miguel and Katerina Gonzalez Seligmann argue that the concept of the Confederación Antillana is articulated and redefined in a historical circularity that parallels the struggles for freedom in the Caribbean, including Haitian

FIGURE 1.4 General Gregorio Luperón, 1866. Colección Alejandro Paulino Ramos 063, Archivo General de la Nación (AGN), Dominican Republic.

independence (1804), Dominican Restoration (1865), Grito de Lares in Puerto Rico (1868), and Grito de Yara in Cuba (1869).[107] The son of a Haitian mother and Dominican father, Luperón was a self-made man of humble origins—a fact that Irmary Reyes-Santos argues led to the obscurity of his contributions to nineteenth-century Caribbean and Latin American intellectual projects.[108] Luperón gained political prominence as a leader in the independence movement against the Spanish occupation, better known as La Guerra de Restauración, or the Dominican War of Restoration (1863–65). But while he has been mostly memorialized as a man of arms, Luperón's intellectual contributions to the projects of dominicanidad, Confederación Antillana, and Latinidad occupied the majority of his life and the bulk of his writing. Throughout the second half of the nineteenth century, Luperón built relationships across the Caribbean with intellectuals and political figures that, like him, found courage and inspiration in Black freedom. He used his own resources to publish *Las Dos Antillas* (later *Las Tres Antillas*), a newspaper dedicated to the "defense and propaganda of the political interests of Cuban and Puerto Rican freedom" and supported—with advice, political leverage, and money—the educational project of Eugenio María de Hostos and multiple political initiatives by Cuban and Puerto Rican exiles living on the island and elsewhere. Multiple Cuban clubs and organizations, including New York–based La Liga, recognized him for his efforts.[109] Historian Emilio Cordero Michel writes that Luperón was "el indiscutible líder histórico de la futura confederación antillana" (the indisputable historical leader of the Antillean Confederation).[110]

In his three-volume *Notas autobiográficas y apuntes para la historia*, published between 1895 and 1896, Luperón outlines his commitment to abolishing slavery and seeking racial justice and independence while denouncing US imperialism, caudillismo, and dictatorships as "evil regression to a form of slavery."[111] Scholars of Luperón read him as a nationalist and, occasionally, as a pan-Caribbean political figure. But to understand him and his political legacies of republicanism in the second half of the nineteenth century, we need to read his works and deeds through his positionalities and his project of dominicanidad. The political and geographic location of the Dominican Republic demanded that its leadership establish the country's values by negotiating and imagining it as part of three territories and political projects: the island of Hispaniola, the Antilles, and Latinidad. These negotiations were grounded on an understanding of mulataje—Black and white racial mixing (as opposed to Hispanicized mestizaje)—that did not privilege whiteness but centered blackness.[112]

To translate Luperón's contributions to Latinidad, Black liberation, and multiracial citizenship, it is necessary to examine each of the sites that shaped his intellectual and political project. First and foremost, Luperón understood that the Dominican Republic shared the island of Hispaniola with Haiti, and with it a colonial past and republican future. The first chapter of his *Notas autobiográficas* begins with a description of the island sharing the "storm" of colonialism and the trauma of slavery.[113] Luperón therefore saw the two nations as indelibly linked—environmentally, economically, and politically interdependent.[114] Unlike the more widely studied nineteenth-century intellectual proponents of Hispanicity and mestizo dominicanidad, such as Manuel de Jesús Galván and César Nicolás Penson, who sought to sever ties with Haiti to erase African heritage and uphold whitewashed mestizaje, Luperón dedicated a big part of his political life to strengthening the relationship between the Dominican Republic and Haiti.[115] In 1867 he signed the Treaty of Peace, Friendship, and Commerce with Haiti, setting a path to reconciliation and cooperation for the two nations. In Haiti, he found military support and moral strength to wage war against Spain and to defend the country against US annexation. From 1863 to 1865, he collaborated with Haiti in the war against Spain, and from 1867 to 1873, he once again relied on Haiti in the fight against US annexation. Haiti was a friend to Luperón, and he understood that friendship as an alliance and a mutual responsibility. He found refuge in Haiti when persecuted—first by Báez in 1868, and again in 1888 by his own friend-turned-dictator, President Ulises Heureaux (Lilís)—before going into exile in St. Thomas.[116] And finally, Haiti was a symbol in and backdrop to his hemispheric project of Latinidad. The Dominican Republic was thus first and foremost part of the island of Hispaniola and a sister nation to Haiti.

For Luperón, Haiti and the Dominican Republic made up the common and legitimate "raza" of postcolonial Hispaniola: "Son éstas la europea y la Africana, que al cruzarse entre sí han producido *otra raza mixta*, participando ambas, según la preponderancia de una u otra sangre la cual tiende por la ley de los climas a volver a la raza primita de la isla" (These [races], the European and the African, as they crossed between each other, produced *another mixed race*, both of which participate, according to the dominance of one or another, in returning to the primitive race of the island in following with the law of nature).[117] In his 1888 presidential campaign, Luperón summoned this notion of "otra sangre" to promote the unity of "Latin American peoples regardless of race."[118] Luperón's unified Hispaniola was thus also a project of Latin American unity grounded on antislavery, anti-colonial, Black-affirming Latinidad.

Luperón's articulation of Hispaniola's "raza mixta," or what his goddaughter Gregoria Fraser, referring to her own subject position as the mediator of the North-South divide, would later refer to as "brownness," might lead the contemporary reader to dismiss his project as yet another example of Latin American mestizaje.[119] Like most Caribbean thinkers of his generation, Luperón struggled with the legacy of Spanish colonialism. But Luperón's use of "raza mixta" to describe the ethno-racial and cultural makeup of the people of Hispaniola summoned not mestizaje (Indigenous and European mixing) but Caribbean mulataje and brownness—*la raza europea y la raza africana*—as the future of Hispaniola and Latin America. José Buscaglia-Salgado theorizes mulataje as a "metaphorical movement" informed not so much by the production of difference that "nurtures the coloniality of power" but "as what Aristotle called an intuitive perception of the similarity in dissimilars."[120] He presents the Caribbean mulato subject as one in movement who escapes the reductive definition of mestizaje: "In every case, the mulatto always moves beyond, not by being alter but by being ultra. Indeed, in a curious antidote to conquest and reduction, the mulatto subject describes a movement of reverse colonization of the ideal that is always more, not less, always additive and forever seemingly shifting. The mulatto subject is the true plus ultra of the Atlantic world."[121] Buscaglia-Salgado's definition of mulataje in the postcolonial Caribbean does not point to racially marked bodies, nor to the problematic racial categories that were used to divide Afro-descendants into castes during the colonial period, but rather to a subversion of those categories. If mestizaje is commonly imagined as the mixture of multiple races that dilutes blackness, Buscaglia-Salgado's definition of mulataje points to a reversal of the colonial order: to the "ultimate realization of all potentiality in the erasure of racial difference."[122] This difference does not erase colonial history but seeks a way forward, undoing colonial structures through ethnic and national unity while naming blackness as central and inseparable from the implicit whitewashing of mulato brownness.

Luperón's use of the word *raza* does not always denote race; rather, it summons mulataje and an anti-colonial project of citizenship and belonging. For Luperón, *raza* functions as a composite of citizenship, ethnicity, and culture. His articulation of Hispaniola's raza as one—rather than two opposing Black and mestizo races, as his contemporaries had done—is radical, particularly when considering the long history of anti-Haitianism that has characterized Dominican intellectualism and political thought since the second half of the nineteenth century. Claiming Haiti and the Dominican Republic *together* as the one (mixed) raza of Hispaniola is a radical assertion of Black and Brown belonging. It is also a political project of anti-colonial independence aimed at severing the trauma of colonialism that produced mulataje via rape, while also insisting on the legitimate place of Black and Brown belonging to the native land: "a volver a la raza primitiva de la isla" through what Buscaglia-Salgado calls the mulato "reversal of the colonial order."[123] Neither mestizo nor white, the postcolonial subject of Hispaniola is the legitimate carrier of its new raza, possessing citizenship that is not bounded by race and the colonial order.

At the time of Luperón's writing in the 1870s, Latin American intellectuals were beginning to center narratives of indigenismo in the project of the Latin American mestizo nation. Indigenismo produced a symbolic narrative of mestizaje that justified the formation of the nation and the production of unique identities and razas. This mestizaje, while symbolically embracing Indigenous heritage, did not translate into actual inclusion or belonging for Indigenous peoples. Rather, as María Josefina Saldaña-Portillo argues, mestizaje erases Indigenous belonging by producing the mestizo subject as the carrier of Spanish aggression and perpetrator of colonial violence: "el hijo de la chingada."[124] Mestizos erase Indigenous claims to land and belonging while simultaneously carrying within themselves the colonial legacy of miscegenation through violence and racial erasure. One lasting effect of the narrative of mestizaje is the erasure of African and Black cultural roots from the nation and, by extension, the region, through a project of whitening that places blackness and indigeneity in the past to imagine a deracinated modern future. Luperón's claiming of mulataje and blackness as a "return to the primitive races" is thus a contra*diction* of mestizaje and a translation of blackness that reminds us that descendants of enslaved people in Hispaniola indeed restored the "native" order of the island not through miscegenation with Indigenous populations but through labor and revolution, by ousting the colonial forces and starting anew in freedom. Rather than promote the idea of heterogeneity and diversity that criollo Juan Pablo Duarte constructed in 1844 as the basis of the Dominican nation—which was eventually co-opted to bolster antiblackness through anti-Haitianism—Luperón upholds African roots and Black belonging while simultaneously acknowledging the violent trauma of colonialism. His is a project of radical hope for racial democracy and inclusion that seeks to replace colonial memory, slavery, and white supremacist mestizaje with the possibility of a raza that would guarantee equality under the law. It was this understanding of racial identity that shaped Luperón's writing and political projects during the last three decades of his life.

Haiti is unquestionably central to Luperón's articulation of mulataje and raza mixta. But for Luperón, Haitian-Dominican unity did not only mean that the two nations shared a colonial history and a common racial present; it also meant they shared the responsibility of ensuring all countries in the region would fight for Black freedom. Silvio Torres-Saillant explains that for Luperón, the borders of the nation-state were not the limits of patriotism. Rather, patriotism was an extension of anti-colonial thought that included the rest of the Antilles.[125] In a letter written to historian José Gabriel García in 1870 during the annexation debate, Luperón expressed his frustration at the "lack of backbone" of Haitian president Sylvain Salnave, who, contrary to his predecessors, did not seem to take a strong stand against US expansionism and in support of Cuban and Puerto Rican independence: "No quisieran ver la anexión Americana [. . .] pero les tienen miedo a los yankees. . . . A esta República le hace falta un hombre de estado que se pusiera a la altura de la situación, no tan solamente de la amenaza que pesa sobre esta isla con la más grave presunción yankee, pero sí que comprendiera la misión que tienen estas dos repúblicas para con las dos islas vecinas de Cuba y Puerto Rico" (They [Haitians] would not want to see the American annexation . . . but they are afraid of the Yankees. . . . That republic is lacking a statesman that would rise to the challenge of the situation, not only to the threat that this island is experiencing in this grave matter of the Yankees, but also for them to understand the mission of these two republics in relation to the neighboring islands of Cuba and Puerto Rico).[126]

Luperón believed that the Dominican Republic, as the first of the Spanish-speaking colonies in the Caribbean to gain independence, had a responsibility to guide and protect Puerto Rico and Cuba in their fights for liberation; he viewed Haiti as a natural ally to that project. He opened his home to many Caribbean freedom fighters, including Puerto Ricans Ramón Emeterio Betances and Eugenio María de Hostos. He collaborated with the former, as previously mentioned, in the creation of the Confederación Antillana and Club Las Dos Antillas, and with the latter in the creation of La Liga de la Paz and the newspaper *Las Tres Antillas*. He gave Hostos his home and personal resources to create the first Escuela Normal on the island, and he backed Máximo Gómez and Antonio Maceo in their revolutionary fights to free Cuba. Luperón's actions in support of Puerto Rican and Cuban liberation are innumerable. They earned him the respect of many of his contemporaries across Latin America and even Europe. In May 1874 Giuseppe Garibaldi offered him a medal of friendship for his work on the republican values of freedom, and in 1882 Victor Hugo hosted a grand reception in Paris in his honor after Luperón received an honorific medal from the French government.[127] In all the recognition Luperón received over the years, what stands out the most is the trust other Caribbean leaders put in him as a conciliator and visionary capable of uniting the Caribbean and Latin America in the anti-colonial struggle for racially inclusive citizenship. In 1895 Hostos wrote a letter to Luperón, who was in exile in St. Thomas at the time, asking for guidance regarding the Cuban independence movement. Calling Luperón the legitimate leader of freedom in the Caribbean, he asks:

> ¿Por qué no toma usted en la dirección el movimiento de las Antillas que Cuba ha vuelto a iniciar, la parte que legítimamente le corresponde como uno de los libertadores americanos? De usted, probablemente, dependería la constitución de un centro directivo que, de acuerdo con el Comité Revolucionario de Cuba y Puerto Rico en Nueva York o Cayo Hueso, reuniera, organizara y de ahí encaminara las fuerzas y recursos revolucionarios de Santo Domingo y Puerto Rico y de la emigración cubana en Puerto Plata y en las islas y tierras circunvecinas.[128]

> [Why don't you take your righteous place as the legitimate Antillean leader, as one of the American liberators, in the struggle that Cuba has reinitiated? It would be up to you, most likely, to build a committee that would direct, following the Revolutionary Committee of Cuba and

Puerto Rico in New York or Cayo Hueso, and organize the revolutionary forces in Santo Domingo and Puerto Rico and the Cuban immigrants in Puerto Plata and the neighboring islands.]

Luperón responded to his friend's query by assuring him that the Cuban fight was in the most "capable hands," and that his role was to uplift that fight by continuing to support the community of exiled Cubans in Puerto Plata and New York—a promise he fulfilled until his death in 1897.

In *An Intellectual History of the Caribbean*, Torres-Saillant argues that the intellectual production and conversations about race, nation, "regional identity, and border crossing" that the members of the Confederación Antillana put forth during the second half of the nineteenth century constituted an early example of what we have come to understand as transnationalism.[129] While, as Torres-Saillant demonstrates, the Caribbean is epistemologically different from the rest of Latin America, Latinidad is both central to and in tension with Caribbeanness. Luperón saw the Dominican Republic—along with Puerto Rico, Haiti, and Cuba—as part of the Latin American project. Language, culture, and the common struggle against colonialism and coloniality were key elements in the construction of Latinidad—which he called "raza" or Latin American brotherhood or unity.

While minimal scholarship has focused on Luperón's Caribbean project, even less emphasis has been put on his understanding of the Dominican people as Latinos and on the Dominican Republic as a part of Latinidad. In the prologue to *Notas autobiográficas*, Luperón provides a brief but clear overview of Latin American political and military struggles for independence. Starting with Mexico, he moves geographically south, explaining the struggles of each country in Central and South America: their triumphs, their challenges, and their political statuses at the time of his writing. In doing so, he places the Dominican Republic within a larger Latin American context. It was through this Latino consciousness that the battle against the newer and imminent threat of US expansionism was waged between 1867 and 1873. Appealing to Latinidad gained Luperón political force while also offering a moral reminder to the United States and Europe that taking the Dominican Republic would infringe upon their own commitment to American liberation. As he wrote to Hostos at the end of his life:

> Para que la nueva república de Cuba, se una a todas las Repúblicas Latinas Américanas y no se eche en brazos de la República Norteamericana, a la que debemos mirar siempre como enemiga y pirata contra las demás naciones americanas. Yo creo que debemos trabajar por una

Confederación política de todas las repúblicas Latinas Americanas contra los filibusteros norteamericanas y los piratas ingleses. Esto es, contra de los Estados Unidos de América e Inglaterra. Los dos más grandes peligros y la mayor amenaza que tienen todas las repúblicas Latinoamericanas. . . . Sí mi querido Hostos: Levante usted su potente voz en la noble Chile, para que toda la América oiga . . . por la liga del principio de la soberanía nacional Americana, por la solidaridad de todas las Repúblicas Latinas Americanas, por su confraternidad con todas las Repúblicas y los pueblos de su raza y por su sólida unión contra todos los filibusteros y piratas, contra todas las tiranías y contra todas las injusticias que vengan de donde venga, para preparar el grandioso porvenir de todas las agrupaciones americanas en una vasta confraternidad política.[130]

[So that the new republic of Cuba unites itself with the Latin American Republics and does not fall in the arms of the North American Republic, which we should look upon as an enemy and pirate of the rest of the American republics. I think we should work toward a political confederation of all the Latin American republics against the North American filibusters and the English pirates. They are both the greatest danger and the greatest threat to Latin American republics. . . . Yes, my dear Hostos, raise your strong voice in that noble Chile, so that all of America will hear it . . . for the solidarity of all Latin American republics, for brotherhood among all Latin republics and the people of its race and for its solid union against all filibusters and pirates, against all tyrannies and all injustices wherever they may be, to prepare for the grand future when all the American groups become one vast political brotherhood.]

But Latinidad does not emerge in Luperón's writings solely as a concept of political unity. Rather, it is an identity that contrasts with Anglo-Saxon culture and identity. While the claim to Latinidad is in many ways grounded on notions of Hispanicity that reveal what Rubén Silié calls a "colonized imagination," I want to highlight the fact that even when his colonial desires colored his conceptualization of Latinidad, Luperón clearly separated what he considers "culture"—language, literature, and the arts—from colonialism: the "subjugation of Latin American sovereignty."[131] In other words, he recognized the inescapability of *Créolité*—the Caribbean racial, linguistic, and cultural dynamics that emerged from encounters of Indigenous, African, European, and Asian people who inhabit the region—and claimed those legacies as part of the raza of the Americas while simultaneously denouncing colonial imposition as a threat to freedom, sovereignty, and color-blind citizenship.[132] The contradictions that shaped his political project of unity, I insist, must not prevent us from recognizing his commitment to Black freedom and racially inclusive citizenship. Rather, these contradictions can help us understand how he saw difference within, beyond, and through race. While difference in the United States was articulated as a Black-white binary, Luperón's project of Latinidad held blackness, Black freedom, and racially inclusive citizenship central to the production of a multiracial, multiethnic community of nations. For Luperón, sovereignty united the Latin American project. But sovereignty, as he saw it, depended first on emancipation and liberation. As such, difference was not imagined as a struggle between multiple races that together made up Latinidad but as a question of power. This becomes clear in his call to arms during the 1871 annexation attempts:

> Dominicanos! Buenaventura Báez has sold you to the Americans in the same manner that Santana sold you to the Spanish, but this time without condition! *Slavery, with all its despotism, the loss of all your interests, the death and your voice threatens and awaits you with all its horrors. . . . The death and extermination of your race* threatens and awaits you with dishonor forever if you do not raise an outcry of reprobation against the assassination of your dearest affections. . . . *Those who do not have a nationality of their own are slaves and objects of traffic for their tyrants. . . .* You know that the impatient American Government, in buying Santo Domingo, buys also a ready man, a man without honor; finally you are aware that every people dragged into bondage, by not matter what means, sooner or later rebel against the foreign will be imposed upon them; and then, either they exterminate or are exterminated.[133]

The equation of imperialism to slavery is striking in Luperón's diction, as is his understanding of race and nationality. Reminding citizens of the very recent colonial history of slavery and subjugation, Luperón translates the meaning of US expansionism through the legacy of European colonialism. Losing one's national identity, he argues, is losing freedom; it is being enslaved—something to be avoided at all costs.

For Luperón, the struggle between Latin America and North America was one of sovereignty versus imperialism. It is precisely this dichotomy that Frederick Douglass misunderstood and mistranslated when he arrived in the Dominican Republic in 1871 as an agent of US empire. Despite the fact that, like Luperón, Douglass was a Black man fighting for Black citizenship, he was unable to translate his project to Dominicanos like Luperón. To Luperón, Douglass was indeed a Black man but nonetheless a "Yanki," and as such a threat to Dominican freedom.[134] Douglass was a Black North American, while Dominican Blacks were Latinos. The difference, as understood by both Luperón and Douglass, marked a hierarchical distinction that would shape the intellectual and political relationship between US Black and Black Latinx subjects for generations to come.

The mutual inability to translate their blackness—to impress upon each other their common struggles for freedom and equality in the face of white supremacy—has thwarted Dominican and US American alliances around racial justice both on the island and abroad. The logic that moved Douglass to side with the US empire in a project that would strip the sovereignty of a Black republic based on a view of Latinidad as inferior, uncivilized, and dysfunctional—like the vision that prevented Luperón from understanding the internal colonialism that produced simultaneous belonging and unbelonging for US Black citizens—continues to complicate the translations and mistranslations of Black Latinidad in the United States today. These mistranslations perpetuate the wedge of "us versus them" that ultimately keeps Black Latinxs and US Blacks from confronting, together, the structures of colonialism that separate them.

Miss Fraser, from Santo Domingo

That Gregoria Fraser was the goddaughter of both Gregorio Luperón and Frederick Douglass is the most beautiful and poetic of all contra*dictions*. A native of Puerto Plata, Luperón's hometown, and the niece of Lewis Douglass, Fraser was born into two Black worlds that zigzagged each other and integrated within her. Fraser grew up with immense privilege, shielded from the hardships of Black childhood. In the Dominican Republic, away from segregation and racial violence, her family enjoyed a class status that allowed them to fully participate in all elements of society. The exemplary lives of her parents meant she grew up surrounded by Black political and economic power and within an ethos of Black feminist possibilities: she was expected, like her mother, to attend university and have a thriving career. Protected by her parents and her padrinos, Fraser was free to learn and dream of becoming whatever she desired. When she moved to the United States, she retained her connection to Latinidad, to the Spanish language, and to the land of her birth. During her long and active career as a musician and educator, she often lectured on Dominican music and customs, insisting on the Dominican

Republic as one of the first "black republics."[135] Perhaps because of a lingering accent or her lifelong commitment to translating her Dominican blackness for an American public that refused to see her, her friends and colleagues knew her throughout her life as "Miss Fraser from Santo Domingo."[136]

Unlike Luperón and Douglass, Fraser's preoccupation with belonging had little to do with state-sponsored notions of citizenship. In the early twentieth century, when she came of age, women's civil rights were dependent upon their relationships to men, particularly via marriage. For Fraser, this meant that she was unable to vote in the United States until the passage of the Nineteenth Amendment in 1920, and in the Dominican Republic her citizenship was "suspended" because of her marriage to a foreign (US) citizen.[137] For Fraser, then, belonging was articulated through a search for and an assertion of her differences and her own lived experiences as a Black woman whose roots were firmly grounded on the "southern republics" rather than through political struggles linked to nation-states.

Fraser's Dominican documents identified her race as "mestiza-mulata." In the United States, she was considered "Negro."[138] But in her own writing, she trades both labels for the descriptor "brown," which as I noted in the opening of this chapter was uncommon at the time: "You see, Sally, *I am brown* and all the other passengers are white Americans. . . . I understood and rejoiced inwardly. *Tomorrow I will be on native soil and being brown will not matter.*"[139] While "brown" did not exist as a racially differentiated category in the early twentieth-century United States, the way Fraser employs the term can be read as an English translation of the multiple forms of dark-skinned mulataje commonly used in the Dominican Republic (morena, india oscura, mulata). Her assertion that her brownness "will not matter" upon landing in the Dominican Republic further contextualizes what the term means to her as a marker of difference from other "white American passengers." Upon arriving to a "brown" country, her brownness would be the norm. Fraser's claiming of "brownness" is thus also a claiming of her translated coexistent blackness and Latinidad.[140] Fraser's brownness is the middle ground on which Luperón's mulato multiethnic unity and Douglass's composite nationality merged. To borrow from Arthur Schomburg, it is the "background of the future" of Black Latinidad that would emerge in the mid-twentieth century and continue in the twenty-first-century Global North.[141]

Most late nineteenth-century and early twentieth-century Black Caribbean diasporic subjects living in the United States claimed Negro identification, thereby embracing political and social struggles while shedding the misunderstood racial dynamics that produced the Caribbean and Latin America as mixed-race or other-than-Black (inferior) republics. For Fraser, who had ancestral familial ties to the United States and was brought up within elite US Black circles, it would have made sense to follow this practice. It is striking that she instead chose to embrace "Miss Fraser from Santo Domingo," and that she continued to embrace that identity even as the years of geographical distance from her country of birth grew. Ginetta Candelario has asserted that Black Latinxs living in the Washington, DC, area in the early twentieth century opted to identify as "Hispanic" in order to escape segregation.[142] Fraser's claim to Dominicanidad, and by extension to Caribbean and Latino identities, was not to distance herself from blackness. On the contrary, she claimed the Dominican Republic as "a black republic." Fraser's blackness and Latinidad were not mutually exclusive but mutually constitutive.

Throughout her adult life in the United States, Fraser embodied the detours that made Douglass and Luperón mirror images in the struggle for color-blind citizenship. A citizen of both the Dominican Republic and the United States, she longed to be seen as human rather than as a representative of her race—for acceptance and recognition as a Black *and* Dominican American woman. Her hopes and dreams of freedom were embedded in nostalgia for Santo Domingo. In 1939, after thirty-six years of absence, Fraser returned to the Trujillo-run Dominican Republic in search of the home she longed for throughout her adult life. Despite encountering the challenges of the dictatorship and its political environment, and having to fight for the recognition of her citizenship, she reclaimed a sense of belonging she had assumed lost, translating her Latina blackness.

> But it is good to be home once more amongst my friends, scenes and customs. . . . Then to think I am living in the same house where I was reared, you youngsters cannot appreciate what that means for you have not broken your house ties and wandered far and long as I have, just think I was away thirty-six years, and to return, find friends and home, be taken into the social, civic and religious life just as if I had never been away seems to me marvelous. For a long time I felt it must be a happy dream and was afraid I would awaken to find myself back at 2019 13th NE.[143]

The idea of "returning to the homeland" is central to the conceptualization of migrant and diasporic subjectivity. As early as 1939, Martinican poet and political figure Aimé Césaire theorized the affective and political implications of "returning" in his *Cahier d'un retour au pays natal*:

> [30] Partir. Mon coeur bruissait de générosités emphatiques. Partir . . . j'arriverais lisse et jeune dans ce pays mien et je dirais à ce pays dont le limon entre dans la composition de ma chair: "J'ai longtemps erré et je reviens vers la hideur désertée de vos plaies." Je viendrais à ce pays mien et je lui dirais: "Embrassez-moi sans crainte . . . Et si je ne sais que parler, c'est pour vous que je parlerai."
>
> [To leave. My heart was humming with emphatic generosities. To leave . . . I would arrive sleek and young in this land of mine and I would say to this land whose loam is part of my flesh: "I have wandered for a long time and I am coming back to the deserted hideousness of your sores." I would come to this land of mine and I would say to it: "Embrace me without fear . . . And if all I can do is speak, it is for you I shall speak."][144]

For Césaire, returning is always a confrontation with the historical forces that enabled his departure—a reunion with heart and flesh that enables enunciation of belonging: "for you I shall speak." Returning "home" is thus intrinsic to and constitutive of diasporic identity. For Gregoria Fraser too, returning home to the Dominican Republic was not merely an act of individual fulfillment; it was also a process of historical self-recognition and validation: to "find friends and a home" from which her diasporic belonging can be spoken into existence through the physical act of homecoming.

Her return to the Dominican Republic is thus a process of re-membering, of piecing together, the promise of Black belonging that brought her two identities—Black Latina and US Black—together. Fraser's birth and upbringing in the Dominican Republic were the result of a transnational Black political movement that was based on the possibility of Black belonging in the Caribbean diaspora. That Frederick Douglass, having failed in his attempt to annex the Dominican Republic, still encouraged Sarah Loguen, Gregoria's mother, to move to Puerto Plata in 1882—and that his son Charles becomes consul in the Dominican Republic as a result of his father's advocacy—demonstrates that the idea of transnational Black belonging in the Dominican Republic persisted even when annexation failed. That the last two decades of the nineteenth century saw a growth in US Black engagement with the Dominican Republic, as the work of Christina Davidson demonstrates, particularly through the AME Church, confirms that for the US Black elite, the Dominican Republic continued to signify a hopeful location for realizing Black futurity.[145] Fraser's life and ethos of Black Latinidad are thus mediated not by the experiences of her own individual vaivén between the Dominican Republic and the United States but by her embodiment of two political dreams for Black belonging, memorialized in her two padrinos' ideologies.

Postscript: Unsilencing the Past

Central to my research as an anti-colonial scholar is an understanding of the official archive as a place that foregrounds the voices of white men and the dominance of colonial powers in the historicization of events, processes, and ideologies that affect colonized, racialized subjects. My previous works have grappled with the contra*dictions* that shape what we in academia deem "truthful" based on the evidence we find in traditional archives and the silences this evidence creates and reproduces. Michel-Rolph Trouillot argues, "Truths derive from mentions or silences of various kinds of degrees. And by silences, I mean an active and transitive process: One silences."[146] These silences are not accidental. Rather, they are intentional in the creation of the archive as a site of exclusion. The larger the archive, the more silences it reproduces. When studying US imperial ventures in the Dominican Republic and Haiti, I am always presented with the challenge of abundance rather than lack. US archives are rich in letters, memos, and other documentation of US Americans and their thoughts about and perceptions of Dominicans. The documentation fills a room; so, too, can the silences this excess reproduces.

While there is some documentation about the annexation debate in Dominican historiography and archives, most of it is mediated by the coloniality of dominicanidad that guided the political actions of the likes of Báez. At times, the dissenting voices of anti-colonial freedom fighters like Luperón are included, but men of privilege and power dominate the archives. One can more or less trace Báez's annexation scheme—how he operated and conspired with American businessmen to sell the country for personal gain. Likewise, with some effort, one is able to reconstruct the formal response by anti-annexation leaders who, while in exile, organized, wrote letters, and waged war. But what the archive silences is the sentiments of average Dominicans who, only four years after the end of the bloody War of Restoration, yet again faced the prospect of annexation and war. I can imagine what it must have been like for my father's great-grandmother, María Frías, a farmer from a *paraje* near San Francisco de Macorís. She must have been so overwhelmed by the uncertainty of a future in which men continued to decide if blood was to be shed, if we were to call ourselves Dominicans, Spaniards,

Haitians, or Americans, if we continued to speak Spanish or if we would need to learn English or French. Or perhaps none of these questions were relevant when food was scarce, and caudillos would not allow her to work her plot of land. Did María Frías care at all who governed the country or what flag was installed in a government building she would never visit? Did it make a difference to her? Maybe it did. Maybe she was invested in the nation-building project. Perhaps she was afraid of the idea of being governed by a foreign power or at the thought of another bloody war. Or maybe she hoped that a change in power would finally put an end to the abuses of the caudillos so she could farm her land and raise her children in peace. While I cannot ever know how most Dominicans experienced the violence of the annexation war during the Báez administration, I can imagine—or perhaps just hope—that the opposition to the annexation represented a voice of dissent against those dominating the country, the debate, and, posthumously, the archive.

It is not only problematic but a gross injustice that most of the scholarship in English about the annexation has been written from the perspective of, and through the voices of, the US American representatives leading the debate. How could the future and destiny of the Dominican Republic mean more to a US senator like Charles Sumner than to the people living the daily consequences of it on the island? Why should we be satisfied with the words of senators and commission members without asking the very basic question, "What did the Dominican people want?"

Sumner was the chairman of the Senate Foreign Relations Committee and a nationally respected abolitionist who had led the congressional battle against slavery and become a sort of martyr for the cause after sustaining injuries at the hands of a brutal assault on the floor of the House of Representatives by cane-wielding South Carolina congressman Preston Brooks in 1856.[147] Historians have focused on Sumner's prominent opposition to Grant's annexation plan more than any other figure in the debate. Sumner's compilation of letters, speeches, and articles is without a doubt the most comprehensive written archive on the annexation debate. Rather than reiterate Sumner's significance, however, I want to highlight his position as an ally amplifying the struggle, armed resistance, and history of liberation and freedom that Dominicans like Gregorio Luperón, José María Cabral, José Gabriel García, and Tomás Bobadilla, among others, were writing and sharing with him and other members of the Senate during the period in which the question of annexation was being contemplated in Washington (1867–72). As Bobadilla clarifies in a letter sent to Sumner on February 4, 1871, from Puerto

Rico, where he was exiled, Sumner was their emissary and ally—a voice for their demands and a representative for their cause. As such, he needed to listen to their version of the facts to adequately represent them.

> Your Excellency, interpreting the true sentiment of the people who entrusted you with their representation in the American Senate, you have raised their voice with authority against the annexation of Santo Domingo as proposed to the cabinet of Washington by General Báez. . . . But in order to afford YE a more thorough knowledge that you may continue advocating of the liberty and the right of the Dominican people, for the sake of their respect which nations owe to each other as well as for the accomplishments of the duty which my friends, my age and my patriotism entrusted me with, allow me to make a faithful statement of the condition of affairs in the Dominican Republic.[148]

The sixteen-page letter, sent while the Commission of Inquiry was conducting its investigation in Santo Domingo at the request of President Grant, provided an abridged version of Dominican struggles for liberation. Insisting on his participation in "every public event in that country" since 1812, and establishing himself as one of the leaders of the "1844 Independence," Bobadilla speaks with the "reason, truth and impartiality of one who considers this act the last of his public life."[149] However, it was not only Bobadilla's old age and long political commitment to Dominican liberation that was implied in this diction—"last" political act—but his belief that should the Dominican Republic fall to the United States, there would be no more restoration; it would lose its sovereignty forever. It was this fear and recognition that fueled the anti-annexation movement from its inception.

As soon as rumors began to circulate in the Dominican Republic that Báez's people were meeting with US representatives to solidify the annexation, a group of Dominican exiles residing on the neighboring island of Curaçao, most likely organized by archivist and writer José Gabriel García, presented a petition to the US Senate demanding that they rescind the annexation efforts and insisting that Báez was a tyrant.[150] Signed on February 7, 1870, by a "group of Dominicans," the letter contained "hostile language" that conveyed revolutionary intentions.[151] On March 18, the same group sent a second letter calling on Dominican patriotism and the will to defend the nation "at all cost" against General Báez and his ambitions.[152] In all letters and memos, the anti-annexationist Dominicans refused to recognize Báez as their president, using the military title "General" instead to denote his position as a dictator and leader of an army that had taken hold of the country by force for the fourth time. As the Senate debate over the annexation was playing out in the United States, the letters continued to pour in to Congress, and in particular to Sumner, each time with additional signatures. Among the most notable correspondences are (1) a letter from Báez dated October 9, 1868, in which he asks Sumner to side with him and "saque a este país de la triste situación en que lo han sumergido los disturbios domésticos y las maquinaciones de toda especie" (take this country out of the sad situation in which domestic disturbances and intrigues of all kind have submerged it);[153] (2) a copy of Luperón's famous *Capotillo Declaration*, an 1871 manifesto against Báez and the annexation that circulated throughout the country and the various enclaves of Dominican exiles in the Caribbean; (3) a letter from Luperón to Grant reminding him of his duty to respect republican sovereignty; and (4) the aforementioned letter from Bobadilla explaining the historical processes that shaped Dominican struggles and denouncing Báez as a "sellout and tyrant."

Reading the English translation of Bobadilla's 1871 letter to Sumner and picking up pieces of the original Spanish in various publications and archives, I hear the voices of these men writing from different Caribbean islands. Their rage, indignation, and disillusionment at having to wage a political fight for their freedom only a short four years after waging a bloody war against Spain are embedded in their correspondence. Bobadilla's diction is particularly touching, as he claims his subject position as an elder who had witnessed multiple wars of independence and who now, exiled in Puerto Rico, saw once more the possibility of annexation and the ultimate threat to sovereignty.

As a scholar who engages with history to analyze social and political events affecting Black Latinx lives, my archival praxis has been to read in contrad*iction*—to find the silences and insist on alternative possibilities for truth. The annexation was indeed stopped, and Sumner was the powerful white ally in the room where these decisions were made; these facts do not change with my reading. My reading of Dominican voices in the archive—unsilencing Bobadilla's words and rage—adds to our understanding of *how* these decisions were made while highlighting the urgency of breaking hundreds of years of silence in American historiography surrounding Black and Brown resistance. Reading the Sumner archive in contra*diction* is a political act against the systematic erasure of Black and Brown people as historical actors. In silencing our past, historians perpetuate the violent erasures that continue to shape our understanding of humanity, knowledge, and epistemology as things that come from Europe and the Global North. Or, as Trouillot puts it, in silencing the past we solidify a version of truth based purely on the colonial and colonizing practices produced through a colonizing discourse of human versus less than human. "The classification of all non-Westerners as fundamentally non-historical," Trouillot writes, "is tied also to the assumption that history requires a linear and cumulative sense of time that allows the observer to isolate the past as a distinct entity."[154] This permits the continued dehumanization of colonized peoples, justifies their exclusion, and reproduces violence.

I am half the age Bobadilla was when he wrote that letter to Sumner, and found myself completing this book in 2020 after the murder of George Floyd brought us to a political déjà vu: watching Black people fight for their lives, fight for the freedom that was promised more than 150 years ago. Living in this moment and writing about Black freedom during Reconstruction makes my reading of history a contra*diction* of the historical praxis of a linear accumulation of fact that Trouillot criticized. As I read Bobadilla, I felt a sense of kinship and a sort of tender sentimental sadness for this eighty-year-old man who had to fight once again to retain a sovereignty twice won through war, and who would die without the assurance that the Dominican Republic would be free from colonialism. I felt the exhaustion and exasperation in his penmanship and his tone. Between the lines, I read his indignity at having to mediate his struggle through an ally because his voice as a Dominican—as a citizen of a contested, deferred free nation of Black and Brown people—would otherwise never be heard. So, I sat with Bobadilla's words and *saw* them. I read them aloud multiple times, enacting and embodying his rage as best I could. I dug into my own rage, my own indignity in 2020—also a moment of deferred promises in which I found myself again writing "I can't breathe" on posters, hoping this will be the last time I had to write it. As I reread Bobadilla, I thought of my great-great-grandmother, María Frías. I thought of my own migration to the United States and my becoming a Black Latina. I thought of Gregoria Fraser's dominicanidad and Black Latinidad, and of Frederick Douglass's contradictory colonizing desires for Black citizenship that led to Fraser's birth in the Dominican Republic. I thought of all the detours and vaivenes that make up this circular "history" that is both decidedly mine and yet foreign. And I saw clearly how it all coexists and how the violence of coloniality that separated Douglass from Luperón and kept them from seeing each other's projects as one is both past and exceedingly present.

2 ARTHUR SCHOMBURG'S HAITI

Diaspora Archives and the Epistemology of Black Latinidad

I don't got to tell you that I'm Black. I expect you to know it. —CARDI B

On August 6, 1902, historian and archivist of Black culture Arthur Schomburg published a letter in the *New York Times* addressing a recent decision by the Bureau of Immigration Commissioner to regulate Puerto Rican immigration to the United States.[1] The short editorial piece, "Questions by a Porto Rican," demanded the "abrogation of immigration restrictions and protocols" for Puerto Ricans.[2] Reminding readers that Puerto Rico, like the Philippines, had been a possession of the United States since the Spanish-American War and that the "United States flag waves over the entire island in supremacy," Schomburg demanded to know: why should Puerto Ricans "be forced to submit to immigration laws?"[3] Suggesting that such restrictions were based on cultural and racial bias rather than legal definitions of citizenship, Schomburg asked: "Does a citizen naturalized in Porto Rico and the citizen naturalized in Ohio differ in any degree of excellence? They are American citizens and as such entitled to the privileges and immunities enjoyed by all citizens of the United

States."[4] Schomburg's editorial is prophetic in its articulation of Puerto Rico's unequal relationship to the United States. His questions reveal that the structures sustaining US citizenship and un/belonging are based on the white supremacist link between colonialism and immigration that—to this day—drives global economies via the exploitation of Black and Brown bodies.

After the Spanish-American War in 1898, the US government was preoccupied with the question of extending full citizenship to its ("racially inferior") colonized subjects.[5] The 1901 decision in the Insular Cases—a series of opinions by the US Supreme Court about the status of US territories acquired in the Spanish-American War—declared Puerto Ricans nonimmigrants without granting them national status and solidified US ambiguity about colonial citizenship, while leaving room for arbitrary decisions such as the one made in 1902 by the Bureau of Immigration Commissioner.[6] This ambiguous Supreme Court pronouncement meant that "Puerto Ricans were not subject to immigration laws as aliens" but were also not welcomed to the mainland as citizens.[7] The Insular Cases thus introduced a form of nationalization without belonging that continues to shape the lives of Puerto Ricans today.

More than a century before the world saw the US government's disavowal of Puerto Rican lives through the inaction that led to the deaths of thousands of people in the aftermath of Hurricane Maria, Schomburg interpellated the government's production of Puerto Rican people as noncitizens and less-deserving humans, linking anti-colonial struggles for liberation with Black freedom struggles in the United States.[8] Calling the United States a vacillator in its relationship to its colonial possessions, Schomburg's op-ed links colonialism and immigration in the production of racialized categories of what Sam Erman calls "almost citizens": people who are US nationals by way of colonialism (including intra-colonialism that shapes the lives of nonwhite Americans) but do not have full rights or access to public life, social benefits, representation, and power in public institutions.[9] The US annexation of Puerto Rico, Hawai'i, Guam, Samoa, and the Philippines brought millions of Black, Brown, Native, and Asian people under US control.[10] But, as Erman argues, this did not translate into a clear path to citizenship and belonging. At the same time, the United States had also not yet extended full rights to all its citizens on the continent: women did not have the right to vote, southern states still had legal segregation, Mexican American children were not allowed to attend the same schools as white children, and Chinese people were banned from immigrating and applying for naturalization.[11] In this climate of unbelonging, Schomburg's question—"Is not Porto Rico, by virtue of the fact that laws of the United States have been extended there, free from the application of the immigration laws?"—expresses more than a concern for his compatriots; it is a call to recognize the effects of US colonialism on the production of a racialized nonwhite category of unbelonging human beings, whom, borrowing from Erman, I call "almost citizens."

Schomburg's long and prolific writing career produced many important pieces that engaged the tensions between race and citizenship. Yet I find this 1902 op-ed, written at the beginning of his scholarly and public life, incredibly compelling in its simple but powerful articulation of the intrinsic link between colonialism and immigration that continues to shape the lives of Global South immigrants of color and their descendants across the globe. Schomburg's intersectional subject position as a US citizen and a Black Puerto Rican man ("being myself a native") makes his writing a revolutionary act in a historical and cultural context that was not yet accustomed to hyphenated identities—when the United States was beginning to imagine itself as a "melting pot" rather than a multiethnic, multiracial society.

The article's implicit critique of US colonialism is, however, tainted with the language of Manifest Destiny that also fueled attempts to annex the Dominican Republic during Reconstruction (see chapter 1) and the global expansion of the US empire at the turn of the twentieth century. Read in tandem with Schomburg's life and work, this short op-ed reveals the emergence of what I call the epistemology of Black Latinidad: a way of knowing that is guided by the intersections of colonialism, diaspora, migration, and blackness that shape the historical processes and experiences of people who are linked—by birth, language, culture, or ancestry—to Latin America but who are also immigrants (whether by their own or their parents' displacement) in the Global North. I argue that we find the epistemology of Black Latinidad at the center of Schomburg's intellectual project of documenting, preserving, and producing a historical narrative for what he conceived of as the (Black) diaspora.

Schomburg's Latino Blackness

Born in Puerto Rico in 1873—one year after slavery was abolished on the island of Puerto Rico—Arturo Alfonso Schomburg migrated to New York at the age of seventeen, motivated by a desire to join the Cuban and Puerto Rican liberation movements.[12] As a Black Caribbean immigrant in New York, Schomburg worked many jobs, from bellhop to elevator operator, to support himself and his studies while also actively working in the Puerto Rican and Cuban independence movements and participating in the political life of Black Caribbean exiles and migrant *clubes* (social and political organizations).[13] Schomburg arrived in New York with letters of recommendation from Puerto Rican cigar makers and independence activists written to Rafael Serra and Gertrudis Heredia, the charismatic leaders of the important New York Black Latinx club La Liga.[14] The letters verified his experience as a typographer and his commitment to liberation and freedom. Through Serra's and Heredia's mentorship and support, Schomburg joined multiple Caribbean clubes, and at the age of eighteen became secretary of Club Las Dos Antillas, an organization that supported the Cuban and Puerto Rican independence movements.[15] As Jossianna Arroyo documents, Schomburg was able to have civic and political interactions in the struggles for racial equality and transnational Black kinship through the multiple connections afforded by clubes and through his membership in the Prince Hall Masonic Lodge.[16]

From his arrival in New York in 1891 until the end of the Spanish-American War in 1898, Schomburg dedicated his time to the struggle for Cuban and Puerto Rican liberation, becoming a fervent supporter of José Martí.[17] In 1898, however, Schomburg laid down the cause of independence and became politically invested in the historization and representation of transnational Black cultures. Soon after this political evolution, Schomburg underwent a personal transformation. He changed his name from Arturo to Arthur, began identifying as Negro, and, aside from a brief visit in 1905, did not return to his native land despite traveling extensively to other parts of the Caribbean, the United States, and the world.[18] Schomburg's biographer, Elinor Des Verney Sinnette, finds this transformation troublesome—a sign of his political volatility.[19] I contend that it helps us understand Schomburg's epistemological journey through Black Latinidad and is emblematic of the contradictory and often confusing experience of translating blackness in the diaspora.

Chapter 1 is framed by the story of Gregoria Fraser, a Black woman born in Puerto Plata, Dominican Republic, to a US Black mother and Black Caribbean father in the late 1880s. Like Schomburg, Fraser was light-skinned and mixed and experienced certain privileges on the island. Fraser moved to the United States around age ten but maintained a close connection to the Dominican Republic through language and culture. Throughout her life, Fraser held on to her memories of the Dominican Republic, insisting on her identity as Dominican, Brown, and Latina. Schomburg's vaivenes through Black Latinidad parallel Fraser's in many ways. Their experiences translating blackness are mediated by the afterlife of slavery and Reconstruction as well as by a transnational Black political and cultural revolution that was very much about claiming the promise of full humanity that had been denied to so many colonized people of color. For Schomburg, as for Fraser, US colonization in the Caribbean had complicated his relationship to citizenship and belonging as a Black Latinx subject living in the United States in the early twentieth century. Their births and upbringing in the Hispanic Caribbean, their blackness, and their migrations to the United States meant that Schomburg and Fraser unbelonged to hegemonic blackness. Yet these shared experiences also allowed them to feel part of a larger transnational community that was defined not solely by citizenship but also by the coexistence of multiple forms of belonging that were mediated by and through diasporic blackness.

The challenges of navigating what Miriam Jiménez Román and Juan Flores call the "triple consciousness" of Black Latinidad—being Black, Latinx, and migrant—have been key to Latinx Caribbean literature since the beginning of the twentieth century.[20] This is a central topic of the foundational Black Latinx novel *Down These Mean Streets* (1967) by Afro-Caribbean writer Piri Thomas. A coming-of-age story that narrates the contradictions of being Black and Puerto Rican in 1940s New York, *Down These Mean Streets* grapples with the challenges facing Black diasporic Caribbean people inhabiting multiple racial paradigms. The son of a light-skinned mother and dark-skinned father, the protagonist, Piri, struggles to find a place in a binary racial system that does not account for multiracial identification and ethno-racial diversity. He ultimately opts to call himself "Negro," in apparent defiance of his Puerto Rican family and cultural identity. But as Yolanda Martínez-San Miguel suggests, rather than defying Puerto Rican identity, Thomas's narrative "interrogates the place of Puerto Ricans within the racial desegregation process in the United States, at the same time that it identifies the limits of these legal measures in the contexts of intracolonial migrations. Neither African American, nor Anglo-American, nor White Hispanic, Thomas defines himself as an unreadable element within US ethnic and racial minorities."[21] I contend that it is precisely through the confrontation with hegemonic blackness in the United States that Black Latinxs like Thomas become aware of their "unreadability." Hegemonic blackness produces Black Latinidad as a category of difference in the Global North, particularly in the United States. Yet, as seen in the cases of Fraser, Thomas, and Schomburg, this confrontation with hegemonic blackness (Anglo blackness, or what I call "Black in English"—blackness that is mediated through US historical, social, political, and cultural experiences) leads to another way of knowing: the epistemology of Black Latinidad. If, as seen in the words of Frederick Douglass studied in chapter 1, Latinidad marked a difference in Black experiences, whether that difference manifested in imagined racial harmony or in the perception of incivility, Schomburg's work attempted to show that rather than fear it and disavow it, Black people should be embracing difference as a way to lift up the race, as evidence of brilliance. Schomburg's embodiment and historicization of difference in Black Others—particularly Black Latinxs—put into practice what much later came to be articulated as the project of diversity and inclusion. Rather than the vacuous liberal scheme we have come to know since the latter part of the twentieth century, Schomburg's project of diversity and inclusion was grounded on research, writing, and the dissemination of subjugated knowledge as a tool to reaching equality and justice within the nation and beyond.[22]

As I argued in chapter 1, Black Latinidad emerged in the nineteenth century in contra*diction* to both European colonialism and US expansion. Insisting that the project of American republicanism must include Black citizenship and belonging, Black Caribbean thinkers like Gregorio Luperón and Ramón Emeterio Betances advocated for Latin American unity that would contrast European and North American white supremacy and colonialism. As the idea of "Latinoamérica" took hold throughout the region, blackness was soon displaced by mestizaje and Hispanicity. By the turn of the twentieth century, the project of a Latin American unity that centered blackness as envisioned by Caribbean thinkers like Luperón and Betances had dissipated, leaving in its place the idea of a "Latin Raza" that, at best, promised color blindness and, at worst, privileged whiteness and Hispanicity as the common ground on which to stand against North American influence.[23] In the nascent US diaspora, Black Latinxs like Schomburg, Fraser, and Thomas thus found themselves outside the hegemonic frameworks that define both Latinidad and blackness in the US imaginary. In the United States, they were perceived as neither Latino (due to their blackness) nor US Black (due to their Latinnness). Their cultural and linguistic links to the Hispanic Caribbean marked them as different and, at times, placed them at odds with hegemonic blackness. Their Latinidad shaped their unbelonging in the United States; their blackness erased them from the imagined Latin Raza of whitewashed mestizos and criollos.

For Schomburg, this dynamic often manifested in perceptions and opinions about his lack of mastery of written English *and* Spanish.[24] Experiencing language policing is, sadly, very common for US and other Latinx peoples in the diaspora. Gloria Anzaldúa writes extensively about the "linguistic terrorism" she experienced as a bilingual Tejana whose native and dominant language is Spanglish.[25] For immigrants who left the homeland at an early age, as did Schomburg, this policing shapes not only their experiences of unbelonging in their new home country but also their relationship to Latin America and the family and friends left behind. Unlike the Second Generations, who are often "forgiven" for their "incorrect" use of the "native" (colonial) language, first-generation and generation-and-a-half immigrants who lose fluency or whose pronunciation and accent changes are perceived as imposters and traitors.

The linguistic experience of immigrant Black Others like Schomburg, Martínez-San Miguel asserts, is also intrinsic to what she calls the "coloniality of the diaspora" that divides national subjects (such as African Americans in the United States) from minoritized citizens from postcolonial/neocolonial spaces, such as Puerto Rico or Martinique, living in the United States or Europe. Remembering Frantz Fanon's classic scene in "L'expérience vécue du Noir" ("The Lived Experience of the Black Man") that narrates his uncomfortable encounter with a child on a train in France, Martínez-San Miguel explains how the coloniality of diasporic Latin American Blacks like Fanon produces them as simultaneously within and outside the nation: "Recognition and misrecognition within the legal boundaries of French citizenship and coloniality and the stereotypical definitions of blackness in First World, post-slavery societies—these are the central narratives of Fanon's book when we revitalize the Antillean dimension of his work. The narrative voice becomes 'unreadable/unintelligible' (Butler, 1990, 17) in the metropolitan context of this scene: the speaking subject is not white, but he is *not only black; he is a French citizen, but he is Martinican too*."[26] Following Martínez-San Miguel's reading of Fanon, I argue that Black Latinidad differs from the experiences of hegemonic Black nationals like African Americans in the United States in their relationship to citizenship and belonging. Marked as foreign due to their legal status and/or cultural or linguistic differences, Black Latinx diasporic subjects struggle to find a political and cultural place within the nation where they reside as immigrants (or as descendants of immigrants) while simultaneously facing similar forms of racism and exclusion to those confronted by African Americans. Today, this dynamic means that a Black Latina undocumented immigrant living in the United States might simultaneously feel excluded from US Black communities because of her cultural and linguistic identities *and* be pulled over by the police for "driving while Black," facing dangers that range from deportation to death. For Schomburg, Black Latinidad meant he was simultaneously Puerto Rican, US American, and Black, yet his Puerto Ricanness, Americanness, and blackness were all constantly questioned. Black Latinx epistemology grows out of this experience of living simultaneously in multiple regimes of coloniality and understandings of blackness while also existing in vaivén between multiple forms of national belonging and unbelonging. In this context of linguistic terrorism, racial unreadability, and mistranslations of Black Latinidad, Schomburg had to negotiate a multiplicity of polities, linguistic regimes, markets, and geographies. Translating blackness across intellectual and social circles, Schomburg founded what is still today the world's most important archive of Black diasporic cultural histories, which has been housed in the New York Public Library since 1926 and laid the groundwork for the project of what we in the US academy understand as Latinx studies.

While most studies about Schomburg have been concerned with his important contributions as an archivist and book collector (see figure 2.1), rarely have researchers read him as a Latino scholar, despite his frequent insistence on his Puerto Ricanness and Hispanicity. Elinor Des Verney Sinnette published the only book-length biography of Schomburg in 1989; in it, she insists on his Puerto Rican identity.[27] Lisa Sánchez González, Jossianna Martínez, and Jesse Hoffnung-Garskof have all traced Schomburg's relationship to the Caribbean and to the political interventions in the Puerto Rican and Cuban independent movements.[28] It was not until the 2010 publication of the edited collection *The Afro-Latin@ Reader* by Miriam Jiménez Román and Juan Flores, however, that Schomburg's Black Latinidad became a main focus for researchers. The book's editors dedicated an entire section to reading Schomburg as "the most illustrious and self-conscious of all Afro-Latin@s in the United States as well as the one whose aspiration and ambiguities seem most deeply exemplary of Afro-Latin@ social experience."[29] More recently, Vanessa Valdés (2017) and Frances Negrón-Muntaner (2021) have claimed him as a Black Latinx scholar. Valdés writes that Schomburg "exemplifies and fully inhabits a subjectivity that today has come to be identified as Afro-Latino, a man who is simultaneously of African and Hispanic heritage."[30] This groundbreaking scholarship on Schomburg's Black Latinidad emerged in great part in reaction to decades of obscurity and silence around Schomburg's intellectual contributions to the studies of blackness (beyond his work as a bibliophile). The growing interest in demonstrating his "Latinness" has been expressed through biographical sketches (Puerto Rican birth, Spanish-speaking ability, and "Hispanic" heritage) and shedding light on Schomburg's dedication to transnational and hemispheric Black histories, a project that, as Negrón-Muntaner argues, focused greatly on Hispanic Blacks; for Shomburg, "Hispanic Blacks and Afro-Latinos . . . encompassed Africans and Afro-descendants subject to the Spanish Empire at any given time—as fundamental to Black history."[31]

While Schomburg's biography is undoubtedly crucial to his scholarly trajectory, I am less interested in proving his Latinidad or debating or specu-

FIGURE 2.1 Portrait of Arthur Alfonso Schomburg, bibliophile, ca. 1910. Schomburg Center for Research in Black Culture, Photographs and Prints Division, New York Public Library.

lating about his Caribbean Puerto Rican US Latino ethnic identification.[32] Rather, my purpose is to show *how* Schomburg's intellectual legacy, his archival ethos, and his political thought are foundational to Black Latinx epistemology and to the field of Latinx studies in the United States. I insist that the very nature of his vacillations, vaivenes, and detours through Latinidad—symbolized in his moving between the names Arturo and Arthur throughout his life—are what make his project decidedly Latinx.[33] Through his thinking, writing, and archival work, Schomburg laid the groundwork for the field of Latinx studies in the United States not only as a site of identity politics but also, and equally important, as a way of thinking and producing knowledge about the world that is guided by processes of disidentification (José Esteban Muñoz), a border consciousness (Gloria Anzaldúa), and the lived experiences of migration/diaspora (Juan Flores and Miriam Jiménez Román), other blackness/brownness, and linguistic/cultural difference.[34] My reading of Schomburg is thus decidedly central to an anti-colonial Latinx studies framework and to establishing a genealogy of what has become the Latinx intellectual and literary canon. Read in tandem with the foundational work of Anzaldúa, Muñoz, Jiménez Román, and Flores, Schomburg's epistemology of Black Latinidad can better allow us to understand the theoretical trajectory and development of the field of Latinx studies as one that has always existed in contra*diction* to North American and European white supremacist knowledge and cultures. Further, locating Schomburg at the center of Latinx intellectual, historical, and cultural discourse allows us to historicize Black Latinx studies as central to Latinidad rather than as the hyphenated, marginalized subfield it has been for nearly a century. In many ways, my reading of Schomburg is an invitation to make blackness central to Latinidad as an analytical framework and to Latinx as an ethno-racial category of human belonging.

Diaspora Archives

Unlike the rigidity of fixed boundaries, diaspora transcends limitation and restraint; it is inherently transgressive, offering an infinite source of potential. —VANESSA VALDÉS, *Diasporic Blackness*

Translating the multiplicity of his own colonial and postcolonial vaivenes through Black Latinidad, Schomburg theorized diaspora thus: "It is the season for us to devote our time in kindling the torches that will inspire us to *racial integrity*. Milton was inspired by the shepherd to his great song. We need it more than the Jews who though not a practical nation, live in theory a nation of most powerful intellects. They live in the very groups of nations who destroyed them. . . . The Negro must strive to follow in the good example of the Jews."[35] Aligning with Jewish people in forging what he called a "nation without a nation," Schomburg articulated an idea of diaspora that imagined Black people as a global collective connected by common intersecting histories, the desire for futurity, and transnational struggles for equality and progress. One of the most remarkable ideas introduced in his theorization of diaspora is that of "racial integrity."[36] The word *integrity* in its most common usage refers to honesty and moral grounding. But another meaning is wholeness or the state of being undivided. Schomburg's call to racial integrity through his evocation of the Jewish diaspora summons his knowledge and understanding of the world he inhabits as a Black Latino—as a nonhegemonic Black man in vaivén. The call for racial integrity—for wholeness—brings together all the parts that make up the Black diaspora; it summons difference to produce unity. To come to racial integrity is to understand how diaspora came to be. It is to recognize that, as Cardi B reminds us, all Black people came into the diaspora "in the same way"—through colonial violence.[37] Yet Schomburg's call to "racial integrity" also urges us to move beyond the pain and common history of slavery and colonialism in order to build a future free of racial violence. For Schomburg, that future cannot and will not be created by the nation-state.

As a Black Puerto Rican man, Schomburg understood the nation, in this case the United States, as a colonializing power that continued to deny equal rights to Afro-diasporic and Global South people in order to exploit them for land and labor and sustain white supremacy. Through his early adulthood, Schomburg saw his native Puerto Rico go from being a Spanish colony to becoming a US American colony. Lisa Sánchez González urges us to understand that this reality shaped Schomburg's archival praxis and intellectual project as well as his identity politics.[38] His call to racial integrity is ultimately an anti-colonial call to make the experiences of nonhegemonic Black others—who, like himself, necessitate translation in order to be seen and heard as a full person—integral to Black futurity. As such, his book and art collections sought not only to legitimate the Black historical and cultural experience through assimilation to Eurocentric knowledge and cultural production, as many Schomburg scholars have demonstrated, but also, and particularly, to historicize the Black Hispanic and the Black Latino subject. He strove to demonstrate their civility and culture vis-à-vis hegemonic blackness. His project of racial integrity through diaspora was thus grounded on and constitutive to Black Latinx epistemology.

Black Latinidad differs from Afro-Latin Americanness in the experience of migration to the United States and Europe. This plurality of diasporas forces Black Latinx people to deal with multiple, often contradictory regimes of coloniality and racial hierarchies: those produced by the Spanish, French, British, and Portuguese colonization of Latin America that shaped their ethno-racial identities and experiences as well as those imposed by US internal coloniality (the Black/white binary) and external colonialism over Latin America and the Pacific. Like many Black immigrants of his generation, Schomburg had a diasporic consciousness that was shaped by the embodiment of his and his family's vaivenes through colonial regimes. Born in Puerto Rico to a Black woman from St. Croix (today, the US Virgin Islands), Schomburg understood the plurality of diasporas: not the one-way forced ancestral movement from Africa to the Americas but a continuum—a vaivén that is both physical and symbolic and that, as Valdés beautifully describes, is a transcendent site of transgression.[39] His call for a diasporic understanding of blackness through the study of "foreign black figures" and the creation of a Black "nation without a nation" poses a contra*diction* of the nation-state and denounces the promise of US citizenship as a colonizing project. That is, he rejects citizenship that is solidified on the exclusion of racialized others, something that he expresses clearly in the 1902 opinion piece that opened this chapter, and demands instead "nothing but equality before the law."[40] In contra*diction* to the project of "almost-citizenship" that the nation reserves for Black, Brown, Indigenous, and Asian colonized subjects, Schomburg's diasporic consciousness offers an invitation to belonging through knowledge-making, lighting "the torches that would inspire racial integrity."[41] This understanding of diasporic belonging is central to how Black Latinx and otherized migrant Black communities structure their political alliances to fight restrictive immigration legislation in the twenty-first century. As we will see in chapters 4 and 5, Second Generation Black Latinx Italians have gained political traction in Italy precisely through an engagement with diasporic blackness that asserts their belonging in the face of state disavowal.[42] For Schomburg, racial integrity through diasporic belonging was a weapon with which to confront the nation-state and to demand equality. To do so, he believed Black people required knowledge, and he set out to create spaces for knowledge-making, learning, and disseminating the history of Black possibility.

When Schomburg arrived in New York at the end of the nineteenth century, he hoped to change the future of his birth country through struggle and political militancy. But during his first decade in New York, Schomburg's goals changed from independent nation building to transnational racial justice. He wrote, "We believe men, no matter of what race, can respect each other without the hobby of raising the dust of social equality. What we demand and are entitled to is plain justice, nothing but equality before the law."[43] His arrival in New York coincided with the emergence of a Black intellectual movement, a growth in Black cultural and political public engagement, and, soon after, the Harlem Renaissance. Schomburg's involvement in Freemasonry, as Arroyo demonstrates, shaped his intellectual development and exposed him to a large transnational community of Black thinkers, artists, and entrepreneurs. It also heralded his insertion into US Black elite circles in the early twentieth century.[44] In 1914 Schomburg became president of the American Negro Academy (founded in 1897 by Alexander Crummell), where he met people like W. E. B. Du Bois. In 1929, after years of traveling to collect art and manuscripts about Black lives abroad, Schomburg was invited by his friend Crummell to curate the Negro Collection at the Fisk University library.[45] In 1932 his long and productive career culminated with his appointment as curator of the Division of Negro Literature, History, and Print at the New York Public Library (which was renamed after Schomburg in 1973). Throughout his time as a curator, collector, and scholar in US Black intellectual circles, Schomburg continued to travel and acquire books and art that built his archive of Black diasporas—an archive that, as Valdés, Negrón-Muntaner, and Sánchez González have argued, was mediated through his Latinidad.[46]

Michel-Rolph Trouillot writes that "history is the fruit of power, but power itself is never so transparent that its analysis becomes superfluous. The ultimate mark of power may be its invisibility; the ultimate challenge, however, the exposition of its roots."[47] Schomburg's profound understanding of the mechanics of history fueled his intellectual project and archival praxis. He possessed a diasporic consciousness grounded on the possibility of knowledge production as a tool for social change: "The white scholar's mind and heart are fired because in the temple of learning they are told how on March 5, 1770 the Americans were able to beat the English; but to find Crispus Attucks it is necessary to go deep into special books. . . . Where is our historian to give us our side of view? We need in the coming dawn the man who will give us *the background of our future*; it matters not whether he comes from the cloisters of the university or from the rank and file of the fields."[48] Schomburg's historical project was thus one of translation and correction—a bifocal revision of Black histories that interrupted the silences imposed by white supremacy within the extant narrative with new information that allowed Black scholars to reclaim the rhetorical and historical space that Black people were entitled to yet denied, inserting Black histories into the dominant narrative. History, for Schomburg, was not just the act of recovering facts but also, and more importantly, a process of drafting a future that carried the potential of liberating Black people.[49] He articulates this most clearly in his famous essay "The Negro Digs Up His Past."[50]

In many ways, "The Negro Digs Up His Past" provides a road map for examining Schomburg's intellectual goals as a historian and archivist; it also articulates what Adalaine Holton calls the "theory of recovery" that shaped the scholar's archival praxis.[51] "The Negro Digs Up His Past" begins by laying out what Schomburg perceives to be the main problem of his time: the lack of historical awareness about Black contributions to humanity. He then offers various examples, including the life and work of Juan Latino (1518–96), a Black professor from Spain, and the biography of Henri Christophe (1767–1820), the leader of the Haitian Revolution, to insist on the need to look outside the borders of the US nation to find the Black people who "labored internationally in the cause of their fellows."[52] The essay introduces what becomes a common trope in Schomburg's writing: the metaphor of history as nourishment and the historian as a farmer. "History must be recovered . . . so that Negro youth can be nourished on its own milk"—that is, so Black people may no longer be deprived of their "spiritual nourishment."[53] For Holton, this metaphor illustrates Schomburg's contention that an archive of Black history is "vital to Afrodiasporic subjectivity and the future of Afrodiasporic peoples."[54] The metaphor of nourishment signals Schomburg's understanding of the significance of history in providing a foundation for Black people's future civic and human development. This task is only possible, Schomburg seems to suggest, through the analysis of transnational Black histories, a historiographic engagement with diaspora, and a redefinition of archival practices and evidence collection.

In many ways, Schomburg's farming metaphor expands the archive. It contains the urgency of historicizing while also conveying the possibility that anyone can become a farmer/historian if the terrain is fertile. Pedigree and accolades do not matter: "it matters not whether he comes from the cloisters of the university or from the rank and file of the fields."[55] Perhaps a reference to his own autodidactic background, Schomburg's suggestion that "anyone can be a historian" is contra*diction* to his own disavowal by hegemonic Black elite scholars like Du Bois and a radical proposal for democratizing knowledge.[56] Farming knowledge, digging up the past, dismantles the traditional notion of the archive as a sacred repository of history and repositions subjugated and otherized knowledge, orality, nontraditional materials, and perhaps even memory as legitimate sources of knowledge-making. The epistemology of Black Latinidad that shapes Schomburg's life and work is an example of this repositioning of subjugated knowledge; it is a manifestation of the "digging" for which Schomburg advocated.[57]

Michel Foucault writes that archives are the "law of what can be said."[58] They are what organize hierarchies of time and statements of truth and are also locations of power that grant historians credibility. For historians, the archive is the place of legitimacy where their "truth" is sanctioned. But as many scholars of critical archival studies have noted, traditional archives, heritage institutions, and historical publications are filled with silences regarding the lives, agency, participation, and cultural production of Black people.[59] The process of silencing, as Trouillot reminds us, begins at the source of creation, not at the archive.[60] Schomburg's archival project centers otherized blackness by compiling a transnational, multilingual assortment of documents and art from all over the world. For Holton, this archival method involves three simultaneous layers of past, present, and future: the recovery of materials, making these materials available to the public, and articulating "a connected web of people of African descent who might draw on each other in their minds or through their actions in their pursuit of social change."[61] Most of all, Schomburg's archive is an anti-colonial intellectual project that centers Black belonging in contra*diction* to white supremacy. Schomburg saw history as threefold: the creation of evidence-based archives (libraries, centers, heritage institutions), the comparative study and interpretation of evidence (through universities and colleges), and the dissemination of information within and outside Black circles (through public appearances and exhibitions). The greatest part of his intellectual work focused on the first task: to set the record straight by collecting evidence, books, pamphlets, art pieces, and material culture that would allow historians to rewrite the white supremacist dominant narrative producing Black people as inferior. This, in turn, would change the course that had led "the Negro man to become a man without a history."[62]

While the dominant archive Foucault refers to is organized around national or colonial axes of power, Schomburg's is an archive of anti-colonial contestation grounded in the notion of a multilingual, multicultural, and interconnected Black diasporic nation without a nation. This archive is organized not on past experiences of domination (slavery) but on the common project of futurity (the nation without a nation): "The American Negro must remake his past in order to make his future. . . . History must restore what slavery took away, for it is the social damage of slavery that the present generations must repair and offset."[63] More than simply identifying a paradigm shift in what Schomburg understood as Negro history, in 1925 he proposed a theoretical framework for a new way of historicizing and producing blackness as a transcendent category by "digging up" the past and using it to contra*dict* white supremacy. This theory was shaped by Schomburg's Black Latinx diasporic consciousness, by his conviction that Black futurity was possible, and by his praxis of translating blackness beyond the national and colonial paradigms to which the world had become accustomed.

Schomburg's plea to "give us the background of our future" moves away from the contractions of the nation-state and state-sanctioned white supremacist institutions to a future grounded on transnational understanding and unity, supported by his belief that history had the power to restore "what slavery took away."[64] However, history is not a matter of debate but "a matter of record."[65] I see Schomburg's "digging" for the future as an exercise in what Jonathan Lear calls "radical hope": an ethics of knowledge-making as a form of political transformation for the future we want to create, not the present we have inherited. Lear writes, "What makes this hope *radical* is that it is directed toward a future goodness that transcends the current ability to understand what it is."[66] Radical hope is not a passive awaiting but rather a praxis, an act of doing. It demands flexibility, openness, and what Lear describes as "imaginative excellence."[67] Radical hope, as Junot Díaz argued, is "our best weapon against despair, even when despair seems justifiable."[68] To hope radically thus means to "act amidst a logic of war and cultural devastation, enacting effective changes for the next generation."[69] Schomburg radically hoped that Black history would produce a fruitful future.

> I am here with a sincere desire to awaken the sensibilities, to rekindle the dormant fibers in the soul, and to fire the racial patriotism by the study of Negro books. We often feel that so many things around us are warped and alienated. Let us see if we cannot agree to arrange a formula or create a basic construction, for the establishment of a substantial method of instruction for our young women and men in the material and the useful. . . . It is the season for us to devote our time in kindling the torches that will inspire us to racial integrity. We need a collection or list of books written by our men and women. If they lack style, let the children of tomorrow correct the omissions of their sires. Let them build upon the crude work. Let them, because of the opportunities that colleges and universities grant, crystallize the crude work and bring it out flawless.[70]

At a moment in which Black Puerto Rican citizenship and belonging were contested everywhere, radical hope moved Schomburg beyond pessimism to imagine Black belonging and futurity. His method, praxis, and episteme remain incredibly relevant a century later.

Schomburg's diasporic consciousness allowed him to conceive of the possibility of a nation without a nation as a symbolic location of belonging from which Black people could be empowered to talk back to the colonial nation-state and demand equality and rights. In Schomburg's view, diasporic movement did not preclude citizenship and belonging to the nation—it expanded it. The problem remained, however, that the national narratives in the Americas erased Black people's participation in the founding of nations. As Schomburg understood it, to be citizens of the Americas, Black people needed to understand their historical belonging in order to claim their rights as citizens: "The American Negro must remake his past in order to make his future."[71] His work as a scholar was to create an archive that would allow future Black subjectivity to claim national authenticity while centering the diaspora. He models this strategy in his writing about Haiti's history.

Scholarship about Latinidad in the United States should begin not with the westward expansion of the United States (the crossing of the US-Mexico border) but with the triumph of the Haitian Revolution in 1804 and its effects on the production of blackness and citizenship in the modern world.[72] As I argue in chapter 1, what we have come to understand as Latinidad is an articulation of difference from/against US Americanness (both Black and white). This difference is intrinsically linked to colonial logics of unbelonging that have determined categories of humans, citizenship, and minoritized nonwhite subjectivities for the larger part of our modern history. The triumph of the Haitian Revolution and its ripple effects in the rest of the American projects of independence, emancipation, and freedom are central and key in the early articulations of Latinidad (in the second half of the nineteenth century) viewed both from the United States and within Latin America.

Schomburg anchored his project of Black American belonging in Haiti, demonstrating his acute understanding of this intricate connection and speaking to his own epistemological journey through Latinidad as a Black Latino subject in vaivén, confronting the weight and the violence of US colonialism. In writing about Haiti, Schomburg delineates the blueprints of a decolonizing Latinx project that centers blackness. Much like Aztlán is the symbolic home of the Chicanx movement, Haiti is the birthplace of Black citizenship in the Americas—Haiti offers an alternative to slavery as the unifying vector of diasporic Black history. For Schomburg, writing about Haiti was thus an important discursive strategy in formulating an ethos of Black Americanness. But this was not always an easy project. The vast proliferation of anti-Haitian narratives that circulated in the United States and throughout the world since the beginning of the nineteenth century—what I have elsewhere called "global anti-Haitianism"—meant that Schomburg needed to engage in a careful and intricate project of translating Haitian blackness through hegemonic discourses of civility and national belonging that would allow him to contra*dict* the white supremacist narrative that for more than a century had produced Haiti as a site of Black incivility.[73]

As the second independent republic in the Americas and the first nation created by descendants of enslaved peoples, Haiti occupies a central place in the political and cultural imaginary of many diverse and often opposing groups. Haiti's success in obtaining liberation despite French oppression served as a model for many young independence movements all over the Americas. Powerful leaders, such as South American Simón Bolívar and

Cuban José Martí, relied on Haitian support in their independence struggles. During the US Civil War, the Union also sought Haitian aid. In all these circumstances, Haiti was perceived as having a strong commitment to the ideals of liberty, justice, and racial equality—principles that guided the liberation movements of all American nations. Yet in the early twentieth century, as Schomburg was writing about the Caribbean nation, Haiti also posed a threat to Eurocentric American national projects and to the burgeoning US empire, which emerged on the back of slavery. Fear of Haiti resulted in reprisal, which came mostly in the form of exclusion from international politics and severe financial sanctions. In 1826, for instance, the United States blocked Haiti from participating in the Congress of Panama.[74] That same year, France recognized Haiti's independence but only after demanding reparations for its losses. French and US economic pressures contributed to Haiti's extreme financial vulnerability, which extended and grew over the long nineteenth century, perduring until today.[75]

At the turn of the twentieth century, the United States became interested in Haiti as a site for colonial investment. In 1908 Haitian president Antoine Simon signed the McDonald Contract, which gave American companies rights to build railroads in Haiti.[76] Soon after, the United Fruit Company and Citibank took control of most of the production and financial activities in the country. The Cacos rebellion of 1911, an insurgent movement protecting the rights of farmers and peasants, performed a coup d'état that ended Simon's presidency and threatened US economic interests.[77] A year later, the United States took over the Customs House as part of a series of negotiations to promote peace and stability in the island. Finally, in 1915 a group of US Marines arrived in Port-au-Prince for what would be the longest and most violent US occupation of Haiti in the twentieth century (1915–34). This intervention, as Mary Renda demonstrates, made Haiti yet another site for the US empire's military experimentations and labor exploitation.[78]

Early twentieth-century US cultural productions, including novels, theatrical performances, and eventually film, represented Haitians as incapable of self-governance, savage, corrupt, and stupid. This ideology is exemplified in Eugene O'Neill's 1920 play *The Emperor Jones*.[79] Based on the figure of Henri Christophe, the first king of Haiti, O'Neill's play tells the story of Brutus Jones, an African American man who escapes prison after having been convicted of murder. Brutus moves to the Caribbean and sets himself up as emperor. The play recounts his story in flashbacks as Brutus makes his way through the forest to escape his former subjects who have rebelled against him. O'Neill's play portrays Brutus as a brute, a criminal, and an "American Negro," not as a Haitian king.[80] Ignoring the historical significance of Christophe, his Caribbean ethnicity, and his contributions to both Haitian and human history, O'Neill instead gives us a savage Haiti—allegorized through Brutus—who threatens the safety of good people and needs to be controlled and civilized.

Unfortunately, these hyperbolic depictions of Haiti and Haitians were not limited to fiction. During the 1915–34 Haiti occupation, the US media represented Haitian men as cruel and violent savages, Haitian women as hypersexual, and Haitian religiosity as uncivilized. These stereotypes continue to circulate in the US media. One of the most egregious recent examples occurred during the aftermath of the 2010 earthquake that devastated the island and took more than 230,000 lives. Days after the earthquake, televangelist Pat Robertson opined that Haitians were suffering because "they had made a pact with the devil" and turned their backs on God.[81] A few days after Robertson's remarks, David Brooks published a column in the *New York Times* in which he explained Haiti's poverty as a byproduct of "progress-resistant cultural influences . . . including the voodoo religion."[82] Both Robertson and Brooks returned to the colonial/imperial discourse of Haiti that, as Renda demonstrates, was used to justify military interventions throughout the twentieth century.

Responding to anti-Haitianism, African American and Afro-Caribbean intellectuals, artists, and writers of the early twentieth century produced a counternarrative that denounced the colonial exploitation of Haiti and exalted the country as a model of valor and civility. James Weldon Johnson, poet, novelist, and field secretary of the National Association for the Advancement of Colored People (NAACP), visited Haiti in 1918 and wrote a powerful critique of the occupation in *The Nation*.

> To know the reasons for the present political situation in Haiti, to understand why the United States landed and has for five years maintained military forces in that country, why some 3,000 Haitian men, women, and children have been shot down by American rifles and machine guns, it is necessary, among other things, to know that the National City Bank of New York is very much interested in Haiti. . . . The military Occupation has made and continues to make military Occupation necessary. The justification given is that it is necessary for the pacification of the country. Pacification would never have been necessary had not American policies been filled with so many stupid and brutal blunders; and it will never be effective so long as "pacification" means merely the hunting of ragged Haitians in the hills with machine guns.[83]

Johnson's essay calls attention to the political and economic causes and consequences of the intervention on Haitian people and economics, demonstrated through historical evidence of the negative impact of US imperialism and global capitalism on the lives of people and to the structures of entire nations. Most importantly, Johnson depicts the occupation as an unequal and immoral act of war that leads to the killing and persecution of innocent civilians.

Like Johnson, many important figures of the early twentieth-century US Black intelligentsia, such as W. E. B. Du Bois, Booker T. Washington, and Langston Hughes, publicly condemned the occupation as immoral and corrupt; others expressed their support for Haiti through positive artistic and literary representations of it as a magical, wonderful place of human liberation. In the play *Popo and Fifina, Children of Haiti* (1932), for instance, written by Arna Bontemps and Langston Hughes, Haiti is portrayed as a country that is uncivilized and poor, yet happy:

> Popo and Fifina were walking barefooted behind two long-eared burros down the highroad to the little seacoast town of Cape Haiti. . . . The sunshine was like gold. The little dusty white road curved ribbon like among the many hills. It was overhung with the leaves of tropical trees. . . . First was Papa himself, a big powerful black man with the back torn out of his shirt. He wore a broad turned-up straw hat and a pair of white trousers; but like all peasants in Haiti, he was barefooted.[84]

In the late spring of 1932, Hughes went to Haiti for the first and only time. He spent three months in Port-au-Prince and Cap-Haïtien. The Harlem Renaissance was over and, as Hughes himself described it, "Negroes are no longer in fashion" in the United States, so he went to the Caribbean in search of new inspiration.[85] During this time, a much more politicized leftist Hughes emerged. He developed a genuine interest in poor and working-class people, though he had experienced neither socioeconomic reality growing up in the United States. He scandalized the manager of the hotel where he stayed in Cap-Haïtien by going out barefoot to meet and talk with fishermen along the waterfront in Okap.[86] Hughes had focused on shoelessness as the primary criterion for separating "the people" from the rest of humanity, and he wanted to talk with "the people" on their own terms—thus no shoes. In his attempt to identify with the "barefooted people," the Haiti Hughes writes about in *Popo and Fifina* is a quasi-fantastic place where tropical beauty reigns and where children, while extremely poor, are happy and satisfied. His narrative falls into what David Kazanjian calls a "colonizing trick" that rearticulates colonial frameworks in the counternarratives that seek to redefine them.[87]

Ironically, many non-Haitian Black writers, like Hughes, ended up constructing Haiti as a tropical fantasy in their efforts to portray it as a source of authentic Africanness. They produce Haiti as an exotic land where magical things happen to Black people against the backdrop of poverty, which emerges as a source of authenticity and pride rather than a result of colonial oppression. The Caribbean Negrista and Négritude movements that brought us the work of Black diasporic scholars and writers like Martinicans Frantz Fanon and Aimé Césaire, Cuban Nicolás Guillén, and Puerto Rican Luis Palés Matos, among many others, situated Haiti as a source of authentic African heritage in the diaspora. Césaire made connections between Africa and the Antilles and concluded that Haiti was the most African of all the Antilles: "I love Martinique, but it is an alienated [assimilated] land, while Haiti represented for me the heroic Antilles, the African Antilles . . . a country with a marvelous history: the first Negro epic of the New World was written by Haitians like Toussaint L'Ouverture, Henri Christophe, Jean-Jacques Dessalines, et cetera."[88] In their efforts to vindicate Haiti in the eyes of the world, Black artists in the United States and the Caribbean at times reproduced a discourse that further alienated Haiti from the modernity and civility that defined citizenship in the Americas, instead rendering it as an extraordinary extension of (uncivilized, magical) Africa. It is in this contradictory environment of disavowal and exaltation—of belonging and unbelonging—that Schomburg's Haiti emerges, interrupting the dominant rhetoric that had produced the country as either a magical place or a site of horror since its independence in 1804.

Schomburg's Haiti is a site of Black pride through which the African diaspora can reclaim "what slavery took away." In writing Haiti, Schomburg follows a twofold strategy: portraying Haitian military ingenuity as a sign of civility and republicanism and highlighting Haitian farming practices to establish Black indigeneity in the Americas. Through his writing, Schomburg shows us that Black people preserved both the nation and the land; their blood literally and figuratively nourished the national projects of the American states.

From the beginning of his intellectual career, Schomburg was preoccupied with Haiti. He wrote numerous articles about its rich histories, the roots of its economic and political challenges, and its seminal role in the various projects of liberation throughout the Americas. In a 1921 article published by the *A.M.E. Church Review*, Schomburg enumerates Haiti's military contributions to the various projects of American independence, from Venezuela to the United States.[89] Marveling over Haitians' commitment to freedom, he writes that the struggles Haiti faced in the twentieth century were not the result of inferiority, as some believed, but the yoke of colonialism—"a case of Might lording over Right."[90] At the time this article was published, the US Marines were occupying the entire island of Hispaniola. Schomburg opposed the occupation as an infringement on Haitian liberties, as did many other Black intellectuals of the moment. But Schomburg's interest in Haiti did not begin or end with the United States' 1915 intervention. Rather, it was a thread that traversed Schomburg's life and career, from his elementary school education in Puerto Rico to his early writings in *Patria*, the Sol de Cuba publication of the late nineteenth century, to his diaspora archives.[91] In 1904, for instance, Schomburg published what is now recognized as his first mainstream article in the business weekly *Unique Advertiser*. "Is Hayti Decadent?" is similar in tone and content to a series of op-eds Schomburg published in the *New York Times* between 1902 and 1904 regarding US expansion over Puerto Rico and the Philippines, in which the author condemns the United States for meddling in the affairs of free countries. He writes, "The time is here when the Haytian Republic must cease the ordinary riots of self-appointed individuals who generally live in exile from attempts to ruin the country through the propagation of internecine wars."[92] Read on its own, "Is Hayti Decadent?" could appear to be an example of what some of Schomburg's critics suggest is a lack of political backbone, particularly when dealing with the effects of colonialism. But read in the context of Schomburg's other writings about Haiti, "Is Hayti Decadent?" fits perfectly into his epistemological construction of an archive of diaspora.

In Schomburg's Haiti, we find a narrative of belonging for Afro-descendants in the Americas rooted in the idea of history as sustenance that shaped his diasporic consciousness and archival praxis. The Haitian Revolution, in particular, gave Schomburg a sense of pride. In it, he found "the milk of sustenance" to feed younger generations of Black people with the possibility of a history of greatness and resistance that shaped not just the small island but an entire world: "The Haitians have rendered to the cause of Independence invaluable and meritorious services. The historians Madiou and St. Mery have chronicled in pages of their books the undisputable facts that over eight hundred Haitians, free men of color fought for the cause of North American Independence. In South America, Simón Bolívar hailed president Pétion with words of the highest praise for the great service he so generously rendered for the cause of South American independence."[93]

Tracing the significance of Black history through the revolutionary wars of the Americas, Schomburg consecrates Haiti as a site of modernity and political advancement, contradicting the narratives of savagery and incivility that dominated public opinion about Haiti during the occupation and until today.[94] By the time Schomburg published "Military Services Rendered" in 1921, scholars had begun to think about the Caribbean as a site of modernity—an intellectual argument that would shape scholarship about the Caribbean throughout the twentieth century.[95] Schomburg's engagement with Haiti's military history as modern can therefore be read not only within Black diasporic intellectual history but firmly and decidedly in conversation with Caribbean and Latinx studies. Strong heroic men who fought for freedom from colonial powers and to end slavery constructed Schomburg's Haiti on the pillars of Western civilizations:

> We may pause here at the close of this awful period and stand in the proud presence of these triumphant black heroes, as the last of their enemies sail slowly away as prisoners of war. With the new flag floating over the fortresses of the Cape, and the victorious army well-equipped and intact, it is Dessalines, the intrepid Dessalines, never beaten . . . who in the name of the black people and Men of Color of Saint Domingo announces: "The Independence of Saint Domingo is Proclaimed. We are restored to our primitive dignity; we have asserted our rights; we swear never to yield them to any power on earth." These were the words of war-worn veterans with swords still unsheathed.[96]

While Haiti's independence from France is the foundational narrative in Schomburg's writing, that moment is important because it consecrated Haiti as a leader in the revolutionary movements of the Americas and in the formation of the New World American nations. What made Haiti special was not its fantastic "Africanness" but its forward-thinking project of nationhood and citizenship. Haiti was the second nation to obtain its independence in the Americas, but it was the first to do so "through an egalitarian movement, through emancipation and freedom, values that all republics have now adopted."[97] Unlike the United States, which built its nation on a foundation of slavery, Schomburg suggests Haiti's is the true model of civilization that all American nations—including the United States after the Civil War—would eventually follow.

Many of Schomburg's critics condemned him for glorifying historical icons and buying into "an aristocratic way of thinking."[98] Sinnette, for instance, states, "Schomburg's writing lacked a broad historical understanding and tended instead to venerate individuals of the race who could serve as models and provide what he called spiritual nourishment for the younger generation."[99] But I contend that Schomburg's strategy was a lot more profound than some critics give him credit for: he was translating Haiti through the language of the colonizer, hoping to infiltrate the official discourse to change "the white scholar's mind."[100] This becomes evident in his narration of Alexandre Pétion (1770–1818): "In South America, Simón Bolívar hailed President Pétion with words of highest praise for the great services he so generously rendered for the cause of South American Independence. The deeds of Haitian sons will live as long as there are true lovers of freedom and the names of Bolívar and Pétion will brilliantly shine and retain their luster as long as that of George Washington."[101]

It would be obstinate to ignore the fact that Schomburg interpolates Western discourses of nation, citizen, and civility in his narration of Pétion. In this, he reminds his readers that Haiti contributed advice, arms, and human power to both the American Revolution and the Civil Wars. Portraying Pétion as a "skillful civil engineer" as well as the "most scientific officer and the most erudite individual among the Negro race, and the equal, if not the superior of many of the American officers now functioning in Haiti," Schomburg insists on his Western education as a symbol of his civility and historical importance.[102] At the center of Schomburg's historical recovery project was the belief that "Negro history is nothing but the missing pages of the world history and that to understand more about who displaced our people from its pages one must study the oppressor."[103] He believed, too, that to speak in silos does nothing to advance the project of racial freedom because racial freedom is about equality, which requires white acceptance of Black lives. Schomburg thus proposed a method of speaking across races, complementing histories where silences stood and correcting where fairness lacked. The challenge he posed for scholars was "to see that the race issue has been a plague on both of our historical houses, and history cannot be properly written with either bias or counter-bias."[104] That is, not only is Schomburg writing Haiti for future Black historians, but he is also challenging the myopic narrative that produces blackness as inferior through the very language and tools of the oppressor. He is thus translating Haiti (and blackness) for white scholars, thinkers, and teachers through the symbols they valued (e.g., West Point / French educated) and through the tropes they recognized as valid evidence of truth. In doing so, Schomburg successfully introduces the white reader to "new sources" for understanding Haiti beyond the colonizing trick that had produced the Caribbean country as an exceptional (savage) place. Producing the source, Schomburg is then able to translate the story to a larger audience, give it historical validity, and serve it as "nourishment" for future Black scholars to "feed on"; that is, he is able to produce the "background of our future."

The Background of Black Futures

What is particularly significant in Schomburg's writing is not solely his assertion of Haitian modernity and civility but his conviction that Haitians—and by extension all Black Americans belong to the Americas—are indigenous to the territory.[105] Throughout his career as a scholar, Schomburg used the metaphor of sustenance to convey the necessity of Black history in strengthening Black belonging. The metaphor encompasses his historical project: planting (sourcing), sowing (archiving), and consuming (producing/disseminating) history. He was determined to revolutionize Black historical thought from the source to the production of knowledge to everyday life understandings of the past. In his 1913 speech "Racial Integrity: A Plea for the Establishment of a Chair of Negro History in Our Schools and Colleges," addressed to the Teachers' Summer Class at the Cheney Institute in Pennsylvania, Schomburg foregrounds historical awareness as key to the future of Black civilization: "It is the season for us to devote our time in kindling the torches that will inspire us to racial integrity. We need a collection or list of books written by our men and women. If they lack style, let the children of tomorrow correct the omissions of their sires. Let them build upon the crude work. Let them, because of the opportunities that colleges and universities grant, crystallize the crude work and bring it out flawless."[106] Schomburg's emphasis on production rather than perfection came from his sense of urgency about the place (and displacement) of Black people in US society. As a Black Puerto Rican immigrant living in the vaivén of citizenship and unbelonging, Schomburg understood all too well that legal and symbolic admission to the nation was intrinsically linked to the historical process of nation-narration. For him, history had the greatest purpose, "returning what slavery took away": humanity, along with legal, symbolic, and historical belonging to the nation.

Schomburg's idea of sustenance solidifies Black belonging in the Americas—not as "displaced" diasporic subjects brought by force to serve but as a "generation of builders" whose belonging to the Americas is ancestral and authentic to this land. Philip Deloria argues that the US independence movement was grounded on claims of Indigenous belonging that legitimated white founders as part of the continent's history.[107] Similarly, in the Hispanic Caribbean and Haiti, Taíno Indigenous mythology allowed criollos to claim authenticity, celebrate mestizaje, and erase blackness from the narrative of the nation. For Schomburg, claiming indigeneity allowed him to insert blackness back into the narrative of nation formation in the Americas:

> The Spaniards not only ill treated the natives but killed them by the thousands. When Father Las Casas landed in Hispaniola, the condition of the natives was so deplorable that he was filled with fear less the Indians become exterminated by the hard laborious work to which they were then subjected. As Negroes had given satisfaction as slaves in Seville, Spain Father Las Casas petitioned the Government that to protect the miserable lives of the Indians, Negroes be brought to the New World as *substitutes* for this laborious work.[108]

Inserting Black history within the rhetoric of European historical dominance in the Americas, Schomburg argues that Africans were brought to America by the Europeans as "substitutes" for enslaved Indigenous peoples. The fact that Africans were brought to the Americas prevented them from claiming authenticity to the land, but the idea that they were "substitutes" for Natives in the cultivation of the land, and later in defending it from oppression through war, legitimates them as authentic to the Americas: Native by proxy.

Much work has been done to critique the troubling narrative of "Native extermination" that founded many American nations. My purpose here is not to defend Schomburg's method but to show how he inhabited the existing dominant discourse as a way of translating blackness into the foundational narratives of the Americas. I will insist, though, on Schomburg's awareness of the troubling nature of foundational narratives, as articulated in his many speeches. He understood that people of color of all ethnicities and histories were excluded from full humanity and citizenship in the official discourse of the nation, but he also believed inclusion could only be accomplished through insertion into the existent dominant paradigms—a strategy that eventually earned his archive a place within the New York Public Library.

Melanie Newton provides a genealogical examination of the concept of Black indigeneity in the Caribbean as one that simultaneously reproduces the myth of Aboriginal disappearance that has produced the Caribbean as a non-Indigenous site in the Americas and presents us with the radical proposition of diasporic Indigenous belonging through substitution even in the "most visionary anticolonial texts."[109] Revisiting seminal scholarship by Sylvia Wynter, Édouard Glissant, Aimé Césaire, and others, Newton argues that the narrative project of Black indigeneity confronted the violence of the plantation that denied Black humanity. Displacing Native people with "indigenous

Black" Caribbean thinkers, Newton argues, produced the Caribbean as an "intertwined" site of diasporic and Indigenous "anticolonial nationalism."[110] For Wynter, this "intertwining" (via Native erasure) is not only necessary but foundational to Caribbean history: "The history of the Caribbean islands is, in large part, the history of the indigenization of the black man."[111] Ultimately, the "indigenization of blackness," as Newton's work demonstrates, while indeed a project of Black belonging, was grounded in the disappearance and erasure of Native communities, languages, and cultures.

Read through Schomburg's Haiti, Black indigeneity reflects the tensions and contradictions of the project of Black citizenship in the early twentieth-century Americas, as Black people grappled with the persistence of colonialism, the dominance of mestizaje, and the increasing climate of antiblackness sustained by scientific racism. In the United States, the early twentieth century brought a rise in antiblackness, lynching, and the continued enforcement of Jim Crow, along with a growth in Black intellectual and cultural production. In Latin America and the Caribbean, as nations solidified their independence and recovered from revolutions and civil wars, the production of citizenship and the project of belonging were increasingly filtered through Hispanicity and mestizaje. Aware of these dynamics of cultural inclusion and civic exclusion, Schomburg advocated for "equality in front of the law" by asserting Black civility and political investment in the project of the nation. On the other hand, Schomburg recognized that the nation had failed Black people and betrayed its promise of inclusive citizenship, as the *New York Times* op-ed that opened this chapter shows. He knew that equality could only be reached through transnational networks of inclusion. His articulation of Haiti as a site for Black indigeneity in the Americas, therefore, is an attempt to translate the symbolic project of belonging (the nation without the nation) into a political project of representation and inclusion (citizenship and political participation) that could challenge Black erasure. Global blackness (diaspora) contradicts local (national) antiblackness, as diaspora transcends and engulfs the nation.

One of the most unambiguous ways Black indigeneity appears in Schomburg's intellectual project of Black belonging is through his narration of Henri Christophe. The Haitian king was, in Schomburg's eyes, an illuminated man of letters, a courageous military chief, and, above all, a true American patriot "who served in the American Revolutionary War against Albion Legions at the Siege of Savannah under General DeGrasse."[112] As in his depiction of Pétion, Schomburg presents Christophe as larger than life, a flawless hero whose image has fallen prey to white supremacist histories—"yet historians have fallen in the same rut of their predecessors to take for granted the already recorded statement."[113] Schomburg attempts to "set the record straight" about Christophe, introducing us to a man who, contrary to O'Neill's Brutus, is a remarkable, intelligent, and honorable human: "Yet the West Indies gave birth to a warrior, a statesman and a king; a man the world someday will find time to deservingly honor the memory of Henri Christophe."[114]

What is truly fascinating about Schomburg's Christophe, though, is not his civility and refinement—characteristics Schomburg always strove to demonstrate in his depictions of Black men—but his intrinsic and instinctual connection to the land via agriculture and farming, a fact that also defined Christophe's political career. Schomburg wrote, "He replaced the arms of warfare for agricultural implements a hundred years before the Soviet Republic made a trial in a five year plan. Soon the virgin soil of Haiti blossomed with flowers and the produce of a kind providence that gave them courage to defend their sovereign nation to this day amid the perils and weakness of the flesh."[115] Nation and land are united in Schomburg's Christophe. To be a true patriot and the leader of the nation, Schomburg suggests, one must be willing to both take up arms and be able to produce food and provide nourishment for its citizens.[116] Black people—whether Haitian or US American—are thus not only capable of being citizens of the nation; they are uniquely positioned to be leaders.

For Schomburg, Haitian farming was a political project; it also shaped Christophe's indigeneity to the Caribbean. According to Schomburg, Christophe's knowledge of the land and of plants and herbs was so vast that he "rarely consulted a physician and seldom took medicine" because he "knew from childhood the value of remedies and what was best for his ailments."[117] Schomburg's engagement with Christophe as an Indigenous figure is congruent with Haiti's own nation narration. In their struggle for independence from France, Black and mulato anti-colonial revolutionaries often summoned Indigenous histories (by invoking the names of Taíno caciques, for example) in their independence manifestos.[118] In fact, the army that fought against the French during the Haitian Revolution called itself Armée Indigène (Indigenous Legion). From the beginning of the Haitian Revolution to the present, Taíno caciques have continued to be upheld by Haitians as symbols of national belonging, anti-coloniality, and freedom.[119]

In writing of Christophe's indigeneity, Schomburg is also attempting to write Black people as legitimate owners of the land not via colonization and exploitation (as Euro-Americans) but because they worked it, defended it, and inherited it—along with bondage and struggle—against colonialism, an argument that is echoed by Wynter half a century later. Wynter argues that Maroons took the place of the Native Arawaks in defending the land against European colonization via rebellion and war, and later as free citizens.[120] Unlike Wynter, who views Indigenous Caribbean people and their cultures as disappeared, Schomburg's Black indigeneity envisions a composite ethnicity in which Indigenous knowledge is passed on to Black people who would then carry the responsibility of autochthonous belonging, becoming anti-colonial Black freedom fighters like Christophe. In this sense, Schomburg's logic of Indigenous belonging, troubling as it may be, is also a spiritual act of possession that facilitates the transfer of Indigenous knowledge through labor (farming/nourishment) and honor (revolutionary war). It is an act not of erasure but of embodiment.

Mestizaje—the mixing of races through colonial violence—traverses Latin American national formations, as we saw in chapter 1. In the Hispanic Caribbean and Haiti, blackness and mulataje are also part of a racial imaginary in which notions of *indigenismo* shape how people imagine themselves culturally, racially, and nationally. At times, Indigenous belonging and mestizaje have been deployed to erase African heritage and blackness. In this context, what does it mean for a Black Caribbean Afro-Latino man to propose indigeneity as a possibility for Black belonging? As Arroyo argues, Schomburg's "transcultural *mulato* subjectivity" shaped his racial discourse as well as his relationship to the United States and Latin America.[121] While Schomburg did not understand himself as Indigenous or mestizo, his "mestizo consciousness" by way of Taíno Caribbean interpellation appears subtly through his writing—particularly in the use of his alias "Guarionex," after the Native Taíno cacique who led a rebellion against Columbus in 1502.[122] Schomburg's choice of Guarionex, a chief from the region that is now the borderland between Haiti and the Dominican Republic, shows his awareness of his own location as an interstitial border subject living between binaries of race, ethnicity, national identity, languages, geographies, and cultures. Unlike other Taíno caciques, Guarionex vacillated between rebellion and appeasement, between taking up arms and finding diplomatic solutions to help his people, until his imprisonment and eventual death at sea. For Arroyo, Schomburg's use of this pseudonym is an example of his transnational identity; for Sinnette, it recalls his affiliation with the clubes (el club Guarionex y Hatuey in Santo Domingo) and is a reminder of his Boricua identity. I contend that given Schomburg's astonishing historical awareness, his choice of Guarionex is an example of what, following Caribbean syncretic religiosity, I have elsewhere called *texto montado* (possessed text), through which the past comes to be recalled in diasporic writing.[123]

In her deeply personal study of African divinity, M. Jacqui Alexander proposes the concept of "embodied memory"—memory passed down to the devout through the spiritual act of possession—as an antidote to "the alienation, separation, and amnesia that domination produces."[124] For Alexander, memory is a "sacred dimension of the self"; "knowledge comes to be embodied through flesh, an embodiment of Spirit."[125] Following Alexander, I have argued that Afro-religious syncretic practices such as spiritual possession contest hegemonic understandings of history by making visible the silenced stories of Black people.[126] Through the act of *montarse*, the subject can interpellate the dominant version of history and reimagine an Other truth that contra*dicts* or complements hegemonic texts or archives. Transplanting this experience to historical evidence, I argue that certain texts are textos montados that produce a more complete, albeit contradictory, version of the truth through the embodied memory of silenced histories, the practice of intertextual knowledge-making, and the incarnation of past understanding through spirit. Syncretic religion traditions in Hispaniola, such as Palos and Liborismo, imagine the spirit of Guarionex as the force of freedom. Schomburg understood historical knowledge as a form of spiritual nourishment. As Schomburg writes about Haiti, he authorizes Christophe as an heir to Indigenous knowledge and assigns that knowledge to himself by claiming historical authority and authenticity through spiritual possession.

One of the most striking elements of Schomburg's epistemology lies in his awareness of the powerful difference between diasporic identity and Indigenous belonging. Black people in the Americas had their citizenship rights deferred while the idea of a "return" to the imagined motherland took root in places like the United States and parts of the Caribbean. Since the early nineteenth century, US politicians as well as Black thinkers had been looking for ways to promote US Black emigration to Africa. As early as 1815, US Black people had migrated to Sierra Leone in search of freedom and a home in which they could thrive. After the Civil War, the American Colonization Society continued to promote emigration. In 1871, as we saw in chapter 1, Frederick Douglass traveled to Santo Domingo to assess the possibility of annexing the island to host "new free Black men."[127]

Schomburg, who traveled extensively to collect archival documentation regarding the African diaspora in Europe and the Americas, was acutely aware of this recent history and its effects on the production of Black (almost) citizenship in the United States. Though he regarded Africa as a space of spiritual strength for Black people in the world, he was also committed to the promotion of civil liberties and equality for Black people in the Americas. As indigenous to this land, Schomburg believed, Black diasporic subjects in the Americas were entitled to citizenship as well as equal civil liberties.[128] The first part of Schomburg's writing about Haiti re-created a glorious historical past, envisioned as an emblem of Black American civilization within the Western historical discourse of war; the second insisted on Black authenticity in the Americas as a process that went beyond books and arms and was linked to the very basic fiber of nation building: the nourishment and sustenance the land produced. While I join scholars like Newton in recognizing how troubling the narrative of Black indigeneity in the Caribbean is in perpetuating the myth of Native disappearance, I insist that we also make room for engaging the sacred and political project of belonging that lay underneath his writing of Black indigeneity. What does it mean to embody the spirit of Guarionex to assert Black belonging? Could this act of knowledge transfer through spiritual possession offer a way out of the pervasive narrative of Indigenous erasure that has shaped the histories of the Caribbean? Can Schomburg's textos montados show us a new way to read intra-ethnic Caribbean anti-colonial solidarity?

Schomburg drew on his multiplicity of identities to formulate his ethics of Black diasporic belonging—to translate his blackness. He sought to create historical bridges to unite the colonized people's experiences in the Americas and beyond, to create a new concept of a nation without a nation. This new nation was based on the principles learned through his involvement in Freemasonry: loyalty, trust, freedom, equality, and independence. He renounced the idea of national borders and "egalitarian" laws based on segregation and oppression. Schomburg's ethic went beyond a desire to rewrite history; he yearned to reconstruct the present in order to secure a better future for Black and colonized people. He wrote before concepts like globalization, transnationality, and border thinking were named as such but lived and thought within those concepts in vaivén. His writing about Haiti reconstructed the world through listening to those who were silenced and giving them the opportunity to speak through him. A man much ahead of his time, Schomburg created archives that provide the source for future belonging.

As economic inequality continues to force poor people in Latin America to migrate to the United States and Europe, the intersections of blackness, indigeneity, migration, and national belonging become more evident, and the questions about their effects on human lives become more urgent. The growing field of Black Latinx studies is well poised to tackle these questions much like Schomburg did: through studying the intersections, contradictions, silences, and vaivenes to produce our own sources and archives, and with them a method for decolonial thinking and freedom. Ultimately, what Schomburg gave us is the gift of optimism: the radical hope that in this large, overwhelming, and seemingly endless struggle for justice and equality for Black, Brown, Indigenous, colonized, and oppressed people across the world, the work we do as scholars—historians and farmers of truth—matters.

PART II. BLACK FEMINIST CONTRA*DICTIONS* IN LATINX DIASPORAS

3 AGAINST DEATH

Black Latina Rebellion in Diasporic Community

¿Quién mató a Sagrario Díaz?
¡La maldita policía!
—PROTEST CHANT

YOLANDA GUZMÁN, 22: frontrunner in the Dominican Revolutionary Party; activist and guerrilla leader; lynched by US-backed constitutional forces on May 2, 1965.

SAGRARIO DÍAZ, 25: student leader and activist; shot by Dominican president Joaquín Balaguer's anticommunist police forces during registration day at the Universidad Autónoma de Santo Domingo on April 4; died on April 14, 1972.

FLORINDA "MAMÁ TINGÓ" SORIANO MUÑOZ, 53: social justice activist and defender of peasant rights; assassinated in Villa Mella, Dominican Republic, by landowner Pablo Díaz on November 3, 1974.

LUCRECIA PÉREZ MATOS, 33: mother and immigrant; murdered by neo-Nazis on November 13, 1992, in Aravaca, Madrid, Spain.

JESSICA RUBI MORÍ, 32: transgender woman and LGBTQI activist from La Romana; brutally murdered by dismemberment in the Dominican Republic on June 4, 2017.

JOANE FLORVIL, 28: mother and immigrant from Juana Méndez, the Haitian-Dominican borderlands; arrested and beaten by Chilean police on August 30, 2017; died in a Santiago hospital on September 30, 2017.

KATHERINA RODRÍGUEZ TAVERAS, 26: immigrant from Mao, Dominican Republic; strangled with her own hair in a park in the outskirts of Naples, Italy, on February 1, 2019. Her family suspects her Italian boyfriend of her murder; no arrests have been made.

The first time I heard the name Sagrario Díaz, I was nine years old. It was the late 1980s, and the ruthless Joaquín Balaguer once again ruled the Dominican Republic.[1] There was a student protest at the Universidad Autónoma de Santo Domingo (UASD), and I was caught in the middle of it as I made my way from La UASD elementary school, on the southeast end of campus, to the Facultad de Humanidades, on the central campus, where my mother worked as a secretary in the literature department. Every day at noon, I walked about a mile through the campus center, Alma Mater, to get to my mother's office. There, I waited for her to finish work so we could take the bus home to El Ensanche La Fé, a working-class neighborhood at the northeast edge of the city center. I often encountered protests along my walk from school (figure 3.1). Sometimes there were police-student confrontations; other times there were peaceful marches. That day the protest was intense. Car tires had been set ablaze on Alma Mater Avenue in central campus, and the police were spreading tear gas to dissipate the crowd of protesters. A young man told me to squat behind him to protect me from the tear gas. Somehow, I was not scared. As he raised his fist and yelled, I found myself joining in the chant: "¿Quién mató a Sagrario Díaz? ¡La maldita policía!" (Who killed Sagrario Díaz? The damn police!). I was not allowed to say "maldita" at home, so I was particularly excited about the opportunity to scream it at the top of my lungs. "¿Quién mató a Sagrario Díaz? ¡La maldita policíaaaa!!!" I did not yet know who Sagrario Díaz was, but I knew in my bones that la maldita policía had killed her. And that, I knew, was not right.

At the age of nine, as I screamed along with college students on the historic site where activist Sagrario Díaz had been killed in 1972—almost a decade before I was born—my eyes burning from tear gas and smoke from the scorching tires, I did not yet understand the single most important real-

FIGURE 3.1 Protests and police occupation of La UASD, 1980. Fondo Editora Hoy, Archivo General de la Nación (AGN), Dominican Republic.

ity that would shape my life and those of so many other Black and Brown women at home and in the diaspora: we are in terrible danger, every day, everywhere. Our partners, our fathers, our government, the police, or even random people can kill us, and once we are gone, that is it. We can be forgotten, erased like we never existed. Unless we are remembered—unless we insist on chanting each other's names, even when we are strangers. Even when saying their names stings and burns.

Sagrario Díaz was a student in the economics department at La UASD. On April 4, 1972, she went to campus with her brother, Fidias, to register for classes for the upcoming term. Shortly after the Díaz siblings arrived, the police occupied campus and blocked all exits. The official police report states they received a tip that communist leader Tácito Perdomo, who had been in exile for months, had arrived in the country with plans to assassinate President Balaguer.[2] Police believed Perdomo was hiding among students at La UASD.[3]

Balaguer, who had been the righthand man of dictator Rafael Leónidas Trujillo during his thirty-one-year regime, took office in 1966, backed by the United States after a tumultuous transition to democracy engulfed the country.

FIGURE 3.2 Fidias Díaz carrying his wounded sister, Sagrario, with help from friends, April 4, 1972. Fondo Editora Hoy, Archivo General de la Nación (AGN), Dominican Republic.

Between 1961, when Trujillo was assassinated, and 1966, when Balaguer took office, the country experienced a coup, a civil war, and a US military intervention. Balaguer became the United States' Caribbean ally in the fight against communism at a moment in which fear of "another Cuba" dominated international politics.[4] Backed by the United States, with support from the Central Intelligence Agency (CIA), Balaguer terrorized the country during the "Terrible Twelve Years" of his first regime (1966–78), operating with impunity as he imprisoned, tortured, disappeared, and murdered people he perceived to be dissidents, communists, or just "troublemakers."[5] La UASD, which had become a site of youth political movements—particularly those associated with the Left—became a special target of the regime. Students and professors were often terrorized and persecuted on and off campus.[6] It was within this climate of fear that the national police occupied the UASD campus on April 4, 1972, injuring many students including Sagrario Díaz, who succumbed to her wounds ten days later (see figure 3.2).[7]

According to testimonies from that day, more than one thousand students crowded in the Aula Magna (central auditorium) and Alma Mater Plaza as professors and deans pleaded with the police to allow students to go home.[8] Fidias Díaz writes that he remembers clearly when the shots started and his sister was hit.

> Fuimos interrumpidos cuando uno de los comandantes baja su brazo derecho y empieza el ametrallamiento contra la familia universitaria. . . . Sagrario y yo estábamos en el primer pasillo de la entrada al Alma Máter, justamente frente a los invasores policiales. Ella y yo, asidos de las manos. . . . Buscamos protección de los tiros más que de las bombas; dimos media vuelta y, en un pequeño jardín del Alma Máter nos fuimos desplazando rozando contra el suelo (la mano derecha de ella asida de la izquierda mía). . . . Los gases lacrimógenos asfixiándonos. . . . Desesperada me dijo: "me estoy asfixiando hermanito" y soltándome la mano hizo el intento de avanzar pero, al levantar la cabeza recibió el impacto mortal de una bala. . . . Intente agarrarla de nuevo por la mano, pero no me respondió.[9]
>
> [We were interrupted when one of the commanders lowered his right arm and the shooting against the university community started. . . . Sagrario and I were in the hallway right after the entrance to the student center, exactly in front of the police perpetrators. She and I were holding hands. . . . We looked for protection from the shooting more so than from the tear gas; we turned around and took refuge in one of the small Alma Mater gardens. We were sliding through, our bodies touching the ground (her right hand holding my left hand). . . . The tear gas was drowning us. . . . Desperate, she said to me: "I am suffocating, brother" and letting go of my hand she tried to move forward but as she raised her head the bullet got her. . . . I tried to hold her hand again, but she did not respond.]

Sagrario Díaz died on April 14, ten days after the attack, at the Clínica Gómez Patiño in Santo Domingo. During the ten days of her hospitalization, high school and college students took to the streets and held strikes, protests, and boycotts. The Dominican Association of Medical Practitioners called for a national strike and issued a harsh statement condemning the violence. Newspapers dedicated ample space to editorial pieces about Sagrario Díaz and state-endorsed violence at the university. This level of national protest was unprecedented during the repressive Balaguer regime.[10] The national media attention and general protests pressured the state to end the police occupation of La UASD and attracted international attention to the human rights violations.[11] Moreover, the outpouring of artistic productions honoring Sagrario Díaz—from poetry to songs to essays—that emerged during the weeks following her assassination consolidated her as an emblem of transnational struggle for democracy and justice.[12]

The assassination of Sagrario Díaz in 1972, more than any other crime of the terrible twelve years of the Balaguer regime, continues to be remembered across multiple generations of students as an example of martyrdom and a symbol of students' fight for democracy across the Americas. Of particular significance is the perdurance of the call-and-response protest chant that first introduced me to Sagrario Díaz in 1988: "¿Quién mató a Sagrario Díaz? ¡La maldita policía!" The slogan, which is still used at times during student demonstrations at La UASD, is a historical contra*diction* of the state-sanctioned violence that operated with impunity for decades.[13] The diction "¿Quién mató?" as uttered by the students in the 1988 demonstration was not a question but a declaration, followed by the defiant contra*diction*, "La maldita policía." Protesters in Brazil revived the chant after the 2017 murder of Black activist Marielle Franco by two former police officers.[14] As with Sagrario Díaz, those chanting "¿Quem matou Marielle Franco?" are not asking a question; they already know the answer. Rather, they are demanding justice while also reminding listeners of the insidious ways the repetition of violence operates in its normalization.[15] Further, "¿Quién mató a Sagrario Díaz? ¡La maldita policía!" replaces the state-sanctioned narrative of exculpation that articulates violence as the result of individual action—the proverbial bad apple—with the more accurate interpellation of the state as the perpetrator of systemic violence. In so doing, the diction "¿Quién mató?" becomes a warning—a pre*diction* of what will happen, over and over, unless we stop it. Revisited in the context of 2020, as police violence against Black people has led to a global call for accountability, "¿Quién mató a Sagrario Díaz? ¡La maldita policía!" also summons the repetition of state-sanctioned violence—particularly against Black women and girls—that has shaped the better part of modern history.

This chapter opens with the names of seven Black women from the island of Haití/Quisqueya—Yolanda Guzmán, Sagrario Díaz, Florinda "Mamá Tingó" Soriano Muñoz, Lucrecia Pérez Matos, Jessica Rubi Mori, Joane Florvil, and Katherina Rodríguez Taveras—whose lives were violently ripped from this Earth by state-sanctioned hate.[16] Some, like Sagrario Díaz, were activists: warrior women who spent their lives trying to make their communities and their country better. Others, like Joane Florvil, were migrants: brave women who left the island of their birth in the hopes of providing better lives for their families, children, and themselves. I have listed only seven names, but the list could go on and on, filling all the pages of this book. The locations could be expanded as well. The list could include Marielle Franco's 2017 murder in Brazil and Breonna Taylor's 2020 murder in the United States.

Writing about the role of late twentieth-century Latin American women's testimonies, Nancy Saporta Sternbach argues that re-membering is the act of "putting together memories, enacting history, chronicling the loss, carrying pictures, and naming the dead. Ultimately, the act of re-membering is really an act of birthing and re-birthing; the offspring is the woman's testimonio."[17] I add that for Black Hispaniola women, re-membering is also a sacred act, a manifestation of living and survival. As you read these names, add those of the women you seek to re-member; consider the overwhelming boundlessness of Black women's deaths and the impossibility of containing the limits of these losses and the extent of their lasting violence. Consider the coexistence of Black women's death and remembrance: the killing of Sagrario Díaz in 1972 and the chant that re-membered her through my nine-year-old body in 1988. This coexistence of death and re-membering is central to Afro-Latinx feminist praxis.

In *The Borders of Dominicanidad*, I proposed the Afro-religious act of possession, popularly known as "montarse" (mounting), as a contra*diction* to silence, erasure, and death.[18] In many Afro-religious traditions in the Caribbean (Palos, Santería, Vodoun, Espiritismo), death is understood as a passage, transformation, and continuation of life on the other side. In these religious epistemologies, life and death coexist; death is another state of being rather than an end. Spirits of the dead can possess the body of a devotee, the two becoming one. The spirit can speak its truth and share wisdom through the possessed body. As M. Jacqui Alexander reminds us, the dead "do not like to be forgotten."[19] I offer possession here as an alternative to the silence of death in all its manifestations—social, cultural, corporeal, and civic—that affect Black women.[20] But rather than a singular event of spiritual practice, I summon possession as Black Dominicana feminist praxis: an exercise in living against death through the insistence of re-membering, piecing together lives, bodies, stories, histories, and legacies in community. For Black Dominicanas, possession is both a verb and a noun. It implies being part of and taken by—the spirit possesses one, and one also takes possession of that which the spirit brings. What Black Dominicanas possess is not a tangible, quantifiable object but a rhizome of multiple collective epistemes. These possessions are both profoundly personal and unequivocally communal: they belong to all of us, and we belong to all of them. We possess and are possessed in community. It is within this feminist praxis of community possession, I argue, that

Black Dominicanas re-member the dead, fight state-sanctioned deaths, and insist on living.

As Christina Sharpe writes, "The ongoing state-sanctioned legal and extralegal murders of Black people are normative and, for this so-called democracy, necessary; it is the ground we walk on."[21] The rate of femicide in the Dominican Republic is the highest in Latin America and the Caribbean.[22] Likewise, rape, abduction, child marriages, and the criminalization of abortion without exception (even when the life of the mother and/or child are in danger, and/or in situations of rape and incest) continue to violate the lives of Dominicanas. State-sanctioned gendered violence against women, girls, and queer people is entangled with global capitalism—often through sex tourism and exploitation—and is a clear manifestation of antiblackness. As Christen Smith argues regarding Brazil, in "Afro-paradise" countries like the Dominican Republic, state-sponsored violence against Black people is paired with the (also violent) exotification and commodification of blackness for foreign consumption and tourism. Black death and Black fantasy are "two sides of the same coin."[23]

For working Black Dominicanas, the path to political representation, equal rights, and liberation in their home country has been barred by centuries of institutionalized misogyny, transphobia and homophobia, the persistence of coloniality, and the interconnections between state-sponsored global capitalism, racism, and xenophobia—or what Sharpe calls "the ground we walk on." For Dominicanas of Haitian descent, as Amarilys Estrella's work shows, death accompanies the work of the living; it's not just the "ground they walk on" but their very sustenance, the only assurance of a future "descanso."[24] Women activists fighting against these intersecting evils, as in the cases of Yolanda Guzmán, Sagrario Díaz, and Mamá Tingó, are often silenced with death. Paradoxically, the Dominican state co-opts their deaths, sanctioning them as patriotic symbols through vacuous ceremonies, floral offerings, and media remembrances of their death while the living walk the ground of deferred death. State-sponsored symbolism does not translate into political empowerment and enfranchisement for Black women, girls, and trans and queer people.

For many Black Dominican queer people and women, migration is the road to survival. At times, as in the cases of Lucrecia Pérez Matos, Joane Florvil, and Katherina Rodríguez Taveras, death follows them across the sea. For others, as in the cases of the activist women whose stories inform this chapter, the diaspora translates death into a political language of Black feminist political power and resistance, forming kinship networks and communities of empowerment and joy. Audre Lorde asserts that feminisms are always plural, always essential, always dangerous, and, most of all, always an alliance against patriarchal hegemony.[25] More recently, Jessica Marie Johnson prompts us to think about the ongoing state of death and violence against Black women as always contrasted with and confronted by kinship and communities of freedom making. [26] Following the Black feminist tradition of struggle, community, and joy, this chapter memorializes the ways Black Dominicanas rebel against death: how their community possession of freedom fuels their fight against state-sponsored physical, political, and social death.

Based on seven years of qualitative research in Italy, New York, and the Dominican Republic working with Black Dominican women-led organizations, this chapter engages the intersections of politics, violence, class, race, and migration as they impact Dominicanas' everyday lives. I specifically center the activist and political work of migrant Dominicanas in Italy from the early 1980s to the present in dialogue with the history of Black women's activism in the transitional years of the post-Trujillo dictatorship in Santo Domingo (1963–80), particularly through involvement in La UASD and contemporary Dominicanyork cultural productions. The revolutionary anti-colonial work of brave Dominicanas from the 1960s to the 1980s has not been studied within the context of Black politics and Black freedom. This omission is in part due to the fact that until the late 1990s, the language of liberation among Dominicanas was articulated through class and anti-dictatorship struggles rather than through blackness.[27] Yet not only did these women understand themselves as Black and part of the African diaspora, as Milagros Ricourt argues, but, as many of the women who shared their stories with me explained, they looked to Black freedom fighters in the United States and elsewhere to shape their political frameworks and aesthetic choices.[28] This chapter translates their struggles to the larger context of global blackness.

Revolutions/Revelations

After the execution of dictator Rafael Leónidas Trujillo in 1961, a revolutionary energy manifested in every demographic of the population. Farmers began to organize to reclaim land ownership, migration to the city and to the United States increased as a form of economic mobility for the poor, and the youth—both working and middle class—began to organize politically through community-based organizations and formal political parties.[29] The youth struggle, as Efraín Sánchez, leader of the Movimiento Popular Dominicano (MPD, Dominican Popular Movement), explains, took place in two arenas: poor and working-class neighborhoods and universities. For working-class youth like Sánchez, who, along with Yolanda Guzmán, became a leader in the Partido Revolucionario Dominicano (PRD, Dominican Revolutionary Party) in the 1960s, the struggle centered on worker's rights, unions, and party organizing.

> Estábamos preocupados por el alcance a los recursos básicos, la dignidad humana que se nos había negado por tanto tiempo; por los derechos de los trabajadores y por la participación ciudadana de la gente trabajadora, algo que a nosotros los pobres se nos había negado desde el inicio de la república.[30]
>
> [We were concerned with access to basic human dignity, which had been denied to us for so long; with workers' rights and the participation of working people in the political processes, something that had been denied to us poor and working people since the beginning of the republic.]

For young, middle-class Dominicans, the fight was both political and ideological. Organizing within La UASD, young Dominicans read Marxist theory together while envisioning a national project very much inspired by the triumph of the Cuban Revolution. A student activist I will call Mariam Almonte, from Villa Altagracia, remembers those early days as a sort of political awakening for the youth in her barrio.

> Yo iba a esos mítines con los ojos cerrados y salía con ellos abiertos. . . . Me acuerdo que yo quería como beberme, inhalar cada artículo, cada libro que leíamos. Pero la cosa no era solo una inquietud intelectual; de hecho a mi ni me importaba tanto eso de la carrera y las notas. La cosa era la acción; el llamado a acción que nos hacían. La inspiración. Estábamos leyendo a Marx y viendo el país como un campo de batalla y los libros como el manual de ejecución. . . . . Nadie iba solo a estudiar, estábamos ahí para crear un país, después de la dictadura. Veíamos ese momento a nuestro país como un lienzo y nosotros como los pinceles.[31]
>
> [I went into the student meetings with my eyes shut and came out with them open. . . . I remember wanting to consume, to inhale every article, every book we read. But it was not just about intellectual development; in fact, I could not care less about a career or school. It was about action—inspiration and a call to action. We were reading Marx and seeing our country as a battleground and his work as a manual. . . . No

one was in school just to study—we were there to fight for the future of a country we were all hoping to create post-Trujillo. We felt the country was a canvas and we had the brushes in our hands.]

In 1962, thanks in great part to the work of young activists and students like Almonte and Sánchez, the revolutionary energy of the moment led to the election of social democratic leader, politician, and writer Juan Bosch as president of the Dominican Republic. Bosch had been in exile since 1942 due to his opposition to the Trujillo dictatorship. During his two decades in exile, Bosch created the PRD and orchestrated strong political resistance against the regime. Bosch's social democratic agenda garnered immense popular support, and he won the election with an overwhelming majority. The military and the Catholic Church, however, opposed Bosch's agenda, which included labor unions and socialist reforms in education, health care, and other services. On September 25, 1963, after only seven months in office, a US-supported coup led by Colonel Elías Wessin y Wessin overthrew Bosch. A three-man military junta then replaced the Dominican Republic's first democratically elected government of the twentieth century. The coup prompted a lot of anger and frustration among the general population and activated unprecedented participation in political activism, culminating in a civil war in 1965. Efraín Sánchez remembers the moment of the coup.

> Nos arrancaron la democracia. Nos la arrebataron. Y no era verdad que nos íbamos a quedar de brazos cruzados. Todos los grupos estaban organizándose. Yo me organicé, caí preso par de veces, pero salía y seguía. Uno se fue radicalizando con la lucha, pero el 65 fue el momento clave de acción.[32]
>
> [They tore away our democracy. They grabbed it from us. And there was no way we weren't going to do anything about it. All the groups were organizing. I organized. I ended up in prison a few times, but once released, I kept going. We became radicalized in the struggle. But '65 was really the key moment of action.]

Known as La Guerra de Abril, the civil war that took place between April 24 and September 3, 1965, began when a group of deserted soldiers, along with civilian PRD supporters, seized the Radio Santo Domingo building, issuing calls of sedition and branding themselves "constitucionalistas" (supporters of the constitution). Their goal was to restore Bosch. During the first days of the conflict, constitucionalistas distributed weapons and Molotov cocktails to their civilian comrades who poured into the city from all over the country to join the effort. To fight the insurgents, Dominican president Donald Reid Cabral appointed Wessin y Wessin as his new chief of staff on April 25. Wessin y Wessin assembled the troops, branding them "loyalistas," and attempted to subdue the revolution with terror. After only four days of battle, and what looked like a clear victory for Bosch, on April 29, US president Lyndon Johnson authorized a large-scale military intervention aimed at preventing the development of what he saw as a potential second Cuban Revolution.[33]

Perhaps because of the overwhelming support it sustained among the peasantry and leftist intellectuals alike, or perhaps because it opens the wound of the democratic republic that could have been and never was, La Guerra de Abril is one of the most studied Dominican events of the twentieth century. In 2015 a transnational commemoration of the fiftieth anniversary of the war was organized by the Dominican state. It included photographic exhibits, publications, public events, and the formal recognition of multiple people in a ceremony held at the national palace.[34] Aside from a handful of mostly middle-class women, all published photographs, books, and public consecrations of the heroes of the 1965 war are of and about men (see figure 3.3).[35] Yet feminist scholarship, feminist testimonies, collective memory, and the testimonies of revolutionary women gathered by journalist Margarita Cordero in the late seventies all demonstrate that the 1965 war would not have been possible had it not been for the women who risked their lives transporting weapons, serving as messengers, tricking US Marines, and engaging in combat.[36] As Cordero explained to me:

> Las mujeres fuimos las que sostuvimos la zonas constitucionales en todos los sentidos. . . . Fuimos las que curamos los enfermos, las que preparamos la comida, y las que hacíamos el amor con los combatientes. . . . Muchas no combatimos, no fuimos excepcionales, pero lo que hicimos tuvo valor para la Guerra.[37]
>
> [We women were the ones who sustained the constitutional areas of the revolution in every sense of the word. . . . We were the ones who took care of the wounded, the ones who prepared the food, and the ones who made love with the combatants. . . . Many of us did not fight in active combat, we were not exceptional, but what we did was valuable for the War.]

Cordero was a member of the Juventud Estudiantil del Catorce de Junio, 14J, or "Jecajú," the student arm of the communist Catorce de Junio party. She was at La UASD in a meeting with fellow students on April 24 when the news

FIGURE 3.3 Guerrilla women marching down Calle El Conde, April 1965. Fondo Milvio Pérez, Archivo General de la Nación (AGN), Dominican Republic. The dark-skinned Black woman marching in the front line (*center*) is Agustina Rivas (a.k.a. Tina Bazuca).

of the revolution first reached her. She recalls, "Nos dijeron que nos quedáramos tranquilos. Nos dijeron que esta no era nuestra lucha. Al principio, el Partido [Catorce de Junio] percibió la revolución como un movimiento de derecha-centro, la gente de Juan Bosch, y nosotros éramos radicales de izquierda, así que nos quedamos en casa" (We were told to stay put. We were told that this was not our revolution. At first, our party [Catorce de Junio] perceived this as a movement of the center-right, the Juan Bosch people, and we were of the radical Left, so we stayed home).[38] Over the course of a few hours, as the revolution gained force, the different political sectors united. The predominantly middle-class communist party, Catorce de Junio, joined the revolution by the evening of April 25 under the direction of General Rafael "Fafa" Taveras.[39] The participation of middle-class women in the days that followed was significant for the organization of the movement and for the coordination of military actions. Women communicated with the different commandos through messengers, and took over the quotidian tasks of care for wounded soldiers. As Taveras told me during an interview, "women were the backbone of this revolution. Without them, there is no Guerra de Abril."[40] However, middle-class women did not, contrary to what some historians have argued, participate in active combat.[41] Rather, the women who fought and died on the front lines were working-class and poor women from the neighborhoods on the outskirts, better known as La Parte Alta. In early May, many of these women—most of them Black and Brown—were killed during the US Marine-supported "Operación Limpieza" (Operation Cleanup).[42]

Yolanda, a seventy-six-year-old Afro-Dominicana who now resides in Italy, lived in 1965 in La Parte Alta's iconic Ensanche Luperón, one of the main battle sites of the US military intervention.[43] Yolanda participated in La Batalla del Puente Duarte on April 27, in which the constitucionalistas overthrew the military and essentially won the war prior to the intervention. She continued to serve the constitucionalistas, working as a messenger and spy in the weeks that followed the intervention. Yolanda recalls the day Operación Limpieza reached her neighborhood as a "brute" massacre that destroyed the bodies and morale of many working people.

> Yo estaba con el pueblo. Con la revolución. . . . Y mi experiencia fue particular como mujer. Porque yo iba a San Isidro a lavar la ropa a los militares americanos. Y ellos me daban comida y cigarillos. Y yo me las llevaba y hasta me llevaba balas y se la llevaba a los muchachos que estaban allá abajo escondidos. . . . Pero después llegó la limpieza y eso fue una masacre, una cosa bruta. . . . Yo estaba con Gladys, mi amiga que le decían La Coronela, y la estaban buscando, y nos escondimos. Nos fuimos a San Francisco y hasta ahí llegaron preguntando. Nos estaban persiguiendo. . . . Y la persecución no terminó con la revolución, no señor. . . . Después llegó Balaguer y toda esa vagabundería siguió. No fue hasta después que me fui a Italia que hallé paz de todo eso. . . . Pero eso fue que hicieron fue una cosa bruta.[44]

> [I was with the people, you know. With the revolution. . . . And my experience as a woman was particular. I would go to the American military and wash their clothes and I would collect food and cigarettes and steal bullets from them and bring them down there to the boys who were hiding. . . . But then the "cleansing" happened, and it was a massacre, a brutality. . . . I was with Gladys, my friend, who went by La Coronela, and they were looking for her and we hid, we went to San Francisco and even then, they followed us. . . . The persecution did not end with the revolution, no sir. I never felt at peace again in the country. They were always after us. Then came Balaguer and all that nonsense continued. It wasn't until I left for Italy that I had peace from that. . . . But it was a truly brute thing they did.]

Despite their contributions, the majority of working-class Afro-Dominicanas like Yolanda have been relegated to obscurity by a male-dominated archive that is more comfortable with the mythification of a handful of light-skinned middle-class women than with acknowledging the tangible and essential roles of many Black and Brown working-class Dominicanas. Cordero argues:

> La Guerra creó muchos mitos. . . . Y hubo muchos mitos creados alrededor de las mujeres. . . . Esas fotos de mujeres con fusiles al hombro montadas en tanquetas . . . son selfies. . . . Las mujeres que participaron en los combates no fueron militantes ningunas. . . . Eran mujeres de la parte norte, mujeres populares. . . . Ajenas a la izquierda que si combatieron.[45]
>
> [The War birthed many myths. . . . There were many myths created about women. . . . But these pictures you see with women holding weapons on their shoulders, riding tanks . . . are selfies. . . . The women who participated in combat were not the militant Left. . . . It was the women from La Parte Alta. . . . It was the women who were not involved in the Left. Those women actually fought in battle.]

One of these "selfies" is the iconic image of Tina Bazuca (see figure 3.4). The famous photo depicts a smiling, light-skinned teenage girl holding a rifle in her right hand and a pair of sunglasses in her left. The caption for the photo, as well as the narrative around its subject, describes her as an "exceptional sixteen-year-old girl, who one day joined the revolution."[46] The photo, which has also become the logo for the highly profitable Tina Bazuca beer made by the artisanal República Brewery (see figure 3.5), shows the teenager wearing a skirt and sandals, seemingly not at all preoccupied with the war she was supposedly fighting. The image, which has become emblematic of La Guerra de Abril, is a misrepresentation. The girl in the photo is, in fact, Julia Cabral Carezzano, a light-skinned upper-middle-class Dominicana whose brother fought in the revolution. Cabral Carezzano posed with her brother's rifle but was not actually involved in the revolution.

But Tina Bazuca did exist. The real "Tina" was twenty-eight-year-old Augustina Rivas, a *rayana* from Dajabón (see figure 3.6).[47] Rivas was born on May 13, 1937, a few days after Trujillo ordered the Parsley Massacre that killed more than twenty thousand people in her hometown.[48] In 1954 she moved with her family to the city in search of work. They lived first in Santiago and later in the Villa Consuelo barrio in Santo Domingo, most likely to work on the many construction projects of Ciudad Trujillo.[49] Those who knew

FIGURE 3.4 Julia Cabral Carezzano, a young girl who posed with her brother's rifle and whose photo was popularized as "Tina Bazuca, guerrilla fighter." Archivo General de la Nación (AGN), Dominican Republic.

her describe Rivas as a "mari-macha" (tomboy/butch) with a hot temper and a real preoccupation with justice. She was a fighter for workers' rights and an active member of the Sindicato de Trabajadores Portuarios de Arrimo (POASI) dockworkers' union.[50] She worked all kinds of jobs not traditionally considered feminine, including security guard and dockworker. During her free time, she volunteered as a boxing coach for children and teenagers and was an active member of her neighborhood workers' organization. When the revolution began, Rivas joined the constitucionalistas, immediately standing out among the women due to her superb combat abilities. Sánchez, who served in the same military commando as Rivas, remembers her as "the only woman capable of taking on the frog-men," the most skilled of the guerrilla fighters: "Era tan buena que la tenían entrenando a los hombres. Nos daba

FIGURE 3.5 República Brewery's "Tina Bazuca" beer bottle. Photo by Carmen Inés Bencosme.

hasta vergüenza pero eso nos hacía ser mas bravos" (She was so good they had her training men. She put us all to shame and made us braver).[51] It was because of her uncanny abilities as a sniper that Rivas earned the nickname "Tina Bazuca." Stories about Tina Bazuca spread like wildfire among the women of the revolution. Yolanda, who never met her, remembers, "Todo el mundo sabía quién era ella aunque no la conocieran. . . . Era una leyenda" (We all knew her even though we didn't know her. . . . She was a legend).[52]

After the revolution, Rivas continued to work for workers' rights with POASI. However, facing persecution during Balaguer's Terrible Twelve Years, she migrated by raft to Puerto Rico in 1976. Unlike Yolanda and other Dominican women veterans who found refuge in the social democratic environment of 1980s Italy, Rivas was quickly deported from Puerto Rico back

FIGURE 3.6 Augustina Rivas, a.k.a. "Tina Bazuca." Photo courtesy of the Tirso Medrano Archive.

to Santo Domingo.[53] After multiple subsequent attempts to migrate and establish herself in the US diaspora, in 1991 Rivas was forced to return to Santo Domingo, where she struggled to find work and support herself and her daughter. Five years later, she died of a massive heart attack at age fifty-nine.

Of the multiple testimonies and stories about La Guerra de Abril that have been entrusted to me over the years, Tina Bazuca's is the most remarkable. She lived an extraordinary life against death from birth, yet her extraordinary life has been obscured by a fictionalized image that mimics and reproduces Dominican colonial desire for whiteness. What does it mean for Dominicans to remember "Tina Bazuca" but not know who she actually was? How do we grapple with the fact that the extraordinary life and contributions of an Afro-Dominicana are only remembered through an invented story about a posed photo of a young light-skinned girl? That the Cabral Carezzano photo has been celebrated and commercialized while the real Tina Bazuca experienced persecution, migration, deportation, hunger, and violence tells us a lot about the Dominican state valuation—or lack thereof—of Black women's lives. It exemplifies the gender-based violence through which Black Dominicanas' deeds and bodies are appropriated and performed through whitewashed representations that are more acceptable to the public. It illuminates Dominican colonial desire for whiteness at the expense of Black lives.

Since the foundation of the Dominican nation, myths about white Dominican women have fueled patriotism and a nationalist agenda at the expense of Black and Brown Dominican women.[54] In the nineteenth century, the image of the white Dominican virgin in need of protection fueled anti-Haitianism and plagued national rhetoric.[55] After the fall of Trujillo in 1961, Patria, Minerva, and María Teresa Mirabal, who were brutally murdered in 1960 as a result of their political work against the regime, became symbols of a new patria in which women could become political actors—through men's protection.[56] The death of the Mirabal sisters, three light-skinned upper-class women from the Cibao region, is often invoked as the single most traumatic event of the Trujillo regime, even when compared to the genocide of more than twenty thousand ethnic Haitians and Afro-Dominicans in Dajabón, the execution of dozens of political dissidents, and the rape and torture of hundreds of women and girls. I do not want to diminish the significance of the Mirabal sisters, either in their political work against the Trujillo regime or as symbols of the struggle to end violence against women. Rather, I want to call attention to the "other women" who are erased from the history of the very nation they helped build: women like Yolanda, who have taken their fight against death to the diaspora precisely because "if I did not leave, I would be dead."[57] We must unsilence these women—poor, Black, Brown, rayana, migrant, trans, queer—in the archives. We need to say their names.

Elsewhere I have discussed the mass emigration of poor and working-class Dominicans to the United States, particularly Puerto Rico and New York, that followed the war and US military intervention in 1965.[58] The significance of the US diaspora, which now constitutes more than 10 percent of the Dominican population, is central to contemporary Dominican studies. Lesser studied, however, are diasporic sites outside the United States that, though smaller in number, are meaningful in translating Dominican blackness to a larger constituency of Latinx and Black political movements. This translation illuminates the political, cultural, and social impact of mid-twentieth-century processes—La Guerra de Abril, the repressive Terrible Twelve Years of Balaguer's regime, the emergence of La UASD as a site of political organizing—and the resulting and continued state-sanctioned social, political, civic, and corporeal deaths of Black Dominicanas. One of these key sites for translating blackness is Italy.

In the late seventies, Italy became an important destination for Dominican women migrants, particularly working-class Dominicanas and women activists associated with the Catholic Left. Migration to Italy opened doors for political enfranchisement for women like Yolanda, who found a space and language for working-class struggles in European social structures. Black migrant women organizing from the late 1970s to the early 2000s influenced national policies and conversations regarding the place of Black, Brown, Muslim, and Asian Italians within the nation. For Dominicanas, participation in Italian organizing and politics allowed them to translate their struggles into a language of Black consciousness and belonging, producing a robust network of support that is now responding to the growing crisis of migrant exploitation resulting from Italian sex tourism and the sex trafficking of Dominican women and girls in Europe.

The political environment for Black migrant women activism in Italy has changed radically since the late 1970s. Italy now faces a continuous influx of refugees and migrants from Syria and the Horn of Africa, and a new wave of anti-immigrant violence propelled by the proliferation of the neofascist and extreme Right discourse of the Lega Nord. But these challenges, as I argue in chapter 5, are also contested by a new wave of political activism by the Second Generation—the children of the women who migrated to Italy in the late twentieth century who have been born on Italian soil yet are often barred from accessing Italian citizenship due to jus sanguinis legislation.[59] It is in great part due to the early struggles of Black and Brown women that a transnational conversation about Italian citizenship, migrant rights, and antiblackness is possible in Italy today.

Diaspora Rebellions

We are the hyphenated people of the Diaspora whose self-defined identities are no longer shameful secrets in the countries of our origin, but rather declarations of strength and solidarity. We are an increasingly united front from which the world has not yet heard. —AUDRE LORDE, Berlin, 1984

Yolanda has lived a life worthy of a novel: she traveled the seven seas on the Onassis boat, fought in a civil war, worked as a spy, and contributed to the founding of the first queer bar in the Dominican Republic.[60] She migrated to Italy in 1989 in search of peace and a better future away from the island and the aftermath of the repression and suppression of the Balaguer regime. But a revolutionary spirit cannot be content with rest while there is injustice, and like many of the activist and revolutionary women who migrated to Italy in the post-Balaguer years, Yolanda has continued to organize for migrant rights in the diaspora, particularly for the protection of young women and girls of color. Her main concern is the liberation of young Latinas, many of them from the Dominican Republic, who are kept in captivity by human traffickers after being sold by family members into prostitution. Unaffiliated with any formal organization, Yolanda and other migrant women work closely with domestic and sex workers to promote the protection and safety of young women and girls through informal networks that operate "very much like a clandestine commando."[61] When someone learns of a young woman in danger, she alerts the community to the woman's location. Yolanda then works quickly and clandestinely to investigate and eventually infiltrate the site to free the woman and take her to a safehouse. When I asked Yolanda why she takes such risks instead of simply contacting the authorities, she explained:

> Esa era mi intención al principio. La primera vez que me di de cuenta que tenían a una muchacha, una jovencita dominicana, en un hotel en Napoli en contra de su voluntad, yo llamé a la policía. Cuando ellos quisieron llegar a investigar, ya la muchacha no estaba ahí. La perdimos. No se sabe a donde se la llevaron. Estos traficantes, ellos están conectados, si me entiendes, son gente que tiene su gente. Yo no me voy a arriesgar a que otra muchacha se pierda. No si es que puedo hacer algo para que eso no pase.[62]
>
> [That was my original intent. The first time I found out that a girl—a young woman from the Dominican Republic—was being held in a hotel in Naples against her will, I contacted the police. By the time they

> arrived to investigate, they had already moved the girl. We lost her. We don't know where she went. These traffickers, they are connected, if you know what I mean, people are tipped off. I am not going to risk losing another girl. Not if I can do something about it.]

Using an old table leg as her only weapon, Yolanda liberated a woman from captivity and forced prostitution. She hopes to continue doing this work as long as "God gives me strength."[63]

While perhaps not as dramatic as Yolanda's rescues, the work of other post-Balaguer Dominican women migrants in Italy has impacted the everyday lives of the people—other women of color and queer migrants—who directly benefit from their activism. Further, it has impacted the national and regional conversations about the rights of Black and migrant women in post-1990 Italy and across Europe. This work has been possible in great part due to the political engagement of migrant women and queer people of color who arrived in Italy on the heels of the Italian feminist movement at the end of the twentieth century.

The past fifty years have seen an increase in the autonomous migration of women—married and unmarried, queer and straight, and often educated—who are the main economic providers for their families. Women and queer immigrants face different opportunities and cope with different risks and challenges than cisgender and/or heterosexual men migrants face, such as vulnerability to human rights abuses, exploitation, and gender-based discrimination. According to data from the United Nations Population Division, obtained mostly from censuses and covering both documented and undocumented migrants, the number of female migrants grew faster than the number of male migrants between 1965 and 1990 in the largest immigrant-receiving countries.[64] Approximately half of all international migrants today are women.[65] Italy offers an important example for studying the growth of women's migration, as more than 70 percent of the immigrant population in Italy is women.[66] The first migrant women to arrive in Italy in the 1960s and 1970s came from Eritrea, Cape Verde, and the Philippines, mostly as domestic workers.[67] As many scholars have argued, their migration was often facilitated by connections with Catholic organizations and as a direct result of Italy's colonial past.[68] Italy is not usually imagined as a colonial power, mainly because it did not exist as a modern nation until 1861. But as we will see in chapter 4, Italy did establish colonies overseas, an enterprise that continued into the twentieth century. By 1914, Italy had annexed Eritrea, Somalia, Libya, and the Dodecanese Islands. Heather Merrill argues that in studying migration and racialization, we need to remember that although Italy has not been historically marked as a colonial power, it formed part of the great colonial expansion in the fifteenth century, which in turn influenced its construction of race, identities, discourses, and practices.[69] This colonial past continues to shape present-day white supremacist Italian immigration legislation.

In the 1980s, the situation of immigrants in Italy gained national attention following the racially motivated killing of a South African immigrant, Jerry Essan Masslo.[70] The event shocked an Italian nation accustomed to imagining itself as nonracist and compassionate, due in part to collective amnesia regarding Italy's own colonialist history. Masslo's murder prompted a public awakening around antiblackness and xenophobia and about the place of immigrants of color within the Italian nation. Soon after, a piece of legislation known as the "Martelli Law" was introduced, granting amnesty to all undocumented immigrants.[71] This law paved the way for many immigrants to become naturalized citizens of Italy, forcing a revision of Italianness to be more inclusive of the new citizens. However, as is the way of immigration reform, there was plenty of opposition to the new law, awakening the Catholic Right. In September 2000, Cardinal Giacomo Biffi, Archbishop of Bologna, asserted that only Catholics should be allowed to immigrate to "preserve the Catholic identity of the nation."[72] Biffi found support among many politicians. His words also sparked a dialogue that contradicted the dominant narrative of the homogenous white Catholic Italy represented in his remarks. Scholars, writers, artists, and the public began to question "the hegemonic construction of an imagined Italian community."[73]

In 1996 blackness, Latinidad, and Italianness intersected on the global stage for the first time with the pageant crowning of Denny Méndez, a naturalized Italian citizen from the Dominican Republic, as Miss Italia. A controversy emerged immediately after a participatory television vote selected Méndez. Two of the pageant judges opposed the coronation on the grounds of Méndez's "inadequately" Italian look: "A black girl cannot be Miss Italia. . . . It is not in the rules."[74] The "rules" referenced by pageant judge Alba Parietti, a former Miss Italia, shed light on the anxiety that the question of race produced among many Italians as the nation struggled with becoming the recipient, rather than the sender, of migrants.[75] The controversy and overt racism among the judges surprised people around the world who were unaccustomed to imagining race and racism as an Italian problem. Méndez's coronation provoked a public dialogue regarding the need for Italy to be more inclusive of its citizens of color. Méndez, for her part, embraced "blackness" and deployed the label "Black" as an international category of unity in her response to the controversy: "*And this beautiful skin makes me very much the sister of many continents*. But most of all I am Italian. I am the new face of a better, more inclusive Italy."[76] Her statement suggests an awareness of the political capital of translating her Black Dominican colonial experience to a larger constituency of immigrant women in Italy.[77] As we can see in the speech act "this beautiful skin," Méndez also understands the political capital of hegemonic blackness as a category of cultural and political belonging and solidarity in the diaspora.

Black Latinx placements and displacements in Italy—and by extension in the European Union—bridge the migratory and colonial experience shaping the racialization and exclusion of citizens of color. Méndez's assertion of Black Latinidad in the Miss Universe pageant called attention to racial diversity—and racism—in contemporary Italy. Her deployment of Spanish and "Latin" cultural markers further called upon the possibilities of what Juan Flores and Miriam Jiménez Román have called Afro-Latinx "triple-consciousness" as a locus for intra-ethnic solidarity.[78] Though Méndez's blackness has been the subject of multiple studies about contemporary Italian racialization, the analytical richness of her triumph lays precisely in her personification of the entanglement of Black Latinidad in present-day constructions and productions of minoritized citizenship. Blackness made her Latinidad visible, and her Latinidad represented blackness.[79] Méndez, who in the Dominican Republic would not typically be understood as Black—though not at the cost of racism—publicly embraced global blackness in her assertion of Italianness. In a clever translation of blackness that very much resembles the hegemonic discourse of multiculturalism Italy had only recently begun to exploit, Méndez's embrace of blackness is an act of political translation of the multiple colonialities that rendered her "inadequate" to represent Italy in the eyes of the judges.

While Latinidad in Italy is always synonymous with *extracomunitari* (foreigner from outside the community), exotic, and foreign, blackness approximates Italy's uncomfortable and oft-silenced colonial relationship with Africa, opening up a political dialogue about belonging and citizenship rights Latinidad has yet to engage. Yet Méndez's performance of blackness is also an example of the social processes through which Black Latinxs make sense of contradictory racial terms amid the globalized economy of inequality they sustain on their very backs. It also points to the urgent need to study Black Latinidad as a locus for articulating racial struggles beyond the hegemonic US Black-white paradigm.

There is not much scholarship on the specificity of Dominican migration to Italy. The little that has been documented, mostly through informal interviews and statistical data, shows that it has been a network migration of mostly women, the majority of whom are from small towns in the southwestern and northern Dominican Republic.[80] As of 2014, the documented population of Dominicans in Italy over age fifteen was 28,804.[81] However, this figure does not reflect the large number of undocumented residents. Like previous generations of women immigrants from Asia, Africa, and other parts of Latin America, Dominicanas largely migrate to Italy as domestic and sex workers. In addition, there are a small number of care professionals (nurses and nurses' aides) as well as *matrimonias* (Dominican women who have married Italian men).

Unlike white and mestiza Latin American migrant women, Dominicans find themselves able to participate in both Black and Latin American social and civic organizations, therefore inhabiting a somewhat privileged space within their marginality. Much like the experiences of Dominicans in Washington, DC, during the 1940s studied by Ginetta Candelario, Dominican immigrants in Italy are racialized as Black (*nera, di colore*). However, their ability to speak Spanish, which in turn facilitates learning Italian, sets them apart from Black African migrants. This duality means that Dominican migrants can be racialized as Black in US or European contexts while at the same time marked as different from hegemonic notions of blackness through language and cultural identity.[82] Through their Black Latina experiences, Dominicanas in Italy quickly form links and alliances within various communities, gaining, as Mercedes Frías recounts, "access to a larger form of sisterhood than the one I had known back home."[83] But for Dominicanas, blackness means more than a transnational space of belonging. It also means their bodies are marked as sites of consumption, corruption, and exoticism.[84]

The increase in women migrants to Italy coincided with the Italian feminist movement, which took off in the late 1970s. As Italian feminists found themselves confronted with the desire to be mothers while also asserting their role in society by working outside the home, and as they gained political representation and social visibility, migrant women came to "solve" their problem by providing in-home care for children and elders. Immigrant women in Italy facilitated the white middle-class feminist agenda, an agenda that largely ignored the needs of migrant women of color. At the same time, Black and Third World feminisms in the United States and other parts of Europe and Latin

America were emerging, insisting on the need to analyze how gender, class, and ethnicity intersect and reproduce power imbalances and oppression.[85]

Immigrant women workers in Italy in the 1970s and 1980s increasingly unbelonged, dually invisible due to their gendered racialization and class status. They were not part of the feminist agenda, despite being such a key element of it. Additionally, they were relegated to domestic or sex work. That is, Asian and Black women were assumed to be domestic or sex workers, as evidenced by the rhetorical equation of "Filippina" and "domestic worker." As Jacqueline Andall argues, while Italian women were asserting their roles as mothers and workers, immigrant women were only viewed as workers, their identities reduced to stigmatized professions.[86] Despite the stigma, immigrant women were not perceived as a threat to the nation, which contributed to a continuum of network migration in the 1980s and 1990s. Needless to say, the preference for foreign workers and the abundance of work opportunities did not necessarily translate into good working conditions or representation.

In this context of hegemonic interpellation, immigrant women in Italy eventually developed systems of support—usually in the form of ethnic, national, and worker organizations—that gave them representation in the larger Italian nation and a space from which to articulate their gender-specific needs. Wendy Pojmann has studied the impact these types of organizations have had in shaping Italian politics and feminism, insisting on their significant role in interpellating Italy's feminist movement.[87] As I have argued elsewhere, the role of immigrant organizations in Italy was key in promoting significant ethnic alliances that led to larger political representation.[88] A twenty-first-century example of this is the 2006 election of Mercedes Frías, a Black Dominicana migrant community organizer, as a representative to Italian parliament.

Post-Balaguer Dominicana activists like Yolanda and Mercedes Frías, who migrated to Italy in the late eighties and early nineties, found their political aspirations intertwined with a local anti-racist feminist political movement led by Black and migrant women. Frías remembers her arrival to Tuscany in 1990 as an opportunity to continue her lifelong commitment to the struggle for women's and workers' rights. It was also the turning point that transformed her activism into a tangible transnational political agenda: "Fueron años productivos de lucha social. Se lograron tantísimas cosas. Colaboramos con tantas mujeres. Con mujeres de toda Europa, de América Latina, de Asia, de África. Fue un momento de gran cambio" (Those were productive years of social struggle. We accomplished so much. We collaborated with so many women. Women from all over Europe, Latin America, Asia, Africa. It was a moment of great change).[89] Frías, like Sagrario Díaz, had been introduced to social justice and activism work as a student at La UASD, where she joined multiple student organizations, including Mujeres en Acción para la Liberación (MOALI) and the National Association of Evangelical Students. Through these organizations, she worked on environmental protection projects and volunteered in ethnic Haitian communities in the outskirts of Santo Domingo, particularly the Black neighborhood of Villa Mella: "En esos años trabajábamos el feminismo de base, educación sobre la salud reproductiva, acceso a recursos básicos. Ese fue mi primer encuentro con el feminismo" (In those times, our work was around very basic forms of feminism: reproductive health and basic access to resources. That was my first encounter with feminism).[90] Frías remembers La UASD as the home of her militancy ("la casa de mi militancia"), where she came of age as an activist politicized around the intersecting identities that shaped her life and her work: being Black, a woman, and working class. In 1990, shortly after completing her degree in geography, Frías migrated to Italy to pursue postgraduate education. Soon after arriving, she became involved with local migrant women organizations, serving first as a translator and then as an advocate and leader for migrant women's rights.

Frías's arrival in Tuscany coincided with a critical historical moment, as Italy began to grapple with its role as an immigrant-receiving nation and the effects of that role on the growth of anti-Black violence. She recalls:

> Esos fueron años mágicos, de grandes luchas sociales. Empezamos a trabajar juntas como mujeres pero al poco tiempo hubo una separación pues nosotras (mujeres inmigrantes de color), empezamos a llamar la atención a nuestras luchas, la lucha de tener cuerpos racializados, de ser pobres, de ser negras e inmigrantes. . . . Las otras [mujeres italianas blancas] no estaban listas para esa conversación. Fue un momento importante aunque difícil.[91]
>
> [These were magical years, years of important social struggles. We began to work together but soon there was a break because those of us who were women of color began to call attention to our intersecting struggles, our struggles of having racialized bodies, of being poor, of being Black and immigrants. . . . The other women [white Italians] were not ready for that conversation. It was an important moment, even if difficult.]

Given her experience working with Haitian migrants in the Dominican Republic and on women's and workers' rights, Frías quickly became a leader in her region, spearheading the creation of multiple migrant women's organizations, including the Nosotras Association, the European Social Forum on

Migrant Women, and the local chapter of the National Organization for Women (NOW). Among her many contributions was Punto di Partenza, one of the largest transnational conferences on migrant women in Southern Europe. In fall 2002, Punto di Partenza brought together women from the Global South and Europe to think, create, and demand the human rights the nation has continued to deny them. Frías also founded the Campus delle culture delle donne, a freedom school devoted to intercultural feminist education. Out of the latter enterprise came multiple publications, including a book about the experience of the campus, *Prendiamo la parola* (Let's take the word).[92] Frías recalls:

> Del Campus surgieron muchas oportunidades para revisar la palabra de la mujer, su contribución, su pensamiento y su política. En esas dos semanas que pasamos estudiando nos convertimos en expertas en nosotras mismas. Los temas fueron tantos: el derecho a la ciudadanía, la diferencia entre el Sur y el Norte y como afecta la vida de las mujeres migrantes de color, las relaciones interculturales, fueron tantos los temas.[93]

> [The Freedom School afforded us so many opportunities for thinking about women's words, their contribution, their thought, and their politics. During those two weeks we spent in school we became experts in ourselves. There were so many topics: the right to citizenship, the differences between the South and the North and how that affected the lives of migrant women of color, intercultural relationships, so many topics.]

One of the most significant accomplishments of Frías's leadership has been Article 18, a constitutional amendment that grants temporary asylum to survivors of sexual assault and human trafficking.[94] The article included a stipulation in which a stamp marked "Article 18" would be attached to their passports or visas, literally marking these women as sex workers or as victims of sex trafficking, further stigmatizing them and exposing them to violence. Frías remembers:

> Ah . . . El Artículo 18. Entonces tú querías hacer tú pero tenías "artículo 18" puesto como un sello en tu pasaporte. . . . Entonces ahí armamos otro rebú, y sobre todo nos dirigimos a las autoridades garante de la parálisis, que nos dio razón. Y esa la ganamos. Así que quitaron eso; hubieron muchas cosas pero esa fue una gran victoria.[95]

> [Ah . . . Article 18. Then you wanted to go on with your life, but you had "Article 18" like a seal on your passport. . . . That's when we started

another revolt and went to the authorities and they saw we were right. That one we won. They took that thing away; there were many things we did but that one—that was a great victory.]

Because of this and other victories, Frías was eventually nominated as the Tuscan candidate for parliament for the Rifondazione Comunista, the Italian communist party.[96] She won, becoming the first Black woman to serve in the Italian parliament.

During our conversations over the years, Frías has shared stories of her time as a community organizer in Italy and the Dominican Republic. Her remarkable life has been shaped by her ability to belong to and cocreate communities of women of color who, more than anything else, desire to live in justice and dignity. Mercedes's political life began in her home, the Dominican Republic, where as a working-class Black woman she dreamed, as did Sagrario Díaz and many others, of change—of a future free of violence. Yet Frías found only violence, exclusion, and the impossibility of fulfilling her full potential as a human being in Santo Domingo. So she opted to leave. Like many, myself included, she later attempted to return, hoping that her years in the diaspora and newfound wisdom would create opportunities to continue her work at home. In the Dominican Republic, though, she was met with disdain and scorn, as Black Dominicanas from the diaspora often are. She was dubbed a troublemaker, and so there was no place for her in the institutional structures of a state that continues to sanction Black women's deaths and exclusion. After three years of trying to establish herself in Santo Domingo, unable to find work, disdained by the very university she had adored as her "home of militancy," Frías returned to Italy.

In the nineteenth century, as we saw in chapter 1, the Dominican Republic was imagined as a site of Black freedom, where Black people from around the world could fulfill their rights as citizens and live as full human beings. In the Dominican Republic, US Black doctor Sarah Loguen Fraser became the first woman to practice medicine, and her daughter, Gregoria Fraser, imagined the multiple possibilities of being Black, woman, and free. A century later, though, women like Frías, Yolanda, and Rivas—and hundreds of other working women activists—saw no other way but to leave, to do elsewhere that which Sarah Loguen Fraser got to do in their land: become full human beings. Or as Marlene de la Cruz of the Milan women's organization Anacaona Mujeres Dominicanas en Italia put it: "Da vergüenza que con tanto talento—con todo lo que podemos lograr en comunidad—tengamos que irnos simplemente porque no nos quieren. Tenemos que recoger nuestro talento e irnos a otra parte donde se nos reconozca, *cambiando una lucha por otra*" (It's a shame that with all our talent—with all that we can collectively accomplish—we have to leave simply because we are not wanted. We have to pick up and bring our talents elsewhere and fight elsewhere for recognition, *trading one fight for another*).[97]

This trade is precisely what drives the work of Anacaona Mujeres Dominicanas en Italia, a women's organization directed by a group of Black Dominican women migrants, most of whom have a history of activism in the post-Balaguer Dominican Republic. Founded in 2009 to "improve the dignity and equality of immigrant women and to protect against gender violence and discrimination," Anacaona is moved by a collective desire to end the cycle of death and violence that led many women and queer people to migrate and seems to follow Dominicanas across the Atlantic.[98] Melania Cruz, a psychologist from Santo Domingo and cofounder of the association, says her determination comes from "solo de ver cuantas de nuestras mujeres siguen sufriendo. Ellas emigran porque no se pueden quedar en casa—en la casa, en el país natal, sus vidas peligran a mano del padre o marido abusador. Y vienen aquí a entrentar más violencia, pero ahora sin apoyo, sin amigos, y sin conocer la ley" (just seeing how many of our women are continuing to suffer. They migrate because they cannot stay home—because home represents a danger to their lives at the hands of an abusive husband or father. And they come here and face similar violence, except now they have no network, no friends, they do not understand the law).[99] Anacaona provides legal and psychological counsel to women migrants facing challenges, including domestic violence, family separation, work discrimination, abuse, and gender-based persecution by sex and human traffickers. It works closely with the municipality and consulates to support women in danger. It also create spaces for community building, celebration, language learning, and childrearing support. Over its decade of existence, Anacaona has succeeded in organizing the Dominicana community in the Milan metropolitan area through solidarity and a feminist network of support—despite the growth of extreme Right politics in northern Italy, and amid the growing global climate of antiblackness. While its efforts often go unnoticed, due in part to its limited access to social media networks and in part to the discreet nature of its work, Anacaona's actions summon the spirit of the Indigenous leader after which it is named: the Taína cacique warrior poet who rebelled against Spanish colonization and died fighting for her right to live, and for her and her people's right to freedom. Like the warrior Anacaona, de la Cruz explains, the women of the association "No seremos gran cosa pero somos efectivas. No estamos en blah blah y mucho bulto, lo de nosotras es la comunidad. Lo de nosotras es no

FIGURE 3.7 Celebration of International Women's Day, Anacaona Mujeres Dominicanas en Italia, March 8, 2015.

dejar a nadie atras. Lo único que tenemos es nosotras y nos tenemos eh" (We might not be flashy, but we are effective. We are not about the noise; we are about the community. About not leaving anyone behind. We are all we got, and we got us).[100]

When I began my research in Italy in 2013, Anacaona Mujeres Dominicanas welcomed me with open arms. The trust and support I received from Anacaona facilitated my research and provided a home in Italy for me and my son. Over the years, I got a front-row seat to witness its actions, care, intention, fight against death, and unwavering commitment to Black women. In its fight I saw the fight of all Dominicanas. Its community rebellion is not radical. It is not about public marches, though Anacaona sometimes marches; it is not about throwing rocks and burning tires, though Anacaona is more than ready to do so if members must; it is not about collecting data and writing books, though its qualitative research and story archive are the most complete archive of dominicanidad I have encountered. Rather, Anacaona's rebellion is grounded on care, a radical hope for change, and the conviction that its members deserve equal rights and dignity wherever they may reside. Its revolution is the manifestation of the simplest and most necessary of feminisms: one that centers Black women and asserts that Black women deserve life (see figure 3.7).

Revisiting the writing of the Black feminists who sustain me—Audre Lorde, bell hooks, Ochy Curiel, Yuderkys Espinosa, Josefina Báez, Angela Davis—one reminder transcends language and history: we, Black women, must rebel in transnational community. Our work, our lives, and our struggle against death are not bound by the borders of nation-states and therefore cannot only be fought within and through national paradigms. Or, as Curiel puts it, "Tenemos que ser anti-nacionalistas para poder hacer luchas comunes" (We must be anti-nationalists to fight our common struggles).[101] My intention in foregrounding the work of migrant women in the Italian diaspora is not intended to romanticize migration as a solution to violence. Death and violence are part of everyday life for migrants. From the state-sanctioned sinking of boats carrying migrants in the Mediterranean to the separation of families and caging of children at the US-Mexico border to the denationalization of ethnic Haitians in the Dominican Republic, violence against migrants is too present, too significant to ignore. What the diaspora, and in particular the Italian diaspora, has afforded Black Dominicanas is the possibility of encountering themselves as part of a larger, stronger, and more visible political network. They are equipped with a language that allows them to name, as Frías does, the "common struggles." In the diaspora, they understand that their exclusion from the nation is exclusion from the world based on colonial structures that still shape citizenship and belonging. In the diaspora, Dominicanas translate their struggles through a language of Black and migrant solidarity. In so doing they are able to build larger networks of inclusion that speak back to the Dominican nation from a global stage. As Black women and migrants, they confront together the structures that led them to migrate in the first place. The diaspora is not always less violent than home; it is simply a larger arena from which to fight against the common enemy. It is a place from which to return, or from which to possess a new form of knowledge in transnational community. For some, the diaspora is just another site of violence and death. For others, it allows them to see the interstices between belonging and unbelonging and become empowered and even comfortable in their own vaivén. As de la Cruz explained to me, "Nos rechazan aquí y nos rechazan allá. Ellos se creen la gran cosa con su rechazo de nosotras. Lo que ellos no saben es que no los necesitamos. Nosotras mismas podemos cargarnos. Quien lo necesita a ellos? *Somos nuestro propio país*" (Rejection here, rejection there. They think they are so big in not wanting us. They just don't get that we don't need them. We got us. Who needs them? *We are our own country*).[102] This country is what Josefina Báez has called El Nié.

A Country of Our Own: From El Nié to the World

In *Carmen: FotonovelARTE* (2020), the Ay Ombe Theatre collective invites us to contradict death and the disavowal of Black Dominicanas from the nation through possession, community, and love. The story opens with a black-and-white photo of a young Black woman, Carmen, doing her hair in front of a mirror and talking to herself in gestures. Thought bubbles in all four corners of the page contain text in what the reader can perceive as loud Dominican Spanish: "Sol, abres la página y comienzo el día, fotonoveliando el resuelve diario" (Sun, you open the page and I start my day, making a *fotonovela* of the daily struggle).[103] Speaking to herself, the protagonist interpellates the sun, that Caribbean character that fills pages of poetry and inflicts castigating sweat on the farm worker. "Sol" is also a term of endearment: "mi sol." Sol is an invitation to life and awakening. As she calls upon the sun, Carmen also interpellates the viewer/reader on the other side of the mirror/page. "Sol!" she declares as she looks at us face-to-face, inviting us into her community of beloveds. Behind that mirror, we sit in complicit contentment, contemplating Carmen's invitation to join in the *sancajeo* (struggle) of her daily life. We can imagine by the tone of the text that this sancajeo is surrounded by a very persistent sense of beauty and joy that can only be found in the quotidian exercises of possessing oneself and being possessed by and through the communal experiences of daily life.

Carmen: FotonovelARTE is the first book of the Levente Visual series, written and directed by Dominicanyork performance artist, poet, and director Josefina Báez and co-produced by members of the Ay Ombe Collective. The series is based on her previous work, *Levente no: Yolayorkdominicanyork*, a feminist narrative centered on the lives of multiple women—most of them Dominican—living in a building in New York City called El Nié. El Nié is both the tangible location between home and the diaspora and the symbolically interstitial space between belonging and unbelonging—neither here nor there—that many marginalized people inhabit.[104] In *Carmen: FotonovelARTE*, Báez and the Ay Ombe Collective take us back to the Dominican Republic and seductively invite us into the everyday life of a Black Dominicana from Santo Domingo: a free and joyous self-proclaimed "levente" woman. The Dominicanism "levente" was traditionally employed as a misogynist insult aimed at controlling women's movement. In defiance, the levente walks freely in the streets, doing as she pleases. To be levente is to walk in danger, to risk being repudiated and reprimanded by the institutions governing women's bodies and social lives. Through Carmen, we confront the misogyny of Dominican culture, the misery of the public health system, the neverending economic crisis, and the powerful ways Black women live in community. *Carmen: FotonovelARTE* challenges its readers in multiple ways. It forces us to confront the historical and rhetorical legacies of femicide and misogyny, from the erasure of Black women to Carmen as a tragic figure in traditional literature and operas. It invites us to explore Santo Domingo in all its beauty and splendor and challenges us to think about community as a form of rebellion—as an antidote to the persistence of death. The form of the text itself, a fotonovela (graphic novel), resists traditional reading, requiring us to pay attention to movement through the images, photographs, and dialogue that jump throughout the pages. It is thus an act of active accompaniment rather than passive reading.

The fotonovela has its roots in the *historietas* (comic books) of turn-of-the-twentieth-century Latin America. Originally, these were illustrated versions of popular works of European literature. Published in serial format, historietas eventually gave way to the fotonovela, which takes contemporary everyday life as its subject matter. Since the mid-twentieth century, fotonovelas have been used across Latin America and Southern Europe as educational tools for vulnerable communities, including women and migrants, to teach literacy and health education and promote civil rights awareness.[105] In the United States, fotonovelas have been central to Latinx communities' struggles for equality. In the 1960s, for example, fotonovelas were a staple of the Chicano movement, particularly in supporting workers' and farmers' rights. *Carmen: FotonovelARTE* is a contemporary rendition of an artistic and activist Latinx tradition that centers Black women's right to live in contra*diction* to the violence and death that dominates both life and literary representations about Black women. The text's backdrop is the proliferation of femicide in the Dominican Republic. As an alternative to death, *Carmen: FotonovelARTE* gives us a glimpse into the life of a Black Dominicana survivor. Carmen's life is so ordinary, her movements throughout the text so quotidian: she gets dressed, takes a bus, watches a volleyball match. Readers may mistakenly dismiss her and the text, particularly given our impatience and preference for multilayered, complicated entertainment. And yet it is in the absence of fantasy or drama that we see the possibility for rebellion. *Carmen: FotonovelARTE* is about common, everyday life as it should be: devoid of drama and violence.

Carmen: FotonovelARTE embodies the history of millions of women who have died at the hands of their partners or the state because they attempted to live their own lives in dignity. In an essay included in the book, feminist scholar Esther Hernández-Medina explains what is at stake in the project.

Nuestra Carmen vive. Vive y con su vida reescribe la historia de millones de mujeres. Como la Carmen de Prosper Mérimée/Georges Bizet, decide, camina, baila, coquetea, seduce con sus ojos y todo su ser, al hombre que quiere querer. La Carmen de Mérimée y Bizet muere. Muerta violentamente por celos. . . . Muerta por querer vivir con desparpajo propio, sus aciertos y desaciertos, por ser y querer su libertad, por amar sin reglas, por hacer lo que como mujer . . . no debe. . . . Nuestra Carmen vive. Y vive apasionada, de forma complete y genuina. . . . Nuestra Carmen vive por ella, para ella y de ella. . . . Y ese es un acto revolucionario, evolucionario para las mujeres. Ha sido considerado un gran crimen vivir para una misma, no vivir para el otro o para la otra, saber decir que no y saber decir que si.[106]

[Our Carmen lives. She lives, and with her life she rewrites the history of millions of women. Like Prosper Mérimée/Georges Bizet's Carmen, she decides, walks, dances, flirts, seduces the man she wants to love with her eyes and her whole being. But Mérimée and Bizet's Carmen dies. She dies violently because of jealousy. . . . Dies because she wanted to live her own life freely, make her own mistakes and triumphs, dies because she wanted to be, she wanted her freedom, she loved without rules, dies because she dares to do what as a woman . . . she was not supposed to. . . . Our Carmen lives. She lives full of passion, completely and genuinely. Our Carmen lives for herself, to herself, and from herself. . . . And that is a revolutionary and evolutionary act for women. It has been considered a great crime for women to live for themselves, instead of for others, to know how to say no and how to say yes.]

Hernández-Medina argues that Báez's Carmen rewrites this violent history, contradicting death with a practice of living grounded on the community-sustained affirmation of the woman-self.

Community is a part of Baez's *Carmen: FotonovelARTE* in three ways: (1) production, (2) narrative structure, and (3) the complicity between the reader and the text. The book is the result of a communal creative project in which three members of the Ay Ombe Theatre collective participated in various roles under the artistic direction of Josefina Báez: Pilar Espinal, Carmen Inés Bencosme, and Esther Hernández-Medina. Espinal, who performs Carmen in the book's photos, is both the muse and the vessel for the character Báez imagines and synthesizes in the fotonovela. An actress, model, and yoga instructor, Espinal was charged with conveying the essence of the levente women of Báez's previous work: the women of El Nié who inhabit the nation building and the literary and cultural representations of women pitted against death for the purpose of entertainment. Wanting to subvert that toxic narrative, Báez gives us a Carmen that, by way of Espinal, is full of joy and love even in the face of adversity. The process, as the women explained to me, was highly communal. Báez says, "I had an idea, and my idea was to have the story of Carmen be told not from what I wanted but from the moment that the DR was living."[107] For Bencosme, photographing Espinal was a highly synchronous act. She says, "We barely had to speak. From the moment Pilar arrived in my office, she was in character. The transformation was instantaneous. Her demeanor, her aura, everything. I did not have to tell her to pose or to move a certain way, I merely had to witness, to be present."[108] The spontaneity of the project allowed Espinal to interact with the everyday life of Santo Domingo. Writing the text, Báez recalls, thus required a lot of adaptability, a "self-editing of the egos" that allowed the communal process to come through: "I wanted every moment to be infused with the beauty and with all that is simple. I wanted to subvert Mérimée's Carmen and have this levente Carmen come out instead. The how, though, was spontaneous at times. It was about Pilar's walks and encounters in the streets. It was about meeting life where life is and capturing it in beauty."[109] Community gave birth to Carmen, and in the process, she became a contra*diction* of death, her life a testimony of Black women living.

The narrative structure of *Carmen: FotonovelARTE* also centers community as key to daily living. Carmen cares for her ill elderly auntie while being sustained emotionally by her cousins and neighbors who share with her the joys and perils of everyday life. But that community does not dilute the "I" of Carmen; rather, it elevates it to its maximum potential. Carmen is able to declare her "yo" because of the "nosotras" that bears her. In this way, the text is a tangible manifestation of the praxis of performance autology developed by Báez over a period of thirty years, which sits at the center of each of the Ay Ombe Collective's projects. Performance autology is a spiritual and physical practice that centers consciousness and awareness of one's body and self through meditation, physical exercise, diet, health awareness, and creative discipline. The artist/participant learns to listen to her body and her needs, first and foremost, and from there enact a life that cares for the whole person, not just the craft.

This revolutionary method is also supported through a community of care. Members of the collective meet annually for retreats aimed at supporting each other's growth as people and creators. For the Ay Ombe Collective members, care is both individual and mutual. It contrasts forms of

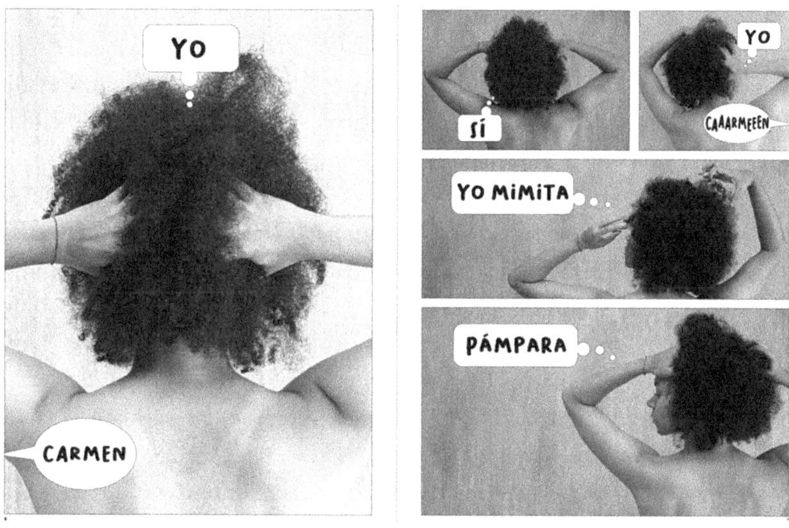

FIGURE 3.8 *Carmen: FotonovelARTE.* Courtesy of Carmen Inés Bencosme.

self-care that promote capitalist consumption. Care is a daily act of presence and consciousness, or, as Báez explains, "It is about meeting life where we are rather than being aspirational. From where we are we can create and craft and live. From where we are and what we have we can be. It is as it is."[110] Espinal's and Bencosme's training in performance autology allowed them to cocreate *Carmen: FotonovelARTE* without much rehearsal or preplanning. Explaining her role in the project, Espinal said, "Our practice and our understanding of our craft every day allowed for all of it to flow in such a way that very little had to be negotiated. I was Carmen, and Carmen had the movements that Pilar has practiced through Ay Ombe, and they all came through at once, effortless. It was a beautiful process, *una chulería.*"[111]

On pages 8 and 9 (see figure 3.8) we find Carmen posing for herself, her back facing us as she massages her afro, seductively turning her head from side to side saying, "Yo, Carmen, Yo Caaarmeeen, Yo mimita."[112] Like a repeated mantra, Carmen's insistent "I" and the simple and individual act of naming herself repeatedly ("Yo Carmen") perform what Hernández-Medina calls the unthinkable act of liberation: the possibility of living by and through herself, against the hegemonic narrative of abnegation that is imposed on Dominicanas by religious and cultural norms that are sustained and institutionalized by the state. The protagonist presents herself—and by extension the multitude of women she represents and embodies—as the agent of her individual destiny and part of the collective. As she does so, she also reminds us that her declaration of freedom has political implications. It is "un pellizco que les recuerda a todos los de los partidos políticos que siempre nos han vendido" (a pinch that reminds all those political party people that have always sold us out).[113] Carmen's "I" is thus in contra*diction* with "civic death."[114]

Báez's literary work is characterized by a feminist framework that centers the personhood and agency of the individual as the center of the collective. Community uplifts the Black woman, who in turn enriches the community by nourishing and cherishing herself. The community is made of life-affirming individuals who come together to cocreate the collective. Báez's feminist arc is particularly central in her 2007 performance text, *Comrade, Bliss Ain't Playing*, which challenges institutionalized determinations of the self—the nation, family, religion, language—affirming, "I am the chosen one," "I am my own tradition," "I am that I am."[115] This manifesto of the self is also a manifesto of migration as a human experience of the self.

> I have been migrating since birth. In fact, migration first comes visible exactly at birth. . . . Migration rapidly wrapped all my existence. . . . Migrating every day. Day to night. To too many places I have arrived. From many places I have left. . . . All ask the same questions: Where are you from? When are you leaving? Where are you going? Like if a "place" would be the thing. What if I tell you that I am that place—where I am, come from and will definitely leave.[116]

These words echo those of Anacaona's cofounder, Marlene de la Cruz: "Rejection here, rejection there. They think they are so big in not wanting us. They just don't get that we don't need them. We got us. Who needs them? We are our own country."[117] Both Báez's text and de la Cruz's words declare liberation from the nation, reclaiming the Black woman as the owner of her body in movement and definer of her own belonging.

In *Comrade, Bliss Ain't Playing*, we find an affirmation of Black women's individuality as a contra*diction* to silencing and death. In *Levente no: Yolayorkdominicanyork*, Báez writes a self-affirming individual woman again, this time as part of a community. She is the "ella-pueblos" (she-people) who embodies multitudes and lives with other women in the interstices of belonging and unbelonging, joy and struggle. Báez locates these interstices in the nation building of El Nié: "We all live in the same building. El Nié. My mother, grandmother, la comadre-mi madrina, el ejemplo, la quiero a morir. Estela La Colora del 3A. La flaca del 6J."[118] As the text names each of the residents of El Nié, we learn their stories and their struggles. In the process, their multiplicity becomes one as their stories are possessed by one another in the nonlinear narrative of Black Dominicanas' fight against death: "Nothing to brag about. This building is full of strong, sometimes sad, lonely women and fatherless children. Eso sí, every apartment cómo casita de muñecas. But then again, that's the real reality. Redundante, dice mi mama. . . . Sooner or later you end up like this. We got it sooner. No sweat. Capicúa big time. Big time capicúa."[119] Carmen lives in apartment 6E. She is a flirtatious and feisty woman who loves music and dancing and who is not afraid of using her sexuality to attract attention. As she leaves home each morning to work in the cigar factory uptown, men from the nearby car repair shop and construction sites come out to catcall her. Rather than shy away or get angry, Carmen

> camina. Sonríe. Se acerca al grupo y le toca el güebo a uno. Le busca en el bolsillo a otro. Y sigue caminando como si nada. Cuando regresa siempre le tiene una sorpresa. Una vez le sacó una teta. Otra vez se puso pintalabios rojo frente a ellos. Le ha cantado. Le ha dicho secretos. El repertorio es inmenso como el Mar Caribe.[120]
>
> [walks. Smiles. She comes near the group and touches one of the men's dicks. Sticks her hand in another man's pocket. Then keeps walking like nothing. When she comes back from work, she always has a surprise for them. One time she took out a tit. Another time she applied red lipstick in front of them. She has sung to them. Told them secrets. The repertoire is as immense as the Caribbean Sea.]

Carmen is a levente. She owns her body and uses it as she pleases. She walks the streets like she belongs. She is not afraid of anyone, nor does she answer to anyone. She is a fierce woman of El Nié who is not confined to the nation's borders. She transgresses, and she owns the streets. Returning "home," Carmen also breaks the dichotomies of migration that seek to confine women's bodies to here or there. Instead, read across Báez's textual and visual interpretations, Carmen is not just a Black migrant woman. She is as she is.

The Levente Visual series, via Carmen, introduces the Black woman's levente body in the public space as a site of belonging against death. In so doing, it confronts the silences and exclusions that for hundreds of years have plagued Dominicanas at home and in the diaspora through the simple act of existing. As Black women, we are often told we need to be more and do more to contrast the intersecting violence of racism and sexism. Carmen, though, shows that the act of being is already radical enough in a world that constantly conspires to end our existence. Carmen's daily levente existence is thus a rebellion against death. Transported to the Dominican Republic, the Carmen we meet in the fotonovela occupies every part of the city: the public buses, the Malecón, the colonial city, the shops, and the streets, her body becoming one with the space. Reclaiming "leventismo" as liberation, Báez's work makes room for women's expressions of love, frustration, anger, joy, and sensuality by portraying them in the simplicity of the quotidian rather than as exaggerated or exceptional characters. Leventes can be vulgar and defiant, speak about politics and sex, love and be angry in the safe space of El Nié. They are also mothers and daughters carrying out daily acts of care, going to work, washing dishes, and cooking.

I have been following the work of Báez and the Ay Ombe Collective since I was fifteen years old. First as a bystander, then as a scholar, and later as a member of the collective, I came to appreciate the aesthetic contributions of Báez's work to both performance art and literature. In previous works, I have analyzed several of her texts and engaged with her ideas—including El Nié—as theoretical contributions to our understanding of the intersections of race, migration, and Latinidad. I am embarrassed to admit that it was not until the publication of *Carmen: FotonovelARTE*, however, that I came to understand the feminist counterdiscourse of Báez's corpus as a Black Latina feminist praxis against death. Reading her oeuvre and engaging with performance autology personally and through interviews with other members of the collective, I am reminded not only of the radical hope for what could be but also of the tangible ways Black women have known how to live in contra*diction* with death despite the national structures and institutional constraints that persist in silencing and erasing us. While the political work to demand inclusion remains essential, the Ay Ombe Collective reminds us that other ways have always been possible, that life belongs to us all and that living is a revolutionary act. This act, embodied also in the lives of Sagrario Díaz, Augustina Rivas, Yolanda, and Mercedes Frías, is all the revolution needed to create a world/community/nation without a nation in which we can thrive. Our living in community is our weapon against despair and our rebellion against death. In community, we—Black women, Black Latinas, Black migrants—are our own nation.

4 THE AFTERLIFE OF COLONIAL GENDER VIOLENCE

Black Immigrant Women's Life and Death in Postcolonial Italy

Coloniality renders racism timeless. —GRADA KILOMBA, *Plantation Memories*

On September 10, 2012, twenty-one-year-old Carolina Payano went out for an *aperetivo* with her husband and their eighteen-month-old daughter in Milan's hip Porta Romana neighborhood. Payano had moved to Italy only two years earlier to join her forty-one-year-old husband, Massimiliano Spelta, whom she had met in her native Santo Domingo at age sixteen.[1] Payano was unhappy in Milan. The Spelta family rejected her because of her race and culture, which they perceived to be backward.[2] Her husband was always traveling for business. The young mother and her child stayed "locked up and alone" in what was still a strange city.[3] "She was so sad," remembers her sister. "All she wanted was to go back to her barrio, to her family and friends."[4] Payano often expressed her disappointment about Italy and her desire to return to the island.[5] She was tired of being judged by the color of her skin and treated like a *sanky panky* (a tourist's sex companion) by her in-laws and strangers alike.[6] But on that September day, Payano was excited to go out with her family. She dressed up, got the baby ready, and posted selfies on social media so everyone would know she was having fun.

As the saying goes, *la felicidad dura poco*. Upon leaving the bar, with the baby in her arms, Payano and her husband were each shot several times in the head and chest. Less than ten seconds later, the couple lay dead on the ground. The unharmed baby cried desperately, covered in blood, until emergency vehicles arrived at the scene. Milan shook with the crime and the media frenzy that followed. As police investigated the murders, eventually linking it to the Spelta family's drug-trafficking business, media reactions centered on Payano—or rather, on her body.[7] The media linked the crime to this "ragazza esuberante straniera" (exuberant foreign girl) whose "exotic" body encapsulated the corruption, criminality, and foreignness of the Caribbean sexscape.[8] It was only a matter of time, said one journalist, before "l'arretratezza di queste persone, i loro modi selvaggi, hanno contagiato la nostra grande città" (the backwardness of these people, their savage ways, infected our great city).[9]

In the days that followed the crime, the media juxtaposed images of Payano's "exuberant" body with photos of tropical sandy beaches and gratuitous assessments of Latin American poverty.[10] In these representations, Payano embodied fantasies about the Caribbean, particularly the fantasy of the exotic (and tragic) mulata caribeña that has circulated in Italy and other parts of the Mediterranean since the mid-sixteenth century.[11] The media represented Payano simultaneously as a symbol of desire, a site for Italian escapades, and the location of poverty and backwardness—a tropical island in need of "civilized sustenance and aid" from the Global North. Representations of Spelta, on the other hand, reflected Italian desire for the Caribbean fantasy. He was "innamorato di Santo Domingo, tanto da sposare una ragazza dominicana di 21 anni" (so in love with Santo Domingo that he married a twenty-one-year-old Dominican girl).[12] Their marriage was seen as impulsive—a side effect of the "tropical fever" that takes over white tourists in the Caribbean.[13] Concurrently inviting the viewer to participate in desiring and rejecting Payano's body, the media comforted the presumed-white Italian audience, reassuring them that the Caribbean fantasy she represented and the legacy of Italian whiteness her motherhood threatened were safe.

As the chapter epigraph by Grada Kilomba reminds us, racism becomes eternal, a quality of certain bodies, through the prevalence of colonial thought in the diaspora.[14] In her posthumous representations in Italian media, Payano enacts the perdurance of the afterlife of colonialism. As Gaia Giuliani argues, Italy's colonial memory is "elliptical"—going back and forth between desire for a past colonialism and the need to address the present, in which

Italians of color are part of the nation. This elliptical desire shapes the everyday experiences of racism and violence against Black Italians and immigrants of color in contemporary Italy.[15] Thus, Payano's embodiment of the "residue" of colonial sexual exploitation is twofold: it translates Italian colonial violence through the recognizable lens of colonialism and its afterlives, and it renders migrant exclusion in the Global North as its "elliptical" manifestation in the present.

Emigration, Colonialism, and White Italianità

Despite the fact that Christopher Columbus was Italian, Italy is not usually invoked in conversations about Global North settler colonialism. On the one hand, this is due to the fact that Italy did not become a unified nation until 1861, and on the other, because of a deliberate and conscious effort on the part of the Italian state to "rehabilitate the national image that had been damaged by the events of World War II" by suppressing colonial memory.[16] By mystifying colonialism, Italy has escaped the kind of anti-colonial critique that proliferates in US, French, and British academies. The fact that Italy has been imagined as an immigrant-sending, Second World, Latin, and, sometimes, an "almost Southern" nation has also permitted it to escape political scrutiny.[17] Yet, while Italians were immigrating to North and South America by the thousands from 1890 to 1950, the Italian empire was establishing colonies in Africa. By 1914, for instance, Italy had annexed Eritrea, Somalia, and Libya. Italy's colonialism in Africa involved "land expropriations, forced removal of masses of people, the creation of internment camps and the ruthless and inhuman military retaliation against resistance movements, the use of gas against civilians and the enforcement of apartheid measures between white Italians and Africans."[18] Italy's colonialism was no different than other European colonialisms in its violence, cruelty, and perdurance. Until recently, though, it has gotten a "pass" in terms of historical and social postcolonial critique.[19]

African colonization helped Italy, as a young nation, form a sense of national identity in a deeply fragmented and culturally diverse territory. Rhetoric of dominance and superiority over its African colonies bridged the north-south divide that continued to disrupt Italian unity after Risorgimento.[20] Italian unification depended upon the internal colonization of the South, and by extension of Italian southerners whom the urban elite and the emerging middle class of the northern and central regions viewed as uncivilized and racially inferior.[21] The perception of southern Italians as racially inferior influenced not only southerners' place within the emerging Italian nation but also the place

Italian emigrants occupied in the racial imaginary of the diaspora, especially in the United States during Jim Crow.[22] Giuliani argues that "southern Italians' violent and uncontrollable ways were a matter of widespread debate in the US and Australian scientific and political circles," which ultimately made Italians appear "unreliable and unfit for citizenship" in the diaspora.[23]

Less than a decade after unification, Italy became the largest emigrant nation in the modern world. Between 1876 and 1976, about twenty-six million Italians migrated to other parts of Europe, the United States, and South America. The racialization of Italians as other than white in the United States has been the subject of numerous studies.[24] While acknowledging the complexities of Italian whiteness/nonwhiteness in the US diaspora is important to our understanding of race and national belonging in the United States, we must also recognize that Italian racialization in the diaspora is entangled with Italy's colonial yearnings in Africa and the depiction of Italian people as benevolent colonizers. That is, Italian emigration allowed the Italian unified nation to imagine itself as a sprawling diaspora, an idea that sustained early colonial expansion. National belonging was thus articulated as inherent to the social and cultural "essence" of Italian people through what is widely referred to as *italianità* (Italianness).

Grounded in Italian colonial Fascism, italianità is a racialized term in which the "essence" of being Italian is imagined as being carried in "the blood" of white Italians. This essence means that Italianness is portable and not lost with emigration. The flip side of this logic is that italianità cannot be acquired, only inherited, a notion that has led to the exclusion of descendants of immigrants of color from belonging to the nation. The discourse of italianità continues to render Italian-born children of immigrants of color "foreigners" by virtue of jus sanguinis legislation and practices of cultural exclusion. Descendants of nonwhite immigrants in Italy are identified as hyphenates and perceived to be foreign. The "immigrant" status of Second Generation descendants of immigrants marks racial difference without naming race. Moreover, Italy has no official language to name racial diversity; Italians are imagined, though unnamed, as white. Consequently, everyone who is not white is presumed foreign, a presumption that materializes in the common cultural practice of asking Italians of color for their "origin."[25] The refusal to culturally and legally admit new citizens of color into the nation, instead prolonging their alignment with the immigrant status of their parents, is an example of colonialism sustaining the internal racial borders of the nation through exclusionary notions of citizenship based on colonial categories of racial exclusion. The category "immigrant" is a present-day manifestation of Fascist colonial racism in postcolonial Italy.

Cultural studies scholar Iain Chambers argues that in Italy, xenophobia "has much to do with the failure and unwillingness to work through a still largely unconscious European past in which colonialism and empire were (and are) distilled into national configurations of identity, culture, modernity, and progress."[26] Similarly, Puerto Rican literary critic Yolanda Martínez-San Miguel invites us to think about the ways colonial and imperial relationships between the Caribbean and Europe and the United States have shaped the experiences of Black diasporic subjects. She argues that "coloniality further complicates the conceptualization of ethnic identities in a postcolonial era by producing subjects who are legal citizens, but who in fact function as marginalized and racialized ethnic minorities in the metropolitan centers of Western Europe and North America."[27] The fact that Italy continues to uphold jus sanguinis citizenship means that descendants of diasporic subjects are not entitled to Italian citizenship at birth and are in turn subjected to a constant process of recolonization.

Three violent colonial histories shape Payano's life in the diaspora, intersecting through her body. The first is fifteenth-century Spanish, French, and British settler colonialism in Hispaniola that led to genocide, slavery, land erosion, and the global production of the Black female body as exotic and for consumption. Second is nineteenth- and twentieth-century North American colonialism that opened doors to sex tourism, labor exploitation of poor Black people, and intra-island border conflicts. And third is twenty-first-century Global North colonialism that manifests in land expropriation, sex tourism, and forced migration of the divested poor. For a Black immigrant woman like Payano, these intersections mean that her body and the histories and geographies that make up her subjecthood, belonging, and home are distilled in the Italian diaspora through a palimpsestic colonial lens. Her migration to Italy was a consequence of the effects of centuries of European and US colonialism in the Dominican Republic. Yet in Italy, her presence summons the ghosts of *another* colonialism: nineteenth-century Italian colonization of the Horn of Africa. The crossings of colonial violence through Payano signal the urgency for historically situated, transnational examinations of the intersections of colonialism, race, and immigration in the new millennium.

Fatima El-Tayeb argues that a translocal approach to "the complex interactions of race, religion, migration and colonialism haunting the presence of minorities of color in Europe might be best explored through a shift away from the vertical look at one ethnic group . . . toward a horizontal perspective crossing various national and ethnic divides."[28] Following El-Tayeb's call, this chapter examines how multiple modes of past and present colonialisms intersect in contemporary Italy through the lived experiences and moving bodies of Black immigrant women. Juxtaposing the figure of the Eritrean *madama* popularized through photographs, music, and postcards during the Italian occupation of Eritrea (1889–1941) with contemporary media and popular representation of the Caribbean sanky panky, I trace the historical junctures of colonial gendered violence in its effects on the everyday lives of Black immigrant women in postcolonial metropolises. I also look at how Black immigrant women bear witness to the violence of colonialism and slavery in the diaspora as their bodies become "affective archives" of colonial violence.[29] As we will see in chapter 5, these memories and images are contra*dicted* through networks of inclusion and political contestation for Black women artists and activists to engage in historical translations of their own coloniality in the diaspora. Asserting their blackness, sexual autonomy, and right to motherhood, Black immigrant women challenge Italian colonial structures and affirm their political belonging to the nation(s) that exclude them.

"Black Females": Racism and Misogyny in Colonial East Africa

Femmine ce ne sono in colonia, nere esuberanti e generose; mancano le donne, le quali non possono essere che bianche. —Renato Paoli, *Nella colonia Eritrea*

As many feminist scholars have argued, the possession of women, and I would specify Black and Brown women, is, as Ann Laura Stoler puts it, not only a "metaphor of colonial power but its currency."[30] Colonial authority and racial distinction are structured in gendered terms. As a result, Black and Brown female bodies are not only icons of sexualized beauty or transactional commodities but also sites of contestation between colonizers and colonized peoples; their images become conflated with colonial domination. Enslaved women, as Marisa Fuentes reminds us, were "dispossessed" of their lives, as their bodies served as sites for capitalist production through sexual violence and labor.[31] The violence enacted on their bodies for the sake of production and reproduction, as Jennifer Morgan argues, dispossessed enslaved women of their relationships to their own bodies and disrupted their connections to motherhood and family.[32] In colonial documents, narratives, and visual representations, naked Brown and Black bodies were objects of conquest, justifying the civilizing mission. Columbus often wrote about the breasts and "beautiful bodies" of Taína natives.[33] Equating them to Eve's naivete and sinfulness, he argued for the need to "Christianize" the natives and "dress them with civilization" to guarantee their salvation.[34] Columbus and other conquerors believed these naked natives, like Eve, had the potential to become "treacherous" carriers of mestizaje. One example of this is La Malinche, the translator, informer, and mistress of Hernán Cortés. La Malinche is the symbolic mother of the mestizo population of Mexico and a complicated, contradictory symbol of miscegenation and racial translation in the Mexican racial imaginary.

At the beginning of the eighteenth century, the myth of the "tragic mulata" as a "fallen woman" began to proliferate in colonial circuits, inundating literary and cultural representations of mixed-race Black women in the colonial Hispanic Caribbean and Brazil.[35] In *The Repeating Body*, Kimberly Juanita Brown argues that the "residue of sexual exploitation on slave women's bodies is the afterimage of black diaspora, the puncture of the past materializing in the present."[36] Symbolic of exoticized, feminized Caribbean blackness, the mulata became a transnational symbol of Cubanía in the nineteenth century.[37] Like the mestiza in Mexico, the figure of the mulata came to quintessentially signify racially unified Caribbean nations. Through her, the violence of colonization was symbolically displaced by the notions of unity and belonging.

Simultaneous to the development of the concepts of mulataje and mestizaje in the Americas, images of Native and Black women appeared in travel narratives, novels, drawings, and magazines that circulated through the colonial circuits of Europe and the United States from the late fifteenth century to the early twentieth century.[38] Through these images, Native, Black, and mulata women were imagined as "sexually dangerous" and devious.[39] Early twentieth-century US American cartography, for example, depicted the naked brown breasts of native Filipinas as markers of their "savage sexuality" to justify imperial intervention.[40] European and US colonialism in the Global South thus produced an archive of nude photography, pornographic literature, and travel narratives that exploited the bodies of women of color for white consumption, while at the same time justifying imperial will in the name of civilization, Christianity, and decency. As postcolonial nations developed in the Americas, these images were transformed into symbols of racial unity that silenced colonial violence and replaced it with the benevolent narrative of hybridity: the mestiza or mulata as the mother of the nation. But as Brown argues, the "afterimage" of the colonial gaze continues to shape Black women's lives and belonging in the nation and the diaspora.[41] The hypervisibility of their oversexualized images, paired with the repetition of Black women's bodies as "objects of articulation for men to write through," renders our subjecthood invisible even when symbolically important to the projects of empire and nation building.[42] The symbol replaces Black women's subjectivities, rendering their unbelonging to the nation.

This cyclical, self-perpetuating, transnational ethos of colonialism operated and continues to operate in Italy and the rest of the Global North through the conceptualization of Black and Brown women as "females" rather than women, that is, as bodies for consumption. Though Italy did not directly partake in the settler colonization of the Americas, it played a key role in the production of white European supremacy in the Global South through epistemological, artistic, political, cultural, and religious economies of Europe in the fifteenth to nineteenth centuries. The figure of Columbus as the great conqueror of the Americas, for example, is central to the republican projects of Latin American mestizaje. Likewise, colonial structures that engendered slavery, miscegenation, the exploitation of Native and Black women, and other colonial cruelties traveled back to Italy, shaping its theories and practices in the nineteenth and twentieth centuries as it colonized Eritrea, Somalia, and Libya.

During the roughly seven decades of Italian colonialism in Eritrea (1882–1941), photographs, stories, and music depicting Black women as adventurous and "looking for white men" were disseminated in the colonial circuits of Europe and North America.[43] Colonial military recruitment ads, postcards, and photographs appealed to Italian men's investment in virility, promising the wide availability of "Black Venuses" as rewards for their service to the patria in the solidification of Africa Orientale Italiana (Italian East Africa).[44] Through extensive state involvement and propaganda that included world's fairs, newspaper ads, music, film, live human exhibitions, and photographs, Africa and Africans became central to defining Italian identity in the newly unified nation.[45] During the first half of the twentieth century, for example, school curricula and textbooks preached Italians' responsibility to civilize "barbaric" Africans in what Giuliani calls the "epic return of modern Rome."[46] By narrativizing their twentieth-century colonization of East Africa as a repetition of the Roman conquest of Libya, the Italian state conceptualized it as the completion of a colonial project and the destiny of the Italian people. The language of historical legitimacy, racial and moral superiority, and "African savagery" depicted Italian colonialism as benevolent and Italians as *brava gente* (good people) whose role in Africa was to "liberate people from slavery (Eritrea) or the Muslim/Turkish yoke" and, in return, "in the (Eritrean) colony, all the disparate dialects of Italy would meld as in a purifying crucible from which a harmonious Italic idiom would emerge vivid, sharp and clear, the same for everyone and familiar to all and for all."[47] As colonization became the unifying language of the emergence of the Italian nation, the representation of Black people as inferior and uncivilized subjects was its most important symbol.

Benito Mussolini often said that Italian colonization of East Africa "was not about subjugation but about expansion."[48] For many Italians, this expansion not only was territorial but also included claiming the bodies of African women. When a land is possessed by force, so are the people who inhabit it. Fascist journalist Indro Montanelli provided one illustration of this argument in his misogynistic and racist assertion that Italian colonizers did not go abroad to kill Africans but "to make love to their women."[49] Colonial propaganda successfully shaped the collective imagination about blackness in Italy, leading to the conceptualization of African women as uncivilized and hypersexual. Images of the so-called Black Venuses—photos of nude Black women imitating Barthélemy Prieur's iconic early seventeenth-century sculpture or referencing Sandro Botticelli's painting—became screens onto which Italian racial fears and erotic stereotypes could be projected.[50] Unlike Botticelli's (white) *Birth of Venus*, which is revered as an emblem of beauty and femininity, Black Venuses were the backdrop for voyeuristic and sexual fantasies of domination that began to appear in sixteenth-century European literary and artistic representation and persisted well into the twentieth century in popular culture, particularly in photography and film.[51] These photographs conveyed the "very ambivalent territory between the artistic portrayals of the aestheticized exotic female body and the pornographic look."[52] The Black Venus photos were taken in photography studios with props and attire that created the illusion of a woman "petrified in time," savage and sexually available for Italian consumption and domination.[53] But as Daniela Baratieri's research demonstrates, pornographic pictures of girls and women were also taken in other settings, including brothels and syphilis hospitals.[54] The advent of photography, as Sandra Ponzanesi argues, gave "visual form to colonial culture" and helped create a "link between the empire and the domestic imagination."[55] For Alessandro Triulzi, this link makes it so that "il passato coloniale del nostro paese . . . non è ancora *passato*" (the colonial past in our country . . . is not yet *past*); that is, it has not become part of the national memory as historical events should, which allows Italy to continue to pretend this violence did not (and does not) happen.[56]

The colonization of Africa coincided with the marketing and wide accessibility of the first portable camera (invented by George Eastman in 1889). By the 1920s and 1930s, at the height of the Fascist colonial regime, the average ranking officer could afford a camera. Based on the high volume of photos that proliferate in the private and public archives of colonial East Africa, we could infer that many of them owned cameras and used them often.[57] As Triulzi argues, the access to photography blurred the lines between the personal and the public and allowed for the production and proliferation of images of East Africa that reflected stories and ideologies that went beyond the national agenda of pacification and militarization.[58] Unlike the visual art and human exhibits of the seventeenth and eighteenth centuries that were reserved for the consumption of the European elite, the popularization of photography made "Black Venuses" available to a colossal economically diverse audience beyond the colonies and extended the perdurance of its violence to the present.[59] In this climate of unfiltered image making, pornographic photography was suddenly accessible beyond the photographic studio, allowing for the mass violation of photographed women. As Susan Sontag argues, "To photograph people is to violate them."[60] I extend that to assert that to photograph colonized others is an act of colonial violence that memorializes and perpetuates that violation for subsequent generations. The perdurance of the images of violence recolonizes postcolonial subjects.

One of the images that proliferates in the colonial photographic archive of the Black Venus is that of the Eritrean madama or concubine. Eritrea was Italy's *primogenita* (firstborn) colony and the economic center of the colonial government. As such, Eritrean women were the first to be sacrificed in the service of the empire. White Italian men who arrived in Eritrea at the turn of the twentieth century usually traveled alone; those who were married often left their wives and kids at home.[61] In the colonies, the military introduced and imposed its own classifications for sexual relationships. Baratieri asserts that among the few Ethiopian words learned by deployed Italian soldiers were "those necessary to assess the social and marital status of women as a prelude to sexual predation."[62] In Eritrea, women were divided into narrow categories of sexual consumption: brothel prostitutes or madamas.[63]

Madamato was a colonial version of Eritrean domestic partnership that existed alongside formal marriage before Italian colonization in which a woman or girl, known as a *dämoz*, would be promised to a man as a companion. In this arrangement, the man had to support the woman and their offspring, providing for all the necessities, including inheritances for the children. Abandonment of a dämoz and her children was culturally unacceptable, and at times prosecuted.[64] Under the Italian colonial regime, madamato was transformed into a colonial institution that was largely unregulated, and which allowed for men to abandon their offspring and discard madamas at their will. As Fascist legislation became concerned with madamato in the 1930s, it became a criminalized practice in ways that served the purpose of the colonial enterprise and without consideration of the personhood of participating girls and women. During the first three decades of the occupation of Eritrea, madamas often lived with Italian men, offering them what Ruth Iyob calls the "comforts of home": keeping house, providing company, and even bearing children.[65] During the occupation of Eritrea, madamas came to signify an Eritrean girl or woman in an exclusively sexual and affective relationship with an Italian man. The Italian empire did not legally recognize madamato. Rather, it was viewed as different from marriage because an African woman in a relationship with an Italian man could not acquire the legal status of wife. Renato Paoli summarizes the Italian sentiment of the time: "Femmine ce ne sono in colonia, nere esuberanti e generose; mancano le donne, le quali non possono essere che bianche" (There are females in the colony, black, exuberant, and generous; but there is a lack of women, who can be only white).[66] Italians denied African women's humanity, rendering them devoid of social and political agency.

Colonial madamato was complex and full of contradictions for the women and girls who participated in it. As Giulia Barrera's research shows, madamas came from all nine of the ethnic groups that made up colonial Eritrea as well as from the neighboring region of Tigray.[67] This diversity meant that madamas had a range of attitudes and ideas about their roles and relationships to Italian men. Likewise, Italian men who participated in madamato came from different regions and social classes. For many women and their mixed-race children, madamato led to exploitation, pedophilia, rape, abandonment, and social ostracism. While there is little documentation on the everyday lives of madamas from their perspectives, oral testimony and literature can help us piece together fragments of their experiences to imagine how they lived.[68] One such fragment is the 1991 novel *L'abbandono: Una storia eritrea*, by white Italo-Eritrean writer Erminia Dell'Oro.[69] The novel memorializes the social ostracism suffered by abandoned madamas and their *métis* (mixed-race) children through the story of Sellass, a young girl who enters a madamato with an Italian soldier only to be abandoned by him after birthing two children. Still a girl herself, Sellass is left to fend for herself, facing rejection and resentment from both Italians, who see her as a corruptor of the race, and Eritreans, who perceive her abandonment as shameful. While there are earlier literary depictions of madamas, including the celebrated novel *Femina Somala* (1933), by Gino Mitrano Sani, and *Tempo di uccidere* (1947), by Ennio Flaiano (made into the successful film *Time to Kill* in 1989), Dell'Oro's is the first Italian novel written from the perspective of a madama and by a woman writer.

As in other forms of colonial concubinage—including present-day Caribbean *sankipankismo*—madamas exchanged sex and companionship for material and economic gain. But while colonial sexual relationships are always hierarchical, we cannot deny that many Eritrean women also had agency and used madamato for social mobility, access, and economic security. Iyob argues that the colonial madama was "an interlocutor between the Italian soldier/settler and the traditional power-brokers," a role that differentiated her from state-sanctioned brothel prostitutes who had very little access to social mobility.[70] While madamas were contractual partners, some acquired higher status as members of colonial households during the first two decades of the occupation, allowing them to inhabit a higher social status within the colonial order. Some madamas, in particular those who were older and more educated, had public lives and gained power and acceptance from other local women. These positions were highly negotiated through their partners' military roles and rankings, their ability to speak Italian, whether or not they had mixed-race children, and, most importantly, the statuses the men negotiated of behalf of the madamas within the local society.

The majority of madamas, though, did not acquire social mobility and were instead treated as objects of desire, or as servants to their partners. Images of madamas as seminude commodified bodies available for white Italian consumption inundated Italian literature, film, and visual arts from the beginning of the Italian occupation of Eritrea at the end of the nineteenth century until the middle of the twentieth century. Artist Enrico De Seta drew a series of racist cartoons depicting Black women as sex slaves and Black men as indolent slave traders (figure 4.1). While De Seta was an anti-Fascist artist, his critique of colonialism came at the expense of Black women. One of his most popular cartoons, "Ufficio postale" (At the post office) (figure 4.2), shows a white soldier holding a packaged bare-breasted Black woman he wants to mail to his friend. The mannequin-like woman is expressionless, while two small Black children watch with curiosity from outside the post office. Another of De Seta's colonial cartoons, "Al mercato" (At the market) (figure 4.1), shows a Black man selling a group of naked women to soldiers "at the most convenient price." At the height of Fascism in the 1930s, the colonial imagination shaped all political responses, producing Africans—and Africa—as exotic and unruly. Whatever the medium, young Black women and girls came to signify the Italian empire. These photos and caricatures—which can still be found in shops all over Italy, Asmara, and on eBay—are tangible evidence of the violence of Italian colonial expansion.

The racist political caricatures of Black women that circulated at the beginning of the twentieth century were juxtaposed with photos of nude madamas.[71] Colonial-era photographs, postcards, advertisements, songs, films,

FIGURE 4.1 Africa Orientale series of postcards by Enrico De Seta, ca. 1930. "Al Mercato" appears in the third row on the right. Courtesy of Elena Rosso.

FIGURE 4.2 Enrico De Seta, "Ufficio postale," 1935–36. The text reads: "I wish to send this souvenir of East Africa to a friend of mine." From a series of postcards, Africa Orientale Italiana. Courtesy of Elena Rosso.

and literature produced madamas as a threat to italianità. In his celebrated *I misteri dell'Africa italiana* (Mysteries of Italian Africa), Tertulliano Gandolfi writes that the madama was the cause of Italian failure and misfortune, for she functioned as an "oasis of degeneration" for the colonial soldier.[72] Gandolfi notes, "Qui si vede l'incretinimento, l'imbestialimento, e il rammollimento degli uomini in modo spaventoso. . . . Forse sarà effetto del clima. Io non avrei mai parlato di madame, se non fosse stato che queste donne su tutte le nostre sciagure africane hanno pesato non poco luttuosamente" (Here we see men turning into fools, into beasts, and we see men softening in frightening ways. . . . Perhaps it is the effect of the climate. I would never have spoken of madamas, had it not been that these women on all our African misfortunes have weighed not a little mournfully).[73]

Madamas, Gandolfi imagines, had the power to seduce and enchant men, but the true danger lay in their potential to produce mixed-race children who could replace white Italians and whose dubious allegiance to italianità could destabilize the racial hierarchy of the colonializing nation: "Questi meticci, del color della cioccolata - che oramai ce ne sono sparsi da per tutto - un giorno saranno loro che ci scaccieranno dalla Colonia in odio ai loro padri, appunto come hanno fatto quelli delle Colonie portoghesi" (These chocolate-colored half-breeds—who are now scattered all over the place—will one day drive us out of the Colony in hatred of their fathers, just as they did in the Portuguese colonies).[74] Stoler writes that colonial concubinage "worked as long as European identity and supremacy was clear."[75] After the 1920s, with the rise of eugenics, colonial concubinage was outlawed throughout African, Asian, and Caribbean colonies and was replaced with a safer, more acceptable structure: legalized prostitution. This shift is most notable during early twentieth-century North American imperial interventions in the Caribbean (1914–34), in which white supremacist and eugenicist theories dominated cultural and political debates about race, physical ability, and miscegenation. Eugenics was implemented, in part, by way of laws that targeted immigration, sanitation, and reproduction. In the United States, for example, in 1907 Indiana passed the first eugenics-based sterilization law in the world. Thirty other US states soon followed. While it took until 1927 for a state eugenics sterilization law to be upheld, in 1921 the US Supreme Court deemed it constitutional to sterilize women in its occupied territories.[76] One effect of eugenics was a heightened fixation on the female body's reproductive potential, which in turn produced a heightened focus on prostitution as a point of national and global anxiety. This was particularly true in relation to questions of race and miscegenation in the Global North's colonies in Africa and the Caribbean. At the height of US eugenics debates, the US empire occupied the Dominican Republic (1916–24), Haiti (1914–34), and Puerto Rico (1898–). The colonial governments of these islands rehearsed a series of eugenics-based laws that led to forced sterilization, the legalization of prostitution, the incarceration of sex workers who tested positive for syphilis, and a ban on interracial concubinage between US soldiers and local women. At the same time, ethnographers and artists produced exoticized pornographic images of Black and Brown Caribbean women that, like those of the East African madamas, circulated all over North America and Europe. As I argue elsewhere, this early twentieth-century commercialized exploitation of Caribbean people, particularly women and queer people, opened the door to sex tourism and the sex trafficking of young adults and minors that continue to this day.[77]

Eugenics and scientific racism manifested most radically in the Italian empire during the rise of Fascism in the 1930s. Between 1937 and 1940, the Fascist regime deployed a series of legislative acts targeting Jews, sexual minorities, women in Italy, and Africans in the colonies. The most significant legislation concerned the enforcement of segregation through the Campo

Cintato (Fenced Camp), which determined a physical segregation of Europeans from Indigenous people in colonial Eritrea. The Campo Cintato (Kombishtato in Tigrinya) served as the model for South African apartheid.[78] Its afterlife perdures in today's Kombishtato neighborhood, an area in the center of Asmara that is the seed of the central government and where the rich and powerful reside.[79] But racial segregation was not restricted only to space; it extended to people. In 1937, for instance, in an effort to control miscegenation, madamato was criminalized. Italian men who engaged in madamato could be punished with up to five years in prison.[80] On May 13, 1940, Italy passed a law, Norme relative ai meticci (L822 1940), prohibiting white Italian men from claiming their mixed-race children and declaring that mixed-race children were "only Africans."[81] This anti-miscegenation act, which was the culmination of a series of laws and political campaigns aimed at criminalizing racial mixing, attempted to regulate not only the legal notions of citizenship but also people's ethnic, racial, and cultural identities.[82] For Barrera, the criminalization and fear of *métissage* (miscegenation) led to the poverty and disenfranchisement of thousands of mixed-race children, who were stereotyped as corruptors of society: "Many held the belief that mixed-race girls tended to become prostitutes while mixed-race boys easily became criminals."[83] This 1940 Fascist colonial legislation, I argue, continues to inform current Italian restrictions on citizenship for children of immigrants in contemporary Italy and shapes the cultural perception of Black and Brown Italians as foreign and unbelonging to the nation.

The conceptualization of mixed-race descendants of colonial sexual relationships as threats to the nation-state is one of the most pervasive legacies of colonialism. The visual and literary representations of colonial sexploitation, as well as the multiple laws aimed at controlling the cultural, ethnic, and political identities of the mixed-race children of white Italian and Black colonized Others, serve as a historical backdrop to the present-day coloniality of diasporic and immigrant women of color like Carolina Payano in contemporary Italy. Understanding how these regimes intersect can help establish the link between colonization and emigration as well as between colonial racism (slavery, apartheid, segregation) and present-day immigration policies and practices (from caging children at the US-Mexico border to shooting at boats of immigrants in the Mediterranean). For Payano, the phantom of Fascist colonialism facilitated the negation of her motherhood, womanhood, and subjecthood in both life and death. It also determined the fate of her daughter, whose cultural identity and link to her maternal family were legally severed in an effort to preserve "her well-being and assimilation" to italianità.[84]

The Afterlife of Colonial Madamato

The "afterimage" (to borrow Brown's adept terminology) of the Eritrean madama as a sexually devious Black Venus that circulated throughout Fascist Italy extended well into the second half of the twentieth century. Throughout the 1970s, for instance, the Italian film industry profited from the portrayal of Africa and Africans as savage and exotic. The work of legendary filmmaker Pier Paolo Pasolini (1922–75), for instance, is marked by metaphors and allusions to an exoticized Africa. While, as Giovanna Trento argues, Pasolini's Africa is intricate and complicated—in part due to his Marxist politics and professed solidarity with the Global South—it is still shaped by Italian "colonial ghosts."[85] Most prominently, his cinematic depiction of Black women as exotic female bodies for consumption is an example of what Moya Bailey calls "misogynoir": the particular misogyny that targets Black women.[86] For example, in Pasolini's *Il fiore delle mille e una notte* (*Arabian Nights*, 1974), which was shot in the Horn of Africa, sexualized nude scenes with the character Zumurrud recall the exoticized photos of early twentieth-century madamas as Black Venus that fueled the colonial enterprise and Italian soldiers' desire. Played by mixed-race Italo-Eritrean actress Ines Pellegrini, Zumurrud is photographed nude, her photos a reminder of the colonial images of the Black Venuses disseminated for soldiers to collect and admire as they sailed to Africa in search of conquest.

Pasolini stated that he had indeed gone to Africa in search of "girls like her [Pellegrini]," a statement that further contextualizes the filmmaker's colonial intertext: "Quando ho visto (durante un casting per 'Il Fiore delle Mille e una notte') una meticcia eritreo-italiana mi sono commosso fin quasi alle lacrime davanti a quei piccoli lineamenti un po' irregolari, ma perfetti come quelli di una statua di metallo." (When I saw [during a casting for "Arabian Nights"] a mixed Eritrean-Italian woman I was almost moved to tears when faced with those small, a bit irregular, features, but perfect as those of a metal statue).[87] Pasolini wrote extensively about his multiple trips to Asmara and other parts of Africa throughout his life. Like other twentieth-century European artists, Pasolini promoted justice and equality for all while also perpetuating sexist and racist stereotypes, casting Black and white women in distinct and restrictive social roles. That Pellegrini appears nude or seminude in many of his films, which coincided with Italy's feminist movement, also signals dissonance with the movement's social and political agenda. Passolini's depictions of Eritrea, as Trento argues, are reminiscing of colonial desire for the Black Venus. His descriptions of Black female actors as well as the camera's gaze on Black women's bodies insist on the sexuality and "natural" grace and beauty of the Other. They are afterimages of colonial desire. In the case of Pellegrini, whom Passolini cast in both *Il Fiore delle Mille e una notte* (1974) and in his last film *Salò* (1975), the actress is transformed into a metaphor for the Global South as an otherized source of possibility for anti-hegemonic revolutions: she is an enslaved woman, but one who has "grace" and agency.[88] But despite Pellegrini's antihegemonic potential, Pasolini's Zumurrud (the character played by Pellegrini), much like the Black Venus of colonial East Africa, appears in the film as a symbol—a body rather than a woman, her lesser humanity further emphasized by her status as a slave.[89] While scholars have argued that Zumurrud embodies power through sexual agency (she is a slave who picks her own master and becomes his lover), her role in the film is important inasmuch as it encapsulates Pasolini's colonial desire.[90] That is, she functions solely as a representation: what matters is her (over)sexualized body through which, Pasolini seems to suggest, she can gain some agency within the structures that render her subhuman.

Zumurrud's sexuality, much like that of higher-status madamas in colonial Eritrea, is weaponized in the film to gain social mobility and access. Unlike her male counterparts, for whom character and personhood exist as separate entities, however, playing Zumurrud defined Pellegrini and shaped her career. In Italy, as in Eritrea, she was perceived as a "fallen woman," someone to desire and possess but not to include in the articulation of italianità or in the project of citizenship and belonging: while Pellegrini was born in Milan to an Italian father and an Eritrean mother, Pasolini describes her as a *meticcia*, a colonial term used to name mixed-race children who were not considered Italian subjects, and professes to have "gone to Africa to find women like her," a statement that further avows the myth of white italianità in the intertext "to find women like her," women who could be objectified and possessed, "we must go to Africa." In post-1990s Italy, this search expanded to other Global South nations like the Caribbean, where sex tourism caters to European men looking for exoticized mixed-race Black women like Pellegrini; women onto which the perduring colonial fantasy of the "fallen and tragic mulata" can be projected.

The afterimage of the "Black female" exemplified in the various characters played by Pellegrini in Pasolini's films extends beyond visual representations in Italian culture, permeating aural archives and collective public memory. One of the most pervasive examples is the perdurance and repetition of the Fascist song "Faccetta Nera" (Little black face) in present-day Italian popular culture. Originally written in Romanesco (Roman dialect) in 1935 by Renato

Micheli, "Faccetta Nera" uses the Black woman as a channel for the realization of fantasy of the Roman conquest of Africa, or what Giuliani calls "the Epic return of modern Rome," through which colonizer and colonized subject are "woven together" into the project of national unity.[91] Invoking Rome as both the site of civilization and the home of the protective patria, the song memorializes the Roman Empire's colonization of Libya in 146 BC as a subtext to Fascist colonization propaganda. It announces a return to an unfinished project of colonization: "Vendicheremo noi Camicie Nere. Gli eroi caduti liberando te!" (We, the blackshirts, will avenge the heroes that died to free you!).[92] Returning to Africa, the "new Roman"—the Fascist Italian citizen—uses his virility to "save" the woman in the song through the "slavery of love," bringing her back to Rome, where she would be safe from the threats of savagery and "bad" slavery: "Moretta che sei schiava tra le schiave . . . Faccetta nera, piccola abissina te porteremo a Roma, liberata . . . Faccetta nera, sarai Romana . . . La tua bandiera sarà sol quella italiana!" (Young moor, a slave among slaves . . . Little black face, beautiful Abyssinian we will take you back to Rome, freed . . . Little black face you will be Roman . . . Your flag will be none other than the Italian one).[93]

Scholars have argued that antiblackness and racial hierarchies became more significant in the colonization of East Africa in the 1930s, during the height of Fascism when Rome served as the central administration from which racial relations were regulated in the African colony, a change from previous decades when colonial governments governed day-to-day activities in the colonies. In this context of centralized policing, the criminalization of racial mixing was intrinsically entangled with Mussolini's project of Italian national unification. For Mussolini, Fascism had to contend with race: "Intendo dire che il Fascismo si preoccupi del problema della razza; I Fascisti devono preoccuparsi della salute della razza con la quale si fa la storia" (I intend to tell you that Fascism must address the problem of race; Fascists should be concerned with the well-being of the race with which history is made).[94] Though the occupation of the Horn of Africa started at the end of the nineteenth century during the Liberal Period, the rise of Fascism under Mussolini pushed colonial racial violence to a new level. For Mussolini, the triumph of the Italian race hinged on its ability to dominate the "inferior races" and expand the empire. As Igiaba Scego points out, Mussolini banned "Faccetta Nera" because he believed it encouraged a kind of benevolent miscegenation—and possible migration—that threatened the purity of the Italian race and the stability of the nation.[95] Soldiers heading to East Africa, though, continued to imagine the "little black face" of the Venus of their fantasies and went searching for her in the Eritrean madama—even against her will. This was the promised reward for their service, and they had the soundtrack and visual images to encourage the mission. Through the conquest of the "little black face," they could prove their virility, their worth as men, and their italianità.

"Faccetta Nera" survived the Fascist regime and colonization and persists in contemporary Italy. Throughout my years conducting research in Italy, I collected numerous anecdotes of Black women's encounters with this song. One interviewee told me that her stepdad woke her up singing this song every day. "I used to love it," she said, "until I learned the history of the song and understood its meaning."[96] Another interviewee, an Italo-Habesha activist, said that during a peaceful demonstration, a journalist began to sing the song to her when she refused to have her photo taken by him.[97] The most notable story I encountered, though, is the July 22, 2015, episode of *Forte e Chiaro* in which Italo-Somali activist Maryan Ismail walks out of the studio after a heated argument with another guest who recited the lyrics of the song.[98] Ismail was speaking out against anti-immigrant racism in Italy on the show when an elderly white Italian man verbally attacked her, weaponizing the song to discipline her into submission. In an example of institutionalized and normalized colonial violence that shapes contemporary understandings of Black Italians' belonging and unbelonging to the nation, the white man who recites "Faccetta Nera" publicly asserts his belonging and Ismail's unbelonging by reclaiming what I would call, following Brown, the aftersound of colonialism, the aural afterlife of colonial violence, as a testament to white supremacy. The permanence of colonial Fascism permeates popular and cultural encounters, recolonizing Black women.

In "Faccetta Nera," the Black woman facilitates national unity by becoming the prize carried back to Rome. She is also the disrupter of unity via her geographical displacement and potential repositioning as an Italian citizen. The man singing at Ismail in this television episode exemplifies the present-day anxiety about the inevitable expansion of italianità to include citizens of color, many of whom were born in Italy to immigrant parents from formerly colonized African countries. In the 1930s, the song offered Black women an invitation to italianità through domination, sexual possession, and migration ("We will take you to Rome as a freedwoman"). Ismail's encounter with present-day colonial Fascism via the song embodies its afterlife: anti-immigrant racism that seeks to expunge Black Italian women from the nation, placing them back into colonial domination. Presumably, the white Italian man believed it to be his duty to punish and discipline Ismail rather than risk the demise of the colonial (Fascist) project of Italian unity. As we will see in the next section, Italian racism is very much preoccupied with maintaining the racial borders of italianità—through legal, cultural, and political channels—by insisting on producing blackness as foreign to the nation and Black people as migrants who exist outside the imagined Italian community. Ismail's defiance of the tacit (colonial) racial order triggered the white Italian man's colonial memory and his imagined duty to the nation. In this context, we can understand the man's invocation of "Faccetta Nera" as an attempt to, echoing Kilomba, recolonize blackness to preserve the border of the nation from "foreign" (Black) intrusion.

Giuliani argues that Italian racism today is grounded on the colonial archive, which shapes public and private conversations about italianità and cultural representations and understandings of Italian belonging.[99] The afterimages and aftersounds of the Black Venus and the Eritrean madama—and by extension of Italian colonial desire for and sexual exploitation of Black women—that flood twentieth- and twentieth-first-century Italian media are tied, as Giuliani argues, to wider social and cultural processes of racialization that render contemporary Black women like Carolina Payano as exotic, indecent, foreign bodies available for consumption, and therefore incapable of belonging to the nation. The fact that images and sounds of sexualized female Black and Brown bodies dominate national—as well as international—representations of Black women in the media and popular culture serves to further sanction Italy's exclusion of Black women through a dual process of hypervisibility and exploitation.

In the wake of the 2020 police murder of George Floyd, a Black man in the United States, we witnessed a global reckoning with the afterlife of colonial antiblackness and slavery as protests erupted all over the world. One of the ways this reckoning manifested was through the defacing and destruction of public monuments of colonial figures, plantation owners, and racist symbols that proliferate in most postcolonial cities. This took place across Italy as well, resulting in damage to many colonial Fascist monuments, including the iconic statue of journalist Indro Montanelli in Milan (see figure 4.3). Montanelli (1909–2001) was a conservative journalist and writer who served two years in a military commando in East Africa during the invasion of Ethiopia (1935–37). He often bragged about having bought, and later sold, a twelve-year-old girl named Destà as his madama. Montanelli often referred to Destà as an "animaletto docile" (docile little animal), a brute, whose smell repulsed him, and whose "mutilated genitals" resisted his ardor to the point that intercourse was only possible after "il brutale intervento della madre" (her mother's brutal intervention).[100] Despite his having raped, enslaved, and

FIGURE 4.3 Defaced statue of Italian journalist Indro Montanelli in Milan, 2020. Photo by Nicola Marfisi.

trafficked a child, public opinion about Montanelli in Italy is highly divided. Some conservative people believe his image should be maintained and revered as an emblem of italianità. Many believe that what he did to Destà was a "normal custom," a manifestation of the time. As one journalist put it, he was "figlio del suo tempo, non certamente un razzista, né stupratore, né pedofilo" (a son of his time, not really a racist, nor a usurper, nor a pedophile).[101]

For years, Italian feminists have protested Montanelli and the legacy he represents by demanding the city of Milan take down his statue.[102] In the aftermath of Floyd's death, protesters once again covered Montanelli's statue with paint and graffiti that included words like "racist" and "rapist." These acts were accompanied by the reemergence in the public sphere, via social media interventions led by anti-racist and feminist activists, of a long and painful controversy that arose in 1969 during Montanelli's appearance on the television show *L'ora della verità*. In the episode, the show's host, Gianni Bisiach, who also lived in East Africa during the Fascist period, asks Montanelli about his "bella moglie indigena" (pretty Indigenous wife). With a smirk, Montanelli, who was often boastful about his escapades in East Africa, responds by opening his arms, shifting his body, and retelling his tale of conquest: "Sì, pare che avessi scelto bene. Era una bellissima ragazza bilena di dodici anni."

(Yes, it looks like I chose well. She was a beautiful Bilen girl, twelve years old.) After saying the girl's age, Montanelli looks at the audience and says, while smiling, "Scusatemi, ma in Africa è un'altra cosa" (Forgive me, but in Africa things are different).[103] Montanelli's diction "in Africa things are different" as he narrates his raping of Destà is both playful and boastful. As if wanting the audience to recognize him as a picaresque hero rather than the pedophile and rapist he is, he elicits laughter from some of the men listening through gestures (opening his arms) and the complicit smirk that culminates with "in Africa things are different." Italian-Eritrean feminist activist Elvira Banotti, who is seated in the audience, then abruptly interrupts Montanelli's speech. Following is an abridged version of their heated exchange on public television.

ELVIRA BANOTTI: Lei ha detto tranquillamente di avere un'amica una sposa diciamo di 12 anni e a 25 anni non si è peritato affatto di violentare una ragazza di 12 anni, dicendo "ma in Africa queste cose si fanno." Io vorrei chiedere a lui, come intende normalmente i suoi rapporti con le donne, date queste due affermazioni.

MONTANELLI: No signorina guardi, sulla violenza nessuna violenza perché le ragazze in Abissinia si sposano a 12 anni. Non è questione.

ELVIRA BANOTTI: Lo dice lei.

MONTANELLI: Ah quindi era l'uso locale.

ELVIRA BANOTTI: Su un piano di consapevolezza dell'uomo, insomma il rapporto con una bambina di 12 anni è il rapporto con una bambina di 12 anni. Se lo facesse in Europa, riterrebbe di violentare una bambina, vero?

MONTANELLI: Sì in Europa sì. Lì no. Eh ma lì no.

ELVIRA BANOTTI: Ecco sì appunto. Quale differenza crede che esista dal punto di vista biologico o psicologico anche? Dal punto di vista del costume.

MONTANELLI: No guardi, li sposano a 12 anni. Non è questione. A 12 anni sposano!

ELVIRA BANOTTI: Ma non è il matrimonio che lei intende, a 12 anni in Africa. Guardi, io ho vissuto in Africa. Quindi il vostro era veramente il rapporto violento del colonialista che veniva lì e si impossessava della ragazza di 12 anni. Senza assolutamente . . .

MONTANELLI: No . . .

ELVIRA BANOTTI: Ma glielo garantisco. Senza assolutamente tener conto di questo tipo di rapporto sul piano umano. Eravate i vincitori. Cioè i militari che hanno fatto le stesse cose ovunque sono stati i vincitori. Ovunque si sono presentati gli uomini, si sono presentati come dei militari. La storia è piena di queste situazioni. No?

MONTANELLI: Signorina vogliamo . . . non so, se lei vuole istruirmi un processo a posteriori.

ELVIRA BANOTTI: No affatto. Guardi, ho soltanto voluto chiederle per inciso come lei intende, dopo le due interpretazioni, come intende i rapporti con le donne.

MONTANELLI: Dipende da cosa ci si mette dentro. Dipende anche da cosa le donne mettono dentro di noi. È tutto un giuoco di specchi.

ELVIRA BANOTTI: Che non è l'essere umano sul piano di paritá. Cioè lei vede sempre la donna in questa funzione e passiva di adulatrice oppure di compagna così che compare e scompare, dell'uomo non l'ha mai vista in una funzione diretta attiva e diversa. Questo è un po' il dramma degli uomini della sua generazione.

MONTANELLI: Può darsi. Della mia generazione? Solo?[104]

[ELVIRA BANOTTI: You said nonchalantly that you had a friend, a spouse let's say, who was 12 years old. And did not hesitate to say that at age 25 you raped a 12-year-old girl, dismissing it by saying "but in Africa these things happen". I would like to ask you, how do you normally see your relationships with women, given your two statements?

MONTANELLI: Look Miss, regarding violence, there was no violence because in Abissinia girls get married at 12 years old. It's not a question of if, . . . but therefore.

ELVIRA BANOTTI: That's what you say.

MONTANELLI: To me . . . it was the local custom.

ELVIRA BANOTTI: At the level of awareness, as a man, a relationship with a 12-year-old child is a relationship with a 12-year-old child. If you did this in Europe you would consider that rape of a child, right?

MONTANELLI: Yes, in Europe, yes.

ELVIRA BANOTTI: Yes, indeed.

MONTANELLI: Over there, no. Over there, no.

ELVIRA BANOTTI: What difference do you think exists from a biological or even psychological point of view?

MONTANELLI: No, look . . .

ELVIRA BANOTTI: From a cultural point of view . . .

MONTANELLI: Over there they get married at 12. It's not a matter of . . . At 12 they get married.

ELVIRA BANOTTI: It's not marriage the way you intend it at 12 years old in Africa. Look, I lived in Africa. So yours was a violent relationship of the colonizer who went there and took possession of the 12-year-old girl. Without . . .

MONTANELLI: No.

ELVIRA BANOTTI: I guarantee you. Without taking into consideration this type of relationship at the human level. You were the winners. The soldiers, that is, they did the same everywhere they were the winners. Anywhere the men showed up, they showed up as soldiers. History is full of situations like this.

MONTANELLI: Miss, I don't know, you want to put me on posthumous trial.

ELVIRA BANOTTI: No, no, not at all. I just wanted to ask you how you see your relationship with women. Especially after those two statements.

MONTANELLI: Depends what you fill it with. Depends what the women put inside us. It's all a game of mirrors.

ELVIRA BANOTTI: It's not an equal relationship. Therefore, you always see the woman in this passive role, as an adulatress, or as a companion so that she appears and disappears. The man never sees her in a direct, active, and different capacity. This is in a nutshell the drama of men of your generation. I think.

MONTANELLI: Maybe. My generation? Only mine? Oh well.]

Given the recurrent antiblackness and violence in public representations of African colonization, Banotti's interruption of Montanelli on television in 1969 is a moment of immense and unprecedented historical import. Born in Asmara to a mixed-race Italo-Eritrean family during the Fascist period, Banotti (1933–2014) grew up in the afterlife of colonialism, experiencing its lasting violence across two continents. Raised in Eritrea, she obtained a college education and began a career in diplomacy. Banotti moved with her family to Rome in the 1960s to pursue a career in journalism. She soon got involved in the emerging women's rights movement and gained a reputation as a controversial feminist activist. Banotti is mostly known for her social justice advocacy around sexuality, rape, and reproductive rights. She was incredibly concerned with the prevalence of rape in Italian society and viewed it as a sign of patriarchal dominance. She spoke publicly about the relationship between colonial violence and rape. Her appearance on *L'ora della verità* is one of the earliest documented interruptions of Italian colonial archives in the public sphere. Banotti speaks from her subject position as a woman who is both African and Italian, sanctioning her intervention as anti-colonial feminism years before postcolonial critique became part of Italian public discourse. In chapter 3, I argued for the possibility of re-membering as a feminist praxis that contra*dicts* state violence and death. Banotti's archival interruption of Montanelli's colonial fantasy—her insistence on unsilencing the rape and violence he inflicted upon Destà—challenges Montanelli as the embodiment of Italian colonial power and the complicity of the spectators and bystanders who listen to his stories of fantasy and conquest and participate in sustaining the normalization of colonial violence in the present.

I have watched the exchange between Montanelli and Banotti more than a dozen times, paying attention to their bodily movements and expressions, listening to every word with obsessive care. Montanelli speaks calmly, smirking and eliciting laughter from the host and audience as he describes how he bought the girl and how she performed her "wifely" duties. Banotti, on the other hand, speaks quickly, decisively, and firmly—almost as if out of breath, trying to quickly fill in the silences in Montanelli's violent speech. She makes sure she is heard, saying, "This man is a rapist," implicitly calling out anyone who may think a Black girl's humanity—or, for that matter, her own humanity—is worth less than a white girl's. Her interruption contra*dicts* the "us versus them" divide that shapes colonial violence and its afterlife. Insisting on her own knowledge as someone who also "spent time in Africa," she questions the logic that a twelve-year-old is developmentally different (more "ready" for sexual relations) depending on location. In so doing, she brings attention to the prevalence of racism in post-Fascist Italy. As she speaks, the camera focuses on her and the rest of the small audience. The white women sitting around her look down or to the side, embodying an "impartial" position and distancing themselves from Banotti and her interruption. Banotti stands alone. She interpellates colonial violence while everyone around her watches in complicit silence. Unstoppable and unabashed by her role as "the Black woman who talks back," Banotti seizes the moment, speaking quickly and forcefully until the program is interrupted by a commercial break—undoubtedly to save the privileged guest and the Italian image he represented from further embarrassment.

I sympathize with Banotti's exasperation. I recognize her fast speech and her abrupt ways. They signal urgency. That urgency persists today, as Black women and girls continue to die and their bodies continue to function as commodities to be traded or discarded. Banotti, as the Black woman in the room, had to be the one to speak truth to power. In 1969 Italy, and still, to an extent, today, the fight against antiblackness and anti-immigrant racism continues to be imagined as Black and Brown people's fight. Banotti's intervention was new, inasmuch as it brought attention to the intersections of race, gender, colonialism, and migration through her words and her body as a person who inhabits, and therefore can translate, Black italianità.

The reappearance and circulation of the 1969 exchange in 2020, in the wake of Floyd's murder, translated Italian blackness—and the horror of living the afterlife of colonialism as a Black immigrant and a Black citizen in Italy—to a global audience. In response, social media and mass media gave Destà a name, a story, a face, and a place in the public archive of anti-colonialism and Black belonging. Despite the outrage that Montanelli has caused among many anti-colonial and feminist critics, we have not yet seen a reckoning that centers the lives, stories, and histories of the women and girls who participated in colonial madamato. In a cultural climate devoid of much vindication, calls from activists and on social media mark a significant rupture in the dominance of the colonial archive in contemporary Italy. They interrupt the afterimage of the Black female body with that of the Black woman/girl, memorializing the violence these women experienced and repositioning the public understanding of history. As a result of these interventions, the iconic Via Indro Montanelli in Palermo was renamed Via Destà. Where her rapist's name used to be, there is now a plaque remembering Destà and condemning colonial violence against women and girls. Dozens of artistic representations, including murals, now honor Destà in the streets of Milan, Palermo, and Rome (see figure 4.4).

Fabienne Le Houérou writes about the proliferation of pedophilia among white Italian men in colonial Eritrea during the Fascist era. She explains that

FIGURE 4.4 Mural about Indro Montanelli and his madama, twelve-year-old Eritrean girl Destà, 2020. Mural and photo by Mr. Cens.

men like Montanelli often adopted girls as young as nine only to exploit them for sex and domestic labor. These girls often came from lower castes or ethnic minorities in areas of conflict. In his interview on *L'ora della verità*, Montanelli recounts that his madama washed all his clothes and showed up with the clean basket, ready to perform her duties, insisting on how "natural" and normal this was for the place and time.[105] Yet as Le Houérou's research demonstrates, for the child victims, the psychological damage was immeasurable: the men became their parents, employers, and abusers all at once.[106] The girls had to obey, serve, and provide sexual pleasure. When the men were done with them, girls like Destà were often abandoned or sold into prostitution. During her two years of fieldwork in Ethiopia and Eritrea in the early 1970s, Le Houérou met and interviewed several Italian men and their young madamas, who were now adults. She explains that when asked how they could marry children, the men, like Montanelli, often cited local customs of child marriage as justification: "like elsewhere, in other European colonial contexts, actors (for example, the French in Africa) in colonial situations or postcolonial contexts, have adapted themselves to the local customs when it was advantageous and comfortable for them: denying the suffering of very young children."[107] Taking advantage of their privilege as colonizers, white Italian men exploited internal ethnic and class conflicts to their advantage, using their power and will to exploit young girls and boys. Gandolfi also comments on the proliferation of "companion boys" called "diavoletti" (little devils) who were "around Massawa soldiers," keeping them "warm at night."[108] Unlike the young madama girls, diavoletti were not sold but were "rented" to the men in what resembles present-day jineterismo: short-term affective relationships based on sex and companionship but not linked to domestic life. Due to social stigma and homophobia, there is very little documentation of the existence of diavoletti; what we do know from the existing research is that Italian officers and civilians often took advantage of both boys and girls in their pedophilic and violent colonization of Eritrea.

Montanelli's narration of his "wife" is representative of the pedophilic colonization—the "*bambine mania*"—in which hundreds of Eritrean children were trafficked and forced to endure physical and sexual violence.[109] Using terms like *imboscati* (hidden or lost in the forest), white Italian men justified their crimes as a sickness: a "fever" that took hold of their bodies when they arrived in Africa, making them ill with bambine mania.[110] When confronted about their crimes decades later, many of these men, like Montanelli, displaced their crimes through the same language of savagery versus civilization that was popular in colonial Fascist Italy. Naturalizing Africa as a land where "these things happen," and producing Black girls as women rather than children, men claimed to be stripped of their own agency by the force of the local "wilderness" and bewitching girl-women.[111] Like the "tropical fever" associated with the Caribbean that journalists wrote about in the wake of Payano's murder, the bambine mania that made "good Italian men" into pedophiles in colonial Africa is a narrative of exculpation, as seen in the public perception of Montanelli, which was produced, narrated, and often accepted in the public sphere as historical truth.

Colonialism and coloniality are intrinsically linked to the everyday fabric of a nation and its citizens. They shape politics and economies as well as attitudes about gender, race, class, and sex. Yet while colonialism visibly, legally, linguistically, politically, and culturally shaped the construction of national identities in colonized countries—as evidenced, for instance, in the dominance of the Spanish language and Hispanism in Spanish-colonized Latin America—the legacy of colonialism in postcolonial Global North cities such as Milan is often invisibilized, sanitized, curated, or legalized. These processes render descendants of colonized subjects and their hybrid colonial cultures foreign and superfluous to the cosmopolitan nation they (unwillingly) helped build. To conjure these ghosts, to make them visible and accountable, it is thus necessary to revisit the past with new eyes, paying attention, as Marisa Fuentes urges us to do, to the fragments of lives of people like Destà amid the dominant archive.[112] In Italy, where colonial amnesia inhibited a reckoning with the colonial past until very recently, the experiences of nonwhite Italians have become entangled with newer forms of anti-immigrant racism that, as seen in Ismail's encounter with the aftersound of "Faccetta Nera," marks Italians of color as foreign, at best, or as menacing threats to the nation, at worst. Italian women of color are forced to confront the simultaneous perdurance and amnesia of colonial violence in their everyday lives. For women of color and Black immigrant mothers, in particular, as I explore in the next section, this violence manifests in societal disavowal of their motherhood that ranges from disapproving looks to confrontation with state authorities that often lead to the loss of custody and other parental rights of their children.[113] This dynamic, I argue, is intrinsically entangled with the legacy of colonialism that engendered fear of mixed-race children in the Fascist era and that perpetuates the idea of italianità as a quasi-sacred essence passed on to children through blood. In the late twentieth and early twenty-first centuries, the perdurance of colonial gendered violence shaped the lives and experiences of many immigrants of color and their children in contemporary Italy.

Black Immigrant Motherhood in the Italian Postcolonial Diaspora

By the time Dominican women started arriving in Italy in the early 1980s, the Dominican Republic had become an important site of commercial sex for white Italian tourists.[114] While there is no single definition of sex tourism, Kamala Kempadoo uses the helpful term *transactional sex* in the context of tourism to "denote sexual economic relationships and exchanges where gifts are given in exchange for sex . . . and an up-front monetary transaction does not necessarily take place."[115] In 1976, when the Dominican National Tourism Plan (an economic project developed under the auspices of the Joaquín Balaguer regime to promote tourism on the island) was first launched, 1,000 out of 1,800 tourists who visited Santo Domingo that year traveled from Italy. Most tourists who arrived on the island between 1976 and 1992 were men traveling alone.[116] Much like the military propaganda surrounding the 1890s colonization of Eritrea, Italian tourist propaganda in the 1970s depicted the Dominican Republic as a paradise for single men: a place where they could realize all their sexual fantasies.

As Medar Serrata argues, the image of the Dominican Republic as a paradise of consumption dates to early colonial narratives that exoticized the island as a natural, savage place.[117] Tourism scholars have long noted the similarities between mass tourism and colonialism. For example, Louis Turner and John Ash's book *The Golden Hordes* (1975) notes that as soon as packaged tourism was extended beyond Europe in the nineteenth century, tourism helped consolidate empire.[118] The book also notes that the economic lure of contemporary mass tourism to newly decolonized countries meant that many were "welcoming back their old masters with open arms."[119] Rooted in histories of colonial desire, which in the Caribbean date back to the fifteenth-century Spanish conquest, the intersection of tourism and sex is an undeniable example of how indicators of global economic power embodied by white middle-class tourists can affect local economies, social structures, and immigration patterns in underprivileged postcolonial regions such as the Caribbean, Brazil, the Philippines, and parts of Africa. At the close of the twentieth century, with the advent of the global marketing industry, the production of the Dominican Republic as a tourist paradise offered up not only the land but also its people. Women, in particular, were featured in official and unofficial Dominican tourist propaganda as one resource available for foreign consumption.

By the time Carolina Payano arrived in Italy in 2010, the Caribbean fantasy had been solidified by four decades of tourist propaganda. At the time of her death, Payano's body and homeland were "naturalized" as an undivided space for Italian consumption. It seemed logical that she, like all vacations, would end and be replaced by other sources of pleasure. In his 1961 essay "The Pitfalls of National Consciousness," Frantz Fanon outlines the tendency of the "national bourgeoisie" in newly decolonized states to organize centers of relaxation and pleasure to meet the wishes of Western bourgeois tourists.

> If proof is needed of the eventual transformation of certain elements of the ex-native bourgeoisie into the organizers of parties for their Western opposite numbers, it is worthwhile having a look at what has happened in Latin America. The casinos of Havana and of Mexico, the beaches of Rio, the little Brazilian and Mexican girls, the half-breed

> thirteen-year-olds, the ports of Acapulco and Copacabana—all these are the stigma of this depravation of the national middle class. Because it is bereft of ideas, because it lives to itself and cuts itself off from the people, undermined by its hereditary incapacity to think in terms of all the problems of the nation as seen from the point of view of the whole of that nation, the national middle class will have nothing better to do than to take on the role of manager for Western enterprise, and it will in practice set up its country as the brothel of Europe.[120]

To Fanon's insights we could add that this European pleasure business also turned people into timeless, unmovable objects frozen in location. That is, if the Caribbean island becomes a brothel, as Fanon suggests, Caribbean women exist only as prostitutes in the European imaginary.

In attempting to translate Payano's displacement from the Caribbean fantasy to metropolitan Italy, the media drew from the archive of colonialism and from Gandolfi's afterimage of the "no-name female body" of the madama: "A Santo Domingo non ti chiamano per nome e cognome: prima di sposarsi Carolina era stata una sanchi panchi. Ragazza non sulla strada e con molta discrezione" (In Santo Domingo they would not call her by first and last name: before getting married, Carolina was a sanky panky. A very discreet street girl).[121] Negating her subjecthood, the media produced Payano as a nameless whore, a projection of the vacation destination Italy is accustomed to imagining and Fanon feared. As Denise Brennan demonstrates in her groundbreaking research on Dominican sex workers in Sosúa, sankipankismo is more than a means of survival: it is an advancement strategy that pivots on a successful "performance of love."[122] Many of these women and men seek to turn a commercialized sexual transaction into a long-term relationship that could lead to marriage, migration, and a way out of poverty. The equation of sankipankismo with "street prostitution" in the Italian media erases the (colonial) entanglements of love, market, and migration that lie at the root of these relationships. The media depiction of Payano as a displaced Caribbean sanky panky shows the difficulties that Italy experiences in grappling with centuries of stereotypical portrayals of objectified Black female bodies and present-day political pressures to create policies and legislations that are inclusive of its citizens of color. The assumption that Payano acquires a name and an identity only through her marriage to an Italian man and migration to Italy further solidifies the perception of the Caribbean—and Caribbean people's bodies—as available for consumption. The striking similarities between the racist portrayal of Payano as a Caribbean sanky without a name and the Eritrean madama as a female non-woman point to the persistence of colonialism in shaping the understanding of blackness in Italy. Furthermore, the portrayal of Payano as a Dominican sanky panky—an assessment that has been denied by her family, friends, and even the Dominican officials involved in the investigation—perpetuates popular and hegemonic perceptions of Black women as sexually deviant and sexually available, and therefore incapable of becoming "Italian women."

Though the investigation eventually found Payano innocent of drug trafficking, news reports continued to insist on her implicit guilt as a carrier of exotic beauty and criminality of the Caribbean sexscape.

> Non si può avere la certezza—continua il testimone—ma qui in Repubblica Dominicana, negli anni, ne abbiamo visti fin troppi di italiani che hanno percorso la stessa strada. Prima le vacanze, poi la familiarità con questo ambiente *in cui è facile entrare in contatto con l'illegalità*; la prospettiva di guadagni facili, rapidi e piuttosto grossi.[123]

> [One cannot be sure—there are ever more testimonies—but in the Dominican Republic, over the years, we have seen too many Italians who have traveled down the same path. First the holidays, then the familiarity with this environment *in which it is easy to come in contact with illegality*; the prospect of easy, quick, and rather big gains.]

Illegality is produced through Payano's very body as an innate force of the Caribbean island that traps and seduces Italian men: "È anche vero però che Carolina era bella, dominicana e aveva 22 anni. Caratteristiche che in un'indagine devono essere tenute in debito conto" (It is also true, however, that Carolina was beautiful, Dominican and was twenty-two years old. Characteristics that must be taken into account in an investigation).[124] According to the media reports, then, her husband's drug trafficking is at least tangentially related to his love affair with Payano, and by extension to the corrupted island she represents and embodies.

But the depiction of Payano's "exotic beauty" and Caribbean foreignness is not only important inasmuch as it helps the white Italian audience understand the "investigation." It also implies Black women's unbelonging to italianità. This unbelonging, in the case of Payano, is articulated as a mutual discomfort that manifests in her inability to assimilate, and by extension her incapability of raising an Italian child who could indeed embody italianità. This argument appears more clearly in an article by Bruna Bianchi published in the daily paper *Il Giorno Milano*. Citing her last Facebook status, in which

Payano complains about feeling out of place among "esta gente del diablo" (these people from hell) and expresses her desire to return home to her neighborhood, Bianchi suggests that Payano is simply not ready for Italian life.[125] Following suit, numerous media outlets hinted at Payano's "differenza culturale" (cultural difference) as evidence of her unbelonging to Italy.[126] One journalist claimed that Payano was a "girl from the Caribbean" accustomed to poverty and to a simpler mode of living. Suggesting that poverty turns corruptive when confronted with the possibilities of wealth in the diaspora, the journalist goes on to say that Caribbean subjects were better off staying home, where poverty has a different face: a face of "dignity."[127] Another article suggested Payano would have had a chance at living, even if in poverty, had she stayed home where she belonged—had she not been "lì nel momento sbagliato" (there at the wrong time).[128] Securing the well-being of the colonial exploitative structures of tourism over *there*, while reminding citizens that the true danger exists when the body that should remain at home is transplanted *here*, the media consistently deployed Payano's motherhood as an aberration—something that did not fit her exoticized "female body"—and her mothering body as unnatural and accidental rather than "sacred," as motherhood is positioned in national narratives of white italianità.

As in other predominantly Catholic nations, the image of the mother in Italian society has been central to the project of nation building and the bloodline belonging of italianità. As Giovanna Grignaffini, Emilia Perassi, Giovanna Faleschini Lerner, Maria Elena D'Amelio, and other Italian scholars have argued, mothers are central to italianità, though the project of the nation has been decidedly patriarchal. Italianità depends on the sacrifice and martyrdom of the abnegate, asexual, devoted virgin mother-woman within the nation.[129] During the Fascist era, this image of the mother-saint who sacrifices for her sons—the patriarchs of the nation—was further solidified through the counterimage of the Black female non-woman whore. For Payano, who was the mother of a mixed-race Italian child, this contradictory rhetoric occupies the symbolic space of a national crisis in which italianità is being questioned and through which the racist legislation impeding citizenship and belonging for Italians of color is being challenged.

The media presumed Payano to be a whore rather than a mother in the mother/whore dichotomy: "Prima di diventare madre, appare una ragazza esuberante, con un seno prorompente che non c'entra affatto con il suo corpo: la chirurgia estetica è il regalo che si fanno le quindicenni, quasi un must in alcuni Paesi dell'America Latina" (Rather than a mother, what appears is an exuberant girl with prominent breasts that do not match her body: cosmetic surgery is a must as a fifteenth-birthday gift in some of these Latin American countries).[130] But the fact that Payano was in fact a mother, and that she died with her baby in her arms—her body physically shielding the child from harm—complicates the dichotomy, challenging both the hegemonic misogyny that denies the possibility of motherhood for sex workers and the antiblackness that fuels the assumption that Payano, because of her race, must have been a prostitute.

The mother/whore dichotomy that shapes narratives about women across history and geographies is complicated in Payano's case by the fact that she is the Black Caribbean mother of an Italian child. Kimberly Juanita Brown writes that Black motherhood complicates notions of citizenship in the afterlife of slavery as the political and the social join in the "flesh" of women's mothering bodies, recalling the violence of slavery and colonialism and its perdurance.[131] In the context of (post)colonial Italy, Payano's motherhood obfuscates the afterimage of the Black Venus through her presence in Milan—rather than a colonial site such as East Africa or the Caribbean. Unlike a madama, who could be displaced and buried in colonial memory (appearing only as a phantom through men's colonial desire, as Destà was in Montanelli's narration), Payano is very much inserted within the Italian nation: her mothering body was a reminder of colonial amnesia, and her child was a contra*diction* of colonial attempts to erase Italian blackness. To contrast the fear elicited by Payano's mothering body, the media naturalized her death as a side effect of her (out-of-place) Black colonized body—as a natural consequence of her transgression.

Milagros Guzmán, vice consul of the Dominican Republic in Milan, handled the repatriation of Payano's body and the custody battle over her child. Referring specifically to the media representation of Payano as a sexualized, non-mother, non-woman female (a present-day incarnation of the madama), Guzmán stated, "There was an unnatural insistence on making sure we found something wrong with this young mother."[132] The murder investigation uncovered evidence that Payano was a victim of the Spelta family and their long-standing drug-trafficking business in the Dominican Republic, and that Massimiliano Spelta, who was two decades her senior, had married her as a minor. It was neither his actions nor her tragedy that the media focused on, however, but her body. They obsessed over her large breasts: "Prima di diventare madre, appare una ragazza esuberante, con un seno prorompente che non c'entra affatto con il suo corpo . . ." (Rather than a mother, an exuberant girl appears, with bursting bosom that doesn't match her body).[133] In fact, her breasts were large because she was a breastfeeding mother, but the media made them perverse, a subject of political and medical debate. Even the doctor who conducted the autopsy was compelled to confirm in a public statement that Payano's breasts were real.[134]

At the time of Payano's murder, Italy was immersed in a conversation about the place of Second Generations within contemporary Italy. The fear of citizens of color raised by immigrant mothers was one of the dominant tropes in the media and on social media as conservatives insisted that italianità was impossible to achieve for children whose foreign mothers lack the cultural abilities to teach them Italianness. While the focus of Second Generation activists, like that of DREAMers in the United States, has been on fighting the legal exclusion of young people, and in particular on the eradication of jus sanguinis citizenship laws that prevent Italian-born people of color from accessing legal citizenship, it is important to note that this exclusion is also based on the concept of "jus culturae": the assumption that children raised by immigrants inherit immigrant ways and therefore cannot assimilate to Italian culture.[135] For Payano, this meant that her motherhood, rather than being an advantage in an otherwise mother-centric nation, represented yet another threat.

As the media struggled to explain Payano's presence in the metropolis, her body was resignified as a sexscape that conjured the colonial African madama and the postcolonial Caribbean sanky. This displacement both reminded the public that Payano was a foreigner and simultaneously assuaged white guilt/fear of Caribbean exoticism to protect Italian capitalist investment in the island. As one newspaper reported it, "Il 27 agosto, qualcosa ha aumentato il conflitto tra gente con pelle e cultura diverse e ha fatto crescere di colpo la nostalgia *di una figlia del mare dei Caraibi, dove la povertà diventa esotica come il luogo e confonde i turisti*" (On August 27, something has increased the conflict between people of different skin colors, growing the homesickness of *this daughter of the Caribbean Sea, where poverty becomes as exotic as the place, confusing the tourists*).[136] Payano's exoticized body belonged over *there*, where the contradictions of mother and whore are "normal." *There*, white Italian tourists could place her within the backdrop of poverty and savagery that presumably produces such contradictions. *Here*, the article suggests, Carolina's (immigrant, sexualized) body simply does not belong.

Melania Cruz, psychologist for the Social Services Branch of the Dominican Consulate in Milan and cofounder of Anacaona Mujeres Dominicanas en Italia (see chapter 3), explains that while in Italy there is the image of the mother as a saint, the mother as the ultimate and most revered woman, that sanctity does not transfer to the immigrant mother.

La percepción general es que nuestras mujeres [inmigrantes de color] solo sirven para dar placer al hombre, y a lo mejor para parir. . . . Por eso es que es aceptable adoptar a niños negros al mismo tiempo que se dejan morir a mujeres migrantes y refugiadas y a sus hijos en el mar.[137]

[The general perception is that our [immigrant of color] women are only good enough to produce pleasure for the men, and maybe to birth the child. . . . We are surrogates rather than mothers. That is why adoption of Black babies is acceptable while migrant and refugee mothers and their children are rejected at sea.]

Violence against Black mothers goes beyond symbolic exclusion from the national paradigm of Italian motherhood. In Italy between January and June 2018, 116 women were killed by their partners or as a direct result of their partners' illegal activities.[138] The Associazione delle Donne in Milan insists these numbers are not complete, as many cases go unreported. More than 3.4 million complaints related to sexual violence and stalking were filed in Italy between 2015 and 2018. What these numbers do not reflect, according to Rossella Amodeo, legal advisor for Anacaona Mujeres Dominicanas Milan, is that immigrant women, particularly those who arrive at a young age, are more vulnerable to abuse from their partners and their partners' families. Often, these abuses, too, go unreported.[139]

In 2015 a Dominican immigrant was detained in the outskirts of Geneva after stabbing her husband. Mireya had been living in subhuman conditions for many years.[140] Upon her arrival from the Dominican Republic, her husband's family had locked her in a small room. They took her newborn baby and only brought him to her for feedings. "She was treated worse than a cow," explained her sister during an interview facilitated by the Dominican Consulate in Milan, which oversaw the case, "because at least cows are allowed to roam free, and their offspring can nurse when they please. They kept her like that for three years. She lost her mind. When we found her, she could barely speak anymore."[141] Mireya was charged with assault and eventually deported to the Dominican Republic. After a long legal battle in which she was unable to regain custody of her child, she died by suicide in Santo Domingo in September 2016. Her white Italian husband's family retains custody of the child, even though the man is not the child's biological father.

Meditating on Mireya's and Payano's cases, Guzmán lamented the fact that their children are being raised by the Italian families that caused their mothers so much suffering.

El hecho de que estos niños nacieran en Italia quiere decir que sus familias en la isla no pueden pedir la custodia o ni siquiera tener la oportunidad de conocer sus nietos o hermanitos. Es una batalla entre David y Goliat. Muchas jóvenes, muchas de ellas que están tratando de salir de la pobreza, son niñas practicamente, se casan con viejos italianos que casi ni conocen. Vienen aquí y sufren toda clase de abuso. Algunas se hayan en situaciones muy precarias y pierden sus hijos. Yo he visto muchas de estas mujeres volverse loca, hasta hacer lo impensable. Es una situación muy precaria aquí. . . . Nuestras mujeres se nos mueren y *no le duele a nadie ni aquí ni allá.*[142]

[The fact that these are children born in Italy means that their families on the island are unable to fight for custody or to even have the chance to meet their grandchildren and siblings. It is a battle between David and Goliath. Many young women, lots of them who are trying to escape poverty, many of them children themselves, marry older Italian men they barely know. They come here and suffer so many abuses. Some of the women find themselves in precarious conditions and often lose their children. I have seen many of these women go mad, do the unthinkable. It is very precarious, our situation here. . . . Our women are dying, and *no one here or there cares.*]

The separation of Black and Brown mothers from their children is sadly not a rare practice, nor is it a new one. Family separation was a common custom and means of controlling and dehumanizing enslaved and Indigenous people in the United States and other parts of the Americas, particularly during the eighteenth and nineteenth centuries. In 2018, as US president Donald Trump's "zero tolerance policy," a plan to tighten immigration control along the US-Mexico border, was implemented, heartbreaking images of family separation became as common in the United States as those of Black bodies killed by the police. Similarly, in Italy, the rhetoric that refugees and immigrants are "invading" summons the colonial history of Campo Cintato that separated Black and Brown people from white colonizers in colonial Asmara. Often, mixed-race children were sent to boarding schools or otherwise forced to Italianize and distance themselves from their Black mothers. In 1937 the ban on colonial concubinage between Italian men and African women in the Horn of Africa paved the way to wider racist Italian legislation enacted against racialized minorities. These colonial manifestations continue to produce power imbalances that deny rights, citizenship, and opportunities for a large part of the population.[143] As Alessandro Triulzi argues, these paradigms of colonial memory are very much present.[144] They function, as Triulzi argues, like a pendulum that alternates between the desire to forget and the nostalgic recollection of a past that is selectively remembered and reenacted, as we have seen in the multiple examples offered in this chapter, through the afterimages and aftersounds of colonial desire for the Black Venus. It is precisely this vacillation between remembering and forgetting that shapes contemporary conversations, attitudes, and legislation about citizenship and belonging for immigrants like Carolina Payano and their Italian children of color. The recent influx of African refugees fleeing former colonies seems to be igniting new racism dressed in the language of border security and economic stability, violently excluding Black and Brown Italians from italianità and rendering them as criminals through the continuous conflation of "immigrant" with "citizen of color" that shapes everyday life in contemporary Italy, an experience I further explore in chapter 5.

Drawing on Jenny Sharpe's notion of slavery as a ghost that haunts present-day racism, Afro-Portuguese scholar Grada Kilomba argues that colonial history haunts us because it has not been properly buried: "The idea of improper burial is identical to the idea of a traumatic event that could not be discharged properly and therefore still exists vividly and intrusively in our present minds. . . . Everyday racism places us back in scenes of a colonial past—recolonizing us again."[145] The Black immigrant bodies of women in the diaspora, like Carolina Payano, are regulated through these haunting colonialities; they are both seen as risky bodies and exist as bodies at risk that must endure colonial violence via legal structures, economic inequalities, and cultural exclusion.[146] Kilomba invites us to decolonize knowledge by summoning the ghosts of the colonial past to the surface, where they can be seen, confronted, mourned, and eventually properly buried. To radically engage with colonialism also requires that we acknowledge the ghost of colonialism that inhabits academia. As Kilomba puts it, it is necessary to privilege the voices and knowledge that "come from the margins," the voices that have been silenced in our archives, and allowing them to become "narrators, writers, subjects and authorities" in their own history and present reality.[147] But how do we include voices that are no longer there? How do we access testimonies and evidence not easily found in dominant archives? How do we humanize the women like Carolina Payano whose lives have been taken and whose bodies have been caricaturized for the comfort and enjoyment of a white audience?

These questions are at the center of contemporary scholarly interventions in the fields of history, critical archival studies, postcolonial/decolonial studies, and transnational ethnic studies. Scholars agree that traditional archives have failed us and that new methods have to be developed in order to read the silences that continue to produce minoritized and colonized peoples as bodies without histories. While scholars agree on the existences of historical silences, though, they do not all agree about how to fill them. As we have seen in Payano's case, when left unfilled, those silences are replaced with the available repertoire of colonial images. For Payano, the silences surrounding the colonial history that shaped her life and her relationship to Italy were filled with the racist colonial images of the Eritrean madama that dominate Italian colonial memory. Both Eritrean madamas and Dominican migrants are silenced and replaced with images of colonial desire that still dominate Italians' understanding of blackness. To conjure the colonial ghosts and fill the silences that sustain the present-day oppression of immigrants and their descendants, Second Generation Italian writers, artists, and activists of color are leading the political struggle through cultural interventions that shatter the silenced history of Italian colonization and translate the struggle of Black Italians to a large global audience through a recognizable language of racial equality, immigrant struggle, African diaspora, and human rights. This dual intervention is creating alternative, contradictory, and complementary archives through the inclusion of past and present nontraditional materials (oral narratives, fiction, songs, and even hearsay). To read these materials, we must recognize the subjective knowledges and epistemes of those who have been silenced. It requires that we *see* Carolina Payano's personhood within the historical, rhetorical, and social sites she inhabited, acknowledging not only the violence that shaped her experiences but the potential yet deferred future that she, as a Black Caribbean migrant, embodied. Archive and method are thus one.

The diverse examples presented in this chapter point to the advantages of developing new frameworks of analysis that can broaden our comparative approaches to race, colonialism, and immigration while paying attention to how the experiences of racialization and immigration manifest in peoples' lives and struggles. They help *see* Carolina Payano, and through her, they help us contra*dict* the violence that continuously erases Black women's humanity, historical agency, and futurity.

5 SECOND GENERATION INTERRUPTIONS

Archives of Black Belonging in Postcolonial Diaspora

Today's fugitives are thus the DREAMers or Black Lives Matter protesters who enact exemplary democratic practices even as their status as citizens is precarious, and as their political activism renders them vulnerable to increased state reprisal. —JULIET HOOKER, *Theorizing Race in the Americas*

In the summer of 2015, I interviewed film director Medhin Paolos (*Asmarina*, 2015) in Milan. While we were talking at Rainbow, a local café in Porta Venezia, a Black street vendor approached us. "Buy this!" he said in English, showing us silk embroidery. When Paolos brushed him off with a polite "No, grazie," the vendor exclaimed, surprised: "Ah! Parli italiano?" Since neither Paolos nor I are white, the vendor had taken us both for American tourists. As one of the leaders of Rete G2, a national organization fighting for citizenship rights for Second Generations (kids of immigrants born in Italy or who migrated at an early age), Paolos is accustomed to justifying her Italian blackness to foreigners and locals alike. She explained to the vendor that her parents are Eritrean. Making himself comfortable next to us, our new friend proudly congratulated Paolos on her English, saying, "A Black person should always speak English." I asked him why. He cast an incredulous look my way, then replied, in English, "Because Black in English is better."

As a light-skinned Black Latina living in the United States, I am all too familiar with the impact of physical appearance and language—including accent, linguistic competency, bilingualism, and diction—on people's constructions and perceptions of racial, ethnic, and national identities. The street vendor's enunciation "Black in English" underscores the connections between language, culture, and race. In Italy, my imperfect Italian and my blackness clearly mark me as a *straniera* (a tourist or foreigner) rather than an *extracomunitaria* (a pejorative term for a noncitizen resident of color; literally "a person out of the community"). I had never been perceived as US American before, despite being a citizen and having grown up in the United States. It was perhaps because of my newly acquired privilege of passing as a Black US American (abroad) that the encounter with the vendor surprised me.

The linguistic constructions of race—and its multiple cultural, political, and semantic translations—can simultaneously exclude (Paolos could not possibly be Black *and* Italian) and include (English made Paolos a better kind of Black, or better at being Black). In the framework of Latinx studies, language and national or ethnic identification are irrevocably linked to race. For Black Latinxs in the United States, for instance, speaking Spanish and performing Latinidad, as Ginetta Candelario's research shows, has at times given them access and privilege denied to Black Anglo-Americans (such as avoiding segregation and Jim Crow practices).[1] At other times, however, Spanish and Latinx linguistic and cultural markers have restricted Black Latinxs' access to representation, political power, and social benefits extended to Black Anglo-Americans (e.g., scholarships, memberships in prestigious organizations, representation in government, etc.).[2] I invoke Black Latinidad here not as a mere example of the implications of "Black in English" but as an epistemological framework for the complexity of translating hegemonic blackness in the afterlives of slavery and colonialism.

As subjects who live within multiple colonial, postcolonial, and intracolonial positionalities, Black Latinxs translate blackness in their everyday lives. One way Latinx Blackness is read as "foreign" in the diaspora is through language. Many of us speak Spanish, Spanglish, Portuguese, or Kreyòl at home. Our existences are often marked by affective relationships to our parents' languages. Those languages in turn shape our engagements with music, art, literature, and history. They also mediate our relationships to recently arrived immigrants and our understandings of ourselves as part of an imagined global community of Latinx people. Latinidad thus coalesces through our historical experiences with European colonialism and its contemporary manifestations: white supremacy, antiblackness, xenophobia, and anti-immigrant violence. But while the linguistic and cultural experiences of Latinidad are bound together by the afterlife of colonialism and its commercialization and exoticization in the Global North, the *Black* in Black Latinidad is a politics of recognition.[3] Black Latinidad offers an important example of how the intersections of colonialism and migration are translated in the contemporary diaspora, calling attention to the contradictions and interdictions that produce Black in English as "better" and shape our understanding of Black citizenship and belonging in the twenty-first century.

The vendor's statement "Black in English is better" emphasizes the ways language (syntax, grammar, inflection, and lexicon) and bodily performance (hairstyle, tattoos, attire, figure, posture, and location) complicate our understandings of race. Paolos's performance of "better" blackness through linguistic competency marked her as decidedly Western and educated—traits our interlocutor associated with the sanitized version of hegemonic blackness that proliferates in the Italian media. Paolos's "better" blackness in turn crystallizes the state's and the media's joint production of acceptable and unacceptable versions of Italian citizens of color.[4]

The fact that in Italy, US blackness is perceived as "better" than Italian blackness points to the ways race (in its multiple linguistic, cultural, and social constructions) and immigration intersect to reproduce categories of exclusion and unbelonging linked to colonial regimes of difference. That is, as we saw in chapters 3 and 4, in Italy, nonwhiteness is assumed to be a marker of foreignness; this presumed foreignness leads to Italians of color being misrecognized as immigrants. Caterina Romeo argues that the Italian media has collaborated with the state to erase blackness from the collective imaginary: "Race—historically a constitutive element in the process of Italian national identity—has 'evaporated' from the cultural debate . . . as a result of the necessity to obliterate 'embarrassing' historical events (Italian colonial history and the racial/racist politics enacted by the Fascist regime, intranational racism, racism against Italian emigrants)."[5] This "evaporation" of race sustains the hegemony of Italian whiteness that led to the vendor's misrecognition of Paolos as a US Black tourist. The foreignness of blackness and, in turn, of anti-Black racism is solidified through Italy's simultaneous engagement with global racism (evidenced by the coverage and debate surrounding the Black Lives Matter movement in the United States) and disengagement from local racism (concretized in the silences surrounding hate crimes against Black immigrants).[6] In contrast, popular Caribbean and US icons of hegemonic blackness—images of exotic and foreign blackness—flood cosmopolitan and urban Italian culture, often reinforcing the idea that Black people (i.e., US Black people) do not experience racism in Italy.[7]

That Black Italianness signifies foreignness, immigration, and unbelonging in Italy while US blackness is conceptualized as "better" points to the global prevalence of US cultural, economic, and political imperialism.[8] As we saw in chapter 1, despite the pervasiveness of racism and inequality in the United States, US imperialism established US blackness as hegemonic—as the lingua franca that connects oppressed communities. But the global hegemony of US blackness also made US antiblackness visible through the history of slavery, the brutal lynching of Black people in the South, segregation, and the present-day police brutality that takes the lives of US Black people in our streets. The hegemony of US blackness became a way to translate the oppression of colonized peoples, migrants, and poor people to the world though recognizable symbols of resistance (e.g., "I Can't Breathe," Black Lives Matter, Black Is Beautiful, Black Power). To be recognized in the diaspora, then, Black migrants and their descendants—be they Black Latinxs or Afro-Italians—must translate their blackness through "better" blackness: the cultural, political, sociological, academic, popular, and historical language of hegemonic US blackness. Doing so offers the possibility of belonging to a larger, more visible network of Black anti-colonial contestations and gains access to history, representation, and political power.

Prior to our encounter with the African vendor, Paolos and I had been discussing the growing popularity of what some call the "Afro Italian" movement: a marketing strategy grounded on cultural, political, and aesthetic representations of hegemonic Black belonging we often associate with the United States (such as hip-hop culture and political figures such as Angela Davis and Malcolm X) led by a small group of Black Italian entrepreneurs and artists.[9] Camilla Hawthorne describes Afro-Italian entrepreneurship as a "complex terrain through which Afro-Italian women seek to advance new representations of Black lives in Italy and transform the meaning of Italianness."[10] However, these emerging expressions of Black Italianness are often interpolated and exploited by the media, the marketing industry, and local politicians in their efforts to appear more inclusive to a younger, intercultural European constituency—a practice that has not effectively produced political, civil, and civic inclusion for Black Italians.[11] Marketing that targets Black Italian consumers employs US-produced slogans like "Black Is Beautiful" and Anglicized terms like "nappy" as well as references to US Black popular culture and history. Paolos describes the result as "a marriage between

Barack Obama, MLK, and Diana Ross."[12] Much like Latinidad in the United States, which produces Latinxs simultaneously as hypervisible and invisible, "Afro Italian" is a convoluted term that profits from and names human and civic exclusion.[13] It is also a term people use to demand access to services and opportunities the state often denies them. For instance, Second Generations use "Afro Italian / Black Italian" to signal solidarity with a larger European community. "Black" in this context names difference and exclusion from Italianness while also appealing to transnational and regional inclusion. "Black Italians" also marks their participation in transnational markets (such as those linked to the natural hair movement), human history (from the struggles for emancipation and freedom from colonial exploitation to political networks organized through transnational Black cultural and political movements), and academic and cultural initiatives (such as Black Europe Summit and Black Europe Summer School). Transnational belonging requires recognizable symbols—often transmitted through marketing and social media—that can translate Italian blackness to a world unaccustomed to imagining Italy as an immigrant-receiving, postcolonial, multiethnic nation.

The power dynamics that rendered Paolos's and my blackness "better" (i.e., foreign) in the eyes of the vendor stem from Italy's colonial histories that, as we saw in chapter 4, frame contemporary Italian engagement with blackness and shape patterns of African postcolonial immigration to Italy. While Italy's role as an immigrant-receiving nation is perceived as new, the Mediterranean country has actually been a hub of immigration—particularly from its former colonies in Africa (Eritrea, Libya, and Somalia)—since the mid-twentieth century.[14] Despite its growing immigrant population (10 percent as of 2019), Italy has not yet learned what to do with the more than 100,000 children of immigrants born in Italy over the past four decades, a reality that shapes contemporary notions of citizenship and belonging in contemporary Europe, as the work of Jean Beaman, Tiffany Florvil, Fatima El-Tayeb, Nana Osei-Kofi, and others illuminates.[15] As Beaman argues in the case of France, "Differential treatment and exclusion are based on racial and ethnic status" that marginalizes individuals because "they are not white."[16] In the case of Italy, the persistence of jus sanguinis citizenship legislation means that Second Generation children of immigrants exist in political limbo, unbelonging to their nation.[17] Many Italian-born children of immigrants are also unable to naturalize, and thus live between Italianness and foreignness. In this context, "better" also refers to Paolos's relationship to the Italian state, determined by her presumed legal citizenship as well as her successful performance of linguistic competency in Italian, cultural assimilation, and secular clothing. Though the vendor felt a sense of kinship with Paolos through what Raimi Gbadamosi calls the "artificial boundaries" of the Black diaspora, as he clearly let us know in sitting down with us to share a drink at the café, he also understood his blackness to be different from—and worse than—Paolos's.[18] As a recent Muslim African immigrant, he experiences the everyday violence of state surveillance amid the widespread fear of terrorism and the ever-growing "refugee crisis."[19] The vendor's misrecognition of Paolos's Italian blackness, then, must be understood within the context of postcolonial racism in which blackness is "evaporated," foreign, ahistorical, and superfluous to the nation—a dynamic also encapsulated in the derogatory term *extracomunitari*, commonly used to refer to people of color in Italy.[20] In *European Others*, El-Tayeb argues, "Race, at times, seems to exist anywhere but in Europe, where racialized minorities have traditionally been placed outside of the national, and by extension continental, community. Europe can thus be situated within the larger context of ideologies of colorblindness that prohibit discourses around racialized oppression."[21] That is, minoritized Second Generation citizens of color like Paolos are produced in the national imaginary as migrant extracomunitari without rights, practices that shape their everyday unbelonging to Italy.

This chapter weaves together colonialism, migration, and blackness through what I call Second Generation interruptions: cultural productions, political interventions, and public art by Second Generation Black Italians that challenge white supremacist constructions of humanity, citizenship, and belonging. "Second Generation" refers to people who are born to immigrant parents, people who migrated at an early age, mixed-race people, and adoptees who experience exclusion from national belonging due to their presumed identities as racialized (Black/Brown/Asian) foreigners due to white supremacist productions of citizenship. As a sociological term, "Second Generation" was first politicized in 2005 in Italy by a multiethnic group of young people that lobbied to overturn jus sanguinis citizenship legislation.[22] Since then, the term has been contested by those who reject the sociological terminology or who want to insist on their subject positions as citizens without having to name their relationship to migration. Borrowing from the brave founders of the Second Generation Network, or Rete G2, I use the term to translate the transnational solidarity of people who migrated as children or were born in the diaspora. My engagement with Black italianità via Second Generation interruptions, in conversation with Black Latinidad, in this chapter is an invitation to think about blackness as global. It also comes with a plea to educate ourselves about the diversity of experiences beyond hegemonic blackness that shape the history and present of collective global blackness.

La mia formazione culturale è italiana, la lingua in cui scrivo è l'italiano (non per scelta, ma per corso naturale) . . . ma il mio vissuto è legato a doppio filo con la madrepatria del cuore, ossia quella Somalia martoriata dei miei genitori.

[My cultural background is Italian, the language in which I write is Italian (not by choice, but by natural course) . . . but my experience is closely linked with the motherland of the heart, that is that battered Somalia of my parents.]
—Igiaba Scego, "Relazione di Igiaba Scego"

Feminist scholar bell hooks writes, "The idea that one has to write, almost as a virtual moral obligation, embodies the belief that history can be interrupted, appropriated, and transformed through artistic and literary practice."[23] For hooks, writing is not only an artistic practice but also an act of archival justice through which the writer "interrupts" the colonial order and provides another perspective of the truth. Interpolating hooks, Grada Kilomba insists that writing is a way of asserting an "authority of [our] own history" for Black subjects who have been excluded from dominant colonialized narratives.[24] For postcolonial, Afro-descendant people living in the Global North, to write is to interrupt coloniality and refocus history from the perspective of colonized, minoritized, racialized subjects to contra*dict* its violence. For immigrant communities of color, too—particularly Second Generations living in the Global North—writing is an important historical-political strategy for intervening in colonized national archives and mainstream globalized culture. The global success and recognition of writers like Junot Díaz, Jhumpa Lahiri, Chimamanda Adichie, Neel Mukherjee, Ocean Vuong, and Marie NDiaye have increased public awareness of the experiences of Second Generation people of color and the role they play as cultural and historical translators of the experiences of transition from colonial to postcolonial, national to global. Unlike their parents, Second Generations write from within the nation—if not always as legal citizens, they write as cultural citizens. They occupy the interstitial space of almost belonging, sitting comfortably in their discomfort, contra*dict*ing white supremacy and the colonial order that led to their parents' migration and their own struggles for cultural and political belonging to the nations in which they came of age and/or were born.

In Italy, Second Generations have been particularly successful in sparking a dialogue about the historical nexus of colonialism, migration, and national belonging, forcing a national conversation about the silenced history of Italian colonialism in East Africa and its impacts on present-day racism and xenophobia. Graziella Parati argues that Second Generations "talk back" to the nation, impelling Italy to recognize its colonial past to make room for a new multicultural Italy.[25] Lorenzo Mari and Polina Shvanyukova also point to the significance of immigrant literature (which at times is a genre that includes Second Generation writers of color whose parents are immigrants) in challenging homogeneous, mainstream interpretations of race, religion, ethnicity, and national identity.[26]

Igiaba Scego's acclaimed 2010 memoir, *La mia casa è dove sono*, is one of the most recognizable literary examples of Second Generation "talking back." Interpolating W. E. B. Du Bois, Scego shows readers how Italianness and blackness coexist in her through the history of colonialism that led to her parents' migration from Somalia and her eventual birth in Rome by writing about her family's story as historical, and about Rome's monuments, neighborhoods, and streets that link Somalia to Italy via colonial violence. The violent history of Italian colonialism in East Africa, which I study in chapter 4, and its everyday manifestations in major cities—from the monuments named after men of arms who destroyed entire villages and raped girls, to streets named after cities in East Africa, to artifacts stolen from the colonies that populate piazzas and museums, to the bodies of newly arrived refugees sleeping outside train and bus stations—shape Scego's experience as a Black woman in contemporary Italy. In turn, through her doubly conscious experience as a Black Somali Italian woman, the author calls attention to the colonial foundations of (white supremacist) italianità and its present-day quotidian manifestations by interweaving personal and national histories that link Italy to Somalia. Scego's writing answers Kilomba's call to own the narrative, to become the history and authority from which to speak back to the nation.

Scego is one of the most recognized of the Second Generation contemporary Black Italian writers. She rose to popularity with the publication of her short stories "Salsicce" and "Dismatria" in the seminal 2005 anthology *Pecore nere* (Black sheep).[27] The collection called attention to the experiences of Black Italians and opened the door for crucial—and overdue—postcolonial critique.[28] In interviews, Scego often describes herself as a "writer *and* citizen." Though she does not identify as an activist, she is often called one by journalists and literary critics because the position from which she speaks makes visible the present-day implications of a colonial past white Italians would like to forget and Black Italians cannot: "My interest in Black Italy, is, first of all, motivated by an interest in myself—a Black woman in this country, born in this country. For me, it has actually been an absolute necessity to dig up history to understand, first, why I am a product of colonialism since my parents came to Italy also because of Italian colonialism and its legacies."[29]

Scego's self-definition as a historically situated citizen is central to the politics of the Second Generation (G2) movement in Italy. As I later discuss, the actions of the G2 movement have centered on raising awareness of the multiple ways statutory belonging to the nation is deferred from, withheld from, and denied to many children of immigrants of color through legal structures based on white supremacist colonial law.[30] To call themselves citizens is a radical act that contra*dicts* white supremacist italianità. Still, Scego writes as a legal citizen, from a somewhat privileged position of *almost* belonging. Born in Rome in 1974 to Somali parents who migrated to Italy following Siad Barre's 1969 coup d'état, Scego became an Italian citizen at age eighteen. In all her writing, she insists on reminding Italy of the perdurance of coloniality that shapes everyday life experiences for postcolonial migrants and their descendants.

Stylistically, Scego's *La mia casa è dove sono* fits the framework of what Gilles Deleuze and Félix Guattari term "minor literature" in "the use of a dominant language and hegemonic cultural terms for political interventions on behalf of an oppressed collective."[31] Scego's literary corpus linguistically and culturally translates Somali history to mainstream Italian popular discourse that conjures the everyday life experiences of growing up in Italy. In her public appearances, Scego often claims her italianità by making reference to popular culture, from music to soccer, and by an insistence on language as a form for cultural belonging.[32] The minoritized narration of Scego's Black experience is also guided by a DuBoisian double consciousness that results not from immigrant assimilation to a majoritarian culture but from an ancestral, visceral, involuntary bond to the colonial oppressor. As she writes in *La mia casa*, "Ho sempre sentito L'Italia profondamente mia" (I have always felt Italy profoundly mine).[33] Scego is Black and Italian because Italy is very much a part of Somalia's history, just as Somalia is a part of Italy's; the two nations are connected by indelible colonial violence.

La mia casa memorializes Italian colonialism as central to the construction of the postcolonial Italian nation, locating that history in Rome through Scego's experience growing up Somali and Italian. Rome's streets are covered with African symbols, most notably in the iconic elephant statue on the Piazza della Minerva (see figure 5.1).[34] As the narrative moves between Rome and Mogadishu through memory and cartographic reconstructions of both cities, the reader follows Scego's vaivén through Black italianità. In the third chapter, "Piazza Santa Maria sopra Minerva," Scego remembers the first time she noticed Africa in Rome. She was walking in the Piazza della Minerva (also known as Piazza Santa Maria della Minerva) with her mother when

FIGURE 5.1 Elephant and obelisk statue in Piazza della Minerva by Gian Lorenzo Bernini in 1667, Rome, 2017. Photo by author.

she noticed the elephant statue. She asked her mom, "Ma siamo in Somalia?" (But are we in Somalia?).[35] Five-year-old Scego had seen so many books about animals that she knew elephants were African: "Mamma rise. Mi disse che no, quella era ancora Roma. La mia confusione durò giorni. Allora Roma è in Somalia? O la Somalia si trova dentro Roma? Quell'elefantino africano nella città confondeva tutte le mie certezze" (Mom laughs. She says no, we are still in Rome. My confusion lasted many days. So Rome was in Somalia? Or is Somalia in Rome? That little elephant in the city confused me).[36] Scego's childhood confusion over the dislocation of the elephant in Rome encapsulates her displaced Black italianità. Remapping Rome through her Somali-Italian eyes, Scego contra*dicts* Italian colonial amnesia while calling out the presence of coloniality in contemporary Italy and the buried histories of unequal African-Italian entanglement that have led to the present-day alienation and dislocation of its citizens of color. East African and Italian histories are intertwined, *La mia casa* shows us, but their entanglement does not equal belonging for Black citizens like Scego. Instead, they must navigate two competing epistemes and cultural regimes. Making sense of elephants in Rome in this climate of historical forgetting is indeed a confusing endeavor.

Colonialism, or rather the relationship between colonialism and present-day Italian antiblackness, shapes Scego's relationship to citizenship and belonging. Her oeuvre, as we see in her celebrated novels *Adua* (2015) and *La linea del colore* (2020), bridges colonialism and Second Generation exclusion. In the middle of that bridge, the author places the experiences of migration and displacement Italy and the world currently recognize as a "crisis" (i.e., the images we have all become accustomed to of boats full of people in the Mediterranean coast of Lampedusa, long lines at borders, children in cages, and other violent illustrations of xenophobia and antiblackness). Her stories and characters are thus always in vaivén, between colonized Africa and postcolonial Italy, past and present.[37] Rather than inhabiting "racially evaporated" italianità, as the "multicultural" nation requires its citizens of color to do, Scego's writing interrupts and redefines italianità as a product of colonialism, white supremacy, Fascism, and antiblackness. In so doing, Scego's corpus breaks the silences of Italian colonialism that lead to the present-day exclusion of Second Generation postcolonial Italian Black subjects from the nation and its archives.

In Somalia, Italy is inescapable: it is in the names of the streets, the light shades of Black skin, and the language people speak.[38] In Italy, Somalia has been swept under the rug, hidden between the lines, erased from books and archives in what I elsewhere call "the footnote condition," through which the stories of colonized and otherized people are disappeared from official archives, national monuments, and hegemonic popular representations of the nation.[39] Only those who already feel the pain of displacement find Somalia in Rome's urban landscapes and historical footnotes. But Somalia, Scego's work reminds us, is also present in the Black bodies of Somali refugees in Rome's streets, train stations, and parks, summoning the presence of Italy's colonialism in the everyday lives of migrants and their descendants. *La mia casa* repositions colonial memory, bringing the footnotes into the main text to force a national dialogue that can lead to her (and other Second Generations') recognition as a citizen of the Italian nation. One of the most memorable ways the repositioning of colonial memory appears in the memoir is through Scego's memories of her "almost white" grandfather, Omar: "Il bianco della sua pelle mi ha posto questi interrogativi irrisolvibili. Il bianco di quella pelle metteva in crisi la costruzione che mi ero fatta della mia fiera identità africana. Nessuno è puro a questo mondo" (The whiteness of his skin has brought forth this unsolvable question. The white in that skin put into question the construction of my own proud African identity. No one is pure in this world).[40] Perhaps because of his light skin, Omar secures a job as a translator for one of the most ruthless Italian generals in the early years of the occupation of Somalia.[41] When Scego learns this, she is surprised and conflicted. She wonders, "Mio nonno allora era fascista?" (Was my grandfather now a Fascist?).[42] The tortuous deliberation that follows resonates with the legacy of italianità many Italians try to forget but which continues to haunt the political climate of the nation as younger generations grapple with the inheritances of Fascism and the need to construct new inclusive structures.[43] Yet it is because of her grandfather's alliance with Fascism that Scego's family survived the displacement and violence of colonialism. Her grandfather's Fascism, symbolized in his light skin, is the painful history and complicated roots of her own italianità. As she grapples with the historical contradictions that led to her family's expulsion from Somalia and saved them from the fate of many other displaced Somalis, Scego inherits her grandfather's trade, translating the past and present that produced her Italian blackness through a historical summoning of colonial memory.

Postcolonial writing like Scego's illuminates the specter of colonial violence in the everyday life experiences of Black Italians. *La mia casa è dove sono* confronts this quotidian violence head-on in Scego's questioning of her own identity: "Sono cosa? Sono chi? Sono nera e italiana. Ma sono anche somala e nera. Allora sono afroitaliana? Italoafricana? Seconda generazione? Incerta generazione? Meel Kalee? Un fastidio? Negra saracena? Sporca negra?" (What am I? Who am I? I am Black and Italian. But also Somali and Black. Then am I African-Italian? Italian-African? Second generation? Uncertain generation? Something else? A nuisance? A Black Saracen? A dirty Negro?).[44] The opening, "Sono cosa?" (What am I?), denounces what Tiffany Florvil calls "the practice of daily racism" through which Black citizens remain inadmissible to the nation as full "human subjects and full citizens."[45] In so doing, "Sono cosa?" calls out to the world for admission into what Arthur Schomburg imagined as "the nation without a nation"—diasporic unity. Scego's contra*diction* of the white supremacist Italian nation is part of the diasporic archives of Black belonging. But the experience of naming herself in relation to the colonializing nation is, to Scego, an absurd, futile, and yet violent exercise of repetition and erasure: "Then am I African Italian? Italian African?" Her almost belonging is symbolized in the shifting of "African" from prefix to suffix attached to the gentilic Italian, marking the unbelonging, and defining her racially in contradistinction to the nation of which she is a citizen. Instead of Afro-Italian, I would suggest, Scego fits more comfortably in the space in between, that space US Latinx scholars, following Gustavo Pérez Firmat, have theorized as "the hyphen," or what I elsewhere have called, following Josefina Báez, El Nié: neither here nor there.[46] Neither African nor Italian, neither colonizer nor colonized, Scego's "cosa?" demands a redefinition of the nation-state and its racial boundaries of belonging. It is not Scego who does not fit italianità but Italy that has failed to be a nation for all its citizens.

The word *cosa* means "what," but it also means thing or object, summoning the incomplete humanity that Lisa Lowe, Sylvia Wynter, and other scholars have argued shapes the experience of colonized Others, particularly Black people, in the diaspora—an experience that converts us into "what" rather than "who" in the eyes of the colonizing white supremacist nation.[47] To answer the loaded question—"Sono cosa?"—Scego moves through multiple, contradictory, and violent euphemisms for racism. The words travel in crescendo through the language of hegemonic identity politics—"afroitaliana? Italoafricana? Seconda generazione? Incerta generazione? Meel Kalee? Un fastidio? Negra saracena?"—ultimately arriving at a direct confrontation with the discourse of racial violence: "Sporca negra?" (A dirty Negro?). This linguistic escalation points to the violence embedded in both politically correct and incorrect labels; they all carry the mark of exclusion. Anticipating white readers' discomfort, the narrator challenges readers to find a "better" name for Italian blackness, pointing to the absurdity of accommodating white privilege at the expense of Black belonging: "Non è politicamente corretto chiamarla così? . . . Allora come mi chiameresti tu?" (Is it not politically correct to call her [the speaker] that? . . . Then what would you call me?).[48]

The terms that name blackness in Italy (*negra, nera, di colore*) are part of a complex national identity process linked to internal as well as external borders guiding Italian nation narration. There is ample scholarship on the internal bordering of Italy, particularly as it relates to race and class.[49] When considering the racialization of immigrants from the Global South and Second Generations in Italy, though, it is helpful to remember that it is intertwined with the "coloring" of southerners in the Italian racial imagination.[50] The growing demands for cultural diversity are thus very much in vaivén, at times in conflict and at others in dialogue, with the hegemonic version of national identity that projects southern Italians as abject to the nation. Scego's confrontation with the language of white privilege through racial slurs and identity politics suggests that naming blackness in Italy is superfluous: all labels carry the implicit exclusion of "Sono cosa?" In such a violent lexical climate, the terms people use to name their exclusion become less important than *how* they use them. Scego's DuBoisian speech act, "Sono nera e italiana," is an assertion of dual belonging that contests political conformity. Like other Second Generation Italian artists, Scego is invested in italianità. Yet this investment also contains an important critique of Italy's disavowal of its postcolonial subjects and the resulting doubly conscious existence of Italians of color. In their analysis of citizenship and belonging in Black Italian writing, SA Smythe argues that Black Italian authors "illustrate how human desires and political demands for belonging exceed the project of citizenship. . . These narratives thus contribute not only to contemporary and postcolonial literature, but also to the study and appreciation of Black aesthetic life, Black experiences, and Black resistance to colonial logics and violent racial regimes across the diaspora."[51] Smythe's argument highlights the inherently anti-colonial project that lays within Black Italian contemporary literature. Second Generation Black Italian literature chronicles the afterlife of colonial violence experienced by migrants and their children in their attempt to become Black Italian citizens.

I contend that this anti-colonial Black Italian project, which is in contra-*diction* to hegemonic italianità, extends beyond literature to other cultural productions such as film, music, and street art (including the recent defacing of colonial statues), activism (particularly Second Generation activism around citizenship legislation), and even the daily interactions between nonwhite ethnic groups across Italian cities that recall and contradict the afterimages and aftersounds of colonial violence that proliferate in present-day Italian media (e.g., in songs like "Faccetta Nera").[52] As Smythe argues, these cultural interventions lead us to think deeper about the intersections of colonialism, blackness, and immigration as they shape notions of belonging and unbelonging for Black citizens in Italy and other parts of the Black diaspora.

Diaspora Archives, Colonial Interruptions

Italy's history of violence toward the peoples it colonized and their Italian children, as we saw in chapter 4, persists in shaping present-day understandings of Italian colonialism and its afterlife. Aside from a few temporary state-sponsored photographic exhibitions in civic museums in Rome and Milan, the historical effects of Italian violence on Eritrea, Somalia, Libya, and Ethiopia have yet to receive national institutional recognition. The only museum specifically dedicated to Italian colonialism is the Museo Civico dell'Italia in Africa 1885–1960 in Ragusa, which is primarily a display of military costumes. There is a public monument, the contested Monumento ai Caduti di Dogali, originally placed outside Rome's Termini railway station and later moved near the Baths of Diocletian, dedicated to the 548 white Italian soldiers killed in the Battle of Dogali between East Africans and Italians during the occupation of Eritrea in 1887.[53] The monument, which is one of the many ancient African obelisks in Rome, rests on a base surrounded by four markers upon which are engraved the names of the fallen soldiers. The obelisk itself is an Egyptian relic from the thirteenth century BC; it was erected by Pharaoh Ramses II in the city of Heliopolis and moved to Rome during the first century by Emperor Domitian. The relic was uncovered during an archaeological excavation in 1719 and eventually dedicated to fallen soldiers shortly after their defeat in Dogali. That an African artistic relic has served to commemorate the loss of white Italian soldiers in a battle against colonization is exemplary of how Italian memory of colonization erases Africa while simultaneously exalting the consolidation of white italianità through imperial will over Africa and Africans. For many years now, multiple activist groups have been advocating for the repatriation of the Egyptian obelisks to Egypt. The "Dogali Obelisk," as it has come to be known, has been at the center of the controversy.[54] Italy's simultaneous lack of institutional memory of Africans who experienced colonial violence and repetitive celebration of white colonizers whitewashes the brutality of colonial rule and impedes the creation of proper institutional representation that could in turn lead to sincere dialogue about present-day racism.

Until recently, colonialism—beyond military memorials—has been ignored in Italian public memory and largely suppressed from critical engagement in any of the country's major heritage institutions. However, a postcolonial critique across different art forms, particularly documentary films and literary works by Second Generations and immigrants from former colonies, has emerged over the past decade, leading to important shifts in the cultural dialogue.[55] Derek Duncan and Ekaterina Haskins both argue that visual interventions are particularly effective in public interpellations of dominant memory because they facilitate evidential recognition and recollection.[56] Parati adds that film—particularly films about the immigrant and diasporic experiences of Italians of color—can effectively talk back to the nation by placing individual migrants' stories at the center of a visual narrative in ways that are more accessible to migrants themselves.[57] She argues that migrants' cultural productions are "counternarratives" to the negative representations of migrants that dominate Italy's public archive. These counternarratives challenge the persistent silences surrounding Italian colonialism and lead to a greater sense of belonging that builds a more inclusive, just, and humanized archive of colonialism and migration.

One of the most significant interruptions of the hegemonic archive of Italian colonial violence is the 2015 documentary film *Asmarina*, directed by Milanese filmmakers Alan Maglio and Medhin Paolos. Through a visually stunning interpellation of Milan via the lives of its Habesha inhabitants, Maglio and Paolos examine the colonial violence that led to Black Italians' doubly conscious existence. The term *Habesha* refers to people who are from Eritrea or Ethiopia or who trace their ancestry to the region. In the Italian diaspora, the term is used to assert cultural and political alliances.[58] Moving through the city of Milan, and in particular the neighborhood of Porta Venezia, the lens introduces a new cartography that is shaped by people rather than monuments. The people—the Habeshas of Porta Venezia—share a sonic and visual archive that comes together in the film through Habesha cultural influence in the city via music, food, and art. The film moves us seamlessly through this alternative Milan, drawing a map that connects colonial history with present-day Milanese life. In its linking of present-day life with colonial memory, *Asmarina* engages with global racial terms and the repositioning of Black Italian alterity as a product of African colonialism, exemplifying how new cultural interventions can force Italy to recognize and publicly confront the "ghosts of colonialism."[59] The film opens with what appears to be a contact sheet of images from an official photographic archive. A hand moves a magnifying glass through a series of numbered slides labeled "Eritrea or Eritreans" as the camera guides our attention to some of them: a smiling girl, children playing, Eritrean women dressed in traditional clothing, a school building, the Asmara airport. Less than a minute into the film, the scene switches to another set of images. While this second set are also photos of Habesha people—children dressed in traditional clothing, people at parties, groups of friends, family celebrations—they are not labeled or numbered; they clearly come from family photo albums. Different sets of hands point at the photos, inviting us to look and perhaps recognize someone. In the background we see a bar, a living room, a kitchen. The juxtaposition of the two sets of photos introduces the film as an archive that interrupts the dominant logic of Italian colonial violence.

Through photography, storytelling, music, and cartography, *Asmarina* bears witness to the intimate and public ways colonial memory permeates Italian life in the present, shaping how Habeshas and other Black Italians experience colonialism in their everyday lives. The use of photography to access memory produces a repository of knowledge in which meaning, affect, and images interact, contradict, and intersect with the public memory of colonialism immortalized in the cartography of the city. Through images and sounds that contradict the violent afterimages and aftersounds of colonial violence,

FIGURE 5.2 Habesha community in Milan, religious celebration. Still from *Asmarina*, 2015.

the film also translates a series of experiences that shape the lives of Habesha people in the diaspora, merging photography (an archive) and memory (the recollection of affective events) to give the viewer a more complete historical account of Habeshas' past and present engagements with Italian colonialism. In the film, people appear as part of a narrative. They have names and stories rather than existing as mere visual representations of violence. In this way, the film translates colonial history, Second Generation struggles, and the so-called European refugee crisis through the lives and stories of living subjects.

One of the film's most important intertexts is the 1985 book *Stranieri a Milano* (Foreigners in Milan), by Lalla Golderer and Vito Scifo. The film juxtaposes the book's black-and-white photos of "foreigners" in Milan with present-day color footage of the ethnically mixed Habesha neighborhood of Porta Venezia. The images are accompanied by testimonies from people who remember the events associated with the photos. The photos in the book show Eritrean, Somali, Salvadoran, and Ethiopian immigrants engaged in various quotidian activities: ceremonies, picnics, taking the train, walking, and going to church. Led by the book's photos, Maglio and Paolos embarked on a quest to find the stories behind Milan's "foreigners." The film that resulted is a web of private and public histories that effectively produces a cohesive visual narrative of Eritrean Italianness that contra*dicts* the nation's silence and erasure of the postcolonial Italian Habeshas living in Italy (see figure 5.2). *Asmarina*'s use of photography, as well as the film's strong social media presence (via

YouTube, Facebook, and Twitter), has consecrated it as an important postcolonial contestation.[60] Moreover, the film's international success is profoundly linked to its recognition as an African diasporic and immigrant cultural product.[61]

The film's first encounter with *Stranieri a Milano* is through the eyes of Elena Woldegabriel, an Italian-born Eritrean-Italian woman. We meet Woldegabriel, along with her mixed-race children and Eritrean-born parents, as they arrive at her parents' apartment. There, the directors share with the family the images and photos from the book. Woldegabriel seems excited to see the photos (see figure 5.3). As she flips through the book, she begins to recognize herself in it, finding pictures of herself as a child and becoming emotional: "These are beautiful! What a beautiful memory."[62] But once her initial excitement subsides, Woldegabriel becomes increasingly upset about the book's title, particularly the choice to define Eritrean Italians as foreigners: "We are foreigners? Even though I speak perfect Italian, was born and grew up here?"[63] As she asks these questions, holding the book and rapidly flipping through the pages, Woldegabriel looks straight at the camera as if asking the viewer why she—as a Second Generation, born and raised in Italy—is perceived as more foreign than actual immigrants, than visitors: "I am more foreign than [a tourist] who comes to visit and does not speak Italian. . . . Those of us who are 'non-European immigrants' are considered bad, others are ok. . . . An American is not considered extracomunitario. . . . But I am."[64] As if answering her own question, Woldegabriel then makes the connection between her own exclusion from italianità and the legacy of colonialism the film is trying to unearth: "Meanwhile we exist in the limbo of distrust they call diversity. . . . And then they speak about colonialism in a romantic tone like they do not know that colonialism is about war, about pain, about destruction."[65] Woldegabriel's reaction to being cast as a "foreigner" in the book calls attention to the history of Italian colonialism that shapes Eritrean postcoloniality—dictatorship, land erosion, destitute mixed-race children, colorism—and that leads Eritreans to immigrate to Italy, to then face exclusion from Italian citizenship and belonging. Colonialism becomes timeless as Kilomba argues and as Woldegabriel articulates in the film, its afterlife erasing Italians of color from the nation.

Woldegabriel's reactions to the photos in *Stranieri a Milano* document the effects of colonialism through what Deborah Thomas has called "affective archives": documentation of memories embodied as ways of knowing and bearing witness to the knowledge violence produces.[66] Woldegabriel cries, laughs, and gets angry. She gets up, sits down, walks to another part

FIGURE 5.3 Elena and her family looking through photos. Still from *Asmarina*, 2015.

of the small apartment, unable to stay put. Her body remembers what the official archives try to silence: the effects and affects of colonialism on her life. Her memory, in turn, begs the viewer's recognition of her Second Generation condition that is the direct result of colonialism: her unbelonging to italianità despite having been born and raised in Italy: "I am much more ostracized having been born and raised here than an Italian who speaks Tigrinya born and raised there [in Eritrea]!"[67] For Woldegabriel, the presence of colonialism is not at all the past but rather her everyday reality that inflicts pain and reproduces her exclusion and recolonizes her existence within the nation-state.

Director Paolos explains that her own Second Generation postcolonial Eritrean-Italian experience was the original impulse for making the film: "We [Eritrean people] have been part of Milan for a very long time. . . . Our histories, Italy's and Eritrea's, are intertwined in ways that are very visible to those who want to see. Yet, our history, our presence, our lives are erased from the narrative. I wanted to bring those histories to light but I wanted to do so in a way that memorializes how people remember it."[68] Calling herself a "story listener," Paolos describes *Asmarina* as a crossroads of stories and histories linked through people.[69] The critique of colonialism *Asmarina* poses shows how diasporic postcolonial subjects appear simultaneously Italian through cultural and linguistic belonging and abject from italianità through the structures of colonialism's afterlife grounded on antiblackness.

Alessandro Triulzi argues that Italian postcoloniality is simply coloniality in that "it continues to reproduce . . . ambiguous displacements of memory in the politically volatile and unresolved public arena of both metropolis and colony."[70] Following Triulzi's reasoning, postcolonial critiques must necessarily attempt to shatter the silenced history of Italian colonial violence and its lasting effects on people. *Asmarina* accomplishes precisely that.

The various texts, testimonies, interviews, and objects in the film create an archive of contra*diction* through which the subjugated knowledge of Habesha people suppressed by the hegemonic Italian memory of colonization comes through. The title, *Asmarina*, for example, references "Asmarina, Asmarina," a 1956 song by Pippo Maugeri that, much like the Fascist song "Faccetta Nera" studied in chapter 4, portrays Eritrean girls and women as exotic beauties—commodities for white Italian men's consumption.

Non so se ti chiami Cicci, Lilly, o Zazà
Sei nata ad Asmara
E sei un fior di beltà.
Fanciulla asmarina,
Sei più bella per me . . .
Asmarina, asmarina,
Di bellezza sei regina,
Se ti vedo da lontano,
Casca quello che ho in mano,
Asmarina, guarda un po'[71]

[I don't know if your name is Cicci, Lilly, or Zazà
You were born in Asmara
You are as beautiful as a flower
My Asmara girl
You are the most beautiful to me . . .
My Asmara girl
You are as beautiful as a queen
If I see you from afar
I drop whatever I'm holding
My Asmara girl, look what you've made of me]

The film's narrative follows the song—and its multiple afterlives—within the Eritrean community, bringing attention to its pervasiveness and the ways Eritrean people subvert its colonial violence. The song—or, rather, the memory of the song—appears at the beginning and throughout the film as multiple generations of Habesha people listen to it and make sense of its meaning. Paolos explains, "If you are Eritrean and a woman, like myself, you have a memory of this song."[72] When interviewing Habeshas in Milan, the song was an important point of entry; it allowed people to confront colonial memory and speak about the personal ways those memories shape their lives in Italy. One of these memories appears thirty minutes into the film as Woldegabriel and her multigenerational family listen to the song together. Woldegabriel, her parents, and her young children all listen with attentive curiosity. At times, Woldegabriel cannot resist her laughter. She finds the tone and its exotifying racism ridiculous. At one point she receives a call from her husband on the phone and plays a verse of the song for him. She asks him in a mocking tone, "Am I your queen? Do I make you shiver when you look at me?" before bursting into laughter.[73]

The most significant contra*diction* of the song, however, appears when the directors play a version of "Asmarina, Asmarina" performed in Tigrinya in 1989 by Eritrean artist Wedi Shawl for the family.[74] Shawl's is an anticolonial version that recovers the city of Asmara as a site of belonging for Eritreans rather than as the nostalgic location of Italian colonial memory that appears to be in the original version. He sings, "Asmara is ours. Ours in our eyes and in our hearts."[75] Changing the chorus from "Asmarina" (a girl or woman from Asmara) to "Asmerana" (our Asmara), Shawl recasts the song as one of liberation and belonging for Eritreans. "Asmerana" is a contra*diction* to Fascism, colonialism, and exoticization as well as a declaration of freedom for Eritrean people. In his introduction to his performance, Shawl warns the audience: "Now I don't want to fool you. I can't speak Italian," before singing a few verses of "Asmarina, Asmarina" to an audience of about ten thousand. As people clap and laugh excitedly, Shawl stops singing the Italian version and tells the audience, "That is how he [Pippo Maugeri] sang it. Now I will sing it in my language." He then switches to Tigrinya and the music switches to a lively funk pop style: "Our Asmara, our Asmara, you're in our eyes and in our hearts." Sung at the Eritrean Festival in Bologna (ፌስቲቫል ኤርትራ ቦሎኛ), an annual event organized by the diasporic Eritrean community in Italy that hosted more than ten thousand exiles, migrants, and Second Generations from all over the European diaspora from 1973 to 1991, the song evinced the characteristic optimism of the festival through which the Eritrean diaspora expressed its support of the Eritrean People's Liberation Front (EPLF).[76] The festival was a place for political strategizing and fundraising where the diasporic Eritrean community could come together to imagine their new independent nation.

As Anna Arnone writes, the festival was "such a formative collective experience that people often refer to it to exemplify what their migration experience was about and how fundamental it was for the Eritrean community in Italy and the diasporic networks. People recall how Eritrean people arrived to Bologna to attend the Festival from other parts of Italy, from European countries but also from other continents. So the Bologna Festival became a symbol of people's participation in the struggle to become an independent state."[77] Shawl's performance of "Asmerana" during the 1989 festival was a call to action in the project of Eritrean nation building and decolonization. Participants remember the festival as a transformative communal experience that brought Eritreans together as a people, building diasporic networks of inclusion across Italy and beyond. Juxtaposing the two versions of the song and the reactions of Eritrean families listening to them, while historicizing the transnational political and cultural significance of the Eritrean Festival in Bologna, the film demonstrates how colonialism and anti-colonial struggles together shape the present-day lives of Second Generation Italians of Eritrean ancestry, creating what I have elsewhere called an archive of contra*diction* from which the suppressed histories of Italian colonialism become visible.[78]

There are many ways for viewers to see the film: through photography, music, cartography, and the stories of the Habesha Italians in the film. The film weaves together a diversity of subjects and stories with military history, archival photography, music, movement, and testimonies of multigenerational, multiethnic Eritrean-Italian families. In doing so, it creates a complicated and unique archive of contra*diction* that tells a more complete story of Eritrean-Italian experiences that not only makes visible the colonial past but insists on the ways Habesha Italians—and by extension other Second Generation Black Italians—continue to be excluded from the nation.

One of the first storytellers to appear in the film is Michele Lettenze, a mixed-race man born in Asmara in 1942 whose migration to Italy in the mid-1960s was facilitated by the very jus sanguinis citizenship legislation that excludes other Eritrean Italians from italianità. During World War II, Eritrea was placed under British administration, eventually becoming part of the Eritrean-Ethiopian Federation, a territory that encompassed both the Italian colony of Eritrea and the Ethiopian Empire. On November 14, 1962, Ethiopian emperor Haile Selassie annexed Eritrea, in defiance of peace treaties and a United Nations resolution. As a result of this tumultuous political environment, Italy issued an order of repatriation that allowed mixed-race children to "return" to Italy. It is in this context that Lettenze received Italian citizenship and was able to migrate at the age of twenty. But Lettenze's father, a white Italian man, did not recognize him as his son, and so he was declared "NN—Nescio Nome" (without a name or child of no one) on his official Italian documents. In the film, Lettenze holds up his repatriation documents while talking about his life as a mixed-race child in segregated Eritrea.

> Until now, all I know of my life is my mother, nothing else. I am a "meticcio," a son of an Eritrean and an Apulian [a man from Puglia]. I never knew my father. He could not recognize me because he was married in Italy. I was raised in the gutter, in poverty. Back then, when poor people like me arrived in the city, we had a curfew, and the police would come and arrest us because we should not go where all the whites went. . . . Then one day they gave me an Italian passport that said "Michele Lettenze, born in Asmara in 1942, son of no one, permanently repatriated from Asmara, Ethiopia"—because back then it was Ethiopia—"to Italia." Once I arrived, I tore the passport because it was not fair to say that. . . . I am the son of an Italian man. It was not fair.[79]

Lettenze's testimony, woven throughout the film, is incredibly powerful in illustrating the insidious ways that colonial violence shaped migration and diaspora for Eritreans. As we meet other people in the film and hear their stories, we can trace just how these histories fit together—how colonialism, racism, segregation, dictatorship, bordering, xenophobia, and migration fit together—and how they shape the everyday lives of postcolonial migrants, mixed-race Italians, and their children both at home and in the diaspora. As I came to understand Habesha history vis-à-vis Italian colonization, I was struck by the similarities between the Dominican Republic–Haiti–US triangle that has occupied my intellectual work and that of Eritrea-Ethiopia-Italy: colonialism is followed by dictatorship, border conflicts, migration to the postcolonial metropolises, internal colonization and racism in the diaspora, and so on. These similarities are not coincidental. Rather, they crystalize the correlation between colonialism and its effects. This correlation also highlights a central argument of this book: it is imperative to examine the relationship between colonialism and immigration to confront present-day antiblackness, xenophobia, and the exclusion of people of color from full humanity within the nation and beyond.

One of the most powerful stories *Asmarina* tells us is that of Tsegehans Weldeslassie, known as Ziggy, a refugee from Eritrea who arrived in Milan in 2007. Throughout the film, we hear how he crossed the Sahara Desert and the Mediterranean Sea to escape the repressive dictatorship in Eritrea, only to arrive in Italy and be denied asylum. "I never imagined leaving my country," he says, "but I had to flee."[80] In 1993, after decades of turmoil and war over independence from Ethiopia, independence was gained via a democratic referendum. Isaias Afwerki of the People's Front for Democracy and Justice was appointed as interim president of the republic. Eritrea also established a 150-member National Assembly, elected by the temporary government, along with a democratic constitution. In 1997, however, Afwerki introduced a new constitution and declared himself president for life. Afwerki's dictatorship has been considered one of the most ruthless in recent history, leading to censorship, poverty, exile, imprisonment, or death for many Eritreans. Lamenting the state of his country, Ziggy remembers the brief moment of hope in 1993 when "we all thought we finally had an independent country."[81] After being imprisoned in Eritrea for dissidence, Ziggy migrated to Italy, risking his life at the hands of smugglers: "I crossed the whole country and arrived in Sudan. . . . The Sudanese then took us to the Libyan border, where human traffickers took charge."[82] It was a dangerous trip through the desert at the hands of merciless traffickers who bought and sold Ziggy "like a bag of goods." But for Ziggy, as for many other dissidents, escaping was the only possibility for survival. He put his life in the hands of human traffickers who cared nothing about his humanity, but the choices were try to survive the journey or perish at home. For Ziggy, migrating allowed him to stay alive, and yet he describes his experiences as surreal: "So when you arrive in Italy and you don't find solutions, you start to feel like this world is not made for us. . . . Then one day you wake up and you're happy because you are alive. And one day you ask yourself, why am I in Italy?"[83] This is exactly the question the film tackles in connecting the experience of present-day refugees with that of Second Generations through archival interventions in the history of the Italian colonization of Eritrea.

Thousands of Eritreans like Ziggy have migrated to Italy en masse since the early twenty-first century.[84] In 2015, prompted by a crisis over the demarcation of the Ethiopia-Eritrea border, migration to Italy increased, provoking Italy to declare a "refugee crisis."[85] Each year from 2015 to 2019, an average of 50,000 refugees from Eritrea formally requested asylum in European Union nations. Nearly 10 percent of those requested asylum in Italy; an average of 5,000 unaccompanied minors also arrived in Italy each year. Nearly 3,000 died at sea between 2017 and 2018 alone. In 2018 more than 100,000 Eritreans fled to Ethiopia; the influx of Eritrean refugees to Ethiopia is about 6,000 per month. The United Nations ranks Eritrea among the top twenty refugee-sending countries and as one of the countries with the worst safety and freedom indicators in the world (seven out of seven indicators of freedom are negative).[86] The filming of *Asmarina* in 2015 coincided with the arrival of large numbers of refugees from Eritrea, Somalia, and Syria in Milan. Paolos remembers that the streets of Porta Venezia, the Habesha neighborhood, "were all of a sudden full of people roaming and trying to find basic help."[87] While Milan offered shelter and asylum to Syrian refugees, it did not do so for Eritrean refugees. Paolos explained, "It became clear to some of us that supporting these newcomers was on us, on the [Habesha] community. We spoke the languages, understood the political contexts both here and there. So why not?"[88] Paolos, along with a handful of other local Habesha Italian activists, including activist Rahel Sereke and athlete Helen Yohannes, organized to provide translation services, medical support, shelter, food, and other necessities to the new arrivals. Their spontaneous efforts eventually led to the creation of the organization Cambio Passo, which, under Sereke's direction, continues to operate in Milan to provide basic needs for refugees of all ethnicities and demand support from the state.[89]

Even though Paolos and Maglio did not originally intend to tackle the growing "refugee crisis" that emerged in 2015, Paolos felt strongly that this "new" part of the Eritrean story had to be included in the film: "I was walking around with Ziggy, whom I knew from the neighborhood, when we began to see what was happening around us [with the growing presence of refugees in Porta Venezia]. We began to respond to the need almost spontaneously, without much organizing."[90] Part of that need was to raise awareness about the repressive political situation in Eritrea that was leading to massive emigration, so Paolos asked Ziggy if he would share his story.[91] Paolos's decision to include an examination of the political situation in Eritrea in the film prompted a backlash against her from the pro-dictatorship community in Milan.[92] This group saw the film as an affront to the liberties and freedoms of Eritrean people; opposition to the film resulted in online and in-person confrontations by way of homophobic insults and trolling against Paolos.[93] The disavowal of *Asmarina* by nationalist Eritreans both at home and abroad points to the place that Second Generations occupy in the political imaginary of the diaspora in both the country of their parents and their new nation. Paolos is a Second Generation born and raised in Milan. She grew up in vaivén between a Habesha political environment fueled by revolutionary sentiment and an Italian society that largely ignored this very formative part of her identity. Like many of us children of immigrants in the diaspora, Paolos had a bifocal experience, colored by the constant translations between languages, cultural experiences, and histories. As an adult, this vaivén becomes the lens through which to articulate her artivism and praxis of "story listening." But

Paolos's value as someone who exists in El Nié, between Eritrea and Italy, is only recognized by each of the parts that make up her hyphenated identity so long as they do not critique the nation. That is, the Second Generation condition as a translator between cultures, languages, and racial formations is only accepted when it serves the project of nation building and when proven through performative practices of respectability, civility, assimilation, and cultural competency. In this context, and through her position as a subject who lives in vaivén, Paolos's critique of the Eritrean state is perceived as a betrayal—one that directly results from her Second Generation position as someone who is not really *one of us*.

But it is precisely because of her position of in-betweenness that Paolos, like Scego and other Second Generations, can appeal to the Italian state on behalf of new immigrants and refugees like Ziggy. Their linguistic, cultural, and political understanding of their parents' home also allows them to translate in vaivén. Sometimes these translations are practical and concrete: they provide support to newcomers in navigating the city and accessing resources. Other times, as *Asmarina* demonstrates, Second Generations translate historical processes and the complicated politics of home to a larger international audience in ways that effect change and promote human rights and social justice. The film is thus part of a larger archive of Second Generation cultural productions that intervenes in the global archive of anti-colonial narratives, linking them through the experiences of blackness and migration.[94]

In *Coloniality of Diasporas*, Yolanda Martínez-San Miguel argues that while "both nationalism and colonialism have been studied by focusing on how ethnoracial categories define political interaction in each of these systems," coloniality in the diaspora further complicates nationalism by producing subjects who are legal citizens of one or multiple nations "but who in fact function as marginalized and racialized ethnic minorities in the metropolitan centers of Western Europe and North America."[95] I add that migrants and refugees and their descendants who question white supremacy, political oligarchy, dictatorship, and corruption become doubly exiled. As I argue elsewhere, migrants from the Global South are always racexiles, forced out of their nations due to the effects of colonialism, and continue to be exiled from receiving nations due to their postcolonial racialized position.[96] But this doubly exiled condition, as Maglio and Paolos's film demonstrates, can also potentially bridge, translate, and interpellate colonialism as a continuum, calling attention to its transnational effects on both people and nations.

Colonial diasporic existence, like colonialism itself, is painful—an "open wound," to borrow Anzaldúa's celebrated metaphor.[97] That wound can only heal through historical recognition that leads to belonging. *Asmarina* intersperses images from the present and past colonial experiences of Eritreans and the multiple voices of interviewees—newly arrived African refugees, white Italian historians, and multiple generations of Eritreans. In doing so, it avows the colonial-migratory nexus as prevalent, ongoing, fluid, and unstoppable, and asserts postcolonial diasporic subjects' belonging—whether or not that belonging is state sanctioned—to multiple nations, histories, and communities. To assert their belonging, *Asmarina* seems to suggest, immigrants, Second Generations, and minoritized citizens must translate their position vis-à-vis the nation in front of the world through interventions that explain the presence of colonized others in ways that allow the viewers to confront the national amnesia around colonial violence. But while the colonial critique is central to *Asmarina*, what makes the film such an interruption of colonial violence and its afterimages is the multiple contra*dictions* that show us Habesha life as integral to italianità through images, sounds, and stories that the film consecrates as archival evidence. In so doing, the film asserts Habesha belonging to italianità, an assertion that necessitates the translations of the individual to collective, of local to global.

"Welcome to Italy": Second Generation Unbelonging and the Struggle for Citizenship Rights

Sociologist Georgia Bianchi outlines four primary dimensions of citizenship: legal status, rights, participation in civic society, and belonging.[98] For Bianchi, citizenship is a "codified relationship between the individual and the state, with each party having rights and obligations to the other."[99] The state guarantees basic rights for the individual, and the citizens agree to their obligations to the state. This focus on rights, Bianchi argues, emphasizes the contract between the citizens and the state and promises "a measure of equality between all citizens."[100] But citizenship goes beyond legal rights and contractual obligations, as Lauren Berlant asserts.[101] Citizenship also encompasses a sense of belonging that is largely affective, closely linked to national identity and to a social and cultural cohesion grounded on what Bianchi calls "an institutionalized form of solidarity."[102] This final dimension of citizenship is therefore "inherently exclusionary, as there must be an in-group and an out-group in order to define who is entitled to citizenship and who is not."[103] The Second Generation, which comprises more than 10 percent of the Italian population, complicates Italian national belonging. Their hyphenated, multilingual, multicultural, racially diverse experiences and identities challenge the hegemonic version of italianità and disrupt the "us versus them" dynamics that delineate the internal and external borders of the nation-state. In the 1990s, Italy saw an emergence of anti-immigrant discourse. Second Generations reacted to being categorized as immigrants and the associated stigma.

The most recent Italian citizenship legislation, Law No. 91/1992, is a restrictive reform of a 1912 law that was drafted to guarantee state control (via taxation) of Italian settler colonialists in African colonies as well as the more than twelve million emigrants living in North America and South America.[104] The 1992 iteration of the law, which was passed amid widespread concern about the growth of immigration in Italy, also includes aspects of a 1937 law dictating that mixed-race children retain the citizenship of their non-Italian parent.[105] In reference to children of immigrants, Article 4.2 states: "Aliens born in Italy who have been legally resident in Italy up to the attainment of their majority shall become citizens if within one year of that date they declare the wish to obtain Italian citizenship."[106] While Italian-born Second Generations are able to apply for citizenship at age eighteen (and only until age nineteen), a positive outcome is not always guaranteed. They must satisfy several restrictive conditions, including continuous and uninterrupted legal residence on Italian soil, proof of parental citizenship status, and economic solvency. They bear a heavy burden of proof and the process entails a lot of bureaucracy. This restriction does not apply to non-Italian citizens of the European community, for whom the only requirement is to have been a legal resident in Italy for at least four years.[107]

Jovanna Rodríguez, whose testimony opens this book, was born in Milan in 1985 to immigrant parents from Lima, Peru. Her grandmother became very ill when Rodríguez was only six years old, and the entire family traveled back to Peru to care for her. Although her grandmother passed away, in a speech given at the "Day of Multicultural Unity" during the Milan Exposition in 2015, Rodríguez recalls this trip as the most beautiful memory of her childhood: "My grandma wanted to meet me before she died. I got to bring her that least bit of joy. I don't regret it. Even if that makes me not Italian, I don't regret seeing her."[108] Rodríguez's summer trip to Peru to meet her dying grandmother made her ineligible for Italian citizenship because it violated the residency requirement of Law No. 91/1992. Explaining the unfairness of being treated as a foreigner in her own country, Rodríguez says, "I speak Italian like anyone else. I know the city like the back of my hand. I studied here. I know more about Italy than the average white Italian. But that makes no difference."[109] Rodríguez's assessment of her own "alien citizenship," to borrow Mae Ngai's terminology, brings attention to the significance of bloodline citizenship laws in sustaining the legal exclusion and unbelonging of Second Generations in contemporary Italy, and to the double consciousness of being raised in a country yet being legally excluded from it. Ngai argues that nations produce "alien citizens": people who are citizens by virtue of birth or cultural assimilation but are presumed "foreign by the mainstream . . . and at times by the state" through structural forms of exclusion based on race as well as cultural and linguistic norms.[110] Writing about denationalized Dominicans of Haitian descent, Amarilys Estrella theorizes this exclusion as "civil death."[111] Navigating everyday life without documents or nationality is an insurmountable task that erases people in tangible and symbolic ways. For Rodríguez, the refusal to legally and symbolically admit her, an Italian-born woman, to italianità, while at the same time readily granting it to descendants of white Italian migrants abroad, crystalizes the Italian colonial structures that sustain the internal borders of the nation through exclusionary legislation based on white supremacy.

Remembering her own experience of the citizenship process, Medhin Paolos recalls, "I was one of the lucky ones. I mean, I was granted citizenship but the whole process, it was very absurd."[112] Paolos, who was also born in Milan, went through the strenuous and incredibly cumbersome citizenship application at age eighteen. She recalls that at the end of the naturalization ceremony, "The agent that performed it gave me a little Italian flag and told me, 'Welcome to Italy.' The whole thing was surreal."[113] The absurdity that produces Paolos and Rodríguez as foreign points to the trouble Italy is having in extending legal and cultural citizenship to its citizens of color. While Rodríguez's emotional appeal garnered applause, her speech also prompted hesitation in the form of people walking away, shaking their heads, or looking down at their feet in the politically mixed audience accustomed to celebrating diversity while simultaneously excluding "diverse" people from italianità. Her plea to her fellow Italians in the audience to recognize her italianità enacted an incisive critique of the racist colonial structures of the modern Italian nation. Rodríguez's intervention and claim to national belonging separate from her racial and ethnic identity (Black/Latina) remind her audience that her exclusion from italianità derives from the legacy of colonialism and Fascism white Italians strive to forget.

In her seminal 2002 essay "Second-Generation Attitude?," Jacqueline Andall argues that the Second Generations in Italy are slowly contesting the racially based exclusionary citizenship laws that have sustained national unbelonging for Italians of color like Rodríguez and Paolos for nearly a century. In her denunciation of racist citizenship legislation, Rodríguez interpolates the political language developed only a few years earlier by Rete G2, the first and largest Second Generation organization in Italy, in its successful 2011 national campaign "L'Italia sono anch'io" (I, too, am Italian). Over the course of fifteen months, and in coordination with seventeen nongovernmental organizations, Rete G2 collected more than 200,000 signatures in support of reforming Law No. 91/1992. The proposed reform would provide an easier path to citizenship for children of immigrants born in Italy, naturalization for legal immigrants, and voting rights in municipal elections for legal residents.

Rete G2's "L'Italia sono anch'io" campaign also raised awareness about the colonial and Fascist legacy of jus sanguinis legal restrictions and the everyday cultural impacts of the law on the lives of Italians of color. Mohamed Tailmoun, cofounder of Rete G2, explained, "What we wanted first and foremost was to change the law, so we wrote a piece of legislation and pushed through various channels through lobbying and public demonstration to get it approved in Congress. But while that process was in place, we also wanted others to know their rights, and to have the knowledge to navigate the arduous process of citizenship approval. For that we needed to reach youth early enough; after all, the window to apply is only a year."[114] Since 2005, Rete G2 activists have traveled all over the country organizing "know your rights" workshops in high schools and community centers aimed at informing young people about the citizenship process. In an effort to reach as many people as possible, they staged public skits, wrote pamphlets and music, created a radio show, and made media appearances (see figure 5.4). This unprecedented large-scale cultural intervention also increased visibility and public awareness about new Italians of color in the mainstream media. Paolos, who cofounded the Milan chapter of Rete G2 in 2006, explained, "We [Second Generation people of color] were claiming Italy as our nation, saying we are Italian, not immigrants, and saying it in perfect Italian. Many people were shocked, but we were out, and they could see us. We were Black and Asian and Brown, but we were Italian and there was no denying that."[115]

One of the most important initiatives of Rete G2 was the 2013 project G.Lab, through which Second Generations of all ethnic origins were able to obtain information and support to apply for Italian citizenship. Led by Paolos and produced in collaboration with the Milan Ministry of Labor and Ministry of Education, G.Lab consisted of a physical office, a help desk, and a hotline operated by volunteers from Rete G2 aimed at informing youth, particularly those under eighteen, about the process of naturalization. G.Lab was particularly successful in working with high schools, preparing students and guidance counselors for job hunting, scholarship applications, and paths to legal citizenship. It was through G.Lab that Rodríguez became aware of

FIGURE 5.4 Annual workshop for Rete G2, Rome, 2007.

her legal situation: "I was in high school and a friend told me about this G.Lab thing. I didn't know what it meant at first, but then I went and these people, Black women, Brown guys, who all spoke Italian like me, explained to me my whole life. . . . I wanted to cry. I felt so validated, and I finally understood these stupid laws. I finally got it."[116] Rodríguez's fortuitous encounter with G.Lab allowed her to enter the process of legalization before her nineteenth birthday. While her citizenship was denied, she was able to obtain a permanent resident permit and legal counsel to appeal her citizenship decision. But more than legal awareness, Rodríguez found validation and support in her experience of unbelonging through Rete G2. As she puts it, "Every day, in every space I move, someone asks me the same question: 'Where are you from?' Those of us who are not white can never be Italian enough, no matter what our papers say. The piece of paper will be good to have but acceptance from the community, from others, that is at the end the real goal."[117] Bianchi's definition of citizenship includes not only rights and legal status but also belonging, measured in acceptance based on shared cultural and social experiences. For the Rete G2 activists, acceptance from the community meant they could collectively demand the other aspects of citizenship they were denied: rights, representation, and protection under the law.

As Maya Llaguno-Ciani, a mixed-race Filipina Italian and cofounder of the Rome chapter of Rete G2, explained to me, "What we look for is recognition.

We are tired of having to answer questions about our origins, of having to be assumed foreign solely because we are not white. It is not only about combating prejudice and xenophobia in general but also about establishing our own legitimate claim to being part of Italianness: something that has been denied to so many of us regardless of our legal status, or birth, or our origins."[118] Rete G2 activists' interventions in mainstream media and social media were as critical as their legal actions in fighting the citizenship legislation. During Rete G2's early years (2005–8), Llaguno-Ciani moderated the "Second Generation Blog," an online forum that was the heart and soul of Rete G2. She says, "The blog connected us to a large network of people all over Italy. We suddenly realized how many of us were out there and how much we had in common."[119] The blog and forum continually clarified the difference between "immigrants" and the "children of immigrants," many of whom are born in Italy and therefore have not immigrated anywhere. While they are supportive of their parents' experiences and immigrant rights, Second Generations have what Andall calls "second-generation attitude": they are more politically involved, more connected to the rest of Europe, and less afraid to protest and demand equal rights.[120] This "second-generation attitude" prompts people like Rodríguez to demand legal inclusion while simultaneously denouncing their exclusion from italianità as racist. In this sense, it translates the global intersections of colonialism and racism that have led to the racially based migration policies that render people foreign in the country in which they were born. More than an attitude, then, the Second Generation possesses a political ethos grounded on the basic principles of human rights, equality, and justice that have been erased through the production of colonial hierarchies. It goes beyond the nation-state, recognizing the regimes of power that categorize some people as disposable. For Rodríguez, this ethos translates her Black Latinidad as a transnational category of political contestation that encompasses her multiple displacements, colonialities, and exclusions. Black Latinidad makes her exclusion visible beyond the nation while simultaneously allowing for her inclusion and visibility through diasporic belonging.

Rodríguez's intersecting racialized identities mark her abjection from the Italian nation. Describing her exclusion as a "racist act . . . an act of war," Rodríguez calls on her fellow citizens to recognize their complicity in "a fake diversity" that upholds white supremacy and its resulting privilege.[121] But Rodríguez's claims to Latinidad *and* blackness, two hegemonic categories produced and disseminated by/through the United States, also bring attention to how citizens and immigrants of color "talk back" to a nation by asserting belonging through affirmations of the very categories often used to exclude them. In the introduction and first section of this book, I articulated and historicized the ways hegemonic blackness shapes notions of belonging and unbelonging for Black Latinx people in the diaspora. In the nineteenth century, as I show in chapter 1, Latinidad came to contrast Anglo-Americanness (both Black and white) at a time of massive colonial expansion. As such, the discourse of Latinidad emerging from the Caribbean, Mexico, Central America, and South America became decidedly anti-colonial. Over the years, what was understood as Latinidad has changed drastically, particularly as the Latinx community in the United States continues to grow. Latinidad has become, in addition to a transnational identity, a brand through which ideas of cultural, racial, and national belonging are traded and commercialized through images and stereotypes that still respond to Eurocentric colonial desires. These images often exclude blackness from Latinidad while privileging whitewashed mestizaje. In this context of racial violence and erasure, for Rodríguez to claim Latinidad is also to translate her unbelonging through an identity marked by both colonial desire and colonial violence.

Despite its vaivenes and contradictions, or perhaps because of them, Black Latinidad, as this book argues, exists in contra*diction* to hegemonic blackness and whitewashed Latino mestizaje, as an affirmation of belonging that denounces Black Latinx double exclusion from hegemonic blackness and Latinidad. As such, Black Latinidad offers an incredibly productive way of translating blackness globally from an interstitial space of unbelonging and belonging. It allows us to see how the afterlife of colonial histories operates in the present day to sustain minoritized subjects' exclusion from the nation through human categories that were created through colonial exclusion. Black Latinxs exist and affirm their existence despite their exclusion from hegemonic notions of Black citizenship and Latino belonging.

Since US culture is globally hegemonic—through music, film, art, brands, and social media—the production of US minoritized identities and their struggles have also become hegemonic. That is, the world recognizes Oprah Winfrey and George Floyd as representative of blackness; in turn, it recognizes Black Lives Matter as a way of contesting antiblackness. In this context of hegemonic identifications, it is not surprising that Black Latinxs in the Italian diaspora, such as Rodríguez, look to the cultural and political production of established Black and Latinx diasporic enclaves in the United States to shape their political and cultural language vis-à-vis the dominant hegemonic and often white supremacist cultures of their new nations. As a Second Generation woman of Peruvian descent from Italy, Rodríguez looks to New Jersey rather than Lima (and to English rather than Spanish) to find a political language with which to talk back to Italy, translating Latinidad through US experiences and political frameworks of blackness for newer diasporas. Black Latinidad offers an important paradigm for understanding how blackness, migration, and colonialism intersect in the diaspora through the very lives and bodies of human subjects. For Rodríguez, Black Latinidad summarizes her struggles and contra*dictions*, connecting her to Black people, Peruvians, immigrants, and Second Generations. It allows her to dislodge citizenship from nation and assert, as Arthur Schomburg called on us to do, racial belonging beyond the nation.

Because of her race, which Rodríguez defines as both Black and Latina, she is denied admission into italianità (a project of national belonging that as we have examined is grounded on ideas of white supremacy and racial purity). But her sense of political belonging to a global network of blackness and Latinidad also provides Rodríguez a political lingua franca from which to translate her own position of exclusion to a larger, more supportive, and more powerful transnational audience. That she gave a speech during the Milan Exposition in English, Spanish, and Italian to an international audience in the context of a day of multicultural unity further affirms the translations of her Black Peruvian Second Generation existence into Black Latinidad. In the face of state disavowal, Rodríguez's political claim to Black Latinidad validates her claim to italianità because, as Beaman argues, the connections between "racial and ethnic minorities with other racial and ethnic minorities worldwide" are intrinsic to the national project.[122] For Rodríguez, this dynamic is encapsulated in the assertion that Black and Latinx are "races, not countries."[123] In asserting her Black Latinidad, Rodríguez makes her disavowal by the state a visible criminal act—a violation of her basic human right to a nationality.

Rodríguez's assertion of Italian Black Latinidad demonstrates how restrictive immigration laws produce new categories of racial difference that shed light on the nation's vision of itself in relation to the world. These "new categories" are linked to the historical processes that have marked the production of what Ngai calls "alien citizens" for the past century: colonialism, exploitation, and migration. Second Generation artists and activists link antiblackness and immigration to the historical contradictions of colonialism and its effects in the current exclusion of citizens of color. In Italy, race and immigration are profoundly intertwined. Dislodging racism thus requires addressing Italy's history of colonialism, Fascism, the North-South divide, and anti-immigrant legislation and its effects on its citizens of color—tasks Second Generation artists have embraced with urgency and determination.

The Second Generation translates their local political struggles through the global language of resistance (e.g., Black Lives Matter, No Human Being Is Illegal, Ni una menos) using cultural, political, and media interruptions of the hegemonic archives of colonialism. In doing so, they disturb the colonial regime that renders them as incomplete citizens, unbelonging to the nation. In this way, Second Generations build transnational, global networks of political alliance and inclusion from which to talk back to the nations that exclude them. The "Second Generation interruptions"—cultural works, artivism, public speeches, and performances that challenge intracolonial structures of oppression—analyzed in this chapter suggest a more productive way to understand the transnational dynamics shaping blackness, immigration, citizenship, and belonging in the present while radically hoping for sustainable interruptions of colonial legacies that can lead to tangible and lasting changes for a future we want rather than the one we inherited.

Contesting Citizenship, Reclaiming Belonging

In her book *The Intimacies of Four Continents*, Lisa Lowe considers the significance of colonialism and its resulting archives. Lowe argues that colonialism categorizes humans according to their closeness with European culture, a practice that marks colonized peoples as less than human because they do not assimilate to European "attributes."[124] The difference between human and less than human, as we see from the examples provided throughout this chapter, continues to define Italy's—and other postcolonial nations'—bordering of citizenship and belonging. Postcolonial nations in the Global North *and* Global South define citizenship through the very colonial classifications that excluded Indigenous, Black, and Asian people, epistemes, arts, cultures, and histories from the category of citizen. This colonized humanism defines humans as racially white and culturally European, anchoring European cultural identity in historical and cultural events such as the colonization of the Americas, the Enlightenment, and the French Revolution. These colonial dynamics shaped the republican enterprises of young postcolonial nations all over the world. After Haitian Independence in 1804, for example, Henri Christophe declared himself king of Haiti, built castles, and demanded that citizens speak French.[125] In Mexico, national institutions silenced Indigenous cultures, languages, and histories and replaced them with an acceptable form of mestizaje that exalted Spanish language and cultural values during the independence and postrevolution periods (1820s and 1920s). In Eritrea, speaking Italian and having European cultural competency became indicators of education and civility during the reconstruction period in the late twentieth century. In the Philippines, Spanish cultural values came to signify class status and dissidence from American colonialism at the end of the nineteenth century. And in the United States, slavery remained legal while Eurocentric values and cultural understandings shaped every aspect of the young nation from politics to education to heritage institutions to markets from its independence in 1776 until 1865.

In the Global North, colonialism shapes national borders and sustains the racially based labor stratification that renders people of color as less than human. It also reinforces white supremacy at every level of the institutional state apparatus. If humanity is defined by its proximity to Europe, then lesser humanity is reserved, as it was during fifteenth- and sixteenth-century colonialisms, for subjects of color presumed to be expendable, durable, and uncivil. The case studies presented in chapters 1 and 4 show the complicated dynamics that emerged in the late nineteenth century as the Global North began to expand its territory to the Global South, while also grappling with the project of multiethnic citizenship within national borders. Colonial expansion abroad went hand in hand with the project of national unity at home, as clearly illustrated in both the United States and Italy. For Italians, colonial expansion in Eritrea, Somalia, and Libya helped rhetorically close the racial divide between the north and the south. The rhetoric of national unity was articulated through a discourse of civilization versus barbarism based on scientific racism that also operated within the nation's borders to divide citizens into racial categories rooted in white supremacy. As we saw in chapter 1 in the case of the project of Dominican annexation, territorial expansion was offered as a "solution" to the "problem" of Black citizenship in the United States. By the turn of the twentieth century, the issue of multiracial citizenship was further complicated as colonized peoples and their descendants became legal citizens of the colonial power and migrated to colonial centers to exercise their rights as citizens only to find those rights denied because while they were citizens on paper, in reality they were violently excluded from the benefits of citizenship white people enjoy freely (receiving good quality education, health care, and housing). In the United States, Black Latinx enclaves emerged in the early twentieth century in New York City, as a result of the Spanish-American War; as an effect of the Jones Act, which granted citizenship to Puerto Ricans in 1917; and following US military interventions in Hispaniola (1914–34, 1965). In the United States, citizens of color demanded their belonging to the nation through armed resistance, peaceful protests, and cultural interventions. Multiple cultural and political movements (e.g., the Harlem Renaissance and the civil rights movement) changed legislation, expanded archives, and increased the visibility of Black people and their cultural contributions. However, these triumphs did not lead to the dismantling of colonial institutional structures, nor did they impede the continued colonization of Black and Brown peoples by the United States abroad. Throughout the late nineteenth and most of the twentieth centuries, the US empire expanded through economic, military, and political interventions in the Caribbean, the Pacific, the Middle East, and Central America. These military, economic, and cultural expansions impacted the economies and politics of Global South nations in Latin America, the Caribbean, Africa, and the Pacific, leading to dictatorships (e.g., Fulgencio Batista in Cuba, Rafael Trujillo in the Dominican Republic, and Jean-Claude and François Duvalier in Haiti), land expropriation (e.g., Panama, El Salvador, Puerto Rico), racially based labor systems (e.g., Haiti), and economic disparity.[126] As previously colonized countries continue to struggle to create democratic governments that provide basic protection and opportunities for their citizens, people are often forced to migrate north to escape poverty and violence and to look for better opportunities for their families.

In this cycle of colonialism and migration, to be a Black citizen in a Global North nation is a privilege; citizens can cross national borders and access state services and institutions, while immigrants experience life-endangering challenges in their attempts to do so. Yet this privilege does not always guarantee belonging. Black people must *do* more; they must prove their worth through performances that range from linguistic capabilities ("Black in English") to purchasing power. Even then, as we saw in the examples of Piri Thomas and Arthur Schomburg in chapter 2 and in Paolos's encounter with the vendor that opens this chapter, for Black postcolonial subjects in the diaspora, belonging necessitates translation through the hegemonic notion of Black citizenship constructed and sustained through the colonial regimes of white supremacy—the "better" blackness associated with US Black success.

Depending on the context, blackness can be perceived as either or both a marker of colonialism and/or a sign of postcolonial "civility" and prosperity. Neither scenario eliminates the experience of racism. As a marker of colonial difference, blackness defines who "looks like a foreigner" and who "looks like a citizen." This is normalized through media, cultural, and historical representations that shape local, national, and global policies and politics of belonging in ways that impact people's relationships to one another, as well as how communities are built, how we protest, shop, and sing, and even the language used to express love.[127] In her study of citizenship and illegal immigration in the United States, Ngai urges us to "rethink American immigration history in the context of global developments and structures" to displace "the colonialists and superpower nations from their self-claimed positions at the center of world history."[128] US expansion in the Caribbean from the late nineteenth to the mid-twentieth centuries, along with its military and economic involvement in Central America throughout the twentieth century, led to massive land expropriation, dictatorships, and violence against vulnerable communities. Similarly, Italy's colonization of Eritrea, Somalia, and Libya from the end of the nineteenth century to the middle of the twentieth century created segregationist systems that engendered ethnic clashes and intensified border conflicts and violence (to this day, Eritrea and Ethiopia are disputing their national borders). Yet Italian, US, and other Global North discourses about immigration and "refugee crises" rarely take into account the relationship between said "crises" and the centuries of colonial exploitation of the Global South. Ngai's call to "rethink American immigration history in the context of global developments" necessarily requires a deeper and more intentional examination of the ways US discourses on race and immigration intersect with other nations' discourses of race and immigration to produce and exclude a global category of racialized subjects.[129]

Race and immigration shape people's lives across geographies and borders, at times reproducing the colonial structures of white supremacy and at other times challenging them. Second Generation descendants of immigrants from the Global South, like Paolos and Rodríguez, can help us better understand how these dynamics operate in people's lives, histories, and social structures. To do so, we must read "across" the colonial divide, as Lowe invites us to do, to search for the ways colonialism is reproduced, interrupted, and contested by the people who experience its effects in their everyday existences: Second Generations in Italy, DREAMers and "DACAmented" people in the United States, and descendants of immigrants in northern and western Europe who struggle with racist anti-immigrant legislation, political exclusion, anti-immigrant violence, and unbelonging in the nations in which they were born or grew up.[130] While the legal structures and restrictions experienced by an undocumented person in the United States differ greatly from those experienced by a documented or undocumented Second Generation in Italy, the same colonial structures produce both groups as foreign and unbelonging to the nations they call home. These colonial regimes also produced and sustained slavery in the Americas, Jim Crow in the United States, apartheid in South Africa, Campo Cintato in Eritrea, and La Sentencia in the Dominican Republic.[131] They also produced the current global border security policies that led to thousands of people drowning in the Mediterranean Sea, families separated at the US-Mexico border, and the deaths of Black migrants in Chile, Israel, Brazil, Spain, Greece, and the Dominican Republic at the hands of police, border patrol, and anti-immigrant militias.[132] Translating these Second Generation experiences into hegemonic blackness allows us to see how antiblackness is a pandemic that transcends time and geography, and invites us to think about global solutions beyond those imagined through the nation-state.

CONCLUSION

Confronting Global Anti-immigrant Antiblackness

On September 30, 2017, Joane Florvil, a twenty-eight-year-old Haitian woman living in Santiago, Chile, died in police custody after sustaining multiple head injuries. Florvil had been arrested on August 30 for allegedly abandoning her two-month-old baby in front of a municipal building.[1] The Black immigrant mother had gone to the police station in the Lo Prado neighborhood to report the robbery of a bag containing her daughter's identification documents. Upon arrival at the station, she tried to ask for help from the security guard at the gate but due to her limited Spanish, the guard could not understand her. She then asked the guard to watch the baby, who was asleep in the stroller, as she went to seek translation help from a nearby construction site that employed Haitian workers. To Florvil, leaving her sleeping baby in the care of the guard was safe; it was also a culturally acceptable practice in both Haiti and many other parts of Latin America (I have held my share of strangers' babies in buses, government buildings, hospitals, and airports in the Dominican Republic). But the guard interpreted Florvil's action as abandonment and reported her to the police. The next day, on August 30, the Chilean police arrested Florvil, charging her with reckless abandonment of a minor.[2] Televisión Nacional de Chile (TVN, Chilean National Television) broadcast a picture of Florvil's arrest, depicting her as a "criminal" and a "bad mother."[3] On August 31, one day after her arrest, Florvil was brought to the hospital to be treated for severe cranial trauma. The police officers in charge alleged that Florvil had "banged her head against the walls" because she was upset about her situation.[4] The young mother remained in the hospital for a month while the state retained custody of her child. On September 30, one month after her arrest, she died in the hospital. Although, according to her lawyer, every time she was conscious Florvil asked to see her daughter, her petition was denied, and she died without ever seeing her baby again. Immigrant advocates and anti-racist organizations continue to demand justice for Florvil. They believe the state is responsible for her death. Whether she died by suicide or as a result of police brutality, Florvil died through either the direct actions or the willful neglect of the xenophobic anti-Black police in charge of protecting her.

I learned about Florvil's story on the social media page of a Chilean friend a few days after her death. My immediate reaction was surprise: how could this be happening in Chile, too? For nearly a decade, I had been tracking Black Caribbean migration to Chile and the effects the migratory changes seem to have on national rhetoric about race and immigration. Throughout the 1990s, Black Caribbean migration to Chile had been small in number (no more than one hundred people per year) and dominated by professionals, students, and artists linked to universities and other formal institutions. But as Chile's economy grew, and as it went from being a country recovering from dictatorship and exile to one that prided itself on modeling equality and democratic values, Chile became an immigration hub. Between 2014 and 2017, the rate of immigration to Chile grew by more than 200 percent and by 2018, 7 percent of the Chilean population was foreign born. Haitians became the third-largest ethnic group in Chile in 2019.[5] Along with immigration, xenophobia and antiblackness are also on the rise in Chile. There were hundreds of hate crimes informally documented by immigrant rights organizations between 2018 and 2019 alone. In addition, labor exploitation, microaggressions, and racism against Black migrants and Second Generation Black Chileans have become commonplace. Black women often report being called prostitutes or being sexually assaulted on public transit and on the streets.[6] Within a period of a little less than a decade, Chile went from thinking of blackness as an exotic commodity associated with the Cuban Revolution and the fantasy of a Caribbean resort vacation to thinking about blackness as a menace to its national essence and a threat to the nation-building project of modernity and democracy, trading one colonial legacy for another.[7]

As I got more acquainted with my rage in the days that followed her death, I scrutinized social media for mentions of Florvil. There was nothing in the mainstream international press, and almost no coverage in English. What happened to Florvil—the violence she suffered—stayed in Chile. In turn, the world continued to view Chile as a Global South nation recovering from a brutal dictatorship and striving to grow its economy, not as a site of antiblackness and white supremacy. But Florvil didn't just die in Chile. For those of us living the cost of global antiblackness, Florvil died—and keeps dying—everywhere; her death echoes the deaths of other Black women across the globe. It haunts us. As I sat in front of my computer, mourning her loss, obsessing about the layers of injustices that led to her death, I could not help but think of another Black woman I had recently mourned, Sandra Bland, who died by hanging on July 13, 2015, while in custody in a Texas jail after being unjustly arrested. The similarities between the two women haunted me. They were both twenty-eight when they died. Both had recently moved to a new place in search of better opportunities. They had both been arrested for crimes they did not commit. They both allegedly took their own lives while in police custody. They were both Black women.

Bland's death inspired protests across the United States. Her case helped raise awareness about how misogyny and antiblackness operate together to invisibilize Black women's suffering, even within Black social movements.[8] She became associated with the #SayHerName movement, cemented by the 2018 HBO documentary feature *Say Her Name: Sandra Bland*. In 2019 video footage of Bland's arrest was publicly released, reigniting activism around the case. In the wake of the police murder of George Floyd in 2020 and the protests that followed, Bland's name reappeared once more in the public sphere, this time garnering international recognition within the larger Black Lives Matter movement.

Like Bland, Joane Florvil's name became a symbol of anti-racist activism in Chile, particularly after the protests that followed Floyd's murder. September 30, the anniversary of Florvil's death, is now Chile's National Day Against Racism. Multiple Chilean anti-racist and immigrant rights organizations are named after Florvil. However, unlike the names associated with the US Black Lives Matter movement, Florvil's remains widely unknown outside Chile. Chilean antiblackness killed Florvil, but because Chile is not imagined as a site of blackness or antiblackness, Florvil's life and death had to be translated through US blackness to become visible to the world—for the world to recognize that her Black life also mattered.

Las vidas negras importan *Everywhere*

Nos parece bastante hipócrita que toda la gente ahora está con el hashtag #BlackLivesMatter, pero que al mismo tiempo no le habla al vecino haitiano. No se sientan contigo en la micro, vas a pedir un trabajo y te dicen que no eres del perfil porque eres negra, o te gritan negra prostituta. Es un doble discurso en que la gente cae muy fácilmente, siento que las redes sociales permiten que el capitalismo utilice las causas sociales a su favor, pero no hay nada de trasfondo. Nosotras estamos tratando de aprovechar la coyuntura, pero el camino es cuesta arriba, en Chile el racismo va subiendo porque también la clase política avala ese avance.

[We think it very hypocritical that everyone now is using the hashtag #BlackLivesMatter but at the same time won't even speak to their Haitian neighbor. They won't sit with you on the bus, you go and ask for a job and then they tell you that you do not fit the profile because you are Black, or they yell "Black prostitute" at you. It's a double discourse people are falling into very easily. I feel like social media allows for the exploitation of social issues by capitalism but there is nothing behind [the hashtag]. We are hoping to take advantage of this moment, but the walk is uphill. In Chile, racism keeps increasing because the political class supports it.]
—Paola Palacios, Black Chilean activist

Translating Blackness comes from a very personal place—from my own subject position as a Black Latina immigrant and scholar living in the United States.[9] As I researched and wrote each chapter, I thought intentionally about what I wanted this book to do in the world. My goals were simple: I wanted to start a conversation about how xenophobia and antiblackness operate together across the globe to exclude human beings, particularly those who identify as Black and migrant, from accessing basic human rights and recognition. Having studied how anti-immigration and antiblackness operate together as the afterlife of colonialism in Latinx border sites such as Haiti–Dominican Republic and United States–Mexico, I was convinced of the need to think about these forms of exclusion as mutually constitutive of the project of citizenship and belonging. When we think about immigration, we inevitably think about the nation-state. After all, immigration is only an "issue" because national bordering is the rubric through which we measure human belonging and citizenship. But what happens when blackness and immigration intersect through the lives and bodies of new minoritized citizen-subjects? How does a Black Latinx subject living in Italy or the United States experience antiblackness? And (how) do they articulate their belonging? Through the stories of the Black migrants and Second Generations in Italy I have shared in the second part of this book, I hope to convey that the nation is no longer sufficient to understand the expansiveness of what I call xenophobic antiblackness through which the violence of the state is mobilized to protect the borders of the nation from foreign intrusion (immigrants) to preserve the internal racial borders of the white supremacist nation (by excluding Black citizenship). Through the lives of the Second Generations in Italy studied in chapter 5, especially, I want to highlight the need to think about blackness and immigration beyond the nation-state, as global categories that shape people's vaivenes across and beyond national borders. I focus on Black Latinidad in dialogue with other minoritized Black identities precisely because Black Latinxs experience these vaivenes as they navigate multiple colonial regimes and racial systems at home and in the diaspora. Their experiences, as I argue in this book, can teach us so much about how race and immigration intersect to reproduce violence and exclusion across national paradigms.

The United States occupies a paramount place in the global imaginary of blackness. The legacies of Black freedom struggles in the United States have shaped how Black communities across the globe think about revolution, anti-colonial struggle, and liberation. While interpellating how US history and radical struggles for freedom have afforded many people a lingua franca with which to articulate and translate blackness, along with a global platform, this book also highlights that US centrality in the articulation of global blackness exists in part because of US colonialism and cultural dominance around the world. As I think about my own process of translating *my* blackness—my radicalization in the struggles for racial justice and migrant rights as well as my formation as a feminist scholar—I understand that none of what I am today would be, had it not been for my own translation through US blackness. It was in, through, against, and in contra*diction* to/with US hegemonic blackness that my own ethical, political, and scholarly commitment to Black Latinidad and Global South blackness came to be. In many ways, then, what this book critiques and posits is a dialogue with the multiple vaivenes of my own translated blackness. My goal is to push us to have uncomfortable, complicated, and imperfect conversations about how the hegemony of US blackness shapes how the rest of the world understands and engages Black Global South peoples, and their art and histories, in ways that at times reproduce colonial structures of silencing and erasure and at others create transnational representation and visibility of nonhegemonic blackness. There is so much more to say about translating blackness through US hegemonic ways of knowing—about the historical and contemporary dynamics that have shaped and continue to shape why and how we think about Black experiences around the world. This book is only an opening to what I hope will be a long and productive dialogue that brings us closer to Joane Florvil, to rethinking our solidarity, struggles, and intellectual contributions to Black futurity.

Thinking transnationally about blackness is by no means a new venture. Rather, as the first part of this book shows, Black internationalism, Pan-Americanism, Afro-diasporic thought, and women of color feminisms invite us to think about transnational blackness in ways that often challenge US hegemony and colonialism and center Global South and minoritized knowledge. *Translating Blackness* engages these earlier intellectual traditions through the works and lives of scholars and artists like Gregoria Fraser Goins, Arturo Alfonso Schomburg, and Gregorio Luperón and through the spirit embodied in Black feminist ethos of the Combahee River Collective, the Junta de prietas, the Ay Ombe Collective, and the transformative work of women of color feminist scholars and activists like Gloria Anzaldúa, Ochy Curiel, Angela Davis, Juderkys Espinosa, Mercedes Frías, Esther Hernández-Medina, bell hooks, Grada Kilomba, Medhin Paolos, Barbara Ransby, Igiaba Scego, and Chandra Talpade Mohanty among many more. Rather than offer a historical survey of these traditions, the goal of *Translating Blackness* has been to expand how we think transnationally about blackness in the twenty-first century, inviting the reader to consider new places and lesser-studied epistemologies and histories that decenter hegemonic blackness while being in dialogue with the important legacies of US Black radical traditions. In this sense, *Translating Blackness* pushes the conversation forward not only in considering newer sites for theorizing blackness, but most importantly, by bringing attention to the urgency of confronting antiblackness and anti-immigration sentiment as intertwined categories of oppression. Black people and migrants of color are dying everywhere, and we can no longer continue to see these issues as local or separate. Antiblackness is a pandemic that has been expanding and spreading across the globe since the fifteenth-century colonization of the Americas. It is time to confront antiblackness and anti-immigrant racism together.

In the summer of 2020, massive protests against police violence and racism took place across the globe in response to the murder of George Floyd in the United States. There were demonstrations in Ethiopia, Nigeria, Colombia, Cuba, Japan, Sweden, Italy, and Brazil, among other places. In all these countries, Floyd's face and the words *Black Lives Matter* written in English appeared on signs, murals, and in protesters' multilingual chants. The global dimension of the protests surprised many people in the United States; in particular, the idea that racism and antiblackness exist in predominantly Black countries like Cuba or Ethiopia was quite shocking to many people. Likewise, newer immigrant destination countries like Chile and Italy were surprised by the "sudden" rise in antiblackness they were experiencing. These countries blamed the violence not on structural white supremacy but on "cultural and ethnic differences" between national subjects and Black immigrants. But xenophobic antiblackness is hardly new, just as police violence in the United States is not a novelty. Rather, these recent iterations are manifestations of ancestral violence grounded on the colonial legacy that shaped the construction of modern nations from Chile to the United States to Italy, and which produce blackness as always foreign, exotic, ahistorical, and unbelonging to the nation-state. As countries become "immigrant hubs" in the new millennium, they also begin to erect internal borders to separate "them" (Black, Brown, and Muslim migrants and their Second Generation children) from "us" (white or mestizo, Christian or secular). As nations like Chile build their figurative border walls to exclude new citizens of color through rhetoric and legislation, they reach back to the repertoire of colonial violence that is foundational to the nation. Immigrants and new citizens of color confront the colonial legacies that sustain white supremacy and antiblackness in the nation, in turn sustaining their exclusions from full citizenship and human rights. That confrontation is never easy, never welcome, always in tension with capitalist ideas of progress and success. And yet that confrontation is the only way to move forward, to truly become a nation—a world—in which Black, Brown, Indigenous, and Asian lives are valued, and white supremacy does not reign. We are far from getting there, as Paula Palacios says in the interview that opens this section—"the road is steep" and we are tired. But Black Latinxs, Black migrants, Second Generations, and immigrants of color invent ways to assert belonging and speak back to the nation, forcing it to confront the presence of colonialism in its institutions, demanding historical justice, reparations, and recognition. This gives me hope that we are heading in the right direction even when it is taking so long.

My goal for this book is to accompany us on our steep walk. Another world is indeed possible if we listen to the voices that, in contra*diction* to colonial and racial violence, have been screaming for centuries and in multiple languages that Black lives, Black knowledges, Black histories, Black cultures, Black struggles, Black resistance, and Black futures are possible.

La lucha sigue.

NOTES

INTRODUCTION

1 Lear, *Radical Hope*, 97.
2 See C. Sharpe, *In the Wake*. In *The Borders of Dominicanidad*, I use contra*diction* to interrogate how history and historical archives produced hegemonic narratives of oppression. I argue that *dictions* can be, and always are, contested. García-Peña, *The Borders of Dominicanidad*, 13.
3 Following Reinaldo Walcott's terminology, Christina Sharpe proposes the "unfinished project of emancipation" as a historical continuum that reproduces the structures of inequality that lead people to live "in the wake" of slavery. C. Sharpe, *In the Wake*, 4–5.
4 García-Peña, *The Borders of Dominicanidad*, 7.
5 In *The Puerto Rican Nation on the Move*, Jorge Duany theorizes Puerto Rico as a nation in vaivén, coming and going, "on the move," 2, 4. He also uses the term as the title to his Spanish collection of essays *La nación en vaivén*.
6 Fanon, *Black Skin, White Masks*, 89.
7 Glissant, *Poetics of Relation*, 7.
8 Benjamin, "The Task of the Translator," 254.
9 See Venuti's introduction to *Rethinking Translation*. See also Venuti, "Translation as Cultural Politics."
10 Anzaldúa, *Borderlands / La Frontera*, 40.
11 Edwards, *Practice of Diaspora*, 5.
12 Sakai, *Translation and Subjectivity*, 11, emphasis added.
13 Figueroa-Vásquez, *Decolonizing Diasporas*, 9.
14 Davis, *Freedom Is a Constant Struggle*, 39.
15 The Nordic Resistance Movement is a neo-Nazi group in Scandinavia. It wants anyone who is not of Northern European descent to leave Sweden.
16 "Colombiana que desafió a los nazis en Suecia."

17 Race as a concept is assumed to be divisive in Sweden. It is very difficult to speak about racism in this context.
18 Tess Asplund, in conversation with the author, January 25, 2020.
19 BBC News, "Tess Asplund."
20 Tess Asplund, in conversation with the author, April 18, 2021.
21 Asplund, in conversation with the author, April 18, 2021.
22 Osei-Kofi, Licona, and Chávez, "From Afro-Sweden with Defiance," 139, emphasis added.
23 Davis, *Freedom Is a Constant Struggle*, 39.
24 Venga Le Cuento, "Entrevista a Maria Teresa Tess Asplund."
25 Osei-Kofi, Licona, and Chávez, "From Afro-Sweden with Defiance," 139.
26 Some of the most notable actions include the confrontation between sixteen-year-old Girl Scout Lucie Myslikova and a neo-Nazi group in the Czech Republic, and Saffiyah Khan, a Birmingham, UK, resident who was photographed smiling bemusedly at an English Defense League protester.
27 Asplund, in conversation with the author, April 18, 2021.
28 Cochran, "Translator Introduction," xxi.
29 Zendaya, "Cardi B Opens Up."
30 López, *Unbecoming Blackness*, 5.
31 López, *Unbecoming Blackness*, 12.
32 Martínez-San Miguel, *Coloniality of Diasporas*, 8–9
33 Hernández, "Undue Process," 3.
34 On October 14, 2010, the University of Georgia Board of Regents voted 14–2 "to prohibit public universities from enrolling students without papers in any school that has rejected other qualified applicants for the past two years because of lack of space." The policy, which keeps academically qualified students from attending the top five public research universities in the state, was based on the belief that undocumented students were taking the seats of citizens in the public university system. However, a study conducted by the very Board of Regents enacting this policy found that undocumented students comprise less than 0.2 percent of all public university students; most undocumented students are enrolled in technical schools and community colleges.
35 Nill, "Latinos and SB 1070," 35.
36 According to the US Census Bureau's "Quick Facts," Athens ranks fifth in the nation in economic disparities between rich and poor.
37 Washington, "Angela Davis on Activism and the Dream Act."
38 I borrow here Christina Sharpe's iconic terminology from her book *In the Wake: On Blackness and Being.*
39 Hartman, *Lose Your Mother*, 6.
40 Wynter, "Unsettling the Coloniality of Being/Power/Truth/Freedom," 260–61.
41 Lowe, *The Intimacies of Four Continents*, 6–7.
42 Over the past couple of years, we have seen a trend in the United States of white people—particularly white women, popularly known as "Karens"—calling the police on Black people engaged in mundane, everyday life activities such as birdwatching or jogging. Those experiences, as seen in the case

of Ahmaud Arbery, an unarmed Black man who was murdered by two white men in Georgia while jogging, are sometimes life threatening.

43 Hernández, "Undue Process," 3.

44 de Genova, "Citizenship's Shadow," 21.

45 de Genova, "Citizenship's Shadow," 17.

46 Hernández, "Undue Process," 8.

47 See Pérez Firmat, *Life on the Hyphen*.

48 de Genova, "Citizenship's Shadow," 19.

49 Duany, *Puerto Rican Nation on the Move*, 4–5.

50 Smythe, "Black Italianità," 13.

51 See Ramírez de Haro et al., *Efectos de la migración internacional*; and Escolano Giménez, "Los procesos migratorios."

52 See Guarnizo, "The Emergence of a Transnational Social Formation"; Guarnizo, "'Going Home'"; and Guarnizo, "The Rise of Transnational Social Formations." See also Pinkus, "Miss (Black) Italy"; Ciarnelli, "Mi spiace per le altre ma sono io Miss Italia"; and Gennari, "Passing for Italian."

53 After I began my graduate studies, I encountered the work of Wendy Pojmann, Heather Merrill, and Jacqueline Andall, among others, which grounded me and provided much guidance as I continued to follow my questions.

54 Schomburg, "The Negro Digs Up His Past," 672.

CHAPTER 1: A FULL STATURE OF HUMANITY

1 Gregoria Fraser Goins, "Biographical Sketch," December 21, 1961, box 36-2, folder 26, Gregoria Fraser Goins Papers, Morland-Spingarn Research Center, Howard University, Washington, DC.

2 In her biographical sketch, Gregoria Fraser Goins refers to Gregorio Luperón as her godfather. In "Miss Doc," she refers to Frederick Douglass in the same way. Gregoria Fraser, "Miss Doc," 141, unpublished manuscript, box 36-4, folder 52, Gregoria Fraser Goins Papers, Morland-Spingarn Research Center, Howard University, Washington, DC.

3 Luft, "Sarah Loguen Fraser," 149.

4 Luft, "Sarah Loguen Fraser," 152; Mayes, *The Mulatto Republic*, 15.

5 Luft, "Sarah Loguen Fraser," 150.

6 Fraser Goins, "Biographical Sketch."

7 Fraser Goins, "Biographical Sketch."

8 Fraser Goins, "Biographical Sketch."

9 I have argued elsewhere that "Black," as a differentiated social category of exclusion, did not exist in the late nineteenth-century Dominican Republic. This is not to say there was no racism. Rather, racism and antiblackness have always been entangled with class, immigration status, gender, and nationality. In the late nineteenth century, the Dominican Republic had Black and Brown (mulato) presidents—something unthinkable in the United States in the late nineteenth century. Yet the light-skinned mulato elite mostly dominated the intellectual class. The entanglement between race, class, and colorism in a

majority Black and Brown nation complicates how blackness is perceived within the nation and by foreign scholars looking in. In the twentieth century, particularly after the Rafael Trujillo regime, the rise of anti-Haitianism further complicated race and racism in the Dominican Republic to the point that the conversation is mostly dominated by interrogations about Dominican xenophobia against Haitians, as if Black identity and African heritage were not integral to dominicanidad. See García-Peña, "Translating Blackness"; and Torres-Saillant, "The Tribulations of Blackness."

10 Fraser Goins, "Biographical Sketch."

11 Even though Gregoria Fraser completed all her coursework, several professors refused to grant her a passing grade and she ended up not receiving her degree. See Fraser Goins, "Miss Doc," 140.

12 This information comes from a journal Fraser Goins kept from her trip back to Santo Domingo, dated 1941. Gregoria Fraser Goins, "Letters to Sally from a South American Republic in Diary Form," 1941, box 36-5, folder 59, Gregoria Fraser Goins Papers, Moorland-Spingarn Research Center, Howard University, Washington, DC.

13 In her book *The Mulatto Republic*, April Mayes cites a letter from Frederick Douglass to Sarah Loguen Fraser in which he encourages her to move to the Dominican Republic. He describes his own experience on the island as one that allowed a Black person like himself to "feel your full stature of manhood." Mayes, *The Mulatto Republic*, 15.

14 Fraser Goins, "Letters to Sally," emphasis added.

15 While mulataje does not exist as an identity category in the United States, my translation of brownness accounts for both its Caribbean location and the naming of racial mixing that led to a light(er)-skinned blackness that, in the Caribbean, afforded privilege and access. See Gregoria Fraser Goins, Diary, 1939, box 36-10, file 107, Gregoria Fraser Goins Papers, Moorland-Spingarn Research Center, Howard University, Washington, DC.

16 See also Hoffnung-Garskof, *Racial Migrations*.

17 See Dixon, *African America and Haiti*; Fanning, *Caribbean Crossing*; V. Smith, "Early Afro-American Presence on the Island of Hispaniola"; and Davidson, "Black Protestants in a Catholic Land." For migration to Puerto Plata specifically, see Ortiz Gamble and Gamble, *Puerto Plata*.

18 García-Peña, *The Borders of Dominicanidad*, 4.

19 Radical Republicans believed that Black people were entitled to the same political rights and opportunities as white people. They also believed that Confederate leaders should be punished for their roles in the Civil War. Their position was in contrast to that of moderate Republicans. The Radical Republican "promise" of a new America that would be inclusive and just to all its citizens never materialized. As Walter Johnson argues in *The Broken Heart of America*, these failed promises are linked to the imperial, racial capitalist project that is reflected at home and abroad through exclusion, mass incarceration, exploitation, subjugation, and racism.

20 Dangerously, this version of blackness is also what positioned Colin Powell, Condoleezza Rice, Susan Rice, and Barack Obama to champion slaughter in the Middle East; drone strikes in Africa; and political suppression in Haiti, the Dominican Republic, Honduras, and Guatemala; as well as massive deportations of Latinx migrants during the first two decades of the twenty-first century.

21 Pitre, "Frederick Douglass and the Annexation of Santo Domingo," 393.

22 See Carta de Gregorio Luperón a José Gabriel García (Jamaica, Correspondencia, septiembre 8, 1868, Legajo 1670, Colección José Gabriel García, Archivo de la Nación, Dominican Republic (hereafter AGN) and "Manifiesto desde el Fuerte de San Luis que informa la voluntad del pueblo dominicano," Marzo 23, 1871, Legajo 1983, in Colección José Gabriel García, AGN.

23 Sawyer, "Racial Politics in Multiethnic America."

24 The use of Black troops in the conquest of Indigenous people in the West—the "Buffalo Soldiers" of the 24th Regiment—was a prelude to that unit's roles in the Philippines and Cuba in 1898.

25 Parks and African Methodist Episcopal Church, *Africa: The Problem of the New Century*, 5. Cited also in M. Mitchell, "'The Black Man's Burden,'" 77.

26 Luperón, *Escritos de Luperón*, 28. All translations are mine unless otherwise indicated.

27 Mayes, *The Mulatto Republic*, 114–15.

28 Luperón, *Escritos de Luperón*, 30.

29 Luperón, *Notas autobiográficas y apuntes históricos*, 151.

30 Martí, *Nuestra América*.

31 F. Douglass, *The Life and Times of Frederick Douglass*, 298.

32 Luperón, *Escritos de Luperón*, 28.

33 See Weinberg, *Manifest Destiny*; and Love, *Race over Empire*.

34 Love, *Race over Empire*, 30.

35 In 1867 the United States purchased the territory of Alaska from the Russian empire and began to assess the possibility of annexing the eastern portion of the Caribbean island of Hispaniola. That is, efforts to annex the Dominican Republic did not begin during Reconstruction. Rather, they were a continuation of a long project of expansion that began during the 1850s and gained strength under the administration of Andrew Johnson. As early as 1845, the United States sent a commission to the Dominican Republic to assess the territory for expansion. In 1854 a group of investors and US Army engineers conducted a survey of the Bay of Samaná as a potential site for a military base. The location of Hispaniola was attractive to investors as well because it fell in the middle of a hot trade zone and could be easily accessible as a military site for regional control. The end of the US Civil War brought a wave of optimism to the project of expansion, leading to multiple explorations under the leadership of William Seward, who served as Secretary of State under Presidents Abraham Lincoln and Andrew Johnson. Seward looked to Mexico, Canada, Central America, and the Caribbean as potential sites for expansion, eventually settling on the island

of Santo Domingo, as the Dominican Republic was then called, as the prime location for the imperial project. Under President Johnson, Seward initiated negotiations with Buenaventura Báez, the nonconsecutive four-term dictator of the Dominican Republic, to lease the Bay of Samaná to the United States for the creation of a US military base. During the administration of Ulysses S. Grant, the plan expanded to the entire country. See Guyatt, "America's Conservatory," 975.

36 See LaFeber, *New Empire.*

37 Grant, "Reasons Why Santo Domingo Should Be Annexed to the United States," 75.

38 Guyatt, "America's Conservatory," 976.

39 Jefferson states, "The slave, when made free, might mix with, without staining the blood of his master. But with us a second is necessary, unknown to history. When freed, he is to be removed beyond the reach of mixture." Jefferson, "Notes on Virginia," 166. See also Love, *Race over Empire,* 46.

40 Love, *Race over Empire,* 45–47.

41 F. Douglass, "Reminiscences of Antislavery Conflict as Delivered during the Lecture Season of 72 and 73," quoted in Polyné, *From Douglass to Duvalier,* 29.

42 Grant, "Reasons Why Santo Domingo Should Be Annexed," 74–76.

43 Love, *Race over Empire,* 48–49. See also Vega, *La cuestión racial,* 112.

44 See Vega, *La cuestión racial,* 99.

45 "Gen. Grant: What He Says about a Third Term," 5, emphasis added.

46 See Love, *Race over Empire*; Guyatt, "America's Conservatory"; Polyné, *From Douglass to Duvalier*; and Vega, *La cuestión racial.*

47 See Eller, *We Dream Together*; and Bosch, *La guerra de restauración.*

48 The category used at the time for light-skinned Dominicans was mulato. As Mayes and others have demonstrated, the term *mulato* was of political significance in the nineteenth-century Dominican Republic, particularly at the moment in which the racial boundaries of a mostly Black and Brown nation were being drawn. I opt to use the terms *light-skinned blackness* or *brownness* to bring attention to the role that colorism, rather than *pureza de sangre,* played—and continues to play—in the Dominican Republic. See Buenaventura Báez, letter to Hon. Charles Sumner, October 9, 1868, Correspondence, Charles Sumner Papers, Harvard University, Cambridge, MA.

49 Throughout the nineteenth century, the Dominican Republic struggled to maintain independence. Under the leadership of white criollo writer and politician José Núñez de Cáceres, the Dominican Republic's first independence was declared on December 1, 1821. Known as the Ephemeral Independence for its short duration (December 1, 1821, to February 9, 1822), the first República del Haití Español did not abolish slavery and thus had scant popular support. Dominican mulato *hateros* (cattle ranchers) and farmers reacted by rallying behind Haitian president Jean-Pierre Boyer to unify the island and abolish slavery. Three years after the unification of 1822, however, following increasing international pressure, Boyer signed the Reparations Act of 1825, in which he promised to pay France 150 million gold francs in compensation for the

European nation's "lost colonial investment" and in exchange for recognition of Haiti's independence. Haiti had won the war against France in 1804, but Europe and the United States had refused to acknowledge the Black nation's sovereignty—a fact that affected President Boyer's ability to participate in international trade. After the passage of the Reparations Act of 1825, Spain, the United States, and England also recognized Haiti's sovereignty, lifting a twenty-one-year economic embargo. To meet French demands, however, Boyer was forced to increase taxation among landowners of East Hispaniola. Widespread discontent over crippling taxes soon resulted in a unified revolutionary front that, under the leadership of French-educated criollo Juan Pablo Duarte, eventually founded the independent Dominican Republic in 1844. But in 1861, fearing unification under the Haitian flag, President Pedro Santana (1801–64), another criollo, sought the support of liberal elites to request that Queen Isabel II reannex Santo Domingo to Spain. Santana rationalized his treason by insisting on the patriotic need to protect the prosperity of the Dominican "Hispanic essence." After a violent two-year Restoration War (1863–65), led by General Gregorio Luperón with support from Haitian allies, the Dominican Republic obtained its third and final independence on August 16, 1865. This recent history of ambivalent independence, which starkly contrasted with Haiti's unwavering sovereignty, allowed US annexationists in 1869 to rationalize the project as one that would forever solve Dominican political problems and eventually lead to island unification under the US flag. See Eller, *We Dream Together*, and García Peña, *The Borders of Dominicanidad*, chapter 1.

50 Cruz Sánchez, *La guerra de los seis años*, 22.
51 Cruz Sánchez, *La guerra de los seis años*, 22. See also Vega, *La cuestión racial*, 101–3.
52 Cruz Sánchez, *La guerra de los seis años*, 49.
53 Núñez Polanco, *Anexionismo y resistencia*, 77.
54 Cruz Sánchez, *La guerra de los seis años*, 49.
55 Luperón, letter to Charles Sumner from Haiti, February 1871, Charles Sumner Correspondence 1829–1874, microfilm (0669), Houghton Library, Harvard University.
56 Luperón, letter to Charles Sumner from Haiti, 1871.
57 Rodríguez Objío, *Gregorio Luperón*, 315–16, emphasis added.
58 To fully understand the significance of Luperón in the project of Dominican anti-colonial liberation, we must also pay attention to his role in fighting against Spanish annexation. See Eller, *We Dream Together*, for a history of 1822–65 that nuances the wars and projects of liberation.
59 Horne, *Confronting Black Jacobins*, 288–315.
60 Horne, *Confronting Black Jacobins*, 291.
61 Horne, *Confronting Black Jacobins*, 291.
62 Howe, "Letter to President Grant, June 1871," 23.
63 Howe, *Letters on the Proposed Annexation of Santo Domingo*, 7. Howe refers directly to a memo sent from Luperón and other exiles to president Grant,

which circulated in the US media in spring 1871 shortly after the commission's visit to the island.

64 I explore this dynamic in *The Borders of Dominicanidad*. The argument that Dominican is "other-than-Black" instead of imagined as mixed race or mulato is central to contemporary Dominican studies. See also the work of Silvio Torres-Saillant, Blas Jiménez, Ginetta Candelario, April Mayes, and Dixa Ramírez.

65 Howe, *Letters on the Proposed Annexation of Santo Domingo*, 17. See also Horne, *Confronting Black Jacobins*, 291.

66 Torres-Saillant, *Introduction to Dominican Blackness*, 5.

67 See Candelario, *Black behind the Ears*; and Ramírez, *Colonial Phantoms*.

68 Howe, *Letters on the Proposed Annexation of Santo Domingo*, 1.

69 Guyatt, "America's Conservatory."

70 Mayes, *The Mulatto Republic*, 19.

71 Douglass, *The Life and Writings of Frederick Douglass*, 259.

72 For more on Douglass and Grant, see Love, *Race over Empire*; and Polyné, *From Douglass to Duvalier*.

73 "Santo Domingo: Arrival of the Tennessee," 1.

74 Blackwell, "Santo Domingo," 1.

75 Douglass, *The Life and Times of Frederick Douglass*, 299.

76 Douglass, *The Life and Times of Frederick Douglass*, 298.

77 Mayes, *The Mulatto Republic*, 20, emphasis added.

78 Polyné, *From Douglass to Duvalier*, 36.

79 Núñez Polanco, *Anexionismo y resistencia*, 67.

80 José Novas cites Douglass as stating that "la población sin educación mantiene un movimiento revolucionario en estado de guerra y cuyos jefes son unos líderes ambicioso" (the uneducated population maintains a revolutionary movement in a state of war led by ambitious leaders). Novas, *Frederick Douglass*, 73–74.

81 Polyné, *From Douglass to Duvalier*, 27.

82 Polyné, *From Douglass to Duvalier*, 27.

83 F. Douglass, "Around the Island of Santo Domingo," (1859) Frederick Douglass Papers, Library of Congress Series: Family Papers, 27, Manuscript/Mixed Material, https://www.loc.gov/item/fmd.01005/. Cited also in Mayes, *The Mulatto Republic*, 20.

84 This change of heart becomes clear during his post in Haiti as minister to the Republic of Haiti and counsel to the Dominican Republic, which Douglass writes about in *The Life and Times of Frederick Douglass*, 438–45.

85 See Polyné, *From Douglass to Duvalier*, chapters 3 and 4; Hooker, *Theorizing Race in the Americas*, 57–66; and Novas, *Frederick Douglass*, 94–96.

86 Jean Louis Rodolphe Agassiz (1807–73) was a Swiss biologist and geologist who immigrated to the United States in 1847, becoming a professor of zoology and geology at Harvard as well as the founder of its School and Museum of Comparative Zoology. Agassiz is known for his resistance to Darwinism, his belief in creationism, and the scientific racism implicit in his writings on human polygenism.

87 Speech by Charles Sumner, March 25, 1870. See Donald, *Charles Sumner and the Rights of Man*, 442–43; Love, *Race over Empire*, 57; and Vega, *La cuestión racial.*

88 Douglass, *The Life and Writings of Frederick Douglass*, 259, emphasis added. See also Polyné, *From Douglass to Duvalier*, 42–43.

89 Douglass, *The Life and Writings of Frederick Douglass*, 259.

90 See García-Peña, *The Borders of Dominicanidad*, chapter 1.

91 M. Mitchell, "'The Black Man's Burden,'" 81. Brandon Byrd also engages this period, looking at the critical role of Haiti in the post–Civil War era. See Byrd, *The Black Republic.*

92 Hammond, "Outpost of Empire, Endpost of Blackness."

93 Hooker, *Theorizing Race in the Americas*, 25.

94 Hooker, *Theorizing Race in the Americas*, 25.

95 Hooker, *Theorizing Race in the Americas*, 26.

96 Douglass, "What to the Slave Is the Fourth of July?," 71–72.

97 Edwards, *Practice of Diaspora*, 7.

98 Luperón, *Escritos de Luperón*, 37.

99 West, "Empire, Pragmatism, and War," n.p.

100 Henry Blanton Parks (1856–1936) was an African American clergyman. He served as bishop of the twelfth Episcopal district of the African Methodist Episcopal Church. In 1896 he was appointed secretary of the church's Missionary department. In his role as secretary of the Missionary department, Parks was influential in promoting African American colonialism during the partition of Africa after the Berlin Conference in 1884 and supported the US invasion of Cuba in 1898.

101 In his now seminal documentary television series and book, *Black in Latin America*, prominent US scholar Henry Louis Gates Jr. describes Dominicans as "not knowing they are Black." This shortsighted depiction has impacted how Dominicans are viewed in the United States and, in particular, through US scholarship, contributing to the further erasure of Dominican Black struggles and histories.

102 "Santo Domingo. Revolution Afloat," *New York Herald*, July 2, 1869, 6.

103 Charles Douglass, "A Colored Hero: General Gregorio Luperón, 1875," scrapbook, Box 36-23, Gregoria Fraser Goins Papers, Morland-Spingarn Research Center, Howard University, Washington, DC.

104 Guridy, *Forging Diaspora*, 5–6.

105 La Sociedad Latinoamericana was founded in 1879 and had chapters in Paris, Madrid, and Germany. See Luperón, *Escritos de Luperón*, 53.

106 See Cordero Michel, "República Dominicana, cuna del antillanismo."

107 Martínez-San Miguel and Gonzalez Seligmann, "Con-Federating the Archipelago," 37.

108 Reyes-Santos, "On Pan-Antillean Politics," 148.

109 He was recognized in March 1876 and became the section director for the Puerto Plata branch of the organization. Luperón, *Escritos de Luperón*, xxii.

110 Cordero Michel, "República Dominicana, cuna del antillanismo," 230.

111 Luperón, *Notas autobiográficas y apuntes para la historia*, 151.

112 Silvio Torres-Saillant argues that the present-day shortsightedness in the American academy that casts Dominicans as negrophobic obfuscates our understanding of the historical significance of Dominican blackness from the early republic to Restoration. See Torres-Saillant, "Blackness and Meaning in Studying Hispaniola."

113 Luperón, *Notas autobiográficas y apuntes para la historia*, 26–27.

114 Luperón, *Notas autobiográficas y apuntes para la historia*, 26–27.

115 I write about Galván and Penson in *The Borders of Dominicanidad*, chapter 1.

116 Unlike other Dominican exiles who took refuge in San Juan, Puerto Rico (then a colony of Spain), or in Europe, Luperón spent his time in Haiti, St. Thomas, and Puerto Limón, Costa Rica, all Afro-diasporic communities.

117 Luperón, *Notas autobiográficas y apuntes para la historia*, 27, emphasis added. See also Reyes-Santos, "On Pan-Antillean Politics," 148.

118 Reyes-Santos, "On Pan-Antillean Politics," 150.

119 Dixa Ramírez writes extensively about the perception/production of the Dominican Republic as a mixed-race nation. Rather than referring to this form of mestizaje here, I am using *raza mixta*, as articulated by Luperón, as a stand-in for the multiplicity of blacknesses that proliferated in the nineteenth century that cannot be encapsulated by the term *mulato*, given that the term denotes a particular form of privilege and political enfranchisement.

120 Buscaglia-Salgado, *Undoing Empire*, xvi.

121 Buscaglia-Salgado, *Undoing Empire*, xvii.

122 Buscaglia-Salgado, *Undoing Empire*, xviii.

123 Buscaglia-Salgado, *Undoing Empire*, xviii.

124 Saldaña-Portillo, *Indian Given*, 14.

125 Torres-Saillant, *An Intellectual History of the Caribbean*, 144–45.

126 Gregorio Luperón, letter to José Gabriel García, March 18, 1870, Colección José Gabriel García, AGN, República Dominicana.

127 Luperón, *Escritos de Luperón*, xx.

128 Hostos, letter to Gregorio Luperón (1895), 230.

129 Torres-Saillant, *An Intellectual History of the Caribbean*, 145.

130 Luperón, letter to Eugenio María de Hostos, November 12, 1895, 238.

131 Silié, "Aspectos y variables de las relaciones entre República Dominicana y Haití"; Silié and Alexandre, "Las relaciones entre Haití y República Dominicana"; Luperón, letter to Eugenio María de Hostos.

132 Créolité is a Francophone Caribbean term that emerged out of cultural and literary studies to name the diversity of the Caribbean experiences beyond the binary of Black and white. Spearheaded by Édouard Glissant and advanced by writers like Patrick Chamoiseau, Jean Bernabé, and Raphaël Confiant, Créolité was in many ways a reaction to the monolithic ideas of the Négritude movement of the early twentieth century. See Bernabé, Chamoiseau, and Confiant, *Eloge de la créolité*.

133 Gregorio Luperón, manuscript translation of letter by Gregorio Luperón, 1871, Charles Sumner Correspondence, 1829–1874, Charles Sumner Archives, Houghton Library, Harvard University, Cambridge, MA. Emphasis added.

134 Luperón, *Escritos de Luperón*, 41.

135 Gregoria Fraser Goins, lecture on "Santo Domingo Country" music, delivered to the Spanish Club at Howard University, May 1, 1935, Gregoria Fraser Goins Papers, Manuscript Collection, box 36-5, folder 58, Morland-Spingarn Research Center, Howard University, Washington, DC. In this lecture, in which she talks about the African roots of Dominican music, she says that the Dominican Republic is one "of the black republics."

136 Gregoria Fraser Goins, letter to her mother, October 20, 1906, box 36-2, folder 36, Gregoria Fraser Goins Papers, Moorland-Spingarn Research Center, Howard University, Washington, DC.

137 Gregoria Fraser married John N. Goins (1873–1930) in 1917. Upon her arrival to Santo Domingo in 1939, she found that her passport had been revoked due to her marriage to a foreign national. She had to pay a fine to have her citizenship reinstated. See box 36-2, folder 28, documents and passport, Gregoria Fraser Goins Papers, Moorland-Spingarn Research Center, Howard University, Washington, DC. See also Mayes, *The Mulatto Republic*, chapters 1 and 6.

138 Gregoria's Cedula Dominicana (national identification card), dated December 26, 1939, gives her race as mestiza, her color as mulata, and her nationality as American. Gregoria Fraser Goins, Cedula Dominicana, box 36-2, folder 35, Gregoria Fraser Goins Papers, Moorland-Spingarn Research Center, Howard University, Washington, DC.

139 Fraser Goins, "Letters to Sally," emphasis added.

140 In this context, "Brown" summons Latinidad; however, this is not the Brown Latinidad theorized by contemporary Latinx studies scholars such as Richard Rodríguez, José Esteban Muñoz, and Lázaro Lima. Despite the similarities of experiences Fraser Goins may share with contemporary Latinxs, particularly in terms of notions of citizenship and belonging, positioning herself within brownness does not reference the interstitial racialized locus of Latinx people in the United States that has come to be associated in the US academy with "brownness."

141 Schomburg, "The Negro Digs Up His Past," 670.

142 Candelario, *Black behind the Ears*.

143 Gregoria Fraser Goins, letter to Misses Eunice and Ophelia Quauder, January 25, 1940, box 36-2, folder 30, Gregoria Fraser Goins Papers, Moorland-Spingarn Research Center, Howard University, Washington, DC.

144 Césaire et al., *Original 1939 Notebook of a Return to the Native Land*, 16–17. English translation cited from this bilingual edition.

145 Davidson, "Disruptive Silences."

146 Trouillot, *Silencing the Past*, 48.

147 See Love, *Race over Empire*, 51.

148 Tomás Bobadilla, letter to Charles Sumner, February 1871, correspondence, Charles Sumner Papers, Houghton Library, Harvard University, Cambridge, MA.

149 Bobadilla, letter to Charles Sumner.

150 Luperón, *Escritos de Luperón*, 30.

151 Tansill, *The United States and Santo Domingo*, 396.

152 Tansill, *The United States and Santo Domingo*, 396.

153 B. Báez, letter to Hon. Charles Sumner, October 9, 1868.

154 Trouillot, *Silencing the Past*, 8.

CHAPTER 2: ARTHUR SCHOMBURG'S HAITI

1 The Bureau of Immigration Commissioner was William Williams, who served at Ellis Island from 1902 to 1905 and again from 1909 to 1914. Williams had served as a soldier during the Spanish-American War until he contracted typhoid fever. In 1902 President Theodore Roosevelt appointed him to the position at Ellis Island, which at the time was the most important port of entry. Williams's main goal was expanding health provisions and tightening control of immigrant entry for persons with "poor physical conditions." Having studied at Harvard at the turn of the century, his provisions were animated by scientific racism and led to more restrictive immigration control against Jews, Asians, and other immigrants of color. See Baynton, "Defectives in the Land," 32.

2 Schomburg, "Questions by a Porto Rican, 8."

3 See also Schomburg, "A Philippines Republic Suggested," 6.

4 Schomburg, "Questions by a Porto Rican," 8.

5 See Erman, *Almost Citizens*; and Meléndez, "Citizenship and the Alien Exclusion in the Insular Cases."

6 Sam Erman writes that the Supreme Court viewed Puerto Ricans as neither citizens nor aliens, a fact that signaled "the possibility that they were noncitizen nationals instead." The Supreme Court held that full constitutional protection of rights does not automatically extend to all places under American control. This meant that people from newly colonized territories such as Puerto Rico and Guam did not have a constitutional right to citizenship. The decision was unprecedented and marked a shift in the project of US colonial expansion. Unlike the project of Dominican annexation studied in chapter 1, in which annexation was imagined as an extension of US citizenship rights, the Insular Cases became a justification for colonialism as they granted authority to the United States to continue its occupation of the territories acquired from Spain in 1898 with complete disregard to the people who inhabited them. See Erman, *Almost Citizens*, 5–6. See also Torruella, "Ruling America's Colonies," 57.

7 Littlefield, "The Insular Cases," 177.

8 A few decades later, this struggle would be clearly articulated by Puerto Rican radicals such as Ana Livia Cordero, a doctor and community organizer who, in the 1950s, "set forth a four-level approach for connecting the Puerto Rican liberation movement with the Afro-American nationalist freedom struggle," movements that Cordero asserted were "intrinsically related" and thus "should work together in common battle." Plácido, "A Global Vision." For more on the effects of Hurricane Maria and the US response (or lack thereof), see Bonilla and LeBrón, *Aftershocks of Disaster*.

9 Erman, *Almost Citizens*, 3.

10 See Thompson, *Imperial Archipelago*.

11 US president Chester A. Arthur signed the Chinese Exclusion Act on May 6, 1882. This was the first law preventing a particular ethnic or racial group from immigrating to the United States.

12 Jiménez Román and Flores, *The Afro-Latin@ Reader*, 64.

13 Sinnette, *Arthur Alfonso Schomburg*, 21.

14 Sinnette, *Arthur Alfonso Schomburg*, 20.

15 Jesse Hoffnung-Garskof writes extensively about La Liga and Rafael Serra, as well as other Black Caribbean immigrants living in New York at the end of the nineteenth century, in *Racial Migrations*. For a more complete picture of the Cuban presence in New York City in the nineteenth century, see Mirabal, *Suspect Freedoms*.

16 Arroyo, "Technologies," 142.

17 Club Las Dos Antillas, "Libro de Actas," Las Dos Antillas Political Club Minutes, October 6, 1895, microfilm, Schomburg Center for Research in Black Culture, New York Public Library.

18 Vanessa Valdés also points to this transformation and the vaivén between Arturo and Arthur in *Diasporic Blackness*, 5. For Frances Negrón-Muntaner, the vaivén leads to an "Afro-Latinx Turn" at the end of his life. Negrón-Muntaner, "Here Is the Evidence," 52–53. See also chapter 2 of Sánchez González, *Boricua Literature*.

19 Schomburg's position on the American presence in the islands was not entirely consistent. The previous year, on November 19, 1903, he wrote to the *New York Times* in support of the Platt Amendment, which continued a US presence in Cuba. In the same letter, he voiced approval of the Panama Canal, referring to it as "our canal." Sinnette, *Arthur Alfonso Schomburg*, 28.

20 Flores and Jiménez Román, "Triple-Consciousness?"

21 Martínez-San Miguel, *Coloniality of Diasporas*, 109.

22 Michel Foucault coined the term *subjugated knowledge* to name all knowledge that has been ignored or marginalized by the dominant culture. Foucault, *"Society Must Be Defended,"* 6. See also Foucault, *The Archaeology of Knowledge and the Discourse on Language*.

23 In the Caribbean and Central America, indigenismo was often used to explain the racial "brownness" of Latin American subjects as well as Latinx difference. Blackness and mulataje were displaced and whitewashed. In the Dominican Republic, for example, "indio" came to replace "negro" as a racial descriptor.

24 It is a big *chisme* among Schomburg scholars and fans that US Black scholars, including W. E. B. Du Bois, dissed Schomburg for his lack of accolades, titles, formal education, and for his Latinized English. There are multiple accounts of similar encounters with Cuban scholars in which Schomburg's Spanish was deemed "imperfect." See Sinnette, *Arthur Alfonso Schomburg*, 196.

25 Anzaldúa, "How to Tame a Wild Tongue," 357.

26 Martínez-San Miguel, *Coloniality of Diasporas*, 106, emphasis added.

27 Sinnette, *Arthur Alfonso Schomburg*.

28 Arroyo, "Technologies"; Hoffnung-Garskof, "The Migrations of Arturo Schomburg"; Sánchez González, "Modernism and Boricua Literature."

29 Jiménez Román and Flores, *The Afro-Latin@ Reader*, 7.

30 Valdés, *Diasporic Blackness*, 1.

31 Negrón-Muntaner, "Here Is the Evidence," 52.

32 To learn more about this debate, see the introduction to Valdés's *Diasporic Blackness*, in which the author gives an incredibly thorough explanation of Schomburg's vaivenes and summarizes the debate.

33 Both Valdés and Negrón-Muntaner talk about the significance of Schomburg's vaivenes through Arthur and Arturo.

34 See Anzaldúa, *The Gloria Anzaldúa Reader*; Flores and Jiménez Román, "Triple-Consciousness?"; and Muñoz, *Disidentifications*. I use the term *identity politics* here as theorized by the Combahee River Collective: the notion that being part of interconnected identities shapes political actions and political empowerment. See Keeanga-Yamahtta, "Interview with Barbara Smith."

35 Schomburg, "Racial Integrity," 6–7, emphasis added.

36 Adalaine Holton also talks about Schomburg's diaspora through a reading of "racial integrity" in "Decolonizing History."

37 Zendaya, "Cardi B Opens Up."

38 Sánchez González, "Decolonizing Schomburg."

39 Valdés, *Diasporic Blackness*, 19.

40 Schomburg, "Racial Integrity," 6

41 Schomburg, "Racial Integrity," 6.

42 I explain this further in chapter 5 through my analysis of the Second Generation movement in Italy. My argument is that translating blackness allows Black Italians to engage with Black Americans and Black Europeans by speaking to global issues of antiblackness through a lingua franca of contestation.

43 Schomburg, "Racial Integrity," 6

44 Arroyo, "Technologies."

45 Sánchez González, "Decolonizing Schomburg," 134.

46 Each of the authors insists on his Hispanic Caribbean, Puerto Rican, and Latinx identity as important in shaping how he thought and acted, the projects he embarked on, and the people he supported throughout his life.

47 Trouillot, *Silencing the Past*, 23.

48 Schomburg, "The Negro Digs Up His Past," 670. Crispus Attucks (ca. 1723–March 5, 1770) may have been an American slave or freeman of Wampanoag and African descent. He was the first casualty of the Boston Massacre and is

widely considered to be the first American casualty of the American Revolutionary War.

49 Holton makes a similar argument in "Decolonizing History" about the significance of a future in Schomburg's project of archiving and recovering.

50 Schomburg, "The Negro Digs Up His Past," 670.

51 Holton, "Decolonizing History," 224.

52 Schomburg, "The Negro Digs Up His Past," 670.

53 Schomburg, "The Negro Digs Up His Past," 670.

54 Holton, "Decolonizing History," 224.

55 Schomburg, "The Negro Digs Up His Past," 670.

56 Bernardo Vega writes that Schomburg did not finish elementary school and was a self-taught scholar. See Vega, *Memoirs of Bernardo Vega*, 106. Although Schomburg wanted to study law, he was unable to do so due to his inability to provide documentation of his schooling in Puerto Rico. See also Sinnette, *Arthur Alfonso Schomburg*, 195–96. Schomburg did not have an advanced degree either, which proved to be a challenge for his intellectual career. Sinnette writes that some of his contemporaries did not think him qualified enough for certain positions, despite admiring his talents. She reports that Du Bois opposed his candidacy as librarian for the collection he helped create at the New York Public Library. Sinnette, *Arthur Alfonso Schomburg*, 199.

57 Valdés offers a discussion on Schomburg's alternative archives through engagement with archive theory in chapter 4 of *Diasporic Blackness*. Negrón-Muntaner talks about Schomburg's exhibits as an important way to share his findings and engage as a scholar in "Here Is the Evidence." Holton proposes the idea of a counterarchive in "Decolonizing History."

58 Foucault, *The Archaeology of Knowledge and the Discourse on Language*, 145.

59 See the work of Saidiya Hartman, Grada Kilomba, Marisa Fuentes, and Hortense Spillers.

60 Trouillot, *Silencing the Past*.

61 Holton, "Decolonizing History," 218–19.

62 Schomburg, "The Negro Digs Up His Past," 672.

63 Schomburg, "The Negro Digs Up His Past," 670.

64 Schomburg, "The Negro Digs Up His Past," 670.

65 Schomburg, "The Negro Digs Up His Past," 670.

66 Lear, *Radical Hope*, 12.

67 Lear, *Radical Hope*, 117.

68 J. Díaz, "Under President Trump," 65.

69 J. Díaz, "Under President Trump," 65.

70 Schomburg, "Racial Integrity," 1.

71 Schomburg, "The Negro Digs Up His Past," 670.

72 I have previously made this argument in the introduction to *The Borders of Dominicanidad*.

73 García-Peña, *The Borders of Dominicanidad*, conclusion.

74 Sanders, "Congressional Reaction," 152.

75 Dubois, *Haiti*, 13.

76 "AMERICAN ROAD FOR HAITI: Right of Way and Unoccupied Lands Go to McDonald Syndicate. Interests in Banana and Other Fruit Concessions Included—Sugar Plant to Be Built," *Washington Post*, August 2, 1910.

77 Charlemagne Peralte led the Cacos insurrection in opposition to the US Marines' "pacification" of Haiti and the use of the "corvee laws" permitting forced labor on foreign-owned lands. The Marines and their proxies killed an estimated fifteen thousand people.

78 It is important to think of the Haitian occupation in relation to the rest of the many military and economic actions that the United States embarked on from 1865 to the 1940s, including those in the Panama Canal, Cuba, Puerto Rico, the Philippines, the Dominican Republic, and so on. See Renda, *Taking Haiti*.

79 Some of these texts include *The Goat without Horns* (1925), by Beale Davis; *Black Majesty* (1928), by John Vandercook; *The Magic Island* (1929), by William Seabrook; and the film *The White Zombie* (1932), directed by Victor Halperin. Renda offers a careful analysis of cultural productions, including Eugene O'Neill's *Emperor Jones*, in *Taking Haiti*. See also Kee, *Not Your Average Zombie*; and Twa, *Visualizing Haiti in U.S. Culture*.

80 O'Neill, *The Emperor Jones*.

81 R. Smith, "Pat Robertson."

82 Brooks, "The Underlying Tragedy."

83 Logan, "James Weldon Johnson and Haiti."

84 Bontemps and Hughes, *Popo and Fifina*, 4–6.

85 Hughes, *The Big Sea*, 334.

86 Hughes, *I Wonder as I Wander*, 13.

87 Kazanjian, *The Colonizing Trick*.

88 Césaire, *Discourse on Colonialism*, 90.

89 Schomburg, "Military Services Rendered by the Haitians."

90 Schomburg, "Military Services Rendered by the Haitians," 199.

91 In her biography of Schomburg, Sinnette recounts that as a child and young teen, Schomburg became interested in Haiti, finding in L'Overture and Haitian independence a refuge against the white supremacist education that taught him that there was "no Black history." Sinnette, *Arturo Alfonso Schomburg*, 14.

92 Schomburg, "Is Hayti Decadent?"

93 Schomburg, "Military Services Rendered by the Haitians," 202.

94 As I was conducting the last round of revisions in the summer of 2021, Haitian president Jovenel Moise was assassinated. The news surrounding Haiti is flooded with racist ideologies, diction, and images that repeat global anti-Haitianism through which Haiti is portrayed as uncivilized, chaotic, and a site of corruption and witchcraft. See García-Peña, *The Borders of Dominicanidad*, chapter 2.

95 See Torres-Saillant, *An Intellectual History of the Caribbean*; and Fumagalli, *Caribbean Perspectives on Modernity*.

96 Arthur A. Schomburg, "Hoover! Haiti! Motion!," microfilm, reel 10, box 12, folder 001, Arthur Alfonso Schomburg Papers, Schomburg Center for Research in Black Culture, New York Public Library.

97 Schomburg, "Military Services Rendered by the Haitians," 201.

98 Sinnette, *Arthur Alfonso Schomburg*, 49.
99 Sinnette, *Arthur Alfonso Schomburg*, 49.
100 Schomburg, "The Negro Digs Up His Past," 672.
101 Schomburg, "Military Services Rendered by the Haitians," 207.
102 Schomburg, "Military Services Rendered by the Haitians," 206.
103 Schomburg, "The Negro Digs Up His Past," 673.
104 Schomburg, "The Negro Digs Up His Past," 673.
105 I am using "Americans" here as Schomburg did, to signify peoples of North America, Central America, South America, and the Caribbean, not solely the United States.
106 Schomburg, "Racial Integrity," 68. The original says "devote our time in kindling." Let us remember that as a native Spanish speaker, Schomburg had these types of peculiarities when speaking or writing English.
107 Deloria, *Playing Indian*.
108 Schomburg, "Military Services Rendered by the Haitians," 199, emphasis added.
109 Newton, "Returns to a Native Land," 108.
110 Newton, "Returns to a Native Land," 119.
111 Wynter, "Jonkonnu in Jamaica," 35.
112 Arthur A. Schomburg, "Henri Christophe," microfilm, reel 1, Arthur Alfonso Schomburg Papers, Manuscripts, Archives, and Rare Books Division, Schomburg Center for Research in Black Culture, New York.
113 Schomburg, "Henri Christophe."
114 Schomburg, "Henri Christophe."
115 Schomburg, "Henri Christophe."
116 Catie Peters writes extensively about the significance of farming in asserting belonging to the Caribbean for "coolies" and South Asians in the nineteenth century. Peters, "A New Race of Cultivators."
117 Schomburg, "Henri Christophe."
118 For French historian Médéric Louis Elie Moreau de Saint-Méry, indigeneity was central to the colony's identity and to the racial makeup of the *affranchis* (freed mulatos), whom he advocated should be free. Moreau de Saint-Méry and W. Cobbett, "A topographical and political description of the Spanish part of Saint-Domingo containing, general observations on the climate, population and productions; on the character and manners of the inhabitants; with an account of the several branches of the government. By M. L. E. Moreau de Saint-Mery. Member of the Philosophical Society of Philadelphia, &c. Translated from the French, by William Cobbett. Vol. I[-II]. Printed and sold by the author, printer and bookseller, no. 84, South Front-Street, (1798)." For more on the study of Haitian indigeneity see Reyes, "Haitian Indigeneity before Africa"; and Fischer, *Modernity Disavowed*, chapter 11.
119 Reyes, "Haitian Indigeneity before Africa."
120 Wynter, "Jonkonnu in Jamaica," 36. See also the discussion of Wynter in Newton, "Returns to a Native Land," 117.
121 Arroyo, "Technologies," 148.
122 Anzaldúa coined the term *New Mestiza* in *Borderlands / La Frontera*.

123 García-Peña, *The Borders of Dominicanidad*, 84–92, 123.
124 Alexander, *Pedagogies of Crossing*, 290.
125 Alexander, *Pedagogies of Crossing*, 290.
126 Garcia-Peña, *The Borders of Dominicanidad*, chapter 2.
127 See also Pitre, "Frederick Douglass and the Annexation of Santo Domingo."
128 James Clifford's article "Diasporas" works the "difference" in terms of legitimization of the claims of diasporic identity and native identities. The section titled "Diaspora's Borders" is especially useful.

CHAPTER 3: AGAINST DEATH

1 Joaquín Balaguer served six terms as president of the Dominican Republic, first from 1966 to 1978, a period known as the "Terrible Twelve Years," and then again from 1986 to 1996. Balaguer was also a public servant and the righthand man of dictator Rafael Leónidas Trujillo from 1930 to 1961; at times, he served as Trujillo's puppet president. See Liberato, *Joaquín Balaguer, Memory, and Diaspora*.
2 F. Díaz, *La UASD ametrallada*, 60.
3 Margarita Cordero, in conversation with the author, July 14, 2020.
4 See Liberato, *Joaquín Balaguer, Memory, and Diaspora*.
5 See Escalante and Muñiz, *The Secret War*; Infante, *12 años de Balaguer*; and Cassá, *Los doce años*.
6 It is estimated that during the Terrible Twelve Years, more than three thousand people were killed and another twelve thousand imprisoned and tortured. The victims were accused of communism or "Leftist tendencies." Among the most notable victims were student activist Amín Abel Hasbún and journalist Orlando Martínez. See "Correspondencia enviada y recibida por diversas personalidades y presos políticos del Movimiento Popular Dominicano, referente a los asesinatos de Amín Abel y Sagrario Día," Colección Rafael Báez Pérez, Cucullo—1958 a 2003, and Prensa Diaria Dominicana (1969–1972), in AGN.
7 There are two advanced graduate students, Genesis Lara (University of California, Davis) and René Cordero (Brown University), currently researching the revolutionary activities at La UASD in the 1960s and 1970s, focusing on women activists. Readers interested in the subject should keep an eye out for these incredibly important historical contributions.
8 F. Díaz, *La UASD ametrallada*, 65.
9 F. Díaz, *La UASD ametrallada*, 67.
10 "UASD: Repudio total a la barbarie," 14. This editorial appears without a byline, a common practice for some of the editorial pieces in this publication during the repressive Balaguer regime.
11 See chapter 50 of Jiménez Maxwell, *Memorias del fracaso de un triunfador*.
12 Venezuelan songwriter Gloria Martín's trova "Sagrario Abierto" describes Sagrario Díaz's transcendence as a Latin American symbol of democracy and courage: "Sagrario se llamó aquí y en mi tierra de otra forma . . . pero todas

fueron muertas por la misma mano de obra." Castañuelas, "Gloria Martín - Sagrario Abierto."

13 In the most recent police-student confrontation at La UASD, on October 1, 2019, the chant was invoked as police shot at protesting students. See Valerio, "Enfrenamiento policías y estudiantes se mudan a la UASD."

14 Marielle Franco (1979–2018) was a Brazilian feminist, politician, and human rights activist shot and killed on March 14, 2018.

15 See Guidotti-Hernández, *Unspeakable Violence*, 7.

16 The colonial name of the island is Hispaniola. I am choosing to use the Indigenous name, Quisqueya, which is also how locals refer to the island.

17 Sternbach, "Re-membering the Dead," 98.

18 García-Peña, *The Borders of Dominicanidad*, 82.

19 Alexander, *Pedagogies of Crossing*, 78.

20 See Estrella, "Muertos Civiles."

21 C. Sharpe, *In the Wake*, 7.

22 United Nations Division for Gender Affairs, "Indicators: Femicide or Feminicide.".

23 C. Smith, *Afro-Paradise*, 4.

24 Estrella, "Muertos Civiles."

25 Lorde, *Sister Outsider*.

26 J. Johnson, *Wicked Flesh*.

27 Curiel and Silva-Reis, "Pensar a tradução e o feminismo negro."

28 Ricourt, *The Dominican Racial Imaginary*.

29 See Hoffnung-Garskof, *A Tale of Two Cities*.

30 Efraín Sánchez, in conversation with the author, February 17, 2018.

31 Mariam Almonte (whose name I have changed to protect her identity at her request), in conversation with the author, February 15, 2018. Almonte was a student activist and later became a spy and messenger for the constitutional forces of the 1965 revolution. Her husband was killed in battle in 1965. Mariam Almonte, in conversation with the author, December 8, 2018.

32 Sánchez, in conversation with the author, February 17, 2018.

33 See McPherson, "Misled by Himself."

34 See "Cincuenta años de la Guerra de Abril" in Archivo General de la Nación, Santo Domingo, AGN, 2015. Additional information can be found on the official webpage of the fiftieth anniversary of the Guerra de Abril, "Memoria de Abril," AGN, accessed November 5, 2020, http://memoriadeabril.com/.

35 Beth Manley talks about the constant erasure of women from the history of political and social movements in the Dominican Republic. See Manley, *The Paradox of Paternalism*, 157–66.

36 Of particular importance is a two-volume collection of documents: Candelario, Manley, and Mayes, *Cien años de feminismos dominicanos*. Also notable are the works of historians Elizabeth S. Manley (*Paradox of Paternalism*) and Neici Zeller *(Discursos y espacios femeninos en República Dominicana, 1880–1961)*, and the feminist scholarly and public interventions of Rosario Castellanos, Yuderkys Espinosa Miñoso, and Ochy Curiel. See also Cordero, *Mujeres de abril*.

37 Margarita Cordero, in conversation with the author, February 19, 2018.
38 Cordero, in conversation with the author, February 19, 2018.
39 In an interview, General Taveras confirmed Cordero's narrative: "At the beginning there was a lot of confusion as to what our [14J's] role was to be. There was the usual power struggle, but also a sense of urgency. I decided to take the leadership in uniting the fronts. It was, after all, one common struggle." Rafael "Fafa" Taveras, in conversation with the author, February 16, 2018.
40 Fafa Taveras, conversation with the author, February 20, 2018.
41 Shortly after the US intervention, the Academia de Mujeres was organized to train women in military combat. The Academia is often cited as a location of women's—mostly middle-class women's—military training. However, by the time the Academia was created in late May, the most intense combat had concluded. The women who fought and died during the first weeks of the revolution leading to Operación Limpieza, with a handful of exceptions, were Black and Brown working-class women.
42 Operación Limpieza took place over roughly May 13–21, 1965, and led to more than one thousand casualties.
43 We will mention the first name only at the request of the interviewee to protect her from potential retaliation.
44 Yolanda, in conversation with the author, October 2, 2017.
45 Cordero, in conversation with the author, February 19, 2018.
46 Resumen Latinoamericano, "República Dominicana."
47 Medrano, "Desmitificando una famosísima foto."
48 Medrano, "Desmitificando una famosísima foto."
49 Hoffnung-Garskof describes this process of internal migration that led to the formation of many of the "Parte Alta" neighborhoods. Hoffnung-Garskof, *A Tale of Two Cities*, 46–47.
50 Sánchez, in conversation with the author, March 12, 2020.
51 Sánchez, in conversation with the author, March 12, 2020.
52 Yolanda, in conversation with the author, October 2, 2017.
53 Medrano, "Desmitificando una famosísima foto."
54 See Vanderplaats Vallejo, *Las madres de la patria*; and Zeller, "The Appearance of All, the Reality of Nothing."
55 See Vanderplaats Vallejo, *Las madres de la patria*, introduction and chapter 1.
56 See Manley, "Of Celestinas and Saints"; and Manley, "'News of "Crazy" Women Demanding Freedom.'" Patria, Minerva, and María Teresa Mirabal were three sisters from the northern Cibao region who opposed the Trujillo regime and were involved in clandestine political activities against the dictator. They were assassinated by the regime on November 25, 1960. Their murders had international resonance. In 1999 the United Nations declared November 25 the International Day for the Elimination of Violence against Women. The assassination of the Mirabal sisters has had a profound effect on Dominican society. The Mirabal sisters have been the subjects of multiple historical and literary texts and films, including Julia Alvarez's acclaimed 1994 novel, *In the Time of the Butterflies*.

57 Yolanda, in conversation with the author, October 2, 2017.
58 García-Peña, *The Borders of Dominicanidad*, chapter 5.
59 See chapters 4 and 5.
60 Yolanda married the captain of the Onassis boat, an elder Greek gentleman forty years her senior, and traveled with him on the boat for nearly a decade. Known as El Bar de Cambumbo, the iconic queer bar first started as a speakeasy in the back of Yolanda's home in el Ensanche la Fe. Yolanda, in conversation with the author, October 2, 2017.
61 Yolanda, in conversation with the author, October 2, 2017.
62 Yolanda, in conversation with the author, October 2, 2017.
63 Yolanda, in conversation with the author, October 2, 2017.
64 United Nations Development Programme (UNDP), *Human Development Report 2009*, 12.
65 UNDP, *Human Development Report 2009*, 25.
66 OECD, *International Migration Outlook 2013*.
67 Merrill, *An Alliance of Women*; and García Peña, "Being Black Ain't so Bad."
68 See Merrill, *An Alliance of Women*.
69 Merrill, *An Alliance of Women*, xvi.
70 Jerry Essan Masslo was a refugee from South Africa who was murdered by a gang in August 1989. His story provoked a strong emotional response throughout Italy and led to the recognition of refugee status by the Italian legislature. Shortly after his tragic death, the first ever anti-racist event organized in Italy took place in Rome. It involved more than 200,000 people, both Italians and foreigners. Masslo's death also inspired several cultural productions, the most significant being the 1991 film *Pummaró*, directed by Michele Placido. See also King and Wood, *Media and Migration*, for more on this period and media representation.
71 The Martelli Law, signed in January 1990, was inspired by the Masslo crime. The law was named after its author, Deputy Prime Minister Claudio Martelli.
72 Reuters, "Cardinal Causes Controversy." See also Parati, *Migration Italy*, 23.
73 Parati, *Migration Italy*, 23.
74 Merrill, *An Alliance of Women*, xviii.
75 See Cristalli, "Denny Méndez." Alba Parietti won the Miss Italia beauty pageant in 1979 and went on to represent Italy in the 1980 Miss Universe competition. She has since become an important television and movie icon. During the week leading up to the 1996 pageant, Parietti was temporarily suspended from the panel for comments suggesting that Méndez's race made her "ineligible to represent the nation." She later claimed that she had been misquoted and was allowed to return as a judge. See Pinkus, "Miss (Black) Italy," 80.
76 See García-Peña, "Being Black Ain't So Bad," 145, emphasis added. See also Agnew, "Denny's Win a Boost for Tolerance."
77 Torres-Saillant, "Diaspora and National Identity," 18.
78 Flores and Jiménez Román, "Triple-Consciousness?"
79 See Phoenix, "Colourism and the Politics of Beauty."

80 See Weyland, *Negociando la aldea global.*
81 World Bank, "Stock of Migrants," 4.
82 Candelario, *Black behind the Ears.*
83 Frías, "La aldea global."
84 See chapter 4.
85 Jacqueline Andall argues that these discourses are extremely relevant to the Italian context as gender is racialized through the emergence of a strong ethnic minority. Andall, *Gender, Migration, and Domestic Service*, 3.
86 Andall, *Gender, Migration, and Domestic Service*, 19.
87 Pojmann, *Immigrant Women and Feminism in Italy*, 6.
88 García-Peña, "Being Black Ain't So Bad."
89 Mercedes Frías, in conversation with the author, June 22, 2020.
90 Frías, in conversation with the author, June 22, 2020.
91 Frías, in conversation with the author, June 22, 2020.
92 Mercedes Frías, in conversation with the author, June 29, 2020. See also Capussotti, "The Experience of the 'Punto di Partenza' Group"; and "Prendiamo la parola: Il campus delle culture delle donne," Florence, 2001, accessed October 3, 2019, http://www.enc.org.
93 Frías, in conversation with the author, June 29, 2020. For more on the Freedom School (El Campus) and publications, see "Punto di Partenza."
94 See Andrijasevic, "I confini fanno la differenza"; and Altin and Saba, "Leggi italiane e servizi sanitari triestini rivolti alle donne immigrate."
95 Frías, in conversation with the author, June 29, 2020.
96 Fikes, "Mercedes Frías."
97 Marlene de la Cruz, in conversation with the author, May 18, 2014, emphasis added.
98 See Anacaona's objective on its Facebook page, https://www.facebook.com/Associazione-Anacaona-Mujeres-Dominicanas-en-Italia-157596721022293/?ref=page_internal.
99 Melania Cruz, in conversation with the author, July 8, 2015.
100 De la Cruz, in conversation with the author, May 18, 2014.
101 Cejas, "'Desde la experiencia,'" 187.
102 De la Cruz, in conversation with the author, June 22, 2018, emphasis added.
103 Báez, *Carmen: FotonovelARTE*, 3.
104 I theorized El Nié in the introduction and chapter 5 of *The Borders of Dominicanidad.*
105 Hinojosa et al., "Salud de la Mujer."
106 Báez, *Carmen: FotonovelARTE*, 96.
107 Josefina Báez, in conversation with the author, June 1, 2020.
108 Carmen Inés Bencosme, in conversation with the author, June 1, 2020.
109 Báez, in conversation with the author, June 1, 2020.
110 Báez, in conversation with the author, June 1, 2020.
111 Pilar Espinal, in conversation with the author, June 1, 2020.
112 Báez, *Carmen: FotonovelARTE*, 8.
113 Báez, *Carmen: FotonovelARTE*, 18.

114 Amarilys Estrella coined the term *muertos civiles*, or civic death, in reference to the dehumanization of ethnic Haitians in the Dominican Republic, particularly after the passing of the 2013 legislation that denationalized people of Haitian descent. See Estrella, "Muertos Civiles."
115 Báez, *Comrade, Bliss Ain't Playing*, 25.
116 Báez, *Comrade, Bliss Ain't Playing*, 79
117 De la Cruz, in conversation with the author, June 22, 2018.
118 Báez, *Levente no*, n.p.
119 Báez, *Levente no*, n.p.
120 Báez, *Levente no*, n.p.

CHAPTER 4: THE AFTERLIFE OF COLONIAL GENDER VIOLENCE

1 Milagros Guzmán (Dominican vice counsel in Milan), in conversation with the author, June 18, 2018.
2 Guzmán, in conversation with the author, June 18, 2018.
3 Guzmán, in conversation with the author, June 18, 2018.
4 Caminero, "Asesinada en Italia quería volver a RD."
5 B. Bianchi, "Omicidio di via Muratori."
6 Guzmán, in conversation with the author, June 18, 2018. "Sanky panky" or "sanqui panqui" is a term used in the Dominican Republic to describe a person who participates in sexual exchanges with a tourist for the duration of their visit. Unlike prostitutes, who are assumed to establish commercial sex exchanges with direct monetary exchange, a sanky panky's relationship with their partner is more complex and varies from couple to couple. Some sanky pankies provide companionship in exchange for participation in the tourist lifestyle (going to restaurants and hotels), while others receive gifts and support for their family (children, parents, etc.). Some relationships continue beyond the vacation and become monogamous. See Brennan, *What's Love Got to Do with It?*
7 Vanni, "Duplice omicidio di via Muratori."
8 B. Bianchi, "Omicidio di via Muratori."
9 "Omicidio Via Muratori."
10 Focarete and Galli, "Loft, viaggi e movida senza uno stipendio."
11 Willis and Williams, *The Black Female Body*, 8.
12 "La bella vita di Spelta."
13 "Tropical fever" is rooted in sexual interactions between colonizers and Black women and girls. Fabienne Le Houérou writes that white Italians viewed their relationship with Black women and girls in colonial East Africa as an illness. They called the women "antchilite," which translates to "toxic attraction." The word encapsulates the violence of the unequal relationship. See Le Houérou, "Gender and Sexual Abuses." For more on sex tourism in the Caribbean, see Kempadoo, *Sun, Sex, and Gold*; Padilla, *Caribbean Pleasure Industry*; Sengupta, "The Economy of Desire"; and Williams, *Sex Tourism in Bahia*.
14 Kilomba, *Plantation Memories*, 11.

15 Giuliani, *Race, Nation and Gender in Modern Italy*, 13.

16 Historian Angelo Del Boca argues that silencing evidence of the violence of the Italian army in the Horn of Africa was a deliberate state attempt to clean up Italy's image and erase the legacy of colonization and Fascism in the metropolis. See Del Boca, *L'Africa nella coscienza degli italiani*, 19–20. Cristina Lombardi-Diop and Caterina Romeo insist that this "suppression of memory" manifests in present-day discourse around immigration, particularly during the recent "refugee crisis." Lombardi-Diop and Romeo, *Postcolonial Italy*, 7.

17 See Parati, *Migration Italy* (2005), 48–53, for a deeper discussion on what she calls "the recolouring of Italian Culture."

18 Lombardi-Diop and Romeo, *Postcolonial Italy*, 7.

19 There has been a recent growth in scholarship about Italian colonialism, particularly in the context of present-day racialization and increasing racial violence. Several anthologies and critical works have been particularly helpful in mapping the legacy of Italian colonialism for an English-speaking audience: Lombardi-Diop and Romeo, *Postcolonial Italy*; Andall and Duncan, *Italian Colonialism*; Andall and Duncan, *National Belongings*; and Parati, *Migration Italy.*

20 Risorgimento (rebirth) was the nineteenth-century political, military, and cultural movement that led to the unification of the Italian state in 1861.

21 Giuliani argues that southerners were believed to belong to a different "racial kinship." Giuliani, *Race, Nation and Gender in Modern Italy*, 39.

22 See Jackson, *Dixie's Italians*; Guglielmo and Salerno, *Are Italians White?*; and Vellon, *A Great Conspiracy against Our Race.*

23 Giuliani, *Race, Nation and Gender in Modern Italy*, 39.

24 See Guglielmo and Salerno, *Are Italians White?*; Ferrari, *Days Pleasant and Unpleasant*; Carnevale, *A New Language, a New World*; Luconi, "The Fascist Racial Turn"; and Richards, *Italian American.*

25 During the seven years of qualitative research I conducted in Milan and its suburbs, I observed with curiosity the common, socially accepted interactions between Black and white Italians in which the latter asked for the former's place of origin. This happened even after Black Italians had said they were born in Milan. I have often heard Second Generation Habeshas refer to their "place of origin" as Eritrea or Ethiopia even when they were born in Italy. This dynamic, though slightly different, also occurs in the United States; Latinx Americans are often perceived to be immigrants.

26 Chambers, *Mediterranean Crossings*, 7.

27 Martínez-San Miguel, *Coloniality of Diasporas*, 4.

28 El-Tayeb, *European Others*, xxiii.

29 Deborah Thomas uses the term *affective archive* to name the ways people bear witness to the violence and survival of the plantation through embodied memories. "Affective Archives, Witnessing, Repair." See also Thomas, *Political Life in the Wake of the Plantation*, 5.

30 Stoler, *Carnal Knowledge and Imperial Power*, 54.

31 Fuentes, *Dispossessed Lives*, 3.

32 Morgan, *Laboring Women*, 122.

33 Sanz, *Diario de Colón*, 10.

34 Sanz, *Diario de Colón*, 8–10, 38.

35 For more on this, see Beltrán, "Representación del cuerpo"; Gilliam and Gilliam, "Negociando a subjetividade de mulata no Brasil"; and Manganelli, *Transatlantic Spectacles of Race*.

36 Brown, *The Repeating Body*, 18.

37 Blanco Borelli, *She Is Cuba*, 5.

38 Willis and Williams, *The Black Female Body*, 8–10.

39 See Balce, "The Filipina's Breast."

40 Balce, "The Filipina's Breast."

41 Brown, *The Repeating Body*, 6–7.

42 Brown, *The Repeating Body*, 7.

43 The Colony of Eritrea was officially established in 1890. In 1941, during World War II, it came under British rule, eventually becoming part of Ethiopia in 1952. Stating that Eritrea was a colony from 1890 to 1941, as historians often do, erases the longer and more complex chronology of Eritrean colonial history, which began with the Italian purchase of Assab in 1869 and continued until the end of the twentieth century. Due to Italian colonialism in the region, Eritrea did not gain independence until 1991. See Le Houérou, "Gender and Sexual Abuses."

44 Africa Orientale Italiana (AOI) was the name the Fascist regime gave to Italy's colonies. The AOI encompassed Somalia, Eritrea, and the Ethiopian regions of Harar, Galla-Sidamo, Amhara, and Scioa.

45 There was a proliferation of exhibitions during the colonial era that displayed colonial subjects. One of the most popular of these live human exhibitions took place during the 1884 Esposizione Generale Italiana in Turin. See Abbattista, "Torino 1884." The display of Black people in live expositions, human zoos, and freak shows proliferated throughout the long nineteenth century in Europe and North America. The most popularized case is that of Saartjie Baartman, a Khoikhoi woman from South Africa who was exhibited all over Europe as the "Hottentot Venus." For more on Baartman, see Gordon-Chipembere, *Representation and Black Womanhood*; R. Mitchell, *Vénus Noire*; and Sharpley-Whiting, *Black Venus*. See also Maseko, *Life and Times of Sara Baartman*.

46 Giuliani, *Race, Nation and Gender in Modern Italy*, 47.

47 Giuliani, *Race, Nation and Gender in Modern Italy*, 46–47.

48 Mussolini, "Il problema dell'emigrazione," 97–98.

49 See "Enzo Biagi Con Indro Montanelli"; and Perilli, "Relazioni pericolose," 155–56.

50 The name comes from French artist Prieur's famous bronze sculpture *Black Venus* (ca. 1600), though sometimes it also references Botticelli's famous painting *Birth of Venus* (1485–86).

51 Black women were represented in Portuguese, Spanish, and Italian literature as early as the fifteenth century. In 1794 British artist Thomas Stothard made a copper engraving, "The Voyage of the Sable Venues," that depicted a seminude sensual image of a Black woman. Deborah Willis and Carla Williams think the

image was inspired by the anonymous 1781 poem "The Sable Venus: An Ode," in which "the Black one" is described as having appeared in Florence ready to love. Willis and Williams, *The Black Female Body*, 9–10. In *Vénus Noire*, Robin Mitchell takes up the symbol of the Black Venus to show how literary and visual depictions of black women in nineteenth-century France helped to shape the country's postrevolutionary national identity, particularly in response to the trauma of the French defeat in the Haitian Revolution.

52 Ponzanesi, "Beyond the Black Venus."

53 Ponzanesi, "Beyond the Black Venus."

54 Baratieri, "'More than a Tree, Less than a Woman,'" 371.

55 Ponzanesi, "The Color of Love," 163.

56 Triulzi, "La costruzione dell'immagine dell'Africa," 166.

57 There are more than seven thousand photographs of colonial Africa currently housed in the Archivio della Società Napoletana alone. See Triulzi, "La costruzione dell'immagine dell'Africa," 165.

58 Triulzi, "La costruzione dell'immagine dell'Africa," 168.

59 While I was able to locate many photographs of madamas in different archives, I decided against including these images given the violence they contain. Most of these photos are of seminude children and young women who, as we know from the archive, were often photographed against their will. They are easily found if the reader chooses to search for them. I presented a version of this chapter during a talk at a university's women and gender studies department. One of the conference attendees questioned my decision not to show the widely available images I describe throughout the chapter. When I explained that the choice was conscious, as I would prefer to avoid inflicting more violence on the women portrayed in the photos and on those of us who would identify with the violence and the trauma, they were confused and became irritable, ending the dialogue by saying, "I think you are making a mistake." The ways we continue to reproduce violence in the name of scholarship and science through the perpetuation of afterimages of colonial violence reflect the urgent need to decolonize academia. See in Archivio Storico del Ex-Ministero Africa Italiana, Archivio Storico Diplomatico, Roma, Italy.

60 Sontag, *On Photography*, 71.

61 Barrera, "Sex, Citizenship, and the State," 161.

62 Baratieri, "'More than a Tree, Less than a Woman,'" 362. See also Labanca and Marchi, *Memorie d'Oltremare*, 24–26.

63 A third category, *antchilite*, was introduced during the Fascist era. Le Houérou, "Gender and Sexual Abuses," 256.

64 See Baratieri, "'More than a Tree, Less than a Woman,'" 365.

65 Iyob, "*Madamismo* and Beyond," 222.

66 Paoli, *Nella colonia Eritrea*, 106.

67 Barrera, "Sex, Citizenship, and the State," 163.

68 I use the term *fragment* to refer to Fuentes's invitation to read the fragments of Black women's lives. Fragments can be used to reconstruct their stories and

histories beyond what colonial archives—archives of epistemic violence—allow. Fuentes, *Dispossessed Lives*, 6.

69 Dell'Oro was born in Asmara in 1938 to an Italian colonial family. At age twenty, she moved with her family to Milan and began a career as a writer. Her first novel, *Asmara addio* (1989), is based on her life growing up in colonial Eritrea and her migration to Italy, a country that shaped her cultural identity but felt foreign to her. Dell'Oro identifies as Eritrean and often writes and speaks publicly about the experiences of being born and raised in a colonial family in segregated East Africa.

70 Iyob, "*Madamismo* and Beyond," 222.

71 See Ponzanesi, "The Color of Love."

72 Gandolfi, *I misteri dell'Africa italiana*, 149. See also Iyob, "*Madamismo* and Beyond," 226.

73 Gandolfi, *I misteri dell'Africa italiana*, 149–50. For more analysis on Gandolfi, see Strazza, "Faccetta nera dell'Abissinia."

74 Gandolfi, *I misteri dell'Africa italiana*, 174.

75 Stoler, *Carnal Knowledge and Imperial Power*, 10.

76 In 1927 the US Supreme Court ruled in *Buck v. Bell* that Virginia's eugenics sterilization law was constitutional. See Briggs, *Reproducing Empire*.

77 García-Peña, *The Borders of Dominicanidad*, 67.

78 Haddas, Asli, Habesha entreprenuer and researcher from Milan, in conversation with the author, June 5, 2017. See also Locatelli, "Beyond Campo Cintato."

79 South Africa introduced apartheid in 1948 as a systematic extension of preexisting racial segregation in the country. Apartheid was characterized by an authoritarian political culture based on *baasskap* (white supremacy) and state repression of Black Africans, Asian South Africans, and other people of color for the benefit of the nation's white minority. The economic and social effects of apartheid continue to this day. See Locatelli, "Beyond the Campo Cintato," 220–21.

80 Research does suggest that madamato continued despite its being criminalized. According to Barrera, there were fifteen thousand registered interracial concubinages in Asmara in 1940. Barrera, *Dangerous Liaisons*, 43.

81 "Norme relative ai meticci." This is happening in the climate of Nazism and antisemitism that, as Tiffany Florvil argues, led to acts of "daily racism" all over Europe and the stripping of citizenship rights for Black Germans. See Florvil, *Mobilizing Black Germany*, 5.

82 Goglia, "Note sul razzismo coloniale fascista."

83 Barrera, *Dangerous Liaisons*, 33.

84 "Le testimonianze."

85 See Trento, *Pasolini e l'Africa, L'Africa di Pasolini*.

86 See Bailey, *Misogynoir Transformed*.

87 Trento, "Pier Paolo Pasolini," 144; Grande, "Ero musa di Pasolini ora servo Madre Teresa."

88 Trento, "Pier Paolo Pasolini," 144–46.

89 Trento, "Pier Paolo Pasoloni, 144.

90 See, for example, Ryan-Scheutz, *Sex, the Self and the Sacred*, 190–91.
91 Giuliani, *Race, Nation and Gender in Modern Italy*, 46.
92 Giuliani, *Race, Nation and Gender in Modern Italy*, 67.
93 Micheli, "Faccetta Nera."
94 Mussolini, "Discorso all'Augusteo," 201–3.
95 Scego, "The True Story of 'Faccetta Nera.'"
96 Marialena Báez, in conversation with the author, July 23, 2017.
97 Anonymous Black Italian activist, in conversation with the author, May 21, 2018.
98 Roberto Poletti, "Questa storia dei profughi finira molto male," *Forte e Chiaro*, July 22, 2015 (mins. 47.44–50.00), TeleLombardia, Milan, https://www.youtube.com/watch?v=ZOt-OwnwGpEApril. In this episode of *Forte e Chiaro*, Poletti invites Ismail to comment on the suspicion of Isis collaborators living in Brescia. The episode aired July 22 and was uploaded on YouTube on October 3, 2015.
99 Giuliani, *Race, Nation and Gender in Modern Italy*, 5.
100 Montanelli, "Quando andai a nozze con Destà."
101 Beppe Severgnini, a columnist at *Corriere della Sera*, the Italian newspaper in which Montanelli's column appeared, characterized the violence and rape as "a common wedding." Severgnini, "Nessuno tolga Montanelli dai suoi Giardini." Marco Travaglio, the editor in chief of *Il Fatto Quotidiano*, actually asserted that Montanelli's actions proved he was not a racist. "Montanelli, Travaglio ad Accordi&Disaccordi."
102 "Indro Montanelli."
103 Indro Montanelli, interview by Gianni Bisiach.
104 Montanelli, interview by Gianni Bisiach.
105 Montanelli, interview by Gianni Bisiach.
106 Le Houérou, "Gender and Sexual Abuses," 261.
107 Le Houérou, "Gender and Sexual Abuses," 261.
108 Gandolfi, *I misteri dell'Africa italiana*, 50–53. See also Baratieri, "'More than a Tree, Less than a Woman,'" 369.
109 Le Houérou, "Gender and Sexual Abuses," 261.
110 Le Houérou, "Gender and Sexual Abuses," 262.
111 This is something we see in the language of Gandolfi, for example. See Bardi, *35 anni vissuti in Eritrea*, 95.
112 Fuentes, *Dispossessed Lives*, 5–6.
113 I have found no data that specifically identify the women of color who lose their children to the state. However, in qualitative interviews with immigrant women, immigrant organizations, and consular representatives as well as with Rossella Amodeo, a family lawyer and activist in Milan, it became clear that this is indeed a serious matter. Two of the women I interviewed between 2015 and 2018 lost their children in what struck me as an excessive, intrusive, and biased process. In both cases, the immigrant mothers did not pose dangers to their children, who had learning disabilities. Rather than offer support to the mothers, the state removed the children and placed them in foster care.

114 As early as 1920, travel narratives, postcards, ads, and rumors about Dominicanas' hypersexuality circulated in Europe and the United States. The Dominican Republic and other Caribbean nations soon came to be imagined as what Denise Brennan calls "sexscapes": sites for negotiating sexual encounters through a global and transnational economy of inequality. By the same token, Dominican subjects came to be imagined as sexually available and sexually proficient commodities for Europeans and North Americans to consume. See Brennan, *What's Love Got to Do with It?*

115 Kempadoo, *Sexing the Caribbean*, 42.

116 World Tourism Organization, "Regional Breakdown of World Tourism Statistics 1976–1980."

117 Serrata, "La ciudad como espectáculo."

118 Turner and Ash, *The Golden Hordes*, 58.

119 Turner and Ash, *The Golden Hordes*, 15.

120 Fanon, *The Wretched of the Earth*, 153–54.

121 Vanni, "Duplice omicidio."

122 Brennan, *What's Love Got to Do with It?*, 21.

123 "Omicidio Via Muratori," emphasis added.

124 Brondoni, "Sparatoria a Milano, 5 ipotesi per un delitto."

125 B. Bianchi, "Omicidio di via Muratori."

126 "Omicidio Massimiliano Spelta e Carolina Payano."

127 "Delitto Spelta."

128 Focarete, "Delitto Spelta, i parenti di Carolina."

129 See Grignaffini, *La scena madre*; Perassi, "Madri e patrie nel romanzo contemporaneo sulla migrazione"; Miscali, "The Transformation of Motherhood"; and Faleschini Lerner and D'Amelio, *Italian Motherhood on Screen*.

130 B. Bianchi, "Omicidio di via Muratori."

131 Brown, *The Repeating Body*, 59–62.

132 Milagros Guzmán, in conversation with the author, July 7, 2015. Guzmán is a graduate of the Instituto Technológico de Santiago (Intec) Women and Gender Studies Program, and the cofounder of the Associazione Anacaona Mujeres Dominicanas en Italia.

133 B. Bianchi, "Omicidio di via Muratori."

134 File Carolina Payano, Caso Payano, 2010–2013, Archivo Consulado Dominicano, Milan, Italy.

135 The term *DREAMer* has been used to describe young undocumented immigrants who were brought to the United States as children, who have lived and gone to school in the United States, and who in many cases identify as US American. The term comes from the Development, Relief and Education for Alien Minors Act (DREAM Act), a bill that was introduced in Congress in 2001 that would have granted legal status to undocumented immigrants who were brought to the United States as children.

136 Focarete and Galli, "Loft, viaggi e movida senza uno stipendio," emphasis added.

137 Melania Cruz, in conversation with the author, June 4, 2015.

138 "Chi sono le donne vittime di violenza."

139 Rossella Amodeo, in conversation with the author, June 27, 2015.

140 Mireya is a pseudonym, since the family member who told me this story asked for anonymity for everyone.

141 Mireya's sister, in conversation with the author, July 30, 2016. The conversation took place in multiple languages (Spanish, Italian, and English), with support from an interpreter. I had previously come to know the details of the case through conversations with consular representatives. In conversation with Melania Cruz, the psychologist who oversaw the case, I commented on the question of linguistic competency. It seems odd to me that this woman, who migrated to Europe as a young adult, seems to have lost fluency in Spanish. Cruz explained that this is a common experience, particularly for people who have been sold into prostitution or experience severe trauma and isolation. I have since encountered several people with similar challenges, including a transgender woman who was severely beaten and imprisoned as well as a woman who was sold as a girl and kept in isolation (except from her solicitors) for more than fifteen years.

142 Milagros Guzmán, in conversation with the author, June 22, 2018, emphasis added.

143 See Lombardi-Diop and Romeo, *Postcolonial Italy*, 1.

144 Triulzi, "La costruzione dell'immagine dell'Africa," 167.

145 Kilomba, *Plantation Memories*, 146; J. Sharpe, *Ghosts of Slavery.*

146 Burns Neveldine, *Bodies at Risk.*

147 Kilomba, *Plantation Memories*, 36.

CHAPTER 5: SECOND GENERATION INTERRUPTIONS

1 Candelario, *Black behind the Ears*, 157–59.

2 Dizidzienyo and Oboler in *Neither Enemies nor Friends* and Vaca in *The Presumed Alliance* write about the tensions that exist among US Black and Latinx communities in the United States. These tensions make coalition-building difficult.

3 As Arlene Dávila's work demonstrates, Latinidad also manifests through our practices of consumption. See Dávila, *Latinos, Inc.*

4 The US production of Asian Americans as a "model minority" materializes this idea of "acceptable citizens of color." See Ty, *Asianfail.*

5 Romeo, "Racial Evaporations," 222.

6 There have been many hate crimes in recent years, the most notable being the mass murder of six African immigrants in Castel Volturno by the Casalesi Clan in 2008 and the killing of Abdul Salam Guibre in Calabria the same year. There was very little media coverage of these crimes. See Hawthorne, "In Search of Black Italia"; Smythe, "The Black Mediterranean and the Politics of Imagination"; and Galindo-Calvo et al., "Islamophobia in Southern Europe."

7 There are several websites and blogs dedicated to the experience of US Black people living in Italy, most notably Tia Taylor's YouTube channel, which contains videos on topics like "Italian men love black women."
8 Florvil makes a similar point in the German context in *Mobilizing Black Germany*, 18.
9 Italy is host to a growing population of Second Generation immigrants. The state privileges Italian descent and makes naturalization very difficult, even for those born on Italian soil. This relegates a large population of Second Generation immigrants to a marginal position, excluded from politics, education, and employment after their eighteenth birthday because of their citizenship status. See G. Bianchi, "Italiani nuovi o nuova Italia?"; Zinn, "'Loud and Clear'"; Hawthorne, "Black Matters Are Spatial Matters."
10 Hawthorne, "Making Italy."
11 The term *Black Italian* or *Afro-Italian* is often kept in English or Italianized English: "Black Italian" or "Afroitaliana." See Hellman, *Journeys among Women*; and Hawthorne, "In Search of Black Italia."
12 Medhin Paolos, in conversation with the author, June 24, 2015.
13 See Dávila, *Latinos, Inc.*, in which the author explains that through marketing processes in which Latino-owned media organizations participate, Latinos are "repackaged" into a commodity that both exploits stereotypical images that reinforce racism and exclusion (such as heteronormative and white supremacist representations of Latinidad that completely erase Indigenous and Black Latinxs) and also speaks to the very people being exploited through a language of cultural unity and familiarity through certain common experiences (language, music, food, religion, etc.).
14 Colatrella, *Workers of the World*, 67–68.
15 See Istituto Nazionale di Statistica, "Population and Households."
16 Beaman, *Citizen Outsider*, 4.
17 Law No. 91/1992 states that people born in Italy to foreign parents must wait until they are eighteen years old to request citizenship. They must then prove that they have lived in Italy, uninterrupted, for their whole lives and that one of their parents was a legal Italian citizen at the time of their birth. They must also demonstrate employment, residency, and no outstanding legal issues. See Frisina and Hawthorne, "Italians with Veils and Afros."
18 Gbadamosi, "Am I Black Enough?," 70.
19 Since 2015, Italy has received an unprecedented number of refugees from Syria, Libya, Eritrea, and Somalia, leading to more restrictive immigration reforms, massive protests, and the loss of many lives at sea. See Guild et al., *The 2015 Refugee Crisis in the European Union*, 4–9; and Smythe, "Black Italianità."
20 Though the racial understanding of the vendor as a Black Muslim and a recent immigrant is very much marked by the Arab/African episteme, I argue that his location and subject position—a street vendor who sells to tourists—and his migrant experience actually make him a very good judge of racial "appearance."

21 El-Tayeb, *European Others*, xviii.

22 See Wessendorf, *Second-Generation Transnationalism and Roots Migration.*

23 hooks, *Salvation*, 152.

24 Kilomba, *Plantation Memories*, 10.

25 Parati, *Migration Italy* (2005), 29.

26 Mari and Shvanyukova, "Re-negotiating National Belonging in Contemporary Italian Migrant Literature," 527.

27 Capitani and Coen, *Pecore nere*. See Clò, "Hip Pop Italian Style," 275–76.

28 One of the most significant contributions to Italian postcolonial studies is Lombardi-Diop and Romeo, *Postcolonial Italy.*

29 Scego said this in correction to a journalist calling her an activist. Riccò, "Igiaba Scego on Writing between History and Literature."

30 See also Parati, *Migration Italy*, 29.

31 Deleuze and Guattari, *Kafka*, 11.

32 Scego, "Relazione di Igiaba Scego."

33 Scego, *La mia casa*, 20.

34 There have been multiple African obelisks around Rome. One of the most famous is the Obelisk of Axum (ሓወልቲ፡ ኣኽሱም), a fourth-century, seventy-nine-foot obelisk from the city of Axum in Ethiopia. In 1937, during the occupation of Ethiopia, Italians took the obelisk to Rome as a war prize. The theft of the obelisk has been an open wound between Ethiopia and Italy and a symbol of colonial oppression for many postcolonial diasporic people living in Italy. In a 1947 United Nations agreement, Italy agreed to return the obelisk. It took more than five decades for Italy to fulfill its promise in 2005.

35 Scego, *La mia casa*, 60.

36 Scego, *La mia casa*, 60.

37 Paynter, "The Spaces of Citizenship," 138.

38 Scego, *La mia casa*, 43.

39 García-Peña, *The Borders of Dominicanidad*, 3.

40 Scego, *La mia casa*, 61.

41 Scego, *La mia casa*, 81.

42 Scego, *La mia casa*, 81.

43 An example of this legacy is the political language of the North League, the right-wing, anti-immigrant, anti-Black political party founded by Umberto Bossi, a minister for Federal Reform in the Berlusconi IV Cabinet. See Garau, *Politics of National Identity in Italy*, 111–13.

44 Scego, *La mia casa*, 33.

45 Florvil, *Mobilizing Black Germany*, 5.

46 Báez, *Levente no: Yolayorkdominicanyork*; Pérez Firmat, *Life on the Hyphen.*

47 Lowe, *The Intimacies of Four Continents*; Wynter, "Unsettling the Coloniality of Being/Power/Truth/Freedom."

48 Scego, *La mia casa*, 33.

49 A lot of research has been done on the South-North divide and racism against southern Italians. See Derobertis, "Southerners, Migrants,

Colonized"; Wong, *Race and the Nation in Liberal Italy*; and Capussotti, "Nordisti contro Sudisti."

50 For more on white italianità and immigrant blackness, see Dal Lago, *Non-persons*.

51 Smythe, "Black Italianità," 3–4.

52 See chapter 4.

53 Henneberg, "Monuments"; Giuliani, *Race, Nation and Gender*; Smythe, "Black Italianità."

54 The battle over the return of ancient relics to Africa, particularly Egypt, became a matter of global conversation in 2003 when another obelisk, a 1,700-year-old Ethiopian artifact that Mussolini's forces seized in 1937, was finally dismantled to be transported back to Ethiopia.

55 Most notable is the literary work of immigrants like Pap Khouma, Christiana de Caldas Brito, and Amara Lakhous, and Second Generations Igiaba Scego and Cheikh Tidiane Gaye. Filmmakers and scholars Dagmawi Yimer, Riccardo Biadene, Leonardo De Franceschi, Valerio Ciriaci, Giusy Buccheri, Suranga Deshapriya Katugampala, and Fred Kudjo Kuwornu have highlighted the intersections of colonialism, antiblackness, and Second Generation exclusion from the postcolonial perspective. Finally, the 2018 digital history project "Postcolonial Italy, Mapping Colonial Heritage" (https://postcolonialitaly.com/), by Markus Wurzer and Daphné Budasz, documents public spaces in an effort to "stimulate a public debate on Italy's silenced colonial history."

56 Haskins, "Between Archive and Participation"; Duncan, "Italy's Postcolonial Cinema and Its Histories of Representation."

57 Parati, *Migration Italy*, 105.

58 I am using the term as the interviewees and communities I engage use it, but I recognize the term is contested by people who assert national boundaries.

59 See Small, "Theorizing Visibility and Vulnerability,"

60 See Bravi, "La storia come strumento d'inclusione sociale."

61 The film has been screened in international festivals, and at colleges and universities across the world. Scholars have also taken an interest in the film. See García-Peña, "Black in English."

62 Maglio and Paolos, *Asmarina*, 8:20 (quoted from English subtitles).

63 Maglio and Paolos, *Asmarina*, 9:44.

64 Maglio and Paolos, *Asmarina*, 9:45.

65 Maglio and Paolos, *Asmarina*, 9:07.

66 Thomas, *Political Life in the Wake of the Plantation*, 5–6.

67 Maglio and Paolos, *Asmarina*, 9:44.

68 Medhin Paolos, in conversation with the author, June 26, 2015.

69 Medhin Paolos, interview by Angela Davis.

70 Triulzi, "Displacing the Colonial Event," 441.

71 Pastacaldi, "Il testo della canzone Asmarina."

72 Medhin Paolos, in conversation with the author, June 24, 2016.
73 Maglio and Paolos, *Asmarina*, 32:10–33:57.
74 For a video recording of the event, see Massawatube, "Wedi Shawl (Bologna)."
75 Massawatube, "Wedi Shawl (Bologna)" (translation by Mihreteab Paolos).
76 The Eritrean Festival in Bologna, known originally as the Festival Eritrea, was first celebrated in Pavía in 1973. Beginning in 1974, it took place in Bologna and eventually came to be known as the Bologna Festival. The Eritrean People's Liberation Front was an armed Marxist-Leninist organization that fought for the independence of Eritrea from Ethiopia. It emerged in 1970 as a far-left group that split from the Eritrean Liberation Front (ELF). After Eritrean independence in 1991, it became the People's Front for Democracy and Justice (PFDJ), which is Eritrea's only legal political party.
77 Arnone, "The Eritrean Festival in the Time-Warp," 75.
78 García-Peña, *The Borders of Dominicanidad*.
79 Maglio and Paolos, *Asmarina*, 20:48–21:06.
80 Maglio and Paolos, *Asmarina*, 43:00.
81 Maglio and Paolos, *Asmarina*, 38:52.
82 Maglio and Paolos, *Asmarina*, 48:06–51:14.
83 Maglio and Paolos, *Asmarina*, 54:52.
84 Eritreans constitute the largest number of asylum seekers in Italy and 25 percent of sea arrivals since 2000. The America Team for Displaced Eritreans, "Recent Statistics."
85 Dearden, "Refugee Crisis"; Day, "EU Refugee Crisis."
86 The America Team for Displaced Eritreans, "Recent Statistics."
87 Medhin Paolos, in conversation with the author, September 12, 2018.
88 Paolos, in conversation with the author, September 12, 2018.
89 Rahel Sereke, in conversation with the author, May 22, 2017.
90 Medhin Paolos, in conversation with the author, July 22, 2017.
91 Paolos, in conversation with the author, July 22, 2017.
92 At the time of the film's release, as a larger number of Eritrean refugees arrived in the city, pro-dictatorship groups were vocal and violent against anti-dictatorship activists. This situation is highly volatile, as tends to be the case in questions of political repression and dictatorships. People become more vocal and less afraid to speak out against the regime from the diaspora as the situation in Eritrea continues to gain attention in the international media.
93 Rahel Sereke, in conversation with the author, September 12, 2018.
94 Other significant Second Generation cultural interventions include the work of Edwidge Danticat, whose writing brought international attention to the massacre of twenty thousand ethnic Haitians in the Dominican Republic in 1937; Jamaica Kincaid, whose writing exposed the corruption of the tourist industry in the Caribbean; and Junot Díaz, whose writing contextualized the thirty-one-year dictatorship of Rafael Trujillo in the Dominican Republic as part of US colonialism.

95 Martínez-San Miguel, *Coloniality of Diasporas*, 7.
96 García Peña, *The Borders of Dominicanidad*, 173.
97 Anzaldúa, *Borderlands / La Frontera*, 25.
98 G. Bianchi, "Italiani nuovi o nuova Italia?," 322.
99 G. Bianchi, "Italiani nuovi o nuova Italia?," 322.
100 G. Bianchi, "Italiani nuovi o nuova Italia?," 330.
101 Berlant, *The Queen of America Goes to Washington City*, 25–26.
102 G. Bianchi, "Italiani nuovi o nuova Italia?," 320.
103 G. Bianchi, "Italiani nuovi o nuova Italia?," 322.
104 Pastore, "A Community Out of Balance," 33.
105 See chapter 4.
106 Republic of Italy, Act No. 91 of 5 February 1992.
107 Republic of Italy, Act No. 91 of 5 February 1992.
108 Rodríguez, speech given at the "Day of Multicultural Unity."
109 Rodríguez, speech given at the "Day of Multicultural Unity."
110 Ngai, *Impossible Subjects*, 2.
111 Estrella, "Muertos Civiles," 43.
112 Paolos, in conversation with the author, June 24, 2015.
113 Paolos, in conversation with the author, September 28, 2018.
114 Mohamed Tailmoun, in conversation with the author, June 8, 2017.
115 Paolos, in conversation with the author, June 24, 2015.
116 Jovanna Rodríguez, in conversation with the author, July 22, 2015.
117 Rodríguez, in conversation with the author, July 22, 2015.
118 Maya Llaguno-Ciani, in conversation with the author, June 10, 2017.
119 Llaguno-Ciani, in conversation with the author, June 10, 2017.
120 Andall, "Second-Generation Attitude?"
121 Rodríguez, speech given at the "Day of Multicultural Unity."
122 Beaman, *Citizen Outsider*, 85.
123 Rodríguez, speech given at the "Day of Multicultural Unity."
124 Lowe, *The Intimacies of Four Continents*, 6–7.
125 See Racine, "During the Reign of Henry Christophe."
126 US intervention in and expansion over the Caribbean began as early as 1804 through its economic embargo against Haiti and continued to grow throughout the long nineteenth century. This included various attempts to purchase the Bay of Samaná in the Dominican Republic, settlements in Haiti and the Dominican Republic, the colonization of Puerto Rico in 1898, and multiple occupations of Cuba, the Dominican Republic, and Haiti throughout the nineteenth and twentieth centuries. Similarly, US military aid and political interventions in Central America disrupted national revolutionary processes. The effects of these interventions are still deeply felt in these nations and have led to people's displacement and forced migration.
127 See Bosworth, Fili, and Pickering, "Women and Border Policing at the Edges of Europe"; and Cisneros, "Contaminated Communities."
128 Ngai, *Impossible Subjects*, 9–10.

129 Ngai, *Impossible Subjects*, 9. See also Milian, *Latining America*; and Roth, *Race Migrations*.

130 The Development, Relief, and Education for Alien Minors Act, also known as the DREAM Act, is a US legislative proposal to grant temporary conditional residency with the right to work to unauthorized immigrants who entered the United States as minors, and later, if they satisfied further qualifications, permanent residency. People eligible for this status are known as DREAMers. Deferred Action for Childhood Arrivals (DACA) is a US immigration policy that allows some individuals with unlawful presence in the United States after being brought to the country as children to receive a renewable two-year period of deferred action from deportation and become eligible for a work permit. DREAMers who have been granted DACA status are known as DACAmented.

131 La Sentencia is a Dominican Republic's Supreme Court ruling passed in 2013 that effectively rendered some 200,000 Dominicans with Haitian roots stateless.

132 For more on the situation in Chile, which has recently begun to receive scholarly attention, see Cruz, "The Other Chile"; and Pavez-Soto and Chan, "The Second Generation in Chile." For more on Greece, see Papadantonakis, "Black Athenians."

CONCLUSION

1 Bustos Bustos, "La discriminación por motivos raciales."

2 The charges were dismissed posthumously. Gonzalez, "Tribunal declaró póstumamente la inocencia de Joane Florvil."

3 See Ruiz Pereira, "Los 30 días de calvario de Joane Florvil."

4 Chile, "Abandona a su bebé en plena vía pública de Lo Prado."

5 In 2002 there were only 50 Haitian nationals registered in Chile. By 2013 the number reached 4,000, and by 2019 there were 179,338 Haitian migrants living in Chile. See Departamento de Extranjería y Migración, Gobierno de Chile, "Información de personas nacidas en el extranjero."

6 The Movimiento Acción Migrante (http://www.mamchile.cl/), a conglomerate of immigrant organizations, is one of the most important sources of information regarding discrimination and immigrant rights actions in Chile.

7 The growth of the extreme right in Chile has followed the trend that we are seeing throughout the world, for example in the presidential elections of Jair Bolsonaro in Brazil and Donald Trump in the United States. Capitalizing on fear and conservative ideas anchored in white supremacy and misogyny, these groups rhetorically link—sometimes in the same sentence—the menace of migrants, abortion, LGBTQ rights, and drug cartels. See Pujols, "Chile."

8 An online petition requesting an investigation into Bland's death garnered thousands of signatures, and she became a popular hashtag (#SandraBland) on social media.

9 Epigraph: Paula Palacios, quoted in Huenchumil, "Los 'George Floyd' de Chile." Palacios is an activist who works for NegroCentricxs, a feminist antiracist organization led by Black Chilean women and Black migrants living in Chile. NegroCentricxs has two main goals: (1) to increase the visibility of Afro Chileans, and (2) migration reform in the Chilean constitution that would facilitate legalization for migrants and a path to citizenship.

BIBLIOGRAPHY

ARCHIVAL COLLECTIONS

Archivio Storico Diplomatico, Roma, Italy
  Archivio Storico del Ex-Ministero Africa Italiana
Archivo General de la Nación Dominicana, Dominican Republic (AGN)
  Colección Báez Pérez, Cucullo
  Colección José Gabriel García
  Guerra de Abril
  Milvio Pérez
  Prensa diaria dominicana
  Universidad de Santo Domingo
Houghton Library, Harvard University, Cambridge, MA
  Papers: Charles Sumner Correspondence 1829–1874
Morland-Spingarn Research Center, Howard University, Washington, DC
  Frederick Douglass Papers
  Gregoria Fraser Goins Papers
Schomburg Center for Research in Black Culture: Manuscripts, Archives, and Rare Books Division, New York Public Library, NY
  Arthur Alfonso Schomburg papers, 1724–1939 [bulk 1904–1938]
US Library of Congress
Frederick Douglass Papers, https://www.loc.gov/collections/frederick-douglass-papers/

PUBLISHED SOURCES

Abbattista, Guido. "Torino 1884: Africani in mostra." *Contemporanea* 7, no. 3 (2004): 369–410.

Agnew, Paddy. "Denny's Win a Boost for Tolerance—or a Mask for Xenophobia?" *Irish Times*, September 11, 1996. https://www.irishtimes.com/news/denny-s-win-a-boost-for-tolerance-or-a-mask-for-xenophobia-1.85013.

Alexander, M. Jacqui. *Pedagogies of Crossing: Meditations on Feminism, Sexual Politics, Memory, and the Sacred.* Durham, NC: Duke University Press, 2005.

Altin, Roberta, and Veronica Saba. "Leggi italiane e servizi sanitari triestini rivolti alle donne immigrate." In *Stato di salute sessuale e riproduttiva delle donne migranti: Difficoltà e buone pratiche,* edited by Giovanni Delli Zotti, 92–95. Trieste: EUT Edizioni Università di Trieste, 2018.

Alvarez, Julia. *In the Time of the Butterflies.* Chapel Hill, NC: Algonquin Books of Chapel Hill, 1994.

The America Team for Displaced Eritreans. "Recent Statistics regarding Eritrean Refugees and Asylum Seekers." Accessed March 29, 2020. https://eritreanrefugees.org/refugee-stats.

Andall, Jacqueline. *Gender, Migration, and Domestic Service: The Politics of Black Women in Italy.* New York: Routledge, 2000.

Andall, Jacqueline. "Second-Generation Attitude? African-Italians in Milan." *Journal of Ethnic and Migration Studies* 28, no. 3 (2002): 389–407.

Andall, Jacqueline, and Derek Duncan, eds. *Italian Colonialism: Legacy and Memory.* New York: Peter Lang, 2005.

Andall, Jacqueline, and Derek Duncan. *National Belongings: Hybridity in Italian Colonial and Postcolonial Cultures.* New York: Peter Lang, 2010.

Andrijasevic, Rutvica. "I confini fanno la differenza: (Il)legalità, migrazione e tratta in Italia dall'est europeo." *Studi culturali* 1, no. 1 (2004): 59–82.

Anzaldúa, Gloria. *Borderlands / La Frontera: The New Mestiza.* San Francisco: Aunt Lute, 1987.

Anzaldúa, Gloria. *The Gloria Anzaldúa Reader.* Durham, NC: Duke University Press, 2009.

Anzaldúa, Gloria. "How to Tame a Wild Tongue." 1987. Reprinted in *Available Means,* edited by Joy Ritchie and Kate Ronald, 357–76. Pittsburgh: University of Pittsburgh Press, 2001.

Arnone, Anna. "The Eritrean Festival in the Time-Warp." *Social Evolution and History* 13, no. 2 (2014): 73–96.

Arroyo, Jossianna. "Technologies: Transculturation of Gender, Race, and Ethnicity in Arturo A. Schomburg's Masonic Writings." In *Technofuturos: Critical Interventions on Latina/o Studies,* edited by Nancy Raquel Mirabal and Agustin Laó-Montes, 141–72. Lanham, MD: Lexington Books, 2007.

Báez, Josefina. *Carmen: FotonovelARTE.* Santo Domingo, DR: I Ombe Press, 2020.

Báez, Josefina. *Comrade, Bliss Ain't Playing: A Performance Theatre Text.* New York: Ay Ombe Theatre / I om be Press, 2008.

Báez, Josefina. *Levente no: Yolayorkdominicanyork.* New York: Ay Ombe Theatre / I om be Press, 2011.

Bailey, Moya. *Misogynoir Transformed: Black Women's Digital Resistance.* New York: New York University Press, 2021.

Balce, Nerissa S. "The Filipina's Breast: Savagery, Docility, and the Erotics of the American Empire." *Social Text* 24, no. 2 (2006): 89–110.

Baratieri, Daniela. "'More than a Tree, Less than a Woman.' Sex and Empire: The Italian Case." *Australian Journal of Politics and History* 60, no. 3 (2014): 360–72.

Bardi, Adelmo. *35 anni vissuti in Eritrea e in Abissinia: Ricordi ed impressioni*. S.l: s.n., 1936.

Barrera, Giulia. *Dangerous Liaisons: Colonial Concubinage in Eritrea (1890–1941)*. Program of African Studies Working Papers 1. Evanston, IL: Program of African Studies, Northwestern University, 1996.

Barrera, Giulia. "Sex, Citizenship, and the State: The Construction of Public and Private Spheres in Colonial Eritrea." In *Gender, Family, and Sexuality: The Private Sphere in Italy, 1860–1945*, edited by Perry Willson, 157–72. New York: Palgrave Macmillan, 2004.

Baynton, Douglas. "Defectives in the Land: Disability and American Immigration Policy, 1882–1924." *Journal of American Ethnic History* 24, no. 3 (2005): 31–44.

BBC News. "Tess Asplund: The Woman Who Faced Down 300 Neo-Nazis - BBC News." YouTube, November 23, 2016. https://www.youtube.com/watch?v=jaNkoMWbPMM&feature=youtu.be.

Beaman, Jean. *Citizen Outsider: Children of North African Immigrants in France*. Berkeley: University of California Press, 2017.

Beltrán, Cristina. "Representación del cuerpo, el género y la 'raza' en *Vida y muerte de la mulata: Una historia que se repite*." *Feminismo/s* 34 (2019): 235–63.

Benjamin, Walter. "The Task of the Translator." In *Walter Benjamin: Selected Writings; Volume 1, 1913–1926*, edited by Marcus Bullock and Michael W. Jennings, 253–63. Cambridge, MA: Belknap Press of Harvard University Press, 1996.

Berlant, Lauren. *The Queen of America Goes to Washington City: Essays on Sex and Citizenship*. Durham, NC: Duke University Press, 1997.

Bernabé, Jean, Patrick Chamoiseau, and Raphaël Confiant. *Eloge de la créolité*. Translated by Mohamed Bouya Taleb-Khyar. Paris: Gallimard, 1993.

Bianchi, Bruna. "Omicidio di via Muratori, lo strano sfogo su Facebook 'Basta, vadano al diavolo.'" *Il Giorno*, September 11, 2012. https://www.ilgiorno.it/milano/cronaca/2012/09/12/770864-milano-omicidio-muratori-facebook-carolina-payano-massimiliano-spelta.shtml.

Bianchi, Georgia E. "Italiani nuovi o nuova Italia? Citizenship and Attitudes towards the Second Generation in Contemporary Italy." *Journal of Modern Italian Studies* 16, no. 3 (2011): 321–33.

Blackwell, Henry B. "Santo Domingo: The Case Stated." *Independent*, April 20, 1871.

Blanco Borelli, Melissa. *She Is Cuba: A Genealogy of the Mulata Body*. New York: Oxford University Press, 2016.

Bonilla, Yarimar, and Marisol LeBrón, eds. *Aftershocks of Disaster: Puerto Rico before and after the Storm*. Chicago: Haymarket, 2019.

Bontemps, Arna, and Langston Hughes. *Popo and Fifina: Children of Haiti*. New York: Macmillan, 1932.

Bosch, Juan. *La guerra de restauración*. Santo Domingo, DR: Ediciones Fundación Juan Bosch, 2016.

Bosworth, Mary, Andriani Fili, and Sharon Pickering. "Women and Border Policing at the Edges of Europe." *Journal of Ethnic and Migration Studies* 44, no. 13 (2018): 2182–96.

Bravi, Luca. "La storia come strumento d'inclusione sociale: Esperienze di Public History of Education." *Pedagogia Oggi* 18, no. 2 (2020): 76–87.
Brennan, Denise. *What's Love Got to Do with It? Transnational Desires and Sex Tourism in the Dominican Republic*. Durham, NC: Duke University Press, 2004.
Briggs, Laura. *Reproducing Empire: Race, Sex, Science, and US Imperialism in Puerto Rico*. Berkeley: University of California Press, 2002.
Brondoni, Cristina. "Sparatoria a Milano, 5 ipotesi per un delitto." *Lettera* 43, September 11, 2012. http://www.lettera43.it/it/articoli/cronaca/2012/09/11/sparatoria-a-milano-5-ipotesi-per-un-delitto/55865/.
Brooks, David. "The Underlying Tragedy." *New York Times*, January 14, 2010.
Brown, Kimberly Juanita. *The Repeating Body: Slavery's Visual Resonance in the Contemporary*. Durham, NC: Duke University Press, 2015.
Burns Neveldine, Robert. *Bodies at Risk: Unsafe Limits in Romanticism and Postmodernism*. Albany: State University of New York Press, 1998.
Buscaglia-Salgado, José. *Undoing Empire: Race and Nation in the Mulatto Caribbean*. Minneapolis: University of Minnesota Press, 2001.
Bustos Bustos, Francisco. "La discriminación por motivos raciales ante el derecho chileno: Un análisis del caso de Joane Florvil." *Anales de la Universidad de Chile* 7, no. 16 (2019): 79–98.
Butler, Judith. *Gender Trouble: Feminism and the Subversion of Identity*. New York: Routledge, 1990.
Byrd, Brandon R. *The Black Republic: African Americans and the Fate of Haiti*. Philadelphia: University of Pennsylvania Press, 2019.
Caminero, Alberto. "Asesinada en Italia quería volver a RD." *El Nacional*, September 14, 2012. http://elnacional.com.do/asesinada-en-italia-queria-volver-rd/.
Candelario, Ginetta E. B. *Black behind the Ears: Dominican Racial Identity from Museums to Beauty Shops*. Durham, NC: Duke University Press, 2007.
Candelario, Ginetta E. B., Elizabeth S. Manley, and April J. Mayes, eds. *Cien años de feminismos dominicanos: Una colleción de documentos y escrituras clave en la formación y evolución del pensamiento y el movimiento feminista en la República Dominicana, 1865–1965*. Santo Domingo, DR: Archivo General de la Nación, 2016.
Capitani, Flavia, and Emanuele Coen, eds. *Pecore nere*. Rome: Laterza, 2005.
Capussotti, Enrica. "The Experience of the 'Punto di Partenza' Group: Women's Diaspora and Politics." *Feminist Review* 87, no. 1 (2007): 85–93.
Capussotti, Enrica. "Nordisti contro Sudisti: Internal Migration and Racism in Turin, Italy: 1950s and 1960s." *Italian Culture* 28, no. 2 (2010): 121–38.
Carnevale, Nancy C. *A New Language, a New World: Italian Immigrants in the United States, 1890–1945*. Urbana: University of Illinois Press, 2009.
Cassá, Roberto. *Los doce años: Contrarrevolución y desarrollismo*. Santo Domingo, DR: Alfa and Omega, 1986.
Castañuelas. "Gloria Martín - Sagrario Abierto." YouTube, April 4, 2016. https://www.youtube.com/watch?v=gvGMRizulKo.
Cejas, Mónica. "'Desde la experiencia': Entrevista a *Ochy* Curiel." *Andamios* 8, no. 17 (September–December 2011): 181–97.

Césaire, Aimé. *Discourse on Colonialism*. New York: New York University Press, 2001.

Césaire, Aimé, A.J. Arnold, and C. Eshleman. *The Original 1939 Notebook of a Return to the Native Land*. Bilingual ed. Middletown, CT: Wesleyan University Press, 2013.

Chambers, Iain. *Mediterranean Crossings: The Politics of an Interrupted Modernity*. Durham, NC: Duke University Press, 2008.

Chile, Aton. "Abandona a su bebé en plena vía pública de Lo Prado, es detenida y termina hospitalizada tras darse cabezazos en la celda." *Publimetro*, August 31, 2017. https://www.publimetro.cl/cl/noticias/2017/08/31/abandona-bebe-plena-via-publica-lo-prado-detenida-termina-hospitalizada-tras-darse-cabezazos-la-celda.html.

"Chi sono le donne vittime di violenza." Istituto Nazionale di Statistica. Accessed February 27, 2021. https://www.istat.it/it/violenza-sulle-donne/il-fenomeno/violenza-dentro-e-fuori-la-famiglia/chi-sono-le-vittime.

Ciarnelli, Marcella. "Mi spiace per le altre ma sono io Miss Italia." *L'Unità*, September 9, 1996. https://archivio.unita.news/assets/main/1996/09/09/page_006.pdf.

Cisneros, J. David. "Contaminated Communities: The Metaphor of 'Immigrant as Pollutant' in Media Representations of Immigration." *Rhetoric and Public Affairs* 11, no. 4 (2008): 569–601.

Clifford, James. "Diasporas." *Cultural Anthropology* 9, no. 3 (1994): 303–38.

Clò, Clarissa. "Hip Pop Italian Style: The Postcolonial Imagination of Second-Generation Authors in Italy." In *Postcolonial Italy: Challenging National Homogeneity*, edited by Cristina Lombardi-Diop and Caterina Romeo, 275–92. New York: Palgrave Macmillan, 2012.

Cochran, Terry. " Translator' Introduction: The Translating Mechanism." In *Culture of the Baroque: Analysis of a Historical Structure*, by José Antonio Maravall, translated by Terry Cochran, xxi–xxxi. Minneapolis: University of Minnesota Press, 1986.

Colatrella, Steven. *Workers of the World: African and Asian Migrants in Italy in the 1990s*. Trenton, NJ: Africa World Press, 2001.

"Colombiana que desafió a los nazis en Suecia está en el país y se encuentra con su familia." Caracol Radio, December 26, 2016. http://caracol.com.co/programa/2016/12/26/6am_hoy_por_hoy/1482764293_815828.html.

Cordero, Margarita. *Mujeres de abril*. Santo Domingo, DR: Centro de Investigaciones para la Acción Femenina, 1985.

Cordero Michel, Emilio. "República Dominicana, cuna del antillanismo." *Clío* 165, no. 71 (January–June 2003): 225–36.

Cristalli, Giordina. "Denny Méndez, venti anni fa la Miss Italia di colore Dalla passerella del concorso di Mirigliani a Los Angeles." *ANSA*, February 26, 2016. http://www.ansa.it/sito/notizie/cultura/2016/02/26/denny-mendez-venti-anni-fa-la-miss-italia-di-colore_1776bf37-c613-4ac4-827d-29997a419aa2.html.

Cruz, Angie. "The Other Chile (Cecilia & Patricia)." *Virginia Quarterly Review* 93, no. 4 (2017): 20–26.

Cruz Sánchez, Filiberto. *La guerra de los seis años: La guerra contra los planes anexionista de Buenaventura Báez, 1868–1874*. Santiago, DR: Editora el Nuevo Diario, 2005.
Curiel, Ochy, and Dennys Silva-Reis. "Pensar a tradução e o feminismo negro: Entrevista com Ochy Curiel." *Revista Ártemis* 27, no. 1 (2019): 241–45.
Dal Lago, Alessandro. *Non-persons: The Exclusion of Migrants in a Global Society*. Translated by Marie Orton. Milan: IPOC di Pietro Condemi, 2009.
Davidson, Christina Cecelia. "Black Protestants in a Catholic Land: The AME Church in the Dominican Republic 1899–1916." *New West Indian Guide / Nieuwe West-Indische Gids* 89, nos. 3–4 (2015): 258–88.
Davidson, Christina Cecelia. "Disruptive Silences: The AME Church and Dominican-Haitian Relations." *Journal of Africana Religions* 5, no. 1 (2017): 1–25.
Dávila, Arlene. *Latinos, Inc.: The Marketing and Making of a People*. Berkeley: University of California Press, 2012.
Davis, Angela. *Freedom Is a Constant Struggle: Ferguson, Palestine, and the Foundations of a Movement*. Chicago: Haymarket, 2016.
Day, Michael. "EU Refugee Crisis: Italy Threatens to Let Thousands Travel North; Migration." *Independent* (UK), June 17, 2015.
Dearden, Lizzie. "Refugee Crisis: Arrivals Rocket in Italy amid Warnings Turkey Deal Could Force Migrants on More Dangerous Routes." *Independent* (UK), March 30, 2016.
de Genova, Nicholas. "Citizenship's Shadow: Obscene Inclusion, Abject Belonging, or the Regularities of Migrant 'Irregularity.'" In *Within and beyond Citizenship*, edited by Roberto G. Gonzales and Nancy Sigona, 17–35. New York: Routledge, 2017.
Del Boca, Angelo. *L'Africa nella coscienza degli italiani: Miti, memorie, errori, sconfitte*. Rome: Laterza, 1992.
Deleuze, Gilles, and Félix Guattari. *Kafka: Toward a Minor Literature*. Minneapolis: University of Minnesota Press, 1986.
"Delitto Spelta." *Corriere della Sera*, September 18, 2012. Expendiente Carolina Payano, Archivo del Consulado Dominicano en Milano.
Dell'Oro, Erminia. *L'abbandono: Una storia Eritrea*. Turin, Italy: Einaudi, 1991.
Dell'Oro, Erminia. *Asmara addio*. Pordenone: Edizioni dello Zibaldone, 1989.
Deloria, Philip J. *Playing Indian*. New Haven, CT: Yale University Press, 1999.
Departamento de Extranjería y Migración, Gobierno de Chile. "Información de personas nacidas en el extranjero residentes en Chile de acuerdo a los datos del XVII Censo de Población de 2002." August 4, 2016. https://web.archive.org/web/20160804090301/http:/www.extranjeria.gob.cl/filesapp/censo__2002_.pdf.
Derobertis, Roberto. "Southerners, Migrants, Colonized: A Postcolonial Perspective on Carlo Levi's Cristo si è fermato a Eboli and Southern Italy Today." In *Postcolonial Italy: Challenging National Homogeneity*, edited by Cristina Lombardi-Diop and Caterina Romeo, 157–71. New York: Palgrave Macmillan, 2012.
Díaz, Fidias. *La UASD ametrallada y Sagrario asesinada*. Santo Domingo, DR: Universidad Autónoma de Santo Domingo, 2007.
Díaz, Junot. "Under President Trump, Radical Hope Is Our Best Weapon." *New Yorker*, November 21, 2016.

Dixon, Chris. *African America and Haiti: Emigration and Black Nationalism in the Nineteenth Century*. Westport, CT: Greenwood, 2000.
Donald, David. *Charles Sumner and the Rights of Man*. New York: Knopf, 1970.
Douglass, Frederick. *The Life and Times of Frederick Douglass*. Mineola, NY: Dover, 2003.
Douglass, Frederick. *The Life and Writings of Frederick Douglass*. Vol. 4. Edited by Phillip S. Foner. New York: International Publishers, 1975.
Douglass, Frederick. "Reminiscences of Antislavery Conflict as Delivered during the Lecture Season of 72 and 73." Manuscript/mixed material. Speech, Article, and Book File, microfilm, reel 14, Frederick Douglass Papers, Library of Congress. http://hdl.loc.gov/loc.mss/mfd.22022.
Douglass, Frederick. "What to the Slave Is the Fourth of July?" 1852. Reprinted in *The Speeches of Frederick Douglass: A Critical Edition*, edited by John R. McKivigan, Julie Husband, and Heather L. Kaufman, 55–92. New Haven, CT: Yale University Press, 2018.
Duany, Jorge. *La nación en vaivén: Identidad, migración y cultura popular en Puerto Rico*. San Juan: Ediciones Callejón, 2009.
Duany, Jorge. *The Puerto Rican Nation on the Move: Identities on the Island and in the United States*. Chapel Hill: University of North Carolina Press, 2002.
Dubois, Laurent. *Haiti: The Aftershocks of History*. New York: Picador, 2012.
Duncan, Derek. "Italy's Postcolonial Cinema and Its Histories of Representation." *Italian Studies* 63, no. 2 (2008): 195–211.
Dzidzienyo, Anani, and Suzana Oboler, eds. *Neither Enemies nor Friends: Latinos, Blacks, Afro-Latinos*. New York: Palgrave Macmillan, 2005.
Edwards, Brent Hayes. *The Practice of Diaspora: Literature, Translation, and the Rise of Black Internationalism*. Cambridge, MA: Harvard University Press, 2003.
Eller, Anne. *We Dream Together: Dominican Independence, Haiti, and the Fight for Caribbean Freedom*. Durham, NC: Duke University Press, 2016.
El-Tayeb, Fatima. *European Others: Queering Ethnicity in Postcolonial Europe*. Minneapolis: University of Minnesota Press, 2011.
"Enzo Biagi Con Indro Montanelli sul FASCISMO e Mussolini 1982 (trasmissione Questo Secolo)." YouTube, October 29, 2009. https://www.youtube.com/watch?v=zPIypUtB-u4&t=44s.
Erman, Sam. *Almost Citizens: Puerto Rico, the US Constitution, and Empire*. New York: Cambridge University Press, 2018.
Escalante, Fabián, and Mirta Muñiz. *The Secret War: CIA Covert Operations against Cuba, 1959–62*. New York: Ocean Press, 1995.
Escolano Giménez, Luis Alfonso. "Los procesos migratorios y su contribución al perfil social del suroeste dominicano: El valle de Neyba (siglos XVIII–XX)." In *Orbis incognitus: Avisos y legajos del Nuevo Mundo*, edited by Fernando Navarro Antolín and Luis Navarro García, 641–49. Huelva, Spain: Universidad de Huelva, 2007.
Estrella, Amarilys. "Muertos Civiles: Mourning the Casualties of Racism in the Dominican Republic." *Transforming Anthropology* 28, no. 1 (2020): 41–57.
Faleschini Lerner, Giovanna, and Maria Elena D'Amelio. *Italian Motherhood on Screen*. Cham: Springer International, 2017.

Fanning, Sara. *Caribbean Crossing: African Americans and the Haitian Emigration Movement.* New York: New York University Press, 2015.

Fanon, Frantz. *Black Skin, White Masks.* New York: Grove, 1952.

Fanon, Frantz. *The Wretched of the Earth.* New York: Grove, 1963.

Ferrari, Robert. *Days Pleasant and Unpleasant in the Order Sons of Italy in America: The Problem of Races and Racial Societies in the United States: Assimilation or Isolation?* New York: Mandy, 1926.

Figueroa-Vásquez, Yomaira. *Decolonizing Diasporas: Radical Mappings of Afro-Atlantic Literature.* Evanston, IL: Northwestern University Press, 2020.

Fikes, Robert. "Mercedes Frías." *Black Past,* January 8, 2014. https://www.blackpast.org/global-african-history/frias-mercedes-1962/.

Fischer, Sibylle. *Modernity Disavowed.* Durham, NC: Duke University Press, 2004.

Flaiano, Ennio. *Tempo di uccidere.* Milano: Rizzoli, 1973.

Flores, Juan, and Miriam Jiménez Román. "Triple-Consciousness? Approaches to Afro-Latino Culture in the United States." *Latin American and Caribbean Ethnic Studies* 4, no. 3 (2009): 319–28.

Florvil, Tiffany N. *Mobilizing Black Germany: Afro-German Women and the Making of Transnational Movement.* Urbana: University of Illinois Press, 2020.

Focarete, Michele. "Delitto Spelta, i parenti di Carolina 'L'ultimo saluto a Santo Domingo.'" *Corriere della Sera, Cronaca* (Milan), September 24, 2021. https://milano.corriere.it/notizie/cronaca/12_settembre_24/delitto-spelta-parenti-carolina-ultimo-saluto-santo-domingo-2111944689082.shtml.

Focarete, Michele, and Andrea Galli. "Loft, viaggi e movida senza uno stipendio, Lei si sfogò in Rete: Non ce la faccio." *Corriere della Sera,* September 12, 2012. https://milano.corriere.it/milano/notizie/cronaca/12_settembre_12/loft-viaggi-movida-sfogo-focarete-galli-2111786141366.shtml.

Foucault, Michel. *The Archaeology of Knowledge and the Discourse on Language.* 2nd ed. New York: Routledge, 2013.

Foucault, Michel. *"Society Must Be Defended": Lectures, Collège de France, 1975–1976.* Vol. 1. New York: Picador, 2003.

Frías, Mercedes. "La aldea global." Presentation, Instituto Tecnológico de Santiago (INTEC), Santo Domingo, DR, May 2006.

Frisina, Annalisa, and Camilla Hawthorne. "Italians with Veils and Afros: Gender, Beauty, and the Everyday Anti-racism of the Daughters of Immigrants in Italy." *Journal of Ethnic and Migration Studies* 44, no. 5 (2018): 718–35.

Fuentes, Marisa. *Dispossessed Lives: Enslaved Women, Violence, and the Archive.* Philadelphia: University of Pennsylvania Press, 2016.

Fumagalli, Cristina. *Caribbean Perspectives on Modernity: Returning Medusa's Gaze.* Charlottesville: University of Virginia Press, 2009.

Galindo-Calvo, Pablo, Beatriz Jiménez-Roger, Francisco Javier Cantón-Correa, and Maria do Nascimento Esteves-Mateus. "Islamophobia in Southern Europe: The Cases of Greece, Spain, Italy, and Portugal." In *Social Problems in Southern Europe,* edited by Francisco Entrena-Durán, Rosa M. Soriano-Miras, and Ricardo Duque-Calvache, 35–50. Northampton, MA: Edward Elgar, 2020.

Gandolfi, Tertulliano. *I misteri dell'Africa italiana*. Rome: Editore, 1910.

Garau, Eva. *Politics of National Identity in Italy: Immigration and Italianità*. New York: Routledge, 2015.

García-Peña, Lorgia. "Being Black Ain't So Bad . . . Dominican Immigrant Women Negotiating Race in Contemporary Italy." *Caribbean Studies* 41, no. 2 (2013): 137–61.

García-Peña, Lorgia. "Black in English: Race, Migration, and National Belonging in Postcolonial Italy." *Kalfou* 3, no. 2 (2016): 207–29.

García-Peña, Lorgia. *The Borders of Dominicanidad: Race, Nation, and Archives of Contradiction*. Durham, NC: Duke University Press, 2016.

García-Peña, Lorgia. "Translating Blackness: Dominicans Negotiating Race and Belonging." *Black Scholar* 45, no. 2 (2015): 10–20.

Gates, Henry Louis, Jr. *Black in Latin America*. New York: New York University Press, 2011.

Gbadamosi, Raimi. "Am I Black Enough?" *Third Text* 12, no. 44 (1998): 69–78.

"Gen. Grant: What He Says about a Third Term—The St. Domingo Question." *Chicago Tribune*, July 26, 1878.

Gennari, John. "Passing for Italian." *Transition* 72 (1996): 36–48.

Gilliam, Angela, and Onik'a Gilliam. "Negociando a subjetividade de mulata no Brasil." *Revista Estudos Feministas* 3, no. 2 (1995): 525–43.

Giuliani, Gaia. *Race, Nation and Gender in Modern Italy: Intersectional Representations in Visual Culture*. New York: Palgrave Macmillan, 2019.

Glissant, Édouard. *Poetics of Relation*. Translated by Betsy Wing. Ann Arbor: University of Michigan Press, 1997.

Goglia, Luigi. "Note sul razzismo coloniale fascista." *Storia Contemporanea* 19, no. 6 (1988): 1223–66.

Golderer, Lalla, and Scifo, Vito. *Stranieri a Milano: Immagini di una nuova immigrazione*. Milano: Mazzotta, 1985.

Gonzalez, María Eugenia. "Tribunal declaró póstumamente la inocencia de Joane Florvil." Defensoría Penal Pública, November 22, 2017. http://www.dpp.cl/sala_prensa/noticias_detalle/8181/tribunal-declaro-postumamente-la-inocencia-de-joane-florvil8.

Gordon-Chipembere, Natasha, ed. *Representation and Black Womanhood: The Legacy of Sarah Baartman*. New York: Palgrave Macmillan, 2011.

Grande, Carlo. "Ero musa di Pasolini ora servo Madre Teresa." *La Stampa*, February 12, 2012.

Grant, Ulysses S. "Reasons Why Santo Domingo Should Be Annexed to the United States." In *The Papers of Ulysses S. Grant*, vol. 20, edited by John Y. Simon, 74–76. Carbondale: Southern Illinois University Press, 1995.

Grignaffini, Giovanna. *La scena madre: Scritti sul cinema*. Bologna: Bononia University Press, 2002.

Guarnizo, Luis Eduardo. "The Emergence of a Transnational Social Formation and the Mirage of Return Migration among Dominican Transmigrants." *Identities: Global Studies in Culture and Power* 4, no. 2 (1997): 281–322.

Guarnizo, Luis Eduardo. "'Going Home': Class, Gender, and Household Transformation among Dominican Return Migrants." *Center for Migration Studies* 13, no. 4 (1996): 13–60.

Guarnizo, Luis Eduardo. "The Rise of Transnational Social Formations: Mexican and Dominican State Responses to Transnational Migration." *Political Power and Social Theory* 12 (1998): 45–96.

Guglielmo, Jennifer, and Salvatore Salerno. *Are Italians White? How Race Is Made in America*. New York: Routledge, 2004.

Guidotti-Hernández, Nicole. *Unspeakable Violence: Remapping US and Mexican National Imaginaries*. Durham, NC: Duke University Press, 2011.

Guild, Elspeth, Cathryn Costello, Madeline Garlick, and Violeta Moreno-Lax. *The 2015 Refugee Crisis in the European Union*. Brussels, Belgium: Centre for European Policy Studies, 2015.

Guridy, Frank Andre. *Forging Diaspora: Afro-Cubans and African Americans in a World of Empire and Jim Crow*. Chapel Hill: University of North Carolina Press, 2010.

Guyatt, Nicholas. "America's Conservatory: Race, Reconstruction, and the Santo Domingo Debate." *Journal of American History* 97, no. 4 (2011): 974–1000.

Hammond, Lauren. "Outpost of Empire, Endpost of Blackness: African Americans, the Dominican Republic, and US Foreign Policy, 1869–1965." PhD diss., University of Texas, Austin, 2014.

Hartman, Saidiya. *Lose Your Mother: A Journey along the Atlantic Slave Route*. New York: Farrar, Straus and Giroux, 2007.

Haskins, Ekaterina. "Between Archive and Participation: Public Memory in a Digital Age." *Rhetoric Society Quarterly* 37, no. 4 (2007): 403.

Hawthorne, Camilla. "Black Matters Are Spatial Matters: Black Geographies for the Twenty-First Century." *Geography Compass* 13, no. 11 (2019): e12468.

Hawthorne, Camilla. "In Search of Black Italia: Notes on Race, Belonging, and Activism in the Black Mediterranean." *Transition* 123, no. 1 (2017): 152–74.

Hawthorne, Camilla. "Making Italy: Afro-Italian Entrepreneurs and the Racial Boundaries of Citizenship." *Social and Cultural Geography* 22, no. 5 (2019): 1–21.

Hellman, Judith Adler. *Journeys among Women: Feminism in Five Italian Cities*. New York: Oxford University Press, 1987.

Henneberg, Krystyna von. "Monuments, Public Space, and the Memory of Empire in Modern Italy." *History and Memory* 16, no. 1 (2004): 37–85.

Hernández, David. "Undue Process: Immigrant Detention, Due Process, and Lesser Citizenship." ISSC Working Paper Series 2003–4.06. UC Berkeley Institute for the Study of Social Issues, University of California, Berkeley, CA, 2005. https://escholarship.org/uc/item/15b1h07r.

Hinojosa, Melanie Sberna, Ramon Hinojosa, David A. Nelson, Angelica Delgado, Bernadette Witzack, Magdalisse Gonzalez, Rene Farias, Syed Ahmed, and Linda Meurer. "Salud de la Mujer: Using Fotonovelas to Increase Health Literacy among Latinas." *Progress in Community Health Partnerships: Research, Education, and Action* 4, no. 1 (2010): 25–30.

Hoffnung-Garskof, Jesse. "The Migrations of Arturo Schomburg: On Being Antillano, Negro, and Puerto Rican in New York 1891–1938." *Journal of American Ethnic History* 21, no. 1 (2001): 3–49.

Hoffnung-Garskof, Jesse. *Racial Migrations: New York City and the Revolutionary Politics of the Spanish Caribbean*. Princeton, NJ: Princeton University Press, 2020.

Hoffnung-Garskof, Jesse. *A Tale of Two Cities: Santo Domingo and New York after 1950*. Princeton, NJ: Princeton University Press, 2007.

Holton, Adalaine. "Decolonizing History: Arthur Schomburg's Afrodiasporic Archive." *Journal of African American History* 92, no. 2 (2007): 218–38.

Hooker, Juliet. *Theorizing Race in the Americas: Douglass, Sarmiento, Du Bois, and Vasconcelos*. New York: Oxford University Press, 2017.

hooks, bell. *Salvation: Black People and Love*. New York: Harper Perennial, 2001.

Horne, Gerald. *Confronting Black Jacobins: The United States, the Haitian Revolution, and the Origins of the Dominican Republic*. New York: Monthly Review Press, 2015.

Hostos, Eugenio María de. "Letter to Gregorio Luperón (1895)." In *República Dominicana y Puerto Rico: Hermandad en la lucha emancipadora, correspondencia 1876–1902*, edited by Vivian Quiles Calderín, 230–40. Río Piedras, PR: Instituto de Estudios Hostosianos, 2001.

Howe, Samuel G. *Letters on the Proposed Annexation of Santo Domingo, in Answer to Certain Charges in the Newspapers*. Boston: Wright and Potter, 1871.

Howe, Samuel G. "Letter to President Grant, June 1871." In *The Papers of Ulysses S. Grant*, vol. 22, *June 1, 1871–January 31, 1872*, edited by John Y. Simon, 23–28. Carbondale: Southern Illinois University Press, 1998.

Huenchumil, Paula. "Los 'George Floyd' de Chile: Los asesinatos y agresiones policiales contra afro descendientes en nuestro país." *Interferencia*, June 4, 2020. https://interferencia.cl/articulos/los-george-floyd-de-chile-los-asesinatos-y-agresiones-policiales-contra-afro-descendientes.

Hughes, Langston. *The Big Sea: An Autobiography*. New York: Hill and Wang, 2015.

Hughes, Langston. *I Wonder as I Wander: An Autobiographical Journey*. New York: Macmillan, 1993.

Hurbon, Laënnec. "American Fantasy and Haitian Vodou." In *Sacred Arts of Haitian Vodou*, edited by Donald J. Cosentino, 181–97. Los Angeles: UCLA Fowler Museum of Cultural History, 1995.

"Indro Montanelli: Statue of Controversial Journalist Defaced in Milan." BBC News, June 14, 2020. https://www.bbc.com/news/world-europe-53042350.

Infante, Fernando A. *12 años de Balaguer: Cronología histórica, 1966–1978*. Santo Domingo, DR: Editorial Letra Gráfica, 2003.

Istituto Nazionale di Statistica. "Stranieri residenti al 1° gennaio: Tutti i comuni." ISTAT 2019 Report on Italian Demographics, February 7. http://dati.istat.it/Index.aspx?lang=it&SubSessionId=2be42f9c-b6bd-4d93-9547-742b1cd591a4.

Iyob, Ruth. "*Madamismo* and Beyond: The Construction of Eritrean Women." *Nineteenth-Century Contexts* 22, no. 2 (2000): 217–38.

Jackson, Jessica Barbata. *Dixie's Italians: Sicilians, Race, and Citizenship in the Jim Crow South*. Baton Rouge: Louisiana State University Press, 2020.

Jefferson, Thomas. "Notes on Virginia." In *The Life and Selected Writings of Thomas Jefferson (1781)*, vol. 234, 173–270. New York: Modern Library, 1944.

Jiménez Maxwell, Joaquín. *Memorias del fracaso de un triunfador*. Santo Domingo, DR: Búho, 2007.

Jiménez Román, Miriam, and Juan Flores, eds. *The Afro-Latin@ Reader: History and Culture in the United States*. Durham, NC: Duke University Press, 2010.

Johnson, Jessica Marie. *Wicked Flesh: Black Women, Intimacy, and Freedom in the Atlantic World*. Philadelphia: University of Pennsylvania Press, 2020.

Johnson, Walter. *The Broken Heart of America: St. Louis and the Violent History of the United States*. New York: Basic Books, 2020.

Kazanjian, David. *The Colonizing Trick: National Culture and Imperial Citizenship in Early America*. Minneapolis: University of Minnesota Press, 2003.

Kee, Chera. *Not Your Average Zombie: Rehumanizing the Undead from Voodoo to Zombie Walks*. Austin: University of Texas Press, 2017.

Keeanga-Yamahtta, Taylor. "Interview with Barbara Smith." In *How We Get Free: Black Feminism and the Combahee River Collective*, edited by Taylor Keeanga-Yamahtta, 60–63. Chicago: Haymarket, 2017.

Kempadoo, Kamala. *Sexing the Caribbean: Gender, Race, and Sexual Labor*. New York: Routledge, 2004.

Kempadoo, Kamala. *Sun, Sex, and Gold: Tourism and Sex Work in the Caribbean*. Lanham, MD: Rowman and Littlefield, 2009.

Kilomba, Grada. *Plantation Memories: Episodes of Everyday Racism*. 4th ed. Münster: Unrast, 2016.

King, Russell, and Nancy Wood, eds. *Media and Migration: Constructions of Mobility and Difference*. New York: Routledge, 2001.

Labanca, Nicola, and Annalisa Marchi, eds. *Memorie d'Oltremare: Prato, Italia, Africa*. Florence: Giunti, 2000.

"La bella vita di Spelta: Donne, calcetto e Santo Domingo." *Lettera 43*, September 11, 2012. https://www.lettera43.it/it/articoli/cronaca/2012/09/11/la-bella-vita-di-spelta-donne-calcetto-e-santo-domingo/55944/.

LaFeber, Walter F. *New Empire: An Interpretation of American Expansion, 1860–1898*. Ithaca, NY: Cornell University Press, 1998.

Lear, Jonathan. *Radical Hope: Ethics in the Face of Cultural Devastation*. Cambridge, MA: Harvard University Press, 2006.

Le Houérou, Fabienne. "Gender and Sexual Abuses during the Italian Colonization of Ethiopia and Eritrea—The 'Insabbiati,' Thirty Years After." *Sociology Mind* 5, no. 4 (2015): 255–67.

"Le testimonianze: La bimba era a terra in braccio alla madre." *Corriere della Sera*, September 11, 2012. http://milano.corriere.it/notizie/cronaca/12_settembre_11/le-testimonianze-la-bimba-era-a-terra-in-braccio-alla-madre-a-be-2111771488944.shtml?fr=correlati.

Liberato, Ana S. Q. *Joaquín Balaguer, Memory, and Diaspora: The Lasting Political Legacies of an American Protégé*. Lanham, MD: Lexington Books, 2013.

Littlefield, Charles E. "The Insular Cases." *Harvard Law Review* 15 no. 3 (1901): 169–90.
Locatelli, Francesca. "Beyond the Campo Cintato: Prostitutes, Migrants, and Criminals in Colonial Asmara (Eritrea), 1890–1941." In *African Cities: Competing Claims on Urban Spaces*, edited by Francesca Locatelli and Paul Nugent, 219–40. Boston: Brill, 2009.
Logan, Rayford W. "James Weldon Johnson and Haiti." *Phylon (1960–)* 32, no. 4 (1971): 396–402.
Lombardi-Diop, Cristina, and Caterina Romeo, eds. *Postcolonial Italy: Challenging the National Homogeneity*. New York: Palgrave Macmillan, 2012.
López, Antonio. *Unbecoming Blackness: The Diaspora Cultures of Afro-Cuban America*. New York: New York University Press, 2012.
Lorde, Audre. "A Burst of Light: Living with Cancer." In *Feminist Theory and the Body*, 149–52. New York: Routledge, 2017.
Lorde, Audre. *Sister Outsider: Essays and Speeches*. Berkeley, CA: Crossing Press, 1984.
Love, Eric T. L. *Race over Empire: Racism and US Imperialism, 1865–1900*. Chapel Hill: University of North Carolina Press, 2004.
Lowe, Lisa. *The Intimacies of Four Continents*. Durham, NC: Duke University Press, 2015.
Luconi, Stefano. "The Fascist Racial Turn: The View from the Italian-American Community in the United States." *Journal of Modern Italian Studies* 24, no. 1 (2019): 32–47.
Luft, Eric v. d. "Sarah Loguen Fraser, MD (1850 to 1933): The Fourth African-American Woman Physician." *Journal of the National Medical Association* 92, no. 3 (March 2000): 149–53.
Luperón, Gregorio. *Escritos de Luperón*. Edited by Emilio Rodríguez Demorizi. Ciudad Trujillo, DR: Imp. de J. R. vda. García sucs, 1941.
Luperón, Gregorio. "Letter to Eugenio María de Hostos, November 12, 1895." In *República Dominicana y Puerto Rico: Hermandad en la lucha emancipadora, correspondencia 1876–1902*, edited by Vivian Quiles Calderín, 238. Río Piedras, PR: Instituto de Estudios Hostosianos, 2001.
Luperón, Gregorio. *Notas autobiográficas y apuntes históricos sobre la República Dominicana desde la Restauración a nuestros días*. Ponce, PR: Imprenta y Librería de M. López, 1896.
Luperón, Gregorio. *Notas autobiográficas y apuntes para la historia*. Vol. 1. Reprint, Santo Domingo, DR: Editorial La Nación, 1961.
Maglio, Alan, and Medhin Paolos, dirs. *Asmarina: Voices and Images of a Postcolonial Heritage*. Milan, Italy, 2015.
Manganelli, Kimberly Snyder. *Transatlantic Spectacles of Race: The Tragic Mulatta and the Tragic Muse*. New Brunswick, NJ: Rutgers University Press, 2012.
Manley, Elizabeth S. "'News of "Crazy" Women Demanding Freedom': Dominican Feminist Activism in a Post-Dictatorial State (1961–1990)." *Caribbean Studies* 47, no. 1 (2019): 3–36.
Manley, Elizabeth S. "Of Celestinas and Saints, or Deconstructing the Myths of Dominican Womanhood." *Small Axe: A Caribbean Journal of Criticism* 22, no. 2 (2018): 72–84.

Manley, Elizabeth S. *The Paradox of Paternalism: Women and the Politics of Authoritarianism in the Dominican Republic*. Gainesville: University Press of Florida, 2017.

Mari, Lorenzo, and Polina Shvanyukova. "Re-negotiating National Belonging in Contemporary Italian Migrant Literature." *Ethnicities* 15, no. 4 (2015): 527–43.

Martí, José. *Nuestra América*. Caracas, Venezuela: Fundación Biblioteca Ayacucho, 1973.

Martínez-San Miguel, Yolanda. *Coloniality of Diasporas: Rethinking Intra-colonial Migrations in a Pan-Caribbean Context*. New York: Springer, 2014.

Martínez-San Miguel, Yolanda, and Katerina Gonzalez Seligmann. "Con-Federating the Archipelago: Introduction." *Small Axe: A Caribbean Journal of Criticism* 24, no. 1 (2020): 37–43.

Maseko, Zola, dir. *The Life and Times of Sara Baartman: The Hottentot Venus*. Brooklyn: Icarus Films, 1998.

Massawatube. "Wedi Shawl (Bologna)." YouTube, October 26, 2016. https://www.youtube.com/watch?v=8CmeZkS7lbk.

Mayes, April. *The Mulatto Republic: Class, Race, and Dominican National Identity*. Gainesville: University Press of Florida, 2014.

McPherson, Alan. "Misled by Himself: What the Johnson Tapes Reveal about the Dominican Intervention of 1965." *Latin American Research Review* 38, no. 2 (2003): 127–46.

Medrano, Tirso. "Desmitificando una famosísima foto de Tina Bazuca: Aquí la verdadera foto de la valiente guerrillera." *Somos Pueblo*, May 11, 2017. https://somospueblo.com/desmitificando-una-famosisima-foto-de-tina-bazuka-aqui-la-verdadera-foto-de-la-valiente-guerrillera/.

Meléndez, Edgardo. "Citizenship and the Alien Exclusion in the Insular Cases: Puerto Ricans in the Periphery of American Empire." *Centro Journal* 25, no. 1 (2013): 106–45.

Merrill, Heather. *An Alliance of Women: Immigration and the Politics of Race*. Minneapolis: University of Minnesota Press, 2006.

Micheli, Renato. "Faccetta Nera." Rome, 1935.

Milian, Claudia. *Latining America: Black-Brown Passages and the Coloring of Latino/a Studies*. Athens: University of Georgia Press, 2013.

Mirabal, Nancy Raquel. *Suspect Freedoms*. New York: New York University Press, 2017.

Miscali, Monica. "The Transformation of Motherhood: From a Neglected Mother to the Mother of a Whole Nation." *Romance Studies: A Journal of the University of Wales* 35, no. 1 (2017): 3–11.

Mitchell, Michele. "'The Black Man's Burden': African Americans, Imperialism, and Notions of Racial Manhood 1890–1910." *International Review of Social History* 44, no. 7 (1999): 77–99.

Mitchell, Robin. *Vénus Noire: Black Women and Colonial Fantasies in Nineteenth-Century France*. Athens: University of Georgia Press, 2018.

Montanelli, Indro. Interview by Gianni Bisiach. *L'ora della verità*, 1969.
Montanelli, Indro. "Quando andai a nozze con Destà." *Corriere della Sera* (Milan), February 12, 2000.
"Montanelli, Travaglio ad Accordi&Disaccordi: 'Rimuovere la statua a Milano? Era figlio del suo tempo, non un razzista.'" *Il Fatto Quotidiano*, June 13, 2020. https://www.ilfattoquotidiano.it/2020/06/13/montanelli-travaglio-ad-accordidisaccordi-rimuovere-la-statua-a-milano-era-figlio-del-suo-tempo-non-un-razzista/5833925/.
Morgan, Jennifer L. *Laboring Women: Reproduction and Gender in New World Slavery*. Philadelphia: University of Pennsylvania Press, 2004.
Muñoz, José Esteban. *Disidentifications: Queers of Color and the Performance of Politics*. Minneapolis: University of Minnesota Press, 1999.
Mussolini, Benito. "Discorso all'Augusteo." In *Scritti e discorsi di Benito Mussolini*, vol. 2, *La rivoluzione fascista*, 201–3. Milan: U. Hoepli, 1940.
Mussolini, Benito. "Il problema dell'emigrazione." In *Scritti e discorsi*, vol. 3, 95–98. Rome: Edizione Definitiva, 1934.
Mussolini, Benito. *Scritti e discorsi di Benito Mussolini*, vol. 2, *La rivoluzione fascista*. Milan: U. Hoepli, 1940.
Negrón-Muntaner, Frances. "Here Is the Evidence: Arturo Alfonso Schomburg's Black Countervisuality." *African American Review* 54, no. 1 (2021): 49–71.
Newton, Melanie. "Returns to a Native Land: Indigeneity and Decolonization in the Anglophone Caribbean." *Small Axe: A Caribbean Journal of Criticism* 17, no. 2 (2013): 108–22.
Ngai, Mae. *Impossible Subjects: Illegal Aliens and the Making of Modern America*. Princeton, NJ: Princeton University Press, 2014.
Nill, Andrea Christina. "Latinos and SB 1070: Demonization, Dehumanization, and Disenfranchisement." *Harvard Latino Law Review* 14, no. 1 (Spring 2011): 35–66.
"Norme relative ai meticci." *L'Italia e le sue colonie africane*, May 13, 1940. Biblioteca Civica A. Mai di Bergamo. http://legacy.bibliotecamai.org/news/iniziative/italia_colonie_africane/DOClegge822.htm.
Novas, José C. *Frederick Douglass: La anexión a los Estados Unidos y otros episodios en la isla de Santo Domingo*. Santo Domingo, DR: J. C. Novas, 1997.
Núñez Polanco, Diómedes. *Anexionismo y resistencia: Relaciones domínico-norteamericanas en tiempos de Grant, Báez, y Luperón*. Santo Domingo, DR: N.p., 1997.
OECD. *International Migration Outlook 2013*. Washington, DC: OECD Publishing, 2013. https://doi.org/10.1787/migr_outlook-2013-en.
"Omicidio Massimiliano Spelta e Carolina Payano: I killer erano professionisti italiani." *BolognaTG24*, September 14, 2012.
"Omicidio Via Muratori: Individuato uno dei killer di Massimiliano Spelta e Carolina Payano." *BolognaTG24*, September 20, 2012.
O'Neill, Eugene. *The Emperor Jones*. New York: Appleton-Century-Crofts, 1921.
Ortiz Gamble, Puig, and Robert S. Gamble. *Puerto Plata: La conservación de una ciudad*. Santo Domingo, DR: Editora Nacional, 2011.

Osei-Kofi, Nana, Adela C. Licona, and Karma R. Chávez. "From Afro-Sweden with Defiance: The Clenched Fist as Coalitional Gesture?" *New Political Science* 40, no. 1 (2018): 137–50.
Padilla, Mark. *Caribbean Pleasure Industry: Tourism, Sexuality, and AIDS in the Dominican Republic*. Chicago: University of Chicago Press, 2007.
Paoli, Renato. *Nella colonia Eritrea: Studi e viaggi*. Milan: Treves, 1908.
Paolos, Medhin. Interview by Angela Davis. Public screening of *Asmarina*, Harvard Art Museum, Cambridge, MA, March 29, 2018.
Papadantonakis, Max. "Black Athenians: Making and Resisting Racialized Symbolic Boundaries in the Greek Street Market." *Journal of Contemporary Ethnography* 49, no. 3 (2020): 291–317.
Parati, Graziella. *Migration Italy: The Art of Talking Back in a Destination Culture*. Toronto: University of Toronto Press, 2005.
Parks, Henry Blanton, and African Methodist Episcopal Church. *Africa: The Problem of the New Century—The Part the African Methodist Episcopal Church Is to Have in Its Solution*. New York: Board of Home and Foreign Missionary Department of the A.M.E. Church, 1899.
Pastacaldi, Paola. "Il testo della canzone Asmarina dell'indimenticabile Pippo Maugeri." *Paola Pastacaldi: Giornalista e scrittrice*. Accessed August 22, 2021. http://www.paolapastacaldi.it/document.php?DocumentID=1071.
Pastore, Ferruccio. "A Community Out of Balance: Nationality Law and Migration Politics in the History of Post-unification Italy." *Journal of Modern Italian Studies* 9, no. 1 (2004): 27–48.
Pavez-Soto, Iskra, and Carol Chan. "The Second Generation in Chile: Negotiating Identities, Rights, and Public Policy." *International Migration* 56, no. 2 (2018): 82–96.
Paynter, Eleanor. "The Spaces of Citizenship: Mapping Personal and Colonial Histories in Contemporary Italy in Igiaba Scego's *La mia casa è dove sono* (My Home Is Where I Am)." *European Journal of Life Writing* 6 (2017): 135–53.
Perassi, Emilia. "Madri e patrie nel romanzo contemporaneo sulla migrazione: Scrittrici italiane e argentine." *Romance Studies: A Journal of the University of Wales* 38, no. 3 (2020): 160–72.
Pérez Firmat, Gustavo. *Life on the Hyphen: The Cuban-American Way*. Austin: University of Texas Press, 2012.
Perilli, Vincenza. "Relazioni pericolose: Asimmetrie dell'interrelazione tra 'razza,' genere e sessualità interrazziale." In *Il colore della nazione*, edited by Gaia Giuliani. Florence: Le Monnier/Mondadori, 2015.
Peters, Catie. "A New Race of Cultivators." PhD diss., Harvard University, 2021.
Phoenix, Aisha. "Colourism and the Politics of Beauty." *Feminist Review* 108, no. 1 (2014): 97–105.
Pinkus, Karen. "Miss (Black) Italy." *Black Renaissance* 2, no. 1 (1998): 80–93.
Pitre, Merline. "Frederick Douglass and the Annexation of Santo Domingo." *Journal of Negro History* 62, no. 4 (1977): 390–400.
Placido, Michele, dir. *Pummaró*. Rome: Cineuropa 92, 1991.

Plácido, Sandy. "A Global Vision: Ana Livia Cordero and the Puerto Rican Liberation Struggle." *Black Perspectives*, December 2016. https://www.aaihs.org/a-global-vision-ana-livia-cordero-and-the-puerto-rican-liberation-struggle/.

Pojmann, Wendy. *Immigrant Women and Feminism in Italy*. New York: Routledge, 2006.

Polyné, Millery. *From Douglass to Duvalier: US African Americans, Haiti, and Pan Americanism, 1870–1964*. Gainesville: University Press of Florida, 2010.

Ponzanesi, Sandra. "Beyond the Black Venus: Colonial Sexual Politics and Contemporary Visual Practices." In *ReSignifications: European Blackamoors, Africana Readings*, edited by Ellyn Mary Toscano and Awam Ampka, 137–47. Rome: Postcart, 2017.

Ponzanesi, Sandra. "The Color of Love: *Madamismo* and Interracial Relationships in the Italian Colonies." *Research in African Literatures* 43, no. 2 (Summer 2012): 155–72.

Pujols, Hector. "Chile: 'Los grupos anti-derechos se fortalecen cuando su discurso es expresado desde el gobierno.'" Interview by *Civicus*, August 30, 2019. https://www.civicus.org/index.php/es/medios-y-recursos/noticias/entrevistas/4022-chile-los-grupos-anti-derechos-se-fortalecen-cuando-su-discurso-es-expresado-desde-el-gobierno.

"Punto di Partenza." Fondo Mariateresa Battaglio, Archivio della donna in Piemonte. Accessed October 7, 2019. https://www.archiviodonnepiemonte.it/fondi-documentari/fondo-mariateresa-battaglino/.

"Quick Facts: Athens-Clarke County (Balance), Georgia." United States Census Bureau. Accessed January 31, 2021. https://www.census.gov/quickfacts/athensclarkecountybalancegeorgia.

Racine, Karen. "During the Reign of Henry Christophe (1811–1820)." *Journal of Caribbean History* 33, nos. 1–2 (1999): 125–45.

Ramírez, Dixa. *Colonial Phantoms: Belonging and Refusal in the Dominican Americas, from the Nineteenth Century to the Present*. New York: New York University Press, 2018.

Ramírez de Haro, Gonzalo, Dolores Brandis, Teresa Cañedo-Argüelles, Teba Castaño, and Luis Escolano. *Efectos de la migración internacional en las comunidades de origen del suroeste de la República Dominicana*. Santo Domingo, DR: Instituto Panamericano de Georgrafía e Historia Sección Nacional de República Dominicana, 2009.

Renda, Mary A. *Taking Haiti: Military Occupation and the Culture of US Imperialism, 1915–1940*. Chapel Hill: University of North Carolina Press, 2001.

Republic of Italy. Act No. 91 of 5 February 1992, Citizenship. National Legislative Bodies, Italy, 1992. https://www.refworld.org/docid/3ae6b4edc.html.

Resumen Latinoamericano. "República Dominicana: A las invisibles por siempre: 'Tina Bazuca.'" January 25, 2018. https://www.resumenlatinoamericano.org/2018/01/25/republica-dominicana-a-las-invisibles-por-siempre-tina-bazuca/.

Reuters. "Cardinal Causes Controversy." *Irish Times*, September 15, 2000. https://www.irishtimes.com/news/cardinal-causes-controversy-1.1103017.

Reyes, Michael C. "Haitian Indigeneity before Africa: Commemorating Columbus and Dessalines in Henri Chauvet's *La fille du Kacik* (1894)." *Research in African Literatures* 50, no. 4 (Winter 2020): 165–81.
Reyes-Santos, Irmary. "On Pan-Antillean Politics: Ramón Emeterio Betances and Gregorio Luperón Speak to the Present." *Callaloo* 36, no. 1 (Winter 2013): 142–57.
Riccò, Giulia. "Igiaba Scego on Writing between History and Literature." Interview by Giulia Riccò. Black Italy Series, Public Books, December 8, 2020. https://www.publicbooks.org/igiaba-scego-on-writing-between-history-and-literature/.
Richards, David A. J. *Italian American: The Racializing of an Ethnic Identity.* New York: New York University Press, 1999.
Ricourt, Milagros. *The Dominican Racial Imaginary: Surveying the Landscape of Race and Nation in Hispaniola.* New Brunswick, NJ: Rutgers University Press, 2016.
Rodríguez, Jovanna. Speech given at the "Day of Multicultural Unity." Multicultural Week, Milan Exposition, Milan, Italy, June 22, 2015.
Rodríguez Objío, Manuel. *Gregorio Luperón e historia de la Restauración.* Santiago, DR: Editora de Santo Domingo, 1939.
Romeo, Caterina. "Racial Evaporations: Representing Blackness in African Italian Postcolonial Literature." In *Postcolonial Italy: Challenging National Homogeneity,* edited by Cristina Lombardi-Diop and Caterina Romeo, 221–36. New York: Palgrave Macmillan, 2012.
Roth, Wendy. *Race Migrations: Latinos and the Cultural Transformation of Race.* Stanford, CA: Stanford University Press, 2012.
Ruiz Pereira, Carla. "Los 30 días de calvario de Joane Florvil." *La Tercera,* October 7, 2017. https://www.latercera.com/noticia/los-30-dias-calvario-joane-florvil/.
Ryan-Scheutz, Colleen. *Sex, the Self and the Sacred: Women in the Cinema of Pier Paolo Pasolini.* Toronto: University of Toronto Press, 2007.
Sakai, Naoki. *Translation and Subjectivity: On "Japan" and Cultural Nationalism.* Minneapolis: University of Minnesota Press, 2008.
Saldaña-Portillo, María Josefina. *Indian Given: Racial Geographies across Mexico and the United States.* Durham, NC: Duke University Press, 2016.
Sánchez González, Lisa. *Boricua Literature: A Literary History of the Puerto Rican Diaspora.* New York: New York University Press, 2001.
Sánchez González, Lisa. "Decolonizing Schomburg." *African American Review* 54, nos. 1–2 (Spring/Summer 2021): 129–42.
Sánchez González, Lisa. "Modernism and Boricua Literature: A Reconsideration of Arturo Schomburg and William Carlos Williams." *American Literary History* 13, no. 2 (2001): 242–64.
Sanders, Ralph. "Congressional Reaction in the United States to the Panama Congress of 1826." *Americas* 11, no. 2 (1954): 141–54.
Sani, Gino Mitrano. *Femina somala.* Napoli: Detken e Rocholl, 1933.
"Santo Domingo: Arrival of the Tennessee." *New York Tribune,* February 22, 1871.
Sanz, Carlos. *Diario de Colón: Libro de la primera navegación y descubrimiento de las Indias.* Madrid: Yagues, 1962.

Sawyer, Mark. "Racial Politics in Multiethnic America: Black and Latina/o Identities and Coalitions." In *Neither Enemies nor Friends: Latinos, Blacks, Afro-Latinos*, edited by Anani Dzidzienyo and Suzana Oboler, 265–79. New York: Palgrave Macmillan, 2005.

Scego, Igiaba. *Adua*. Firenze: Giunti, 2015.

Scego, Igiaba. *La linea del colore: Il Grand Tour di Lafanu Brown*. Milan: Bompiani, 2020.

Scego, Igiaba. *La mia casa è dove sono*. Milan: Rizzoli, 2010.

Scego, Igiaba. "Relazione di Igiaba Scego." IV Forum internazionale sulla letteratura della migrazione, 2004. http://www.eksetra.net/studi-interculturali/relazione-intercultura-edizione-2004/relazione-di-igiaba%20scego/.

Scego, Igiaba. "The True Story of 'Faccetta Nera.'" Translated by Antony Shugaar. Words without Borders, April 2016. https://www.wordswithoutborders.org/article/april-2016-women-write-war-the-true-story-faccetta-negra-igiaba-scego.

Schomburg, Arthur A. "Is Hayti Decadent?" *Unique Advertiser*, August 1904.

Schomburg, Arthur A. "Military Services Rendered by the Haitians in the North and South American Wars of Independence." *A.M.E. Church Review* (1921): 199–212.

Schomburg, Arthur A. "The Negro Digs Up His Past." *Survey*, March 1, 1925, 670–73.

Schomburg, Arthur A. "A Philippines Republic Suggested." *New York Times*, September 24, 1901.

Schomburg, Arthur A. "Questions by a Porto Rican." *New York Times*, August 6, 1902, 8.

Schomburg, Arthur A. "Racial Integrity: A Plea for the Establishment of a Chair of Negro History in Our Schools and Colleges, etc." Paper presentation, Negro Society for Historical Research, Yonkers, NY, July 1913.

Sengupta, Ipshita. "The Economy of Desire: Globalisation, Gender and Sex Tourism in the Caribbean." *SSRN Electronic Journal*, July 28, 2010. https://doi.org/10.2139/ssrn.1649999.

Serrata, Medar. "La ciudad como espectáculo: Santo Domingo ante la mirada de los primeros turistas." In *Diálogos culturales en la literatura iberoamericana: Actas de XXXIX Congreso del Instituto Internacional de Literatura Iberoamericana*, edited by Concepción Reverte Bernal, 463–77. Madrid: Verbum, 2014.

Severgnini, Beppe. "Nessuno tolga Montanelli dai suoi Giardini." *Corriere della Sera*, June 22, 2020. https://www.corriere.it/esteri/20_giugno_11/proteste-statue-nessuno-tolga-montanelli-suoi-giardini-f35060ec-ab4f-11ea-ab2d-35b3b77b559f_amp.html.

Sharpe, Christina. *In the Wake: On Blackness and Being*. Durham, NC: Duke University Press, 2016.

Sharpe, Jenny. *Ghosts of Slavery: A Literary Archeology of Black Women's Lives*. Minneapolis: University of Minnesota Press, 2003.

Sharpley-Whiting, T. Denean. *Black Venus: Sexualized Savages, Primal Fears, and Primitive Narratives in French*. Durham, NC: Duke University Press, 1999.

Silié, Rubén. "Aspectos y variables de las relaciones entre República Dominicana y Haití." *Futuros: Revista Trimestral Latinoamericana y Caribeña de Desarrollo Sustentable* 3, no. 9 (2005): 3–20.
Silié, Rubén, and Guy Alexandre. "Las relaciones entre Haití y República Dominicana." *Ciencia y Sociedad* 18, no. 3 (1993): 231–37.
Sinnette, Elinor Des Verney. *Arthur Alfonso Schomburg: Black Bibliophile and Collector*. Detroit, MI: Wayne State University Press, 1989.
Small, Stephen. "Theorizing Visibility and Vulnerability in Black Europe and the African Diaspora." *Ethnic and Racial Studies* 41, no. 6 (2018): 1182–97.
Smith, Christen A. *Afro-Paradise: Blackness, Violence, and Performance in Brazil*. Urbana: University of Illinois Press, 2016.
Smith, Ryan. "Pat Robertson: Haiti 'Cursed' after 'Pact with the Devil.'" CBS News, January 13, 2010. http://www.cbsnews.com/8301-504083_162-12017-504083.html.
Smith, Valerie E. "Early Afro-American Presence on the Island of Hispaniola: A Case Study of the 'Immigrants' of Samaná." *Journal of Negro History* 72, nos. 1–2 (1987): 33–41.
Smythe, SA. "Black Italianità: Citizenship and Belonging in the Black Mediterranean." *California Italian Studies* 9, no. 1 (2019): 1–19.
Smythe, SA. "The Black Mediterranean and the Politics of Imagination." *Middle East Report* 286 (Spring 2018). https://merip.org/2018/10/the-black-mediterranean-and-the-politics-of-the-imagination/.
Sontag, Susan. *On Photography*. New York: Farrar, Straus and Giroux, 2011. Kindle.
Sternbach, Nancy Saporta. "Re-membering the Dead: Latin American Women's 'Testimonial' Discourse." *Latin American Perspectives* 18, no. 3 (1991): 91–102.
Stoler, Ann Laura. *Carnal Knowledge and Imperial Power: Race and the Intimate in Colonial Rule*. Berkeley: University of California Press, 2010.
Strazza, Michele. "Faccetta nera dell'Abissinia: Madame e meticci dopo la conquista dell'Etiopia." *Humanities* 1, no. 2 (2012): 116–33.
Tansill, Charles Callan. *The United States and Santo Domingo, 1798–1873: A Chapter in Caribbean Diplomacy*. Baltimore: Johns Hopkins Press, 1938.
Thomas, Deborah A. "Affective Archives, Witnessing, Repair. Deborah A. Thomas in Conversation with Nydia A. Swaby." November 24, 2020. https://www.youtube.com/watch?v=zLwkF2gTWmg.
Thomas, Deborah A. *Political Life in the Wake of the Plantation: Sovereignty, Witnessing, Repair*. Durham, NC: Duke University Press, 2019.
Thomas, Piri. *Down These Mean Streets*. New York: Knopf, 1967.
Thompson, Lanny. *Imperial Archipelago: Representation and Rule in the Insular Territories under U.S. Dominion after 1898*. Writing Past Colonialism. Honolulu: University of Hawai'i Press, 2010.
Torres-Saillant, Silvio. "Blackness and Meaning in Studying Hispaniola." *Small Axe: A Caribbean Journal of Criticism* 10, no. 1 (2006): 180–88.
Torres-Saillant, Silvio. "Diaspora and National Identity: Dominican Migration in the Postmodern Society." *Migration World Magazine* 25, no. 3 (1997): 18–22.
Torres-Saillant, Silvio. *An Intellectual History of the Caribbean*. New York: Palgrave Macmillan, 2006.

Torres-Saillant, Silvio. *Introduction to Dominican Blackness*. New York: CUNY Dominican Studies Institute, 2010.

Torres-Saillant, Silvio. "The Tribulations of Blackness: Stages in Dominican Racial Identity." *Callaloo* 23, no. 3 (2000): 1086–1111.

Torruella, Juan R. "Ruling America's Colonies: The Insular Cases." *Yale Law and Policy Review* 32, no. 1 (2013): 57–95.

Trento, Giovanna. *Pasolini e l'Africa, L'Africa di Pasolini: Panmeridionalismo e rappresentazioni dell'Africa postcoloniale*. Milan: Mimesis, 2010.

Trento, Giovanna. "Pier Paolo Pasolini in Eritrea: Subalternity, Grace, Nostalgia, and the 'Rediscovery' of Italian Colonialism in the Horn of Africa." In *Postcolonial Italy: Challenging the National Homogeneity*, edited by Cristina Lombardi-Diop and Caterina Romeo, 139–55. New York: Palgrave Macmillan, 2012.

Triulzi, Alessandro. "La costruzione dell'immagine dell'Africa e degli africani nell'Italia coloniale." In *Nel nome della razza: Il razzismo nella storia d'Italia*, edited by Alberto Burgio, 165–81. Bologna: Il Mulino, 1999.

Triulzi, Alessandro. "Displacing the Colonial Event: Hybrid Memories of Postcolonial Italy." In "Colonial and Postcolonial Italy," special issue, *Interventions: International Journal of Postcolonial Studies* 8, no. 3 (2006): 430–43.

Trouillot, Michel-Rolph. *Silencing the Past: Power and the Production of History*. Boston: Beacon, 1995.

Turner, Louis, and John Ash. *The Golden Hordes: International Tourism and the Pleasure Periphery*. London: Constable, 1975.

Twa, Lindsay J. *Visualizing Haiti in U.S. Culture, 1910–1950*. Burlington, VT: Ashgate, 2014.

Ty, Eleanor. *Asianfail: Narratives of Disenchantment and the Model Minority*. Urbana: University of Illinois Press, 2017.

"UASD: Repudio total a la barbarie." *Revista Ahora* (Santo Domingo), no. 440 (1972): 14.

United Nations Development Programme. *Human Development Report 2009: Overcoming Barriers: Human Mobility and Development*. New York: Palgrave Macmillan, 2009. http://hdr.undp.org/sites/default/files/reports/269/hdr_2009_en_complete.pdf.

United Nations Division for Gender Affairs. *Indicators: Femicide or Feminicide*. Gender Equality Observatory for Latin America and the Caribbean, 2019. https://oig.cepal.org/en/indicators/femicide-or-feminicide.

Vaca, Nicolas. *The Presumed Alliance: The Unspoken Conflict between Latinos and Blacks and What It Means for America*. New York: Rayo, 2004.

Valdés, Vanessa K. *Diasporic Blackness: The Life and Times of Arturo Alfonso Schomburg*. Albany: State University of New York Press, 2017.

Valeri, Mauro. *Black Italians: Atleti neri in maglia azzurra: l'Italia multirazziale*. Palombi Editori, 2006.

Valerio, Tony. "Enfrenamiento policías y estudiantes se mudan a la UASD." Vigilanteinformativo.com, October 1, 2019. https://vigilanteinformativo.com/https-vigilanteinformativo-com-enfrentamiento-policias-y-estudiantes-se-mudan-a-la-uasd/.

Vanderplaats Vallejo, Catharina. *Las madres de la patria y las bellas mentiras: Imágenes de la mujer en el discurso literario nacional de la República Dominicana, 1844–1899*. Miami: Ediciones Universal, 1999.

Vanni, Franco. "Duplice omicidio di via Muratori, un ergastolo e una assoluzione." *Repubblica* (Milan), July 3, 2015. http://milano.repubblica.it/cronaca/2015/07/03/news/omicidio_muratori_sentenza-118266120/.

Vega, Bernardo. *La cuestión racial y el proyecto dominicano de anexión a Estados Unidos en 1870*. Santo Domingo, DR: Academia Dominicana de la Historia, 2019.

Vega, Bernardo. *Memoirs of Bernardo Vega: A Contribution to the History of the Puerto Rican Community in New York*. Edited by César Andreu Iglesias. New York: Monthly Review Press, 1984.

Vellon, Peter G. *A Great Conspiracy against Our Race: Italian Immigrant Newspapers and the Construction of Whiteness in the Early Twentieth Century*. New York: New York University Press, 2017.

Venga Le Cuento. "Entrevista a Maria Teresa Tess Asplund." YouTube, December 30, 2016. https://www.youtube.com/watch?v=HyY39_F6vfc.

Venuti, Lawrence, ed. *Rethinking Translation: Discourse, Subjectivity, Ideology*. Vol. 2. New York: Routledge, 2018.

Venuti, Lawrence. "Translation as Cultural Politics: Regimes of Domestication in English." *Textual Practice* 7, no. 2 (1993): 208–23.

Washington, Derek. "Angela Davis on Activism and the Dream Act." SoundCloud, March 2011. https://soundcloud.com/derekwashington314/full-edited-angela-davis.

Weinberg, Albert Katz. *Manifest Destiny: A Study of Nationalist Expansionism in America*. New York: Barakaldo Books, 2020.

Wessendorf, Susanne. *Second-Generation Transnationalism and Roots Migration: Cross-Border Lives*. New York: Routledge, 2016.

West, Cornel. "Empire, Pragmatism, and War: A Conversation with Cornel West." Interview by Eduardo Mendieta. *Logos* 3, no. 3 (2004). http://www.logosjournal.com/west_interview.pdf.

Weyland, Karen. *Negociando la aldea global con un pie aquí y otro allá: La diáspora femenina dominicana y la transculturidad como alternativa descolonizadora*. Santo Domingo, DR: Instituto Tecnológico de Santiago (INTEC), 2006.

Williams, Erica Lorraine. *Sex Tourism in Bahia: Ambiguous Entanglements*. Urbana: University of Illinois Press, 2013.

Willis, Deborah, and Carla Williams. *The Black Female Body: A Photographic History*. Philadelphia: Temple University Press, 2002.

Wong, Aliza S. *Race and the Nation in Liberal Italy, 1861–1911: Meridionalism, Empire, and Diaspora*. New York: Palgrave Macmillan, 2006.

World Bank. "Stock of Migrants and Level of Education of Dominican Emigrants to OECD and Latin American Countries." In *Migration and Remittances Factbook 2011*, 233–36. Washington, DC: World Bank, 2011.

World Tourism Organization. "Regional Breakdown of World Tourism Statistics 1976–1980." *Journal of Travel Research* 21, no. 2 (1982): 47.

Wynter, Sylvia. "Jonkonnu in Jamaica: Towards the Interpretation of Folk Dance as a Cultural Process." *Jamaica* 4, no. 2 (June 1970): 34–48.

Wynter, Sylvia. "Unsettling the Coloniality of Being/Power/Truth/Freedom: Towards the Human, after Man, Its Overrepresentation—An Argument." *CR: The New Centennial Review* 3, no. 3 (2003): 257–337.

Zeller, Neici M. "The Appearance of All, the Reality of Nothing: Politics and Gender in the Dominican Republic, 1880–1961." PhD diss., University of Illinois at Chicago, 2010.

Zeller, Neici. *Discursos y espacios femeninos en República Dominicana, 1880–1961*. Santo Domingo, DR: Editorial Letra Gráfica, 2012.

Zendaya. "Cardi B Opens Up." *CR Fashion Book*, December 21, 2018. https://www.crfashionbook.com/celebrity/a15956294/card-b-zendaya-cr-fashion-bookinterview/.

Zinn, Dorothy Louise. "'Loud and Clear': The G2 Second Generations Network in Italy." *Journal of Modern Italian Studies* 16, no. 3 (2011): 373–85.

INDEX

Page numbers in italics refer to figures.

abolitionism, 22, 29, 36, 40–41, 49–50, 75
Academia de Mujeres, 260n41
activism, 146, 158, 193, 238, 259n31, 268n113, 274n92; Afro-Chilean, 277n9; Afro-Dominican, 113–32, 258nn6–7; Afro-Italian, 133–44, 172, 174–75, 178–79, 188, 192, 200, 206–7, 217, 221–27, 272n29; antiracist, 9–10, 235–36; Black Chilean, 236, 277n9; Brazilian, 259n14; and gender, 115–33, 138–44, 258n7, 259n35; Habesha, ix, 217; immigrant rights, 14–16, 24–25; LGBTQI, 114; Puerto Rican, 82; Second Generation, 25, 188, 192, 200, 206, 221–27. *See also* feminism
Adichie, Chimamanda, 199
affective archives, 158, 210, 264n29
African Americans, 53, 83, 85, 86–97, 249n100. *See also* US Blacks
African Methodist Episcopal (AME) church, 29, 51, 59, 73, 249n100; *A.M.E. Church Review*, 99
Africa Orientale Italiana (Italian East Africa), 160, *165–66*, 265n44
Afro Chileans, 114, 118, 120, 233–37, 277n9. *See also* Black Chileans
Afro-descendant people, x, 18, 64, 86, 100, 199
Afro Italians, 196–97, 204–5, 271n11. *See also* Black Italians; Second Generation (G2)
Afro-Latin Americanness, 19, 89
Afropessimism, 23
Afro-Portuguese people, 191
afterimages, 159; and Italian colonialism, 169–70, 173, 179, 184, 187, 191, 208, 219, 266n59
Afwerki, Isaias, 216
Agassiz, Jean Louis Rodolphe, 248n86
agency, 92, 149–50, 163–64, 170, 181, 192
Alaska, 245n35
Albion Legions, 105
Alexander, M. Jacqui, 108, 119
alien citizenship, 220–21, 226
Almonte, Mariam (pseudonym), 122–23, 259n31
almost belonging, 201, 203–4
almost citizens, 80–81, 90, 108
Alvarez, Julia, 260n56
American (term), ix
American Colonization Society, 40, 108
American Negro Academy, 90
American Revolution (US), 102, 254n48
Amhara, 265n44
Amodeo, Rossella, 189, 268n113
Anacaona Mujeres Dominicanas en Italia, 141–*43*, 150, 188–89, 269n132
Andall, Jacqueline, 138, 221, 224, 243n53, 262n85
Anglo-Americanness, 34, 225

Anglo-Americans, 13, 35–38, 83, 194
Anglo blackness/Black in English, 83, 193–95
Anglophone Caribbean, 4
Anglo-Saxon identity, 54, 68
annexation, 247n58; of the Dominican Republic by US, 23, 35–78, 81, 108, 228, 245n35, 246n49, 252n6; of Eritrea by Italy, 134, 155; of Eritrea by Ethiopia, 214
antiblackness, 4, 22, 195–96, 254n42; and colonialism, 4, 171, 177, 212–13, 215, 273n55; Dominican, 37, 65, 243n9; global anti-Haitianism, 64–65, 95, 97, 131, 243n9, 256n94; and immigration, 12, 14–16, 24, 212–13, 215, 233–39; Italian, 132, 135–36, 142, 158–92, 203, 212–13; and mestizaje, 8, 24, 62–65, 84, 104–5, 107, 225; resistance to, 12, 20, 26, 142, 173, 225, 231; and sexual violence, 120, 158–82. *See also* Jim Crow; Karens; La Sentencia (2013); lynching; Parsley Massacre (1937); racial segregation; racism; slavery; white supremacy
anticolonialism, 6, 10, 14, 19–20, 34, 121, 196, 225, 237; anticolonial nationalism, 105; and Arthur Schomburg, 80, 87–89, 93, 109; and Indigeneity, 104–7; and Italian empire, 155, 179, 206, 213–14, 218; and US empire, 36, 38–39, 47, 48–50, 53, 57, 59–70, 74, 247n58
anticommunism, 113, 116, 258n6
anti-fascism, 164
Antilles, 41–42, 62, 65, 99
anti-nationalism, 144
anti-racism, 10–11, 14, 19, 58, 138, 174, 234–35, 261n70, 277n9
antisemitism, 267n81
Anzaldúa, Gloria, 6, 84, 87–88, 218, 238, 257n122
apartheid, 155, 168, 230, 267n79. *See also* Jim Crow
Arbery, Ahmaud, 242n42
archives, 3, 8, 17, 26, 131, 241n2; affective archives, 158, 210, 264n29; archival interruptions, 25; archival praxis, 77, 89, 91, 100; and Arthur Schomburg, 23–24, 79–110, 255n49, 255n57; and methodology of book, 2, 74–77; racially gendered, 127, 143, 158–62, 170, 173, 178–79, 182, 184, 191–92, 266n59, 266n68; and Second Generations, 193–231. *See also* libraries
Argentina, 55
Argentines, 55, 57
Aristotle, 63
Arizona SB 1070, 15
Armée Indigène, 106
Arnone, Anna, 214
Arroyo, Jossianna, 82, 86, 90, 107
Arthur, Chester A., 253n11
Ash, John, 183
Asian Italians, 132, 138, 222
Asian people, 12, 18, 80, 132, 138, 222, 227, 239, 252n1, 257n116; and almost citizenship, 90; and apartheid, 267n79; Asian feminists, x; colonial concubinage in, 167; and créolité, 68; indentured servants, 17; and model minority discourse, 270n4; and racialization, 198
"Asmarina, Asmarina" (song), 212–13
Asplund, Tess, 9–12
assimilation, 9, 18, 38, 55, 89, 99, 227; and italianità, 168, 185, 188, 197, 201, 218, 221
Associazione delle Donne, 189
asylum, 21, 140, 215–17, 274n84. *See also* refugees
Attucks, Crispus, 91, 254n48
Ay Ombe Collective, 238; *Carmen: FotonovelARTE*, 145–52
Aztlán, 95

baasskap, 267n79. *See also* white supremacy
Báez, Buenaventura, 44–47, 50, 52–53, 60, 63, 69, 74–77, 245n35
Báez, Josefina, 144, 205; *Carmen: FotonovelARTE*, 145–52; *Comrade, Bliss Ain't Playing*, 150; *Levente no: Yolayorkdominicanyork*, 145, 150; Levente Visual series, 145, 151
Bailey, Moya, 169
Balaguer, Joaquín, 113–15, 126, 133–34, 138, 142, 182, 258n10; Terrible Twelve Years (1966–78), 116–18, 129, 132, 258n1, 258n6
bambine mania, 181
Banotti, Elvira, 175–79
Baratieri, Daniela, 161–62
barbarism discourse, 34, 36, 40, 49, 54–55, 60, 160, 228

Barre, Siad, 201
Barrera, Giulia, 163, 168, 267n80
Baths of Diocletian, 207
Batista, Fulgencio, 229
Battle of Dogali, 207
Bazuca, Tina. *See* Rivas, Agustina (Tina Bazuca)
Beaman, Jean, 197, 226
Bencosme, Carmen Inés, 147–49
Benjamin, Walter, 6
Berlant, Lauren, 219
Berlin Conference (1884), 249n100
Berlusconi, Silvio, 272n43
Bernabé, Jean, 250n132
Betances, Ramón Emeterio, 36, 60, 66, 84
Bianchi, Bruna, 185–86
Bianchi, Georgia, 219, 223
Biffi, Giacomo, 135
Bisiach, Gianni, 174
Bizet, Georges, 147
Black (term), ix
Black Anglo-Americans, 34, 194
Black Chileans, 114, 118, 120, 233–37, 277n9. *See also* Afro Chileans
Black Colombians, 9–10
Black Europe Summer School, 197
Black Europe Summit, 197
Black Freedom Schools, 14
black fugitive democratic ethos, 56–57
"Black Haiti," 41
Black immigrant motherhood, 182–92
Black in English/Anglo blackness, 83, 193–95
"Black Is Beautiful," 196
Black Italians, 22, 155, 172, 192, 196–208, 214, 254n42, 264n25, 271n11. *See also* Afro Italians; Second Generation (G2)
Black Latinx studies, 109
Black liberation, 11, 30, 36, 47, 57, 62
Black Lives Matter, 12, 37, 193, 195, 225, 227, 235, 237–38
#BlackLivesMatter, 14, 236
Black man's burden, 35
Black Panamericanism, 36
Black Power movement, 10–12, 196
Black Puerto Ricans, 13, 23, 81, 89, 94, 103
Black Venus, 161–62, 169–70, 173, 187, 191, 265nn50–51
Blackwell, Henry, 50
Black/white binary, 33, 69, 83, 89, 250n132
Bland, Sandra, 235, 276n8. *See also* #SayHerName
Bobadilla, Tomás, 47, 75–78
Bolívar, Simón, 95, 100, 102
Bolsonaro, Jair, 276n7
Bontemps, Arna: *Popa and Fifina, Children of Haiti*, 98
bordered identities, 17
Boricuas. *See* Puerto Ricans (Boricuas)
Bosch, Juan, 123–25
Bossi, Umberto, 272n43
Boston Massacre (1770), 254n48
Botticelli, Sandro: *Birth of Venus*, 161, 265n50
Boyer, Jean-Pierre, 246n49
Brazil, 118–20, 159, 231, 238, 259n14, 276n7; Copacabana (Rio de Janeiro), 184; Rio de Janeiro, 183
Brennan, Denise, 184, 269n113
Brooks, David, 97
Brooks, Preston, 75
Brown (term), ix–x
Brown, Kimberly Juanita, 159, 169, 187
brownness, 63–64, 71, 87, 244n15, 251n140, 253n23
Buck v. Bell (1927), 267n76. *See also* eugenics; sterilization
Buffalo Soldiers (24th Regiment, US Army), 245n24
Buscaglia-Salgado, José, 63–64
Byrd, Brandon, 249n91

Cabral, Donald Reid, 124
Cabral, José María, 44, 47, 75
Cabral Carezzano, Julia, 127–28, 131
Cacao, Beto, 15
caciques, 106–7, 142
Cacos Rebellion (1911), 96, 256n77
California, 42
Cambio Passo, 217
Campo Cintato (Kombishtato), 168, 190, 230
Campus delle culture delle donne, 140
Canada, 245n35
Candelario, Ginetta, 72, 137, 194
Cape Verde, 134

capitalism, 7, 43, 98, 120, 149, 158, 188, 236, 239; colonial, 15–16; racial, 244n19
Capotillo Declaration (1871), 77
Cardi B, 13, 79, 89
Caribbean Confederation, 38
Caribbean studies, 101
Casalesi Clan, 270n6
caste, 41–42, 53, 64, 180
Catholic Church, 123, 134, 186; Catholic Left, 132; Catholic Right, 135
Catorce de Junio Party, 124–25
caudillos, 38, 44, 62, 75
Cedulas Dominicanas, 251n138
Central Intelligence Agency (CIA), 116
Césaire, Aimé, 72–73, 99, 104
Chambers, Iain, 157
Chamoiseau, Patrick, 250n132
Chávez, Karma, 10
Cheney Institute, 103
Chicago Tribune, 42–43
Chicanx movement, 95, 146
Chile, 68, 231, 234–36, 238–39, 276n132, 276nn5–7, 277n9; Santiago, 114, 127, 233, 269n132
Chilean Constitution, 277n9
Chinese Exclusion Act (1882), 253n11
Christophe, Henri, 91, 96–97, 99, 105–8, 227
Citibank, 96
citizenship, 2, 12, 14, 17, 109, 140, 144, 181, 193, 237, 239, 251n140, 270n4; alien, 90, 220–21, 226; almost, 80–81, 90; Chilean, 277n9; color-blind, 44, 53–55, 69, 72; Cuban, 35, 38; Dominican, 33, 38–39, 53, 71–72, 78, 141, 251n137; French, 85, 197; gendered, 16, 18, 71, 80, 263n13; German, 267n81; Haitian, 33, 35, 38, 41, 95, 99, 101–2; and Indigeneity, 18, 90, 107; Italian, x, 21, 25, 132, 135–36, 156–57, 168, 170–72, 179, 184–206, 210, 214, 218–31, 271n9, 271n17; jus sanguinis, 132, 156–57, 197–98, 214, 222; and marriage, 71, 251n137; minoritized, 13, 18–20, 85, 136, 198–99, 219, 225, 236; naturalization, 18, 79–80, 135, 197, 221–22, 271n9; Puerto Rican, 13, 18, 24, 38, 79–83, 94, 103, 228, 252n6; racially inclusive, 38–39, 62–66, 69, 184, 244n19; Swedish, 10; US, 18, 23–24, 33–37, 39–44, 48–59, 70–72, 79–83, 85, 90, 94, 103–6, 108, 194, 228, 242n34, 244n19, 251n137, 252n6. *See also* La Sentencia (2013); Law No. 91 (1992)
civil rights, 12, 16, 23, 71, 146
civil rights movement, 3, 23, 229
Clifford, James, 258n128
Club Las Dos Antillas, 66, 82
coalition, 10, 15, 37, 270n2
Cochran, Terry, 13
Colombia, 238; Cali, 9
colonial amnesia, 135, 182, 187, 202, 219
colonial memory, 65, 154, 173, 187, 191–92, 203–4, 208, 213
colonizing trick, 98
Columbus, Christopher, 107, 155, 158–60
Combahee River Collective, 238, 254n34
Commission of Inquiry for the Annexation of Santo Domingo to the United States of America, 23, 36, 49, 50, 76
communism, 115–16, 124–25, 141, 258n6. *See also* anticommunism
composite nationality, 56–57, 64, 71
concubinage, 162–82, 190, 267n80. *See also* madamas/madamato
Confederación Antillana, 60–62, 66–67
Confederacy, 244n19
Confiant, Raphaël, 250n132
Congress of Panama (1826), 96
constitucionalistas, 123–24, 126, 128
contra*diction*, 2, 6, 11, 14, 70, 84, 118, 226, 237, 239; and archives, 25, 74, 77–78, 212, 214; and Arthur Schomburg, 92–93, 95; and Black citizenship, 33, 35, 38–39, 45, 90, 204; and Black feminist praxis, 24, 146–52, 158, 178, 187, 192; and colonialism, 4, 23, 25, 187, 199, 202, 204–14, 219; definition, 241n2; and Gregoria Fraser Goins, 33, 35, 39, 70; and italianità, 201, 204–14, 219; and Latinx studies, 88; and mestizaje, 65; and montarse, 108, 119; and translating blackness, 9, 57
Cordero, Ana Livia, 253n8
Cordero, Margarita, 124, 127, 260n39
Cordero, René, 258n7
Cordero Michel, Emilio, 62
Corriere della Sera, 268n101
Costa Rica: Puerto Limón, 250n116

counterhegemony, 6, 19
counternarratives, 97–98, 207
coups, 96, 116, 123, 201
Créolité, 68, 250n132
criollos, 38, 53, 65, 84, 103, 246n49
critical archival studies, 92, 191
Crummell, Alexander, 90
Cruz, Melania, 142, 188, 270n141
Cuba, 40, 47, 57, 61–62, 100, 116, 229, 238; and Black citizenship, 35, 38; colonialism in, 36, 48, 60, 65–68, 81–82, 86, 245n24, 249n100, 253n19, 256n78, 275n126; Havana, 183
Cubanía, 159
Cuban Independence, 65, 66, 81–82, 96
Cuban Revolution, 122, 124, 234
Cubans, 18, 35, 38, 60, 62, 96, 99, 253n15, 254n24; exiled, 61, 67
Curaçao, 76
Curiel, Ochy, 144, 238
Czech Republic, 242n26

D'Amelio, Maria Elena, 186
dämoz, 162
Danish (language), 29
Danticat, Edwidge, 274n94
Darwinism, 248n86
Davidson, Christina, 73
Dávila, Arlene, 270n3, 271n13
Davis, Angela, 8, 10, 16, 144, 196, 238
decolonial studies, 191
decolonization, 95, 110, 183, 191, 214, 266n59
Deferred Action for Childhood Arrivals (DACA, 2012), 230, 276n130
de Genova, Nicholas, 17, 19
DeGrasse, François Joseph Paul, 105
de la Cruz, Marlene, 141–42, 144, 150
De Las Casas, Bartolomé, 104
Del Boca, Angelo, 264n16
Deleuze, Gilles, 201
Dell'Oro, Erminia: *Asmara Addio*, 267n69; *L'abbandono: Una storia eritrea*, 163
del Monte, Félix María, 55
Deloria, Philip, 103
deportation, 15, 42, 85, 129, 131, 189, 245n20, 276n130
descanso, 120
De Seta, Enrico, 164–66
Dessalines, Jean-Jacques, 99, 101
Destà, 173–82, 187
Development, Relief, and Education for Alien Minors Act (DREAM Act, 2001), 188, 193, 230, 269n135, 276n130
diasporic consciousness, 89, 91, 93–94, 100
diavoletti, 181
Díaz, Fidias, 115–17
Díaz, Junot, 199, 274n94
Díaz, Pablo, 113
Díaz, Sagrario, 113 20, 138, 141, 152, 258n12
dictatorship, 218, 230; Chilean, 234–35; Dominican, 44, 60, 62–63, 72, 76, 114–15, 121, 123, 216, 229, 245n35, 258n1, 260n56, 274n94; Eritrean, 210, 215, 217, 274n92. See also *individual regimes*
discrimination, 8, 13, 17, 50, 134, 142, 276n6. *See also* alien citizenship; almost belonging; almost citizens; antiblackness; antisemitism; apartheid; eugenics; exoticism; gender-based violence; global anti-Haitianism; homophobia; italianità; Karens; La Sentencia (2013); Law No. 91 (1992); linguistic terrorism; minoritization; misogynoir; misogyny; model minority discourse; muertos civiles; negrophobia; patriarchy; pureza de sangre; racial segregation; racism; sexual violence; slavery; transphobia; white supremacy; xenophobia
(dis)enfranchisement, 41, 50, 58, 120, 132, 168, 250n119
disidentification, 87
Dodecanese Islands, 134
domestic violence, 142, 180, 189, 190
domestic workers, 137–38
Dominican Association of Medical Practitioners, 117
Dominican Civil War, 24, 116, 123, 133
Dominican Constitution, 123
dominicanidad, 3–4, 55, 61–62, 74, 78, 119, 243n9
Dominican Independence, 29, 43, 47–48, 61–62, 64, 66, 76–77, 246n49. *See also* Ephemeral Independence
Dominican National Tourism Plan, 182

Dominican Republic, 3, 5, 20, 215, 233, 247n58, 248n84; activism in, 113–32, 259n35; antiblackness in, 37, 55, 65, 221, 230, 243n9, 250n112, 263n114, 274n94, 276n131; Bay of Samaná, 40, 44, 47, 50–*51*, 245n35, 275n126; and Black citizenship, 33, 53, 71–72; blackness in, 31, 243n9, 246n48, 248n64, 250n119, 251n135, 253n23; Cibao, 131, 260n56; Cuidad Trujillo (Santo Domingo), 127; Dajabón, 127, 131; dictatorships in, 44, 60, 62–63, 72, 76, 114–15, 121, 123, 216, 229, 245n35, 258n1, 260n56, 274n94; El Ensanche La Fé, 114; Gregoria Fraser Goins in, 30–34, 70–74, 78, 82, 244n13, 251n138; Haitian-descendent people in, 1, 120, 131, 139, 144, 221, 263n114, 274n94, 276n131; immigrants from, 2, 21–22, 24–25, 32–34, 37, 44, 114, 120–21, 126, 129, 132–52, 154, 157, 182–92, 230, 250n116; Independencia Province, 21; Jimaní Basin, 21; La Romana, 114; La Sentencia (2013), 144, 221, 230, 263n114, 276n131; Mao, 114; Neyba Valley, 21; Postrer Río, 21, 66–67; Puerto Plata, 30–34, 60, 70, 73, 82, 249n109; relations with Haiti, 47–49, 54–55, 62–65, 243n9; San Francisco de Macorís, 74; Santo Domingo (city), 1, 31, 113–14, 117, 121, 123, 127, 130, 139, 141–42, 145–46, 148, 153–54, 183–84, 189; state violence in, 24, 113–18, 120–32, 258n1, 258n6, 260n56; Terrible Twelve Years (1966–78), 116–18, 129, 132, 258n1, 258n6; tourism in, 120, 132, 154, 182–83, 188, 263n6, 269n114; and US empire, 23, 35–78, 81, 108, 157, 167, 228, 245n35, 246n49, 252n6, 256n78, 275n126; Villa Altagracia, 122; Villa Mella, 113, 139. *See also* Santo Domingo (historical name)
Dominican Republic–Haiti border, 107, 114, 236
Dominican Revolutionary Party, 113
Dominicans, 18, 29, 36, 39, 74–75; Black Dominicana feminist praxis, 119–21, 152; and Black Latinidad, 16, 67, 70, 82, 249n101; and blackness, 30–32, 250n112; diasporic activism by, 132–52; exiled, 44, 63, 66, 76–77, 115, 123, 247n63, 250n116; of Haitian descent, 1, 120, 131, 139, 144, 221, 230, 263n114, 274n94, 276n131; in Italy, 21–22, 24–25, 132–52, 154, 182–92; as other-than-black, 48, 72, 248n64; and race, 37–38, 44, 48–49, 53, 55, 62–65, 69, 71–72. *See also* Dominicanyork people
#Dominicans, 37
Dominican studies, 132, 248n64
Dominican Supreme Court, 276n131
Dominican War of Restoration (La Guerra de Restauración, 1863–65), 44, 61, 74, 247n49, 250n112
Dominicanyork people, 121, 145, 150
Domitian, Emperor, 207
Douglass, Charles, 53
Douglass, Frederick, 4; "What to the Slave Is the Fourth of July?," 57
Douglass, Lewis, 31, 70
DREAMers, 188, 193, 230, 269n135, 276n130
drug trafficking, 154, 185, 187, 276n7
Duany, Jorge, 3, 19–20, 241n5
Duarte, Juan Pablo, 36, 44, 65, 126, 246n49
Du Bois, W. E. B., 90, 92, 98, 200–1, 206, 254n24, 255n56
Duncan, Derek, 207
Duvalier, François, 229
Duvalier, Jean-Claude, 229
Dzidzienyo, Anani, 270n2

Eastman, George, 161
eBay, 164
Economic Justice Coalition, 15
Edwards, Brent, 6, 58
Egypt, 207, 273n54
El Bar de Cambumbo, 133, 261n60
El Club Guarionex y Hatuey, 107
Ellis Island, 252n1
El Nié, 34, 144–45, 147, 150–52, 205, 218, 262n104
El Salvador, 209, 229
El-Tayeb, Fatima, 157, 197–98
emancipation, 12, 38–40, 42, 49, 69, 95, 101, 197; unfinishedness of, 2, 16, 241n3
embodied memory, 108
emigration, 41, 132, 156, 168, 195, 220; from Cuba, 66; from the Dominican Republic, 21–22, 24–25, 32, 34, 44, 120–21, 132–52, 157, 182–92, 230, 250n116; from Eritrea,

21, 134, 178, 197, 208–19, 267n69, 271n19, 274n84, 274n92; from Ethiopia, 209; from Latin America, 60; from Mexico, 15, 54; from the US, 40–41, 47, 50, 59, 108
engaged scholarship, 15
England, 40, 55, 68, 91, 242n26, 246n49; Birmingham, 242n26. *See also* Great Britain
English (language), 29, 84, 225–26, 235, 238, 254n24, 257n106, 270n141, 271n11; Black in English, 83, 193–95; scholarship in, 75, 264n19; translations into, 71, 77; and white supremacy, 13
English Defense League, 242n26
Enlightenment, 227
Ensanche Luperón, 126
Ephemeral Independence, 246n49
Eritrea, ix, 9, 227, 264n25, 274n76; annexation by Ethiopia, 214; Asmara, 164, 168–69, 178, 190, 208, 212–15, 267n69, 267n80; Assab, 265n43; immigrants from, 21, 134, 178, 197, 208–19, 267n69, 271n19, 274n84, 274n92; Italian colonization of, 25, 134, 155, 158–92, 197, 206–7, 228, 230, 265nn43–44; Massawa, 181. *See also* Campo Cintato (Kombishtato)
Eritrean Constitution, 216
Eritrean-descendant people, 21, 134, 178, 193, 197, 208–19, 264n25, 267n69, 274n84, 274n92
Eritrean-Ethiopian Federation, 214
Eritrean Festival in Bologna (ፌስቲቫል ኤርትራ ቦሎኛ), 213–14, 274n76
Eritrean Independence, 216, 265n43, 274n76
Eritrean Liberation Front (ELF), 274n76
Eritrean National Assembly, 216
Eritrean People's Liberation Front (EPLF), 213, 274n76
Erman, Sam, 80–81, 252n6
Escuela Normal (Dominican Republic), 66
Espinal, Pilar, 147–49
Espinosa, Juderkys, 238
Espinosa, Yuderkys, 144
espiritismo, 119
Esposizione Generale Italiana (1884), 265n45
Estrella, Amarilys, 120, 221, 263n113
Ethiopia, ix, 180, 215, 238, 274n76; annexation of Eritrea, 214; Axum, 272n34; border with Eritrea, 216, 230; immigrants from, 209; Italian colonization of, 162, 173, 206, 265nn43–44, 272n34, 273n54
Ethiopian-descendant people, 9, 208–9, 264n25. *See also* Habesha people
Ethiopian Empire, 213
eugenics, 167, 267n76. See also *Buck v. Bell* (1927); sterilization
Eurocentrism, 55, 89, 96, 225, 228
European Social Forum on Migrant Women, 139–40
European Union, 20, 136, 216; Article 18, 140–41
Eve (biblical), 158–59
exile, 74, 82, 100, 234; Cubans in, 61, 67; Dominicans in, 44, 63, 66, 76–77, 115, 123, 247n63, 250n116; Eritreans in, 213, 216; Latinx, 60; Puerto Ricans in, 61; racexiles, 218
exoticism, 99, 120, 154, 159, 234; and colonialism, 25, 136–37, 157–92, 195–96, 212–13, 239
expansionism, 38–40, 45, 57–58, 67, 69, 245n35. *See also* Manifest Destiny
extracomunitari, 136, 194, 198, 210

"Faccetta Nera," 170–73, 182, 206, 212
Facebook, 185, 210
Faleschini Lerner, Giovanna, 186
Fanon, Frantz, 4, 85, 99, 183–84
farming, 74–75, 96, 106, 110, 121, 145–46, 246n49, 257n116; in Schomburg's work, 92, 99, 106–7
fascism, 132; Italian colonial, 156, 161–86, 195, 203–4, 212–13, 221–22, 226, 264n16, 265n44, 266n63. *See also* anti-fascism; "Faccetta Nera"; Lega Nord; Mussolini, Benito
Faustino Sarmiento, Domingo, 55
feminism, x, 70, 158, 199, 237, 259n36; Black Chilean, 277n9; Black Dominican, 119–21, 124; Black Italian, 139–52, 175–76; Black Latina, 24–25, 119; Brazilian, 259n14; Italian, 134, 137–52, 169, 174–79; Third World, 127, 137; white, 137; women of color, 238
Figueroa-Vásquez, Yomaira, 8

Filipinos, 18, 138, 159, 223
first-generation migrants, 85
First World, 85
Fish, Hamilton, 44
Fisk University Library: Negro Collection, 90
Flaiano, Ennio: *Tempo di uccidere*, 163
flesh (Spillers), 187
Flores, Juan, 83, 86–88, 136
Florida, 40; Cayo Hueso (Key West), 65–66
Florvil, Joane, 114, 118, 120, 233–35, 237
Florvil, Tiffany, 197, 204, 267n81, 271n8
Floyd, George, 37, 78, 173–74, 179, 225, 235, 238
footnote condition, 203
Forte e Chiaro, 172, 268n98
fotonovelas, 145–49, 152
Foucault, Michel, 92–93, 253n22
France, 55, 85, 102, 155, 257n118, 265n50; Calais, 40; citizenship in, 85, 197; French colonialism, 19, 40, 49, 89, 95–96, 101, 106, 157, 181, 246n49, 265n51; Paris, 31, 60, 66, 249n105
Franco, Marielle, 118–19, 259n13, 259n14
Fraser, Charles, 29–30
Fraser Goins, Gregoria, 53, 141, 238, 244nn11–12, 251n135; godfathers/padrinos of, 29, 34–35, 39, 63, 70, 74, 243n2; marriage, 251n137; racial/class identity of, 28–34, 63, 70–74, 78, 82–84, 251n138, 251n140; vaivenes, 23, 31–34, 39, 78, 82
"free Black problem," 40
freedom schools, 14–15, 140
Freedom University Georgia, 14–15
Freemasonry, 82, 90, 109
French (language), 29, 75, 227
French Revolution, 227
Frías, María, 74–75, 78
Frías, Mercedes, 137–41, 152, 238
Fuentes, Marisa, 158, 182, 266n68

Galla-Sidamo, 265n44
Galván, Manuel de Jesús, 55, 62
Gandolfi, Tertulliano, 166, 181, 184
García, José Gabriel, 58, 65, 75–76
García, Luiso, *11*
García Peña, Lorgia: *The Borders of Dominicanidad*, 3–4, 119, 241n2, 247n49, 249n90, 250n115, 255n72, 256n94
Garibaldi, Guiseppe, 66
Garibay, Elizabeth, 1–3, 7, 15
Gates, Henry Louis, Jr., 249n101
Gautier, Manuel María, 44
Gbadamosi, Raimi, 198
gender, 3, 97, 243n9, 260n41, 262n85, 265n51; and activism, 115–33, 138–44, 258n7, 259n35; and citizenship, 16, 18, 71, 80, 263n13; and colonialism, 24–25, 153–92, 212, 263n13, 265n45, 266n59; and immigration, 21, 24–25, 113–92, 268n113; and racialized motherhood, 182–92; and state violence, 115, 118–26, 131, 234–35, 242n42, 260n56, 268n113, 270n141; terminology, x; and tourism, 182–86, 268n114. *See also* feminism; gender-based violence; misogynoir; misogyny; patriarchy; sexual violence; transphobia
gender-based violence, 131, 134, 142; and colonialism, 25, 153–92, 266n59, 268n101. *See also* misogynoir; misogyny; patriarchy; sexual violence
genealogy, 3–4, 23, 88, 104
generation-and-a-half migrants, 85
Georgia, 7, 14, 16, 242n34, 242n42; Athens, 15, 242n36; Atlanta, 2; Pinewoods, 15
ghosts of colonialism, 157, 169, 182, 191–92, 208
Giuliani, Gaia, 154, 160, 264n21
Gladys "La Coronela," 126
Glissant, Édouard, 5, 104, 250n132
global anti-Haitianism, 64–65, 95, 97, 131, 243n9, 256n94. *See also* La Sentencia (2013)
global blackness, 5, 20, 26, 105, 121, 136, 198
Global North, x, 5–6, 8, 56, 71, 77, 140; and belonging/unbelonging, 17–19; citizenship in, 227–29; and colonialism, 22, 24, 56, 154–55, 157, 160, 167, 182, 195, 199, 227–30; hegemonic blackness in, 83; immigration to, 22, 24, 34, 81
Global South, 12, 140, 235, 237–38; and belonging/unbelonging, 6; citizenship in, 227; colonialism in, 81, 89, 159–60, 169–70, 228–30; emigration from, 4, 21, 24, 81, 205, 218, 230
Goins, John N., 251n137
Golderer, Lalla: *Stranieri a Milano*, 209–11

Gómez, Máximo, 66
Gonzalez Seligmann, Katerina, 60
grammar of blackness, 6
Grant, Ulysses S., 35, 60, 245n35, 247n63; and Dominican Republic annexation, 40–50, 53, 58, 76–77, 245n35, 247n63
Great Britain, 47, 155, 265n51; British colonialism, 19, 89, 157, 214, 265n43. *See also* England
Greece, 231, 261n60
Grignaffini, Giovanna, 186
Grito de Lares (1868), 61
Grito de Yara (1869), 61
Guam, 80, 252n6
Guarionex, 107–9. *See also* Schomburg, Arthur (Arturo)
Guarnizo, Luis, 21
Guatemala, 245n20
Guattari, Félix, 201
Guibre, Abdul Salam, 270n6
Guillén, Nicolás, 99
Gulf of Mexico, 40, 42
Guridy, Frank, 36, 60
Guyatt, Nicholas, 40, 49
Guzmán, Milagros, 187, 189, 269n132
Guzmán, Yolanda, 113, 118, 120, 122

Habesha people, ix, 172, 208–19, 264n25, 267n78
Haiti, 40, 57, 74, 215, 227, 229, 245n20, 248n84, 249n91; and Arthur Schomburg, 23, 91, 94–109, 256n91; and Black citizenship, 33, 35, 38, 41; Cap-Haïtien, 98; earthquake (2010), 97; global anti-Haitianism, 64–65, 95, 97, 131, 243n9, 256n94; and Gregorio Luperón, 61–67, 250n116; Juana Méndez, 114; and Latinoamericanism, 3; Môle Saint-Nicolas, 54; Port-au-Prince, 96, 98; relations with the Dominican Republic, 47–49, 54–55, 62–65, 243n9; and US annexation of the Dominican Republic, 47–50, 53–55, 246n49; US colonialism in, 97, 167, 256nn77–78, 275n126
Haitian-descendent people, 48; in Chile, 233–34, 276n5; in the Dominican Republic, 1, 120, 131, 139, 144, 221, 263n114, 274n94, 276n131
Haitian Independence, 60–61, 96, 99–101, 106, 227, 246n49, 256n91
Haitian military, 48, 99
Haitian Revolution, 91, 95, 100, 106, 265n51
Haitians, 1, 44, 61, 65, 75, 96–103, 105–6, 131, 229, 246n49, 256n94
Haiti–Dominican Republic border, 107, 114, 236
Hammond, Lauren, 56
Harar, 265n44
Harlem Renaissance, 12, 90, 98, 229
Harrison, Benjamin, 54
Hartman, Saidiya, 16
Harvard University: School and Museum of Comparative Zoology, 248n86
Hasbún, Amín Abel, 258n6
Haskins, Ekaterina, 207
Hawai'i, 80
Hawthorne, Camilla, 196
hegemonic blackness, 5–8, 11–12, 49, 83–84, 136, 198, 225, 231, 237–38; definition, 4
Heredia, Gertrudis, 82
Hernández, David, 14, 16
Hernández-Medina, Esther, 146–47, 149, 238
Heureaux, Ulises "Lilís," 63
Hispanic Caribbean, x, 3, 24, 33, 83–84, 103, 159, 254n46
Hispanicity, 8, 62, 68, 84, 86, 105
Hispaniola/Quisqueya, 3, 39, 104, 108, 118–19, 157; and Gregorio Luperón, 62–65; name, 259n16; and US empire, 3, 23, 37–59, 100, 228, 245n35
Hispanism, 182
Hispanoamérica (term), 49
historietas, 146
historiography, 77, 92
Hoffnung-Garskof, Jesse, 86, 253n15, 260n49
Holton, Adalaine, 91–92, 254n36, 255n49, 255n57
homophobia, 120, 181, 217. *See also* sexual violence
Honduras, 245n20
Hooker, Juliet, 56–57, 193
hooks, bell, 144, 199, 238
Horne, Gerald, 47, 49

Horn of Africa, 132, 157, 169, 171, 190, 264n16
Hostos, Eugenio María de, 60–61, 66–68
Howe, Samuel G., 48–50, 247n63
Hughes, Langston: *Popo and Fifina, Children of Haiti*, 98–99
Hugo, Victor, 66
human rights, 16, 56, 117–18, 134, 140, 192, 218, 224, 226, 236, 239
human trafficking, 132–34, 140, 142, 167, 174, 181, 216
Hurricane George, 21
Hurricane Maria, 80
hybridity, 159, 182
hyphenated identities, 18, 81, 88, 133, 156, 205, 218–19

identity politics, 87, 205, 254n34
Il Fatto Quotidiano, 268n101
Il Giorno Milano, 185
illegality, 14, 17–18, 185, 189, 229
immigrant-receiving nations, 18, 22, 134, 139, 197, 218
immigrant rights, 3, 14, 16, 24–25, 132–33, 224, 234–35, 237, 276n6
immigrant-sending nations, 25, 155, 216
immigration, 264n25, 272n43, 276n6; and antiblackness, 12, 14–16, 24, 139, 212–13, 215, 233–39, 243n9; Black immigrant motherhood, 182–92, 268n113; and Black Latinidad, 2–25, 57, 194–95, 224, 226, 236–37; from the Dominican Republic, 2, 21–22, 24–25, 32–34, 37, 44, 114, 120–21, 126, 129, 132–52, 154, 157, 182–92, 230, 250n116; from Eritrea, 21, 134, 178, 197, 208–19, 267n69, 271n19, 274n84, 274n92; from Ethiopia, 209; and gender, 21, 24–25, 113–92, 268n113; from Haiti, 1, 114; to Italy, x, 21–22, 24–25, 113–14, 121, 126, 129, 132–201, 205–27, 230, 264n16, 270n6, 271n9, 271nn19–20, 273n55; and linguistic terrorism, 84–85; and marriage, 134; from Mexico, 15, 54; and postcolonialism, 18, 182–231; and Puerto Rican status, 79–81, 89, 103; and racism, 14–17, 135–92, 195–200, 220–30, 238; to the US, 15–19, 21, 32–34, 37, 70–74, 82–83, 85, 109, 121, 130, 132, 156–57, 168, 188, 190, 229–31, 248n86, 249n101, 252n1, 253n11, 253n15, 269n135, 276n130; zero-tolerance immigration policy, 190. *See also* Second Generation (G2)
indentured servants, 17
indigenismo, 64, 107, 253n23
Indigenous Peoples, x, 8, 17, 64, 99, 110, 142, 239, 245, 271n13; and citizenship, 18, 90; and colonialism, 16, 174; and Créolité, 68; and dispossession, 55; indigenization of blackness, 103–9, 257n118; and mestizaje, 63–65, 107, 227; and racial segregation, 168, 190. *See also* Native Americans; Native Peoples; *individual nations and communities*
Instagram, 37
Insular Cases (1901), 80, 252n6
International Day for the Elimination of Violence against Women, 260n56
International Women's Day, *143*
intra-ethnic solidarity, ix–x, 8, 109, 136
Irish Americans, 18
Isis, 268n98
Ismail, Maryan, 172–73, 182, 268n98
Israel, 231
Italian (language), 270n141
Italian Americans, 18
Italian Army, 264n16
italianità, 155–58, 179, 185–88, 191, 198–207, 210–11, 224, 226; and citizenship, 214, 219–21; and colonialism, 166–74, 182
Italian Parliament, 138, 141
Italian unification, 155–56, 171, 264n20
Italo Eritreans, 163, 169–70, 175, 178. *See also* Habesha people
Italo-Somali people, 172
Italy, 261n70, 262n85, 265n51, 274n84; Afro-Italian activism in, 133–44, 172, 174–75, 178–79, 188, 192, 200, 206–7, 217, 221–27, 272n29; antiblackness in, 132, 135–36, 139, 142, 158–92, 203, 212–13; blackness in, 5, 20, 22, 90, 132, 135–37, 155, 158–231, 254n42, 261n75, 264n25, 271n7; Bologna, 135, 213–14, 274n76; Castel Volturno, 270n6; citizenship in, 132, 135, 156–57, 168, 188, 190–91, 197, 210, 214, 219–27, 271n17; Dominican immigrants in,

21–22, 24–25, 121, 126, 129, 132–52, 154, 182–92; feminism in, 134, 137–52, 169, 174–79; immigration to, x, 21–22, 24–25, 113–14, 121, 126, 129, 132–201, 205–27, 230, 264n16, 270n6, 271n9, 271nn19–20, 273n55; Italian colonialism, 5, 25, 134–35, 142, 155–92, 195–219, 228, 230, 236, 238–39, 263n13, 264n16, 264n19, 265nn43–45, 266n59, 267n69, 272n34, 273n54; Italian fascism, 156, 161–86, 195, 203–4, 212–13, 221–22, 226, 264n16, 265n44, 266n63; Liberal Period, 171; Milan, 1, 25, 141–42, 153–54, 170, 173–74, 179, 182, 185, 187–89, 193, 206, 208–17, 220–22, 226, 264n25, 267n69; Naples, 114, 133; Palermo, 179; Porta Venezia, 193, 208–9, 217; Ragusa, 206; Second Generations in, x, 5, 25, 90, 132, 192–231, 236–37, 254n42, 264n25, 271n9; and sex tourism, 25, 132, 153–54, 158, 170, 182–86, 188, 263n13; Tuscany, 138–39, 141; whiteness in, 135–36, 137, 154–58, 166–74, 179, 182, 185–88, 191, 195, 198–207, 210–11, 220–26, 263n13. *See also* Campo Cintato (Kombishtato)

Iyob, Ruth, 1630164

Japan, 238

Jefferson, Thomas, 40, 246n39

Jewish people, 88, 167, 252n1

Jim Crow, 2, 12, 15–16, 34, 105, 156, 194, 230. *See also* racial segregation

Jiménez Román, Miriam, 83, 86–88, 136

Johnson, Andrew, 245n35

Johnson, James Weldon, 97–98

Johnson, Jessica Marie, 121

Johnson, Lyndon, 124

Johnson, Walter, 244n19

Jones Act (1917), 228

joy, 32, 120–21, 145, 148–52, 220

jus culturae, 188

Juventud Estudiantil del Catorce de Junio 14J (Jecajú), 124

Karens, 242n42

Kazanjian, David, 98

Kempadoo, Kamala, 182

Khan, Saffiyah, 242n26

Khoikhoi People, 265n45

Kilomba, Grada, 153–54, 173, 191, 199–200, 210, 238

knowledge-making, 2, 7, 35, 144, 178; and antiblackness, 24, 26, 77; and Arthur Schomburg, 87–93, 103, 107–9; and colonialism, 77, 191–92, 208, 210, 212, 238; resisting hegemonic knowledge, 6, 26, 238–39; shared knowledge, 5; subjugated knowledge, 84, 92, 212, 253n22

Kombishtato. *See* Campo Cintato (Kombishtato)

Kincaid, Jamaica, 274n94

King, Martin Luther, Jr., 197

Kreyòl (language), 194

Ku Klux Klan, 34

Ku Klux Klan Act (1871), 42

La Batalla del Puente Duarte, 126

La Guerra de Abril (1965), 123–29, 131–32

La guerra de los seis años (1868–74), 45

La Guerra de Restauración. *See* Dominican War of Restoration (La Guerra de Restauración, 1863–65)

Lahiri, Jhumpa, 199

La Liga, 62, 82, 253n15

La Liga de la Paz, 66

La Malinche, 159

La Parte Alta, 126–27

Lara, Genesis, 258n7

Las Dos Antillas/Las Tres Antillas, 61, 66

La Sentencia (2013), 144, 221, 230, 263n114, 276n131

La Sociedad Latinoamericana, 60, 249n105

Latin (term), 49

Latin American people (term), ix

Latin difference, 36–38, 49

Latino (term), 49

Latino, Juan, 91

Latinoamerica, 84

Latinoamericanism, 3

Latinoamericano (term), 49

Latin Raza, 84

Latinx (term), x, 49

Latinx studies, 3–4, 22, 86, 101, 109, 194, 251n140; Schomburg's role in, 87–88

Law No. 91 (1992), 220, 222, 271n17

Lear, Jonathan, 2, 93–94

Lega Nord, 132, 272n43

Le Houérou, Fabienne, 179–81, 263n13
Lerner, Faleschini, 186
Lettenze, Michele, 214–15
Lewis, John, 16
Liberia, 40
Liborismo, 108
libraries, 86, 90–93, 104, 255n56. *See also* archives
Libya, 134, 155, 160, 171, 197, 206, 216, 228, 240, 271n19
Licona, Adela, 10
Lima, Lázaro, 251n140
Lincoln, Abraham, 245n35
linguistic terrorism, 84–85
Llaguno-Ciani, Maya, 223–24
Lloyd, Linda, 15–16
Loguen, Jermain Wesley, 29
Loguen Fraser, Sarah, 29–32, 53, 73, 141, 244n13
Lombardi-Diop, Cristina, 264n16
López, Antonio, 13, 36
L'ora della verità, 174, 178, 180
Lorde, Audre, 120, 133, 144
Louisiana: New Orleans, 40
L'Ouverture, Toussaint, 99
Love, Eric, 40
Lowe, Lisa, 17, 205, 227, 230
Luperón, Gregorio, 71–72, 238, 247n63, 250n116; and anti-colonialism, 44–48, 53, 58, 59–62, 74, 75, 77–78, 247n49, 247n58; and Black Latinidad, 22–23, 34–39, 62–70, 84, 250n119; godfather to Gregoria Fraser Goins, 29, 34–35, 39, 70, 74, 243n2
lynching, 105, 113, 196

MacDonald Contract (1908), 96
Maceo, Antonio, 66
madamas/madamato, 158, 162–88, 192, 266n59, 267n80
Maglio, Alan: *Asmarina*, 208–19
Malcolm X, 10, 196
Mandela, Nelson, 4, 10
Manifest Destiny, 34, 40, 81
Manley, Beth, 259n35
Mari, Lorenzo, 200
Marley, Bob, 4
Maroons, 107
marriage, 30, 137, 154, 184, 215, 261n60; of children, 120, 176–81, 187, 190, 268n101; and citizenship, 71, 251n137; and immigration, 134; and madamato, 162–63, 176–81
Martelli, Claudio, 261n71
Martelli Law, 135
Martí, José, 36, 38, 60, 82, 96
martial law, 42
Martín, Gloria: "Sagrario Abierto," 258n12
Martínez, Orlando, 258n6
Martínez-San Miguel, Yolanda, 13, 60, 83, 85, 157, 218
Martinique, 72, 99
Marxism, 122, 169; Marxism-Leninism, 274n76
Masslo, Jerry Essan, 135, 261n70
matrimonias, 137
Maugeri, Pippo, 212–13. *See also* "Asmarina, Asmarina" (song)
Mayes, April, 36, 38, 49, 52, 244n13, 246n48
Mediterranean Sea, 144, 154, 168, 197, 215, 231
melting pot discourse, 18, 81
Méndez, Denny, 21–22, 135–36, 261n75
Mérimée, Prosper, 147–48
Merrill, Heather, 134, 243n53
mestizaje, 48, 71, 137, 160, 227, 250n119, 251n138; erasing blackness, 8, 24, 62–65, 84, 104–5, 107, 225; gendered, 159
mestizo consciousness, 107
mestizo dominicanidad, 62
mestizos, 38, 62, 64, 84, 107, 159, 239
methodology of book, 2–3, 6–8, 20–22, 74–75. *See also* genealogy; historiography
meticci, 166, 168–70, 215
métis people, 163
métissage, 168. *See also* miscegenation
Mexican-descendant people, 2–3, 80
Mexicans, 15, 18, 54, 57, 183
Mexico, 3, 41, 67, 183, 225, 245n35; Acapulco, 184; immigrants from, 15, 54; mestizaje in, 159, 227
Mexico-US border, 3–4, 95, 144, 231, 236
Micheli, Renato, 170–71

Milan Exposition (2015), 220, 226
Milan Ministry of Education, 222
Milan Ministry of Labor, 222
minoritization, 7, 14, 17, 20, 95, 192, 201, 225, 237–38; and citizenship, 13, 136, 198–99, 219; and coloniality of diaspora, 13, 85; gendered, x, 3; and hyphenated identities, 18
minor literature, 201
Mirabal, Nancy, 36
Mirabal sisters (Patria, Minerva, and María Teresa), 131, 260n56
Mireya (interviewee), 189, 270nn140–141
miscegenation, 40, 64–65, 159–60, 167–68, 171. *See also* métissage
misogynoir, 169. *See also* misogyny; patriarchy; racism
misogyny, 120, 145–46, 161, 169, 173–82, 187, 235. *See also* misogynoir; patriarchy; sexual violence
Miss Universe pageant, 21, 135, 136, 261n75. *See also* Méndez, Denny
mistranslation, 4, 6, 8, 35, 37, 69–70, 86
Mitchell, Michele, 56
Mitchell, Robin, 265n51
model minority discourse, 270n4
Mohanty, Chandra Talpade, 238
Moïse, Jovenel, 256n94
Monroe Doctrine (1823), 40–41, 45–48
Montanelli, Indro, 161; rape of Destà, 173–82, 187, 268n101
montarse, 108, 119
Monumento ai Caduti di Dogali (Dogali Obelisk), 206–7
Moreau de Saint Méry, Médéric Louis Elie, 257n118
Morgan, Jennifer, 158
Movimiento Acción Migrante, 276n7
Movimiento Popular Dominicano (MPD), 121
muertos civiles, 263n114
Mujeres en Acción para la Liberación (MOALI), 139
Mukherjee, Neel, 199
mulataje, ix, 33, 49, 62–65, 71, 107, 159, 244n15, 253n23
mulato/as, 13, 48, 63–64, 71, 107, 154, 159, 170, 243n9, 246n49, 251n138; affranchis, 257n118; as term, x, 246n48, 250n119. *See also* tragic mulata trope
multiculturalism, 33, 93, 136, 200, 203, 219–20, 226
multiethnic blackness, 13
multiethnicity, 9, 13, 69, 71, 81, 197–98, 214, 228
Muñoz, José Esteban, 87–88, 251n140
Museo Civico dell'Italia in Africa, 206
Muslims, 12, 132, 160, 198, 239, 271n20
Mussolini, Benito, 161, 171, 273n54
Myslikova, Lucie, 242n26

Nation, The, 97
National Association for the Advancement of Colored People (NAACP), 97
National Association of Evangelical Students, 139
National Black Convention (1871), 51
National City Bank of New York, 97
National Day Against Racism, 235
nationalism, 35, 62, 131, 218, 253n8; anticolonial, 105; Eritrean, 217; as European construct, 58; US, 55–56. *See also* anti-nationalism
National Organization for Women (NOW), 140
Native Americans, 16, 55
Native Peoples, 18, 55, 80, 104–5, 107, 109, 158–60. *See also* Indigenous Peoples; *individual nations and communities*
Naturalization Act (1890), 18
NDiaye, Marie, 199
Negrista movement, 99
Négritude movement, 99, 250n132
NegroCentricxs, 277n9
Negrón-Muntaner, Frances, 86, 91, 253n18, 254n33, 255n57
negrophobia, 59, 250n112. *See also* antiblackness
neocolonialism, 13
neo-Nazis, 9, 113, 241n15, 242n26, 267n81. *See also* Nordic Resistance Movement; white supremacy
New Jersey, 5, 225
new mestiza, 258n122
Newton, Melanie, 104–5, 109
New World, 99, 101, 104

New York City, 40, 66, 228, 253n15; Bronx, 37; Cubans in, 62, 67; Dominicans in, 31, 37, 121, 132, 145, 150; Manhattan, 37; Puerto Ricans in, 13, 81–83, 90
New York Public Library, 86; Schomburg Center for Research in Black Culture, 86, 91, 104
New York State, 47; Rochester, 57
New York Times, 79, 97, 100, 105, 253n19
Ngai, Mae, 220–21, 226, 230
Nigeria, 238
Nissage Saget, Jean-Nicolas, 45
Ni una menos, 227
No Human Being Is Illegal, 227
#NoHumanBeingIsIllegal, 14
Nordic Resistance Movement, 9, 241n15
Norme relative ai meticci (L822, 1940), 168
Nosotras Association, 139
Novas, José, 248n80
Núñez de Cáceres, José, 246n49
Núñez Polanco, Diómedes, 52
Nuyoricans, 13, 83

Obama, Barack, 197, 245n20
Obelisk of Axum (ሓውልቲ ኣኽሱም), 272n34
Oboler, Suzanne, 270n2
Old World, 46, 60
O'Neill, Eugene: *The Emperor Jones*, 96–97, 106, 256n79
Operación Limpieza, 126, 260nn41–42
Osei-Kofi, Nana, 10, 197
other-than-black, 48, 72, 248n64

Palacios, Paola, 236, 239
Palés Matos, Luis, 99
Palos, 108, 119
Pan-Africanism, 23, 50, 58
Panama, 96, 229; Darién Province, 40
Panama Canal, 253n19, 256n78
Paoli, Renato, 158, 163
Paolos, Medhin, 193–98, 221–22, 229–30, 238; *Asmarina*, 208–19
Parati, Graziella, 199, 207
Parietti, Alba, 135, 261n75
Parks, Henry Blanton, 37, 59, 249n100
Parsley Massacre (1937), 127, 274n94
Partido Azul, 44
Partido Revolucionario Dominicano (PRD), 122–23
Pasolini, Pier Paolo, 169–70
Patria, 100
patriarchy, 121, 178, 186. *See also* gender-based violence; misogyny; sexual violence
Payano, Carolina, 25, 153–55, 157, 168, 173, 181, 183–89, 191–92
pedophilia, 163, 174–75, 179, 181
Pellegrini, Ines, 169–70
Pennsylvania, 103
Penson, César Nicolás, 55, 62
People's Front for Democracy and Justice (PFDJ), 216, 274n76
Peralte, Charlemagne, 256n77
Perassi, Emilia, 186
Perdomo, Tácito, 115
Pérez Firmat, Gustavo, 18, 205
Pérez Matos, Lucrecia, 113, 118, 120
Perry, Raymond, 44
Peru: Lima, 5, 220, 225
Peruvian-descendent people, 1, 5, 220, 225–26
Pétion, Alexandre, 100, 102, 105
Philippines, 79–80, 100, 134, 183, 228, 245n24, 256n78
Piazza della Minerva, 201–2
Pierre, María, 1, 3
Pimentel, Antonio, 44
Platt Amendment (1903), 253n19
Pojmann, Wendy, 138, 243n53
police, 15, 133, 154, 171, 259n13; killings by, 14, 37, 113–19, 173, 190, 196, 231, 233–35, 238–39, 259n14; and racism, 17, 85, 196, 234–35, 238–39, 242n42
Polyné, Millery, 36, 53
Ponzanesi, Sandra, 161
pornography, 159, 161–62, 167
Portugal, 265n51; Portuguese colonialism, 19, 49, 89, 167
Portuguese (language), 194
postcolonialism, 13, 85, 88; and gender-based violence, 153–92; in Hispaniola, 63–64; and immigration, 18, 182–231; in Italy, 20, 22, 25, 153–231, 272n34, 273n55
postcolonial studies, 191, 272n28
Powell, Colin, 245n20

Prendiamo la parola, 140
Prieur, Barthélemy: *Black Venus*, 161, 265n50
Prince Hall Masonic Lodge, 82
prisons, 17, 96, 101, 107, 116, 123, 168, 216, 258n6, 270n141
Puerto Rican Independence, 65, 81–82
Puerto Ricans (Boricuas), 60, 99, 107, 157, 253n8; and diasporic identity, 13, 23–24, 79–82, 85–89, 94, 100, 103, 254n46, 255n56; and US citizenship, 18, 24, 79–83, 94, 103, 228, 252n6; and vaivén, 19, 103. *See also* Nuyoricans
Puerto Rico, 21, 38, 129, 132, 253n8; and Arthur Schomburg, 13, 23–24, 79–82, 85–89, 94, 100, 103, 254n46, 255n56; San Juan, 250n116; and US empire, 18, 48, 56, 60–61, 65–67, 75–82, 100, 167, 229, 252n6, 256n78, 275n126; and vaivén, 241n5
Punto di Partenza, 140
pureza de sangre, 246n48

queerness, x, 120, 131, 133–34, 142, 167, 261n60
"¿Quién mató?," 11314, 118
Quisqueya. *See* Hispaniola/Quisqueya

racexiles, 218
racial ambivalence, 38
racial integrity, 88–90, 94, 103, 254n36
racial justice, 3, 14, 35, 62, 70, 237
racial segregation, 14–16, 70, 72, 80, 83, 109, 194, 196, 267n79; and colonialism, 167–68, 230, 267n69; in Eritrea, 215. *See also* apartheid; Campo Cintato (Kombishtato); Jim Crow
racism, 4, 7, 256n94, 267n81, 271n13; Chilean, 233–36; and colonialism, 4–5, 25, 35, 42–43, 54, 135–92, 195–200, 212–13, 215, 230, 273n55; Dominican, 37, 65, 243n9; and immigration, 14–17, 135–92, 195–200, 220–29, 230, 238; Italian, 25, 132, 135–92, 195–200, 203–7, 212–13, 215, 220–29, 268n101; resistance to, 4, 10–11, 14, 19, 25, 58, 138, 174, 234–35, 261n70, 277n9; scientific, 54, 105, 167, 228, 248n86, 252n1; in Sweden, 9–10, 242n17; as "the ground we walk on," 120; US, 14–17, 31–32, 42–43, 54, 85, 105, 244n19, 252n1. *See also* antiblackness; anti-racism; eugenics; "Faccetta Nera"; global anti-Haitianism; italianità; Jim Crow; Karens; Lega Nord; lynching; misogynoir; Nordic Resistance Movement; racial segregation; white supremacy; xenophobia
radical hope, 2, 19, 34, 65, 93–94, 110, 143, 152
Radical Republicans, 244n19
Radio Santo Domingo, 123
Ramírez, Dixa, 250n119
Ramses II, Pharaoh, 207
Ransby, Barbara, 238
rayanas, 127, 131
raza (term), 49, 64, 67
raza mixta, 63–65, 250n119
raza unida, 38
Reconstruction, 23, 29–59, 78, 81–82, 245n35
refugees, 132, 189, 191, 200, 203, 215, 274n92; refugee crisis (2015), 11–12, 209, 216–19, 230, 261n70, 264n16, 271n19. *See also* asylum
relational memory work, 10
re-membering, 24, 73, 119–20, 178
Renda, Mary, 96–97, 256n79
reparations, 96, 239, 246n49
Reparations Act (1825), 246n49
República Brewery: Tina Bazuca beer, 127, *129*
República del Haití Español, 246n49
republicanism, 34, 49, 160, 227, 244n19; and Arthur Schomburg, 99; and Frederick Douglass, 36, 39, 41, 53–55; and Gregorio Luperón, 45, 47, 62, 66, 77, 84
Republican Party, 50
Restoration War (1861–65), 44, 61, 74, 246n49, 250n112
Rete G2 (Second Generation Network), 193, 198, 221, 224; G.Lab, 222–23; L'Italia sono anch'io campaign, 222
returning what slavery took away, 93, 99, 103
Revolutionary Committee of Cuba and Puerto Rico, 66–67

Reyes-Santos, Irmary, 61
Rice, Condoleezza, 245n20
Rice, Susan, 245n20
Ricourt, Milagros, 121
Rifondazione Comunista, 141
Risorgimento, 155, 264n20
Rivas, Agustina (Tina Bazuca), *125*, 127–31, 141, 152
Robertson, Pat, 97
Rodríguez, Jovanna, 1, 3, 5, 7, 220–26, 230
Rodríguez, Richard, 251n140
Rodríguez Taveras, Katherina, 114, 118, 120
Roman Empire, 171
Romanesco (language), 170
Romeo, Caterina, 195, 264n16
Roosevelt, Theodore, 252n1
Ross, Diana, 197
Rubi Mori, Jessica, 114, 118
Russia, 245n35

"Sable Venus: An Ode, The" (poem), 265n51
Sahara Desert, 215
Sakai, Naoki, 7
Saldaña-Portillo, María Josefina, 64
Salnave, Sylvain, 65
Salvadorans, 209
Samoa, 80
Sánchez, Efraín, 121–23, 128
Sánchez González, Lisa, 86, 89, 91
#SandraBland, 276n8
Sani, Gino Mitrano: *Femina Somala*, 163
sankipankismo, 153, 158, 163–64, 184–85, 188, 263n6
Santana, Pedro, 69, 246n49
Santería, 119
Santo Domingo (historical name), 36, 41–54, 66–67, 69, 71–72, 76, 107–8, 244n12, 245n35, 246n49, 251n137. *See also* Dominican Republic
Sarmiento, Domingo Faustino, 57
Sawyer, Mark, 37
#SayHerName, 235
Say Her Name: Sandra Bland, 235
Scego, Igiaba, 171, 199–206, 218, 238, 272n29, 273n55
Schomburg, Arthur (Arturo), 22, 204, 226, 229, 238, 253n19, 257n105; and anticolonialism, 80, 87–89, 93, 109; and archives, 23–24, 79–110, 255n49, 255n57; "background of our future," 71, 91, 93, 103; and farming, 92, 99, 106–7; Guarionex alias, 107–9; and Haiti, 23, 91, 94–109, 256n91; "Is Hayti Decadent?," 100; and Latinx studies, 87–88; "Military Services Rendered," 101; "The Negro Digs Up His Past," 91; and Puerto Rican diasporic identity, 13, 23–24, 79–82, 85–89, 94, 100, 103, 254n46, 255n56; on racial integrity, 88–90, 94, 103, 254n36; on unbelonging, 80–81, 83–85, 99; use of Spanish, 84–86, 241n5, 254n24, 257n106; and vaivén, 23–24, 82, 85–89, 95, 103, 109–10, 253n18, 254nn32–33
Schurz, Carl, 47
Scifo, Vito: *Stranieri a Milano*, 209–11
Scioa, 265n44
Second Generation (G2), 5, 18, 90, 192, 239, 264n25, 273n55, 274n94; and archival interruptions, 25–26, 193–231; and citizenship, 132, 188, 197–98, 201, 219–31, 271n9; definition, x, 198; and Italian colonialism, 206–19; and language, 85; racialization of, 156, 193–97, 199–206, 234, 236–37, 254n42. *See also* Rete G2 (Second Generation Network)
second-generation attitude, 221, 224
Second World, 155
Secure Communities program, 15
Seiter, Joseph Carl, 31
Selassie, Haile, 214
Sereke, Rahel, 217
Serra, Rafael, 82, 253n15
Serrata, Medar, 183
Severgnini, Beppe, 268n101
Seward, William, 245n35
sexscapes, 185, 188, 269n114
sex tourism, 25, 120, 132, 157, 167, 170, 182. *See also* transactional sex
sexual violence, 64, 120, 140, 163, 200, 270n141; in Chile, 234; and colonialism, 158–82; in the Dominican Republic, 120, 131; by Indro Montanelli, 173–82, 187, 268n101; in Italy, 178, 189; under slavery, 158. *See also* gender-based violence; human trafficking

sex work, 133, 137–38, 140, 167, 184, 187. *See also* concubinage; madamas/madamato; sankipankismo; transactional sex
Sharpe, Christina, 2, 16, 120, 241n3, 242n38
Sharpe, Jenny, 191
Shawl, Wedi, 213–14
Shvanyukova, Polina, 200
Siege of Savannah (1779), 105
Sierra Leone, 108
Silié, Rubén, 68
Simon, Antoine, 96
Sindicato de Trabajadores Portuarios de Arrimo (POASI), 128
Sinnette, Elinor Des Verney, 82, 86, 101, 255n56, 256n91
slavery, 12, 30, 75, 81, 85, 104, 190–91, 196, 228; afterlife of, 15–16, 20, 24, 82, 173, 187, 194; and Black diasporic identity, 14, 95–96, 99; and colonialism, 16–24, 35–40, 47–48, 53–54, 57–58, 62–65, 69, 89, 101, 230; and gender-based violence, 157–60, 164, 168–74, 187; returning what slavery took away, 93, 99, 103; wake of, 2, 39, 42, 241n3. *See also* abolitionism
Smith, Christen, 120
Smythe, SA, 20, 206
socialism, 25, 123
social justice, 9, 15, 113, 138, 178, 218
Social Services Branch of the Dominican Consulate in Milan, 188
Sol de Cuba, 100
solidarity, 142, 169, 197, 219, 237; anticolonial, 14, 38, 109; Black diasporic, 14, 35, 38, 58–60, 133, 136, 144; intra-ethnic, ix–x, 8, 109, 136; Latin American, 68; transnational, x, 7–8, 11, 58–60, 198
Somalia, 21, 134, 199, 217, 271n19; Italian colonialism in, 134, 155, 160, 197, 200–6, 228, 230, 265n44
Sontag, Susan, 162
Soriano Muñoz, Florinda "Mamá Tingó," 113, 118, 120
South Africa, 4, 135, 168, 230, 265n45, 267n79
South Carolina, 75
Southern Cone, 55
southern races (term), 49
sovereignty, 38, 44–45, 47, 49, 53, 68–70, 76–78, 106, 246n49
Soviet Union, 106
Spain, 69, 231, 265n51; Madrid, 21, 113; Spanish colonialism, 19, 45, 49, 53–54, 60–63, 66, 86, 142, 157, 182–83, 247n58
Spanglish (language), 84, 194
Spanish (language), 1, 66, 70, 75, 77, 136, 137, 182, 194, 233; and Arthur Schomburg, 84–86, 241n5, 254n24, 257n106; Dominican, 145; and Gregoria Fraser Goins, 29; and immigration, 270n141; and racism, 13; and Second Generation Black Latinidad, 225–28
Spanish–American War, 34, 56, 79–80, 82, 228, 252n1
Spelta, Massimiliano, 153–54, 187
St. Croix, 89
sterilization, 167, 267n76. See also *Buck v. Bell* (1927); eugenics
Sternbach, Nancy Saporta, 119
Stoler, Ann Laura, 158, 167
Storum, Caroline, 29
Stothard, Thomas, 265n51
St. Thomas, 44, 63, 66, 250n116
subjugated knowledge, 84, 92, 212, 253n22
Sudan, 216
Sumner, Charles, 45, 50, 54, 75–78
Sweden, 238; Borlänge, 9
Switzerland, 248n86
syncretic religious traditions, 107–8
Syracuse University, 29–32, 34
Syria, 21, 132, 217, 271n19

Taínos, 103, 106–7, 142, 158
Taveras, Rafael "Fafa," 125, 260n39
Taylor, Breonna, 119
Taylor, Tia, 271n7
Televisión Nacional de Chile (TVN), 234
terminology of book, ix–x
Terrible Twelve Years (1966–78), 116–18, 129, 132, 258n1, 258n6
Texas, 42, 235
textos montados, 107–9
theory of recovery, 91
Thomas, Deborah, 210, 264n29
Thomas, Piri, 13, 84, 229; *Down These Mean Streets*, 83

Tigray, 163
Tigrinya (language), 168, 211
Time to Kill, 163
Torres-Saillant, Silvio, 65, 67, 250n112
tragic mulata trope, 154, 159, 170
transactional sex, 182
transatlantic triangulation, 4
translating blackness, definition, 8–9, 11–13
translation, definition, 6–8
transnational Black solidarity, 58–60, 73, 82, 197
transnational ethnic studies, 191
transphobia, 120, 270n141
Travaglio, Marco, 268n101
Treaty of Peace, Friendship, and Commerce (1867), 62
Trento, Giovanna, 169
triple-consciousness, 83, 136
Triulzi, Alessandro, 161–62, 190–91, 212
tropical fever discourse, 154, 181, 263n13
Trouillot, Michel-Rolph, 74, 77–78, 91–92
Trujillo, Rafael Leónidas, 72, 115–16, 121, 123, 127, 131, 229, 243n9, 258n1, 260n56, 274n94
Trump, Donald, 190, 276n7
Turner, Louis, 183
Twitter, 37, 210

unbelonging, 6–8, 10, 12, 14–19, 22, 26, 95, 225, 230, 239; and Arthur Schomburg, 80–81, 83–85, 99; and Black citizenship, 57; and the Dominican Republic, 32–33, 41–42; and El Nié, 144–45, 150; and Gregoria Fraser Goins, 32–34, 83; in Italy, 138, 160, 168, 172, 185–86, 195–98, 204–6, 211, 219–27; and vaivén, 2–3, 19, 26, 32–33, 80, 85, 144
Uncle Sam, 42–*43*
Underground Railroad, 29
undocumented migrants, 1, 7, 14–16, 85, 134, 137, 230, 242n34, 269n135. *See also* Deferred Action for Childhood Arrivals (DACA, 2012); Development, Relief, and Education for Alien Minors Act (DREAM Act, 2001)
Unique Advertiser, 100
United Fruit Company, 96
United Nations, 214, 216, 260n56, 272n34; Population Division, 134
United States, x, 2, 29–30, 119, 197, 205, 215, 244n15, 247n63, 257n105, 264n25, 269n114; academia in, 86, 155–56, 249n101, 251n140; activism in, 137, 146, 173, 195, 235; Black Latinidad in, 3–4, 5–8, 16, 22, 37, 70–74, 78, 83–90, 95–101, 194, 224–25, 228, 270n2; blackness in, 4–14, 17–19, 24, 32–44, 69, 83–85, 105–8, 136–37, 194–96, 225–26, 235–39, 242n42, 243n9; citizenship in, 18, 22–24, 33–37, 39–44, 48–59, 70–72, 79–83, 85, 90, 94, 103–6, 108, 194, 228, 242n34, 244n19, 251n137, 252n6; Dominicans in, 21, 32–34, 37, 70–74, 82–83, 121, 130, 132, 249n101; extreme right in, 276n7; immigrants in, 15–19, 21, 32–34, 37, 70–74, 82–83, 85, 109, 121, 130, 132, 156–57, 168, 188, 190, 229–31, 248n86, 249n101, 252n1, 253n11, 253n15, 269n135, 276n130; model minority discourse in, 270n4; relationship with Puerto Rico, 13, 18–19, 24, 48, 56, 60, 66–67, 79–89, 94, 100, 103, 167, 228–29, 252n6, 253n8, 256n78, 275n126; US empire, 3–4, 14, 18, 22–24, 34–70, 74–84, 89–90, 95–100, 113, 115–16, 123–26, 132, 157, 159, 167, 228–30, 245n35, 246n49, 249n100, 252n6, 253n19, 256nn77–78, 260n41, 275n126
Universidad Autónoma de Santo Domingo (UASD), 113–18, 121–23, 132, 139, 258n7, 259n13
University of Georgia, 14; Board of Regents, 242n34
unreadability, 83, 85–86
US Americans, 52, 95, 269n135; and blackness, 33, 57, 70, 85, 106, 159, 194; definition, ix; and Latinidad, 34, 49, 85; and US empire, 75, 89, 159
US Army, 245n35; Buffalo Soldiers (24th Regiment), 245n24
US Black imperialism, 59
US Blacks, 82, 95, 106, 141, 254n24; and citizenship, 33–36, 39–59, 70, 90–91, 229; and class, 72–73; definition, ix; and global blackness, 8–14, 195–96, 229, 235, 237–38; and Latinidad, 13–16, 23, 32–33,

35–38, 58, 70, 84–85, 237–38, 270n2; and migration, 15–16, 85, 108, 271n7; and US empire, 34–36, 39–59, 70, 73
US Bureau of Immigration, 79–80, 252n1
US Census Bureau, 242n36
US Civil War, 34–35, 38–40, 96, 101, 102, 108, 244n19, 245n35, 249n91
US Congress, 35, 48, 222, 269n135; House of Representatives, 75; Senate, 45, 50, 54, 60, 76–77; Senate Foreign Relations Committee, 47, 49, 75
US Constitution, 167, 252n6, 267n76; Fifteenth Amendment, 40, 42, 49, 53; Fourteenth Amendment, 36, 40, 49; Nineteenth Amendment, 71; Thirteenth Amendment, 40
US Independence, 35, 103
US Marines, 51, 96, 100, 124, 126, 256n77
US–Mexico border, 3–4, 95, 144, 231, 236
US Navy, 46–47
US Supreme Court, 80, 167, 252n6, 267n76
US Union (Civil War), 96
US Virgin Islands, 89

Vaca, Nicolas, 270n2
vaivén, 54, 144, 225, 237; and Arthur Schomburg, 23–24, 82, 85–89, 95, 103, 109–10, 253n18, 254nn32–33; and belonging/unbelonging, 2–6, 19, 26, 32–33, 80, 85, 144; and the Dominican Republic, 20, 22–23, 25, 31–34, 39, 74, 78; and Frederick Douglass, 4, 54, 58, 78; and Gregoria Fraser Goins, 23, 31–34, 39, 78; and Italy, 22, 25, 201, 203, 205, 217–18; and Puerto Rico, 19, 24, 85–89, 103, 241n5
Valdés, Vanessa, 86, 88–89, 91, 253n18, 254nn32–33, 255n57
Vasconcelos, José de, 57
Vega, Bernardo, 255n56
Venezuela, 99, 258n12
Venuti, Lawrence, 6
vodoun, 119
voting, 45, 47, 52, 135, 242n34; gendered, 71, 80; racialized, 40, 42, 49–50, 56, 222
Vuong, Ocean, 199

Wade, Benjamin, 50
Walcott, Reinaldo, 241n3
Wampanoag People, 254n48
Washington, Booker T., 98
Washington, DC, 46–47, 72, 75–76, 137
Washington, George, 102
Weldeslassie, Tsegehans "Ziggy," 215–18
Wessin y Wessin, Elías, 123–24
West, Cornel, 58
West Indies, 48
White, Andrew, 50
White Hispanics, 83
white supremacy, 5, 13, 20, 37, 105, 195, 224–25, 228–30, 237, 271n13; Chilean, 235, 276n7; Dominican, 70; European, 58, 84, 88, 160; Italian, 25, 135, 160, 172, 198–205, 221, 226; North American, 84, 88, 167; resistance to, 9–12, 25, 37, 65, 91, 93, 95, 198–205, 218, 239, 256n91; South African, 267n79; US, 37, 42, 70, 89, 276n7. *See also* italianità; Karens; Ku Klux Klan; Lega Nord; lynching; neo-Nazis; Nordic Resistance Movement; racial segregation; racism; slavery; xenophobia
Williams, Carla, 265n51
Williams, William, 252n1
Willis, Deborah, 265n51
Woldegabriel, Elena, 210–*11*, 213
women (term), x
women of color (term), x
Wood, Fernando, 47–48
World War II, 155, 214, 265n43
Wynter, Sylvia, 16–17, 104–5, 107, 205

xenophobia, 4, 157, 195, 199; and antiblackness, 12, 120, 135, 203, 215, 224, 234, 236, 243n9. *See also* italianità; Lega Nord; racism

Yankees, 36, 39, 46–47, 65, 70
Yohannes, Helen, 217
Yolanda (interviewee), 126–34, 138, 141, 152, 261n60
YouTube, 210, 271n7

Zendaya, 13